Jane's

Aircraft
Recognition Guide

D1044594

Fourth Edition published in 2005 by **Collins**

HarperCollins Publishers
77-85 Fulham Palace Road
Hammersmith
London w6 8jb
UK
www.collins.co.uk

HarperCollins Publishers Inc
10 East 53rd Street
New York
NY 10022
USA
www.harpercollins.com

www.janes.com

ISBN: 0-00-718332-1
ISBN-10: 0-06-081894-8 (in the US)
ISBN-13: 978-0-06-081894-4 (in the US)

HarperCollins books may be purchased for
educational, business or sales promotional
use. For information in the United States,
please write to: Special Markets
Department, HarperCollins Publishers,
Inc., 10 East 53rd Street, New York, NTY
10022.

The name of the "Smithsonian",
"Smithsonian Institution", and the sunburst
logo are registered trademarks of the
Smithsonian Insitution.

Printed and bound in Scotland by Scotprint

06 07 08   10 9 8 7 6 5 4 3 2

Aircraft
Recognition Guide

Günter Endres
&
Michael J. Gething

Collins

CONTENTS

CONTENTS

CONTENTS

CONTENTS

PRIVATE LIGHT AIRCRAFT

CONTENTS

CONTENTS

CONTENTS

CONTENTS

MILITARY TRAINING AIRCRAFT

CONTENTS

COMBAT SUPPORT AIRCRAFT

CONTENTS

MILITARY HELICOPTERS

CONTENTS

FOREWORD

This latest edition of *Jane's Aircraft Recognition Guide* is firmly entrenched in the 21st century with its revised 'portrait' format, all-colour illustrations and the same compilers on the flight deck as the Third Edition.

Let us remind the reader what exactly this book sets out to provide and, also, what it does not. It is an aide memoire for individuals interested in aviation who visit airfields, airports or air shows to assist in identifying the aircraft they will see. It sets out to illustrate a very wide variety of aircraft and helicopters likely to be found at such locations and events around the world.

It is not a pocket-sized edition of *Jane's All The World's Aircraft*, however. To this end, there are no entries for the likes of Unmanned Aerial Vehicles or the huge variety of light general aviation, sports or homebuilt aircraft produced in single figures, which would fill a book twice this size.

The previous edition of *Jane's Aircraft Recognition Guide* – the first under our steward-ship – was compiled afresh, sourced from *Jane's All The World's Aircraft, Jane's Aircraft Upgrades* and *Jane's World Air Forces*. As benefits a guide bearing the Jane's marque, we have returned to source and updated the entries, hopefully correcting the few (human) mistakes which infected the original Third Edition, while updating a large number of the photographs used to illustrate the book.

Readers should note, however, that specifications remain rounded up or down to one decimal place (in the case of metric) and without

fractions (in Imperial measures). After all, at the distances involved in aircraft recognition, what difference can 0.002m or 3/4 inch make in identifying the type of aircraft? We can well remember that, during the mid-1960s, the skill was to detect the subtle differences between the Boeing 707, Convair 880 and DC-8 airliners, all three types being roughly of the same overall size and configuration, in order to confirm identity.

Indeed, it is identification of aircraft types that is the *raison d'être* for this minor tome. While aircraft recognition goes back almost one hundred years, it has only been practised as an 'art form' since the Second World War when, with radar in its infancy, visual identification of 'ours' and 'theirs' was a vital requirement for air defence.

In the UK, this skill resided, principally, in the Royal Observer Corps, which was an integral part of the RAF's reporting and control organisation. In the latter years of the 20th century, its importance faded and the Corps was disbanded in 1991. The fascination with aviation, be it civil or military has not faded. Indeed, its popularity as an enthusiast pastime in the UK, much of continental Europe and the United States continues unabated.

Another trend that has arisen in recent years is the contraction of the aerospace business itself, leading to a vast reduction in the number of aircraft manufacturers. In parallel, there has been the longevity, well beyond original plans, of many types of aircraft.

Thus we see many aircraft flying built by companies that no longer exist... but the DC-3

Dakota/C-47 Skytrain will forever be a Douglas rather than a Boeing product (via the McDonnell Douglas Corporation). In applying 'common sense' to this contraction of the industry, aircraft are labelled with what we believe is the obvious manufacturer, with either the original or current name in parentheses afterwards. Hence we have the Aerospatiale Alouette III rather than the original Sud Aviation or current Eurocopter identity. The overall rule applied is that if production has ceased, the main manufacturer name is prime, with the current holder of design authority secondary. Where a manufacturer has been taken over during production of a type, the new company name is used with the original name secondary.

Our revised re-categorisation of the many types remains. For instance, many advanced jet trainers have a light ground attack role and previously were included as Combat Aircraft. Such types now reside under Military Training Aircraft, where their prime role is better reflected. We have also, where applicable, included the military versions of a basic civil type under its latter category if it is mainly a civil aircraft, and vice versa. This has reduced the number of essentially duplicate entries between military and civil types.

Another feature of the aerospace industry is the quantum growth in the use of initials for all manner of long-winded names, titles and techniques, as well as short-hand phrases, only some of which are in common usage. Most of these comprise the *lingua franca* of aviation. Mindful that many readers may have this book as their first-ever reference to aircraft and aviation, we have updated the Glossary which allows these sometimes incomprehensible abbreviations and acronyms to be de-coded and explained.

Since the last issue, we have added further reference material showing national military insignia and civil registration listings.

In compiling this book, we acknowledge the considerable assistance of the many public relations personnel of the aerospace industry and operators (civil and military) whom we have consulted for information and photographs. You are too numerous to single out but you know who you are and we thank you.

Within the Jane's and HarperCollins organisations, we thank Keith Faulkner, Michael Johnson, Simon Michell, David Palmer, Andreas Schindler and Samantha Ward among others, for their help.

We would also like to thank those of our peers who have provided the few elusive images to complete this guide: *Air Forces Monthly*, Gerd Beilfuss, Ian Bostock, Art Brett, Piotr Butowski, Horacio J. Clariá, Tomás Coelho, Barrie Compton, Elias Daloumis, Rainer Eixenberger , Andy Graf, Grzegorz Holdanowicz, Craig Hoyle, Jamie Hunter, Paul Jackson, Dmitry Kudryn, David McIntosh, Toni Marimon, Shawn Miller, Lothar Müller, John Olafson, Thomas Posch, Nigel Steele, Michael Stroud, Henry Tenby, Tsen Tsan Tung, Theodore Valmas, Paolo Valpolini, Alan Warnes, Rogier Westerhuis, Sokol Ymeri and Harima Yoshihiro.

Günter Endres and Michael J. Gething, 2005

CIVIL
JET
AIRLINERS

Airbus A300 France/Germany/Spain/UK

Twin-turbofan medium-haul airliner

First flown on 28 October 1972, the A300 was the first aircraft to be built by the multi-national Airbus consortium. The introduction into service in June 1984 of the A300-600 represented a major step-up, featuring advanced technologies including a two-crew cockpit. Total delivered: 508.

VARIANTS

A300B2-100: Baseline model with GE CF6-50 turbofans
A300B2K: Krüger flaps and higher T-O weight
A300B2-200: Re-designation of A300B2K
A300B4-100: Increased range capability
A300B4-200: Higher T-O weight
A300B4-300: Introduced P&W JT9D turbofans
A300B4-600: Two-crew cockpit
A300B4-600R: Two-crew cockpit and increased range
A300C4-200: Convertible version of A300B4
A300C4-600: Convertible version of A300B4-600
A300F4-200: All-cargo version of A300B4-200
A300F4-600R: All-cargo version of A300B4-600R
Many early B2 and B4 models converted to cargo

SPECIFICATIONS: A300-600R

Accommodation: 2 + 361
Cargo/baggage: 147.4 m³ (5,206 cu.ft)
Max speed: M0.85 (484 kt; 895 km/h)
Range: 4,160 nm (7,700 km)

DIMENSIONS

Wingspan: 44.8 m (147 ft 1 in)
Length: 54.1 m (177 ft 5 in)
Height: 16.5 m (54 ft 3 in)

FEATURES

Low/swept wing with small winglets; twin underwing GE CF6-80C2 or P&W PW4000 turbofans; swept tailfin and low-set tailplane; widebody fuselage

Airbus A310 France/Germany/Spain/UK

Twin-turbofan short/medium-haul airliner

Shorter version developed from the A300 at instigation of Swissair and Lufthansa, major innovations including a new advanced-technology wing, smaller horizontal tailplane and digital two-crew cockpit. First flown on 3 April 1982 and entered service with Lufthansa on 12 April 1983. Total delivered: 255.

VARIANTS

A310-200: Baseline model
A310-200C: Convertible passenger/cargo version
A310-300: Increased fuel capacity and range, plus wingtip fences
A310-300ER: Additional centre tanks for extra long range
Many early aircraft since converted to cargo

SPECIFICATIONS: A310-300

Accommodation: 2 + 280
Cargo/baggage: 102.0 m^3 (3,605 cu.ft)
Max speed: M0.85 (484 kt; 895 km/h)
Range: 4,350 nm (8,050 km)

DIMENSIONS

Wingspan: 43.9 m (144 ft 0 in)
Length: 46.7 m (153 ft 1 in)
Height: 15.8 m (51 ft 10 in)

FEATURES

Low/swept wing with wingtip fences; twin underwing CF6-80, JT9D or PW4000 turbofans; swept tailfin and low-set tailplane; widebody fuselage

Airbus A318 France/Germany/Spain/UK

Twin-turbofan short-haul airliner

Short-bodied version of single-aisle A319, formally announced at the Farnborough Air Show in September 1998. Final assembly started at Hamburg on 9 August 2001, with first flight with P&W engines taking place on 15 January 2002 and with CFM56-5s on 29 August 2002. Entered service with Frontier Airlines on 29 July 2003. Total delivered: 12 (ordered 51).

VARIANTS

A318-100: Baseline aircraft

SPECIFICATIONS

Accommodation: 2 + 129
Cargo/baggage: 21.9 m^3 (773 cu.ft)
Max speed: M0.82 (470 kt; 870 km/h)
Range: 1,500nm (2,778km)

DIMENSIONS

Wingspan: 34.1m (111 ft 10 in)
Length: 31.5m (103 ft 3 in)
Height: 12.6m (41 ft 3 in)

FEATURES

Low/swept wing with winglets; twin underwing P&W PW6000 or CFM56-5 turbofans; swept tailfin and low-set tailplane

Airbus A319 France/Germany/Spain/UK

Twin-turbofan short-haul airliner

Short-fuselage version of A320, officially launched in June 1993 and first flown at Hamburg on 29 August 1995. Entered service with Swissair on 30 April 1996. First ACJ (Airbus Corporate Jetliner) variant was announced at 1997 Paris Air Show and made its maiden flight on 12 November 1998. First delivery to customer 8 November 1999. A319LR delivered to PrivatAir May 2004. Total delivered: 564.

VARIANTS

A319-100: Baseline passenger model
A319LR: Intercontinental version with up to four additional fuel tanks and ACJ features
ACJ: Corporate jet with typically 58 passengers and customer-specific interior

SPECIFICATIONS

Accommodation: 2 + 145
Cargo/baggage: 27.6 m^3 (976 cu.ft)
Max speed: M0.82 (470 kt; 870 km/h)
Range: 1,830 nm (3,390 km)

DIMENSIONS

Wingspan: 34.1 m (111 ft 10 in)
Length: 33.8 m (111 ft 0 in)
Height: 11.8 m (38 ft 7 in)

FEATURES

Low/swept wing with winglets; twin underwing CFM56-5 or IAE V2500 turbofans; swept tailfin and low-set tailplane

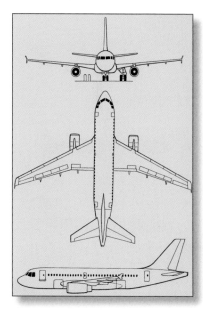

Airbus A320 France/Germany/Spain/UK

Twin-turbofan short-haul airliner

First member of single-aisle Airbus family launched on 23 March 1984. Made maiden flight with CFM56-5 engines at Toulouse on 22 February 1987, and with IAE V2500 engines on 28 July 1988. First deliveries to Air France on 28 March 1988. Total delivered: 1247.

VARIANTS

A320-100: Initial version, only 21 built
A320-200: Standard version featuring wingtip fences and wing-centre fuel tank

SPECIFICATIONS

Accommodation: 2 + 180
Cargo/baggage: 38.8 m^3 (1,370 cu.ft)
Max speed: M0.82 (470 kt: 870 km/h)
Range: 2,800 nm (5,185 km)

DIMENSIONS

Wingspan: 34.1 m (111 ft 10 in)
Length: 37.6 m (123 ft 3 in)
Height: 11.8 m (38 ft 9 in)

FEATURES

Low/swept-wing with winglets; twin underwing CFM56-5 or IAE V2500 turbofans; swept tailfin and low-set tailplane

Airbus A321 France/Germany/Spain/UK

Twin-turbofan short-haul airliner

Stretched version of A320 launched on 24 November 1989. First flight with V2530 lead engine on 11 March 1993, followed by CFM56-powered alternative in May that year. Type entered service with Lufthansa on 18 March 1994. Alitalia took delivery of first CFM56 - powered model on same day. Total delivered: 289.

VARIANTS

A321-100: Initial version
A321-200: Extended-range with additional centre tank (ACT), reinforced structure and higher thrust engines

SPECIFICATIONS

Accommodation: 2 + 220
Cargo/baggage: 52.0 m³ (1,838 cu.ft)
Max speed: M0.82 (470 kt; 870 km/h)
Range: 2,325 nm (4,306 km)

DIMENSIONS

Wingspan: 34.1 m (111 ft 10 in)
Length: 44.5 m (146 ft 0 in)
Height: 11.8 m (38 ft 9 in)

FEATURES

Low/swept-wing with winglets; twin underwing CFM56-5 or IAE V2500 turbofans; swept tailfin and low-set tailplane

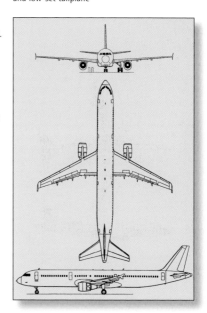

Airbus A330 France/Germany/Spain/UK

Twin-turbofan medium/long-haul airliner

Developed simultaneously with four-engined A340. Launched on 5 June 1987 and made its first flight with GE CF6-80 engines on 2 November 1992 and with Rolls-Royce Trent 700s on 31 January 1994. Entered service with Air Inter in January 1994. Total delivered: 282.

VARIANTS
A330-200: Shortened fuselage, extended-range
A330-300: Baseline version
A330 Enhanced: Improved model with FBW-controlled rudder, flightdeck with new LCDS and updated passenger cabin
A330MRTT: Proposed aerial tanker/transport

SPECIFICATIONS: A330-300
Accommodation: 2 + 440
Cargo/baggage: 46,715 kg (102,958 lb)
Max speed: M0.86 (493 kt; 912 km/h)
Range: 5,620 nm (10,400 km)

DIMENSIONS
A330-300: Wingspan: 60.3 m (197 ft 10 in)
Length: 63.7 m (208 ft 11 in)
Height: 16.8 m (55 ft 3 in)

FEATURES
Low/swept wing with winglets; twin underwing GE CF6-80, P&W PW4000 or Rolls-Royce Trent 700 turbofans; swept tailfin and low-set tailplane; widebody fuselage

Airbus A340 France/Germany/Spain/UK

Four-turbofan long-haul airliner

Launched 5 June 1987 in a combined programme with A330. First flight of -300 and -200 models on 25 October 1991 and 1 April 1992 respectively, followed by service entry of both with Lufthansa in January 1993. Stretched -600 first flown on 23 April 2001 and ultra long-range A340-500 on 11 February 2002, entering service respectively with Virgin Atlantic on 5 August 2002 and Emirates on 3 December 2003. Total delivered: 261.

VARIANTS

A340-200: Short-fuselage, longer-range version
A340-300: Higher-capacity version of A340-200
A340-300E: Extended-range with additional centre fuel tank (ACT)
A340-500: Ultra-long range stretch
A340-600: Further stretch, higher-thrust engines and four-wheel central landing gear

SPECIFICATIONS: A340-300

Accommodation: 2 + 440
Cargo/baggage: 45,915 kg (101,915 lb)
Max speed: M0.86 (493 kt; 912 km/h)
Range: 7,100 nm (13,150 km)

DIMENSIONS

Wingspan: 60.3 m (197 ft 10 in)
Length: 63.6 m (208 ft 8 in)
Height: 16.8 m (55 ft 3 in)

FEATURES

Low/swept wing with winglets; four underwing CFM56-5 or Rolls-Royce Trent 500 turbofans; swept tailfin and low-set tailplane; widebody fuselage

Airbus A380 France/Germany/Spain/UK

Four-turbofan high-capacity long-range airliner

Development of this double-deck airliner was begun under the designation A3XX in April 1996, with formal launch as the A380 on 19 December 2000. First metal was cut on 23 January 2002 and first flight scheduled for early 2005. Singapore

Airlines will put the passenger A380 into service in March 2006, with the freighter to follow in June 2008. Total ordered: 129.

VARIANTS
A380-700: Potential short-fuselage version
A380-800: Baseline passenger variant for 555 passengers in three classes
A380-800F: All-cargo version with 150-tonne payload capacity
A380-900: Potential stretch for up to 950 passengers in high-density configuration

SPECIFICATIONS: A380-800
Accommodation: 2 + 555
Cargo: 150,000 kg (330,690 lb) (-800F)
Max speed: Mach 0.89
Range: 8,000 nm (14,815 km)

DIMENSIONS
Wingspan: 79.65 m (261 ft 4 in)
Length: 72.75 m (238 ft 8 in)
Height: 24.08 m (79 ft 0 in)

FEATURES
Low/swept wings with winglets; four underwing Engine Alliance GP7200 or Rolls-Royce Trent 900 turbofans; swept high tailfin with swept low-set tailplane; double-deck fuselage

Antonov An-72/74 'Coaler' Ukraine

Twin-turbofan light STOL transport

Developed as tactical transport replacement for the An-26 in service with the Soviet air force. The most significant design feature is the considerable increase in lift achieved through the Coanda effect whereby the engine exhaust gases are blown over the high wing's upper surface. First flown on 31 August 1977, but did not enter production until December 1989. Total delivered: 160+.

VARIANTS

An-72-100: Civilianised version with upgraded avionics
An-74: Improved multi-role transport
An-74T-100: As -200, with navigator station
An-74T-200: Freight version with increased payload
An-74T-200A: Longer hold, roller conveyors and loading winch
An74TK-100: As TK-200, with navigator and flight engineer station
An-74TK-200: Passenger/cargo convertible
An-24TK-200 Salon: Executive version for 10-16 passengers

SPECIFICATIONS

Passengers: 3 + 68
Cargo: 10,000 kg (22,046 lb)
Max speed: 380 kt (705 km/h)
Range: 1,160 nm (2,150 km)

DIMENSIONS

Wingspan: 31.9 m (104 ft 8 in)
Length: 28.1 m (92 ft 2 in)
Height: 8.7 m (28 ft 5 in)

FEATURES

High/swept wings; twin ZMKB Progress D-36 turbofan engines mounted high on wing and close in to sides of fuselage; upswept rear fuselage with ramp/door; swept T-tail; tricycle landing gear retracting into large side fairings

Antonov An-74-300 Ukraine

Twin-turbofan short-haul transport

Announced in mid-1998 and demonstrated for the first time at the Paris Air Show in June 2001 after making its maiden flight in April 2001. This new model differs considerably from the earlier An-74 version, the most noticeable being the replacement of the overwing engines by conventionally podded engines under the wing. Certificated in September 2002.

VARIANTS
An-74TK-300 : Baseline passenger transport
An-174: Proposed stretched fuselage

SPECIFICATIONS
Passengers 2 + 68
Cargo 10,000 kg (22,046 lb)
Max speed: 391 kt (725 km/h)
Range: 1,890 nm (3,500 km)

DIMENSIONS
Wingspan: 31.9 m (104 ft 8 in)
Length: 28.1 m (92 ft 2 in)
Height: 8.7 m (28 ft 5 in)

FEATURES
High/swept wing with slight anhedral; twin underslung ZMKB Progress D-36 turbofan engines; upswept rear fuselage; swept T-tail; tricycle landing gear retracting into large side fairings

Antonov An-124 'Condor' Ukraine

Four-turbofan outsize freight transport

Under development in the late 1970s as outsize freighter, capable of take-off and landing from unprepared fields and provided with front and rear loading access with fold-down hydraulic ramps. Prototype first flew on 26 December 1982 and the type entered service in January 1986. Set several world records for payload/distance flights. Total built to date: 55.

VARIANTS

An-124: Basic military transport
An-124-100: Standard civil transport
An-124-100M: As An-124-100, but with Western avionics and increased take-off weight
An-124-200: Proposed version with GE CF6-80C2 turbofans
An-124-300: Proposal with extended fuselage and wingspan and two-crew glass cockpit
Military models being converted for civil freighter use

SPECIFICATIONS

Passengers 6 crew + 12 cargo handlers
Cargo 150,000 kg (330,700 lb)
Max speed: 467 kt (865 km/h)
Range: 2,430 nm (4,500 km)

DIMENSIONS

Wingspan: 73.3 m (240 ft 6 in)
Length: 69.1 m (226 ft 9 in)
Height: 21.1 m (69 ft 2 in)

FEATURES

High/swept anhedral wing; four ZMKB Progress D-18T turbofans; clamshell doors aft of rear loading ramp; upward-opening nose section with fold-down ramp for front loading; retractable undercarriage with 24 main wheels

BAe (BAC) One-Eleven UK

Twin-turbofan short-haul airliner

Thomas Posch

Decision to proceed with development of former Hunting H.107 project taken in March 1961. Prototype first flew on 20 August 1963 and type entered service with British United Airways on 9 April 1965. Later produced under licence in Romania. Total delivered: 230 (in UK), 9 (in Romania).

VARIANTS

Series 200: Initial version
Series 300: Increased fuel in centre tank and structural modifications
Series 400: Based on Srs 300 but optimised for US operators
Series 475: Combining wings of Series 500 with fuselage of Series 400
Series 500: Stretched version with more powerful engines
Rombac 495: Romanian-built version of Series 475
Rombac 560: Romanian-built version of Series 500

SPECIFICATIONS: SERIES 500

Accommodation: 119
Cargo/baggage: 20.1 m³ (710 cu.ft)
Max speed: M0.82 (470 kt; 870 km/h)
Range: 1,480 nm (2,745 km)

DIMENSIONS

Wingspan: 28.5 m (93 ft 6 in)
Length: 32.6 m (107 ft 0 in)
Height: 7.5 m (24 ft 6 in)

FEATURES

Low/swept wing; twin, rear-mounted Rolls-Royce Spey turbofans; swept T-tail and tailplane; ventral airstairs

BAe 146/Avro RJ UK

Four-turbofan short-haul regional jet

Former Hawker Siddeley H.S.146 project re-launched on 10 July 1978 and first flown on 3 September 1981. Entered revenue service with Dan-Air on 27 May 1983. Avro RJ developed from 146 with major changes including uprated engines and digital avionics; first flight on 23 March 1992. Further improvements, including new Honeywell AS977 turbofans, incorporated in RJX, first flown on 28 April 2001, but programme abandoned in November 2001. Total delivered: 389 (219 BAe 146, 170 Avro RJ).

VARIANTS
146-100: Baseline version with ALF502 turbofans
146-200: Longer fuselage and higher weights
146-300: Further stretch for increased capacity
Statesman: Executive model
146-300ARA: Atmospheric Research Aircraft
RJ70: Short version for up 70-94 passengers, LF507 turbofans
RJ85: Lengthened version for 85-112 passengers
RJ100: Further stretch for 100-116 passengers

SPECIFICATIONS: RJ85
Accommodation: 2 + 112
Cargo/baggage: 18.3 m³ (644 cu.ft)
Max speed: M0.72 (412 kt; 763 km/h)
Range: 1,080 nm (2,000 km)

DIMENSIONS
Wingspan: 26.3 m (86 ft 5 in)
Length: 28.6 m (93 ft 8 in)
Height: 8.6 m (28 ft 3 in)

FEATURES
High/swept wing; four underwing ALF 502 or LF 507 turbofans; swept T-Tail and swept tailplane; retractable landing gear in fuselage panniers

Boeing 707/720 USA

Four-engined medium/long-haul airliner

First Boeing jet airliner to enter service. Prototype, designated 367-80, first flew on 15 July 1954. First 707 with longer fuselage and powered by four P&W JT3C-6 turbojets entered service with Pan American across the Atlantic on 26 October 1958. The 720 was similar in general appearance but with lighter structure, and slightly shorter fuselage matching that of the 'short-body' 707-120. Total delivered (including military): 878 (707), 154 (720).

VARIANTS

707-120: First production version available in

both 'long-body' and 'short-body' versions, P&W JT3C turbojets
707-120B: More powerful development with JT3D turbofans
707-220: Identical to –120 but powered by JT4A turbojets
707-320: Intercontinental range, increased wingspan and longer fuselage
707-320B: More powerful JT3Ds and other refinements
707-320C: Convertible with forward cargo door and loading system
707-320C: All-cargo version with passenger facilities eliminated
707-420: As –320 but with Rolls-Royce Conway turbofans
720: basic model with P&W JT3C-7 turbojets
720B: Improved version with JT3D turbofans
Most 707s still in service have been converted to freighters

SPECIFICATIONS: 707-320B

Accommodation: 3 + 219
Cargo/baggage: 50.3 m³ (1,775 cu.ft)
Max speed: M0.94 (540 kt; 1,000 km/h)
Range: 5,000 nm (9,265 km)

DIMENSIONS

Wingspan: 44.4 m (145 ft 9 in)
Length: 46.6 m (152 ft 11 in)
Height: 12.9 m (42 ft 5 in)

FEATURES

Low/swept wings; four underwing P&W or Rolls-Royce turbojets or P&W JT3D turbofans; swept tailfin with antenna at top; low-set tailplane; small ventral fin (except -320B/C)

Boeing 717 USA

Twin-turbofan short-haul airliner

Art Brett

Originally developed by McDonnell Douglas as MD-95, announced at Paris Air Show in June 1991. Design taken over by Boeing in 1997 and renamed. Prototype first flew on 2 September 1998 and type entered service with AirTran Airways in September 1999. Total delivered: 125.

VARIANTS

717-200: Standard production version
717-300: Proposed 'stretch' for around 130 passengers

SPECIFICATIONS

Accommodation: 2 + 117
Cargo/baggage: 26.5 m³ (936 cu.ft)
Max speed: M0.76 (438 kt; 811 km/h)
Range: 1,920 nm (3,556 km)

DIMENSIONS

Wingspan: 28.5 m (93 ft 4 in)
Length: 37.8 m (124 ft 0 in)
Height: 8.9 m (29 ft 1 in)

FEATURES

Low/swept wings; twin, rear fuselage-mounted Rolls-Royce Deutschland BR 715 turbofans; swept T-tail and tailplane

Boeing 727 USA

Three-turbofan short-haul airliner

David McIntosh

Launched on 5 December 1960 and designed for maximum commonality with 707, permitting similar cabin layouts. Advanced aerodynamics and greater wing sweepback. First flown on 9 February 1963, and entered service with Eastern Air Lines on 1 February 1964. Total delivered: 1,832.

VARIANTS

727-100: Initial production version
727-100C: Convertible passenger/cargo with reinforced flooring and large forward cargo door
727-100QC: Quick-change alternative with palletised seats
727-200: Stretched model replacing –100s as standard aircraft
727-200 Advanced: Further refinements and improved cabin interior
727-200F: Pure freighter with strengthened fuselage structure and windows blocked out
Many aircraft since fitted with 'hushkits'

SPECIFICATIONS: 727-200

Accommodation: 3 + 189
Cargo/baggage: 43.2 m³ (1,525 cu.ft)
Max speed: M0.95 548 kt (1,014 km/h)
Range: 2,370 nm (4,392 km)

DIMENSIONS

Wingspan: 32.9 m (108 ft 0 in)
Length: 46.7 m (153 ft 2 in)
Height: 10.4 m (34 ft 0 in)

FEATURES

Low/swept wing; three P&W JT8D turbofan engines, one atop and integral with tail and two on side of rear fuselage; highly-swept T-tail and tailplane

Boeing 737-100/200 USA

Twin-turbofan short-haul airliner

Design of the 'Baby' Boeing started on 11 May 1964, featuring a conventional layout with underwing engines. Made first flight on 9 April 1967 and entered service with launch customer Lufthansa on 10 February 1968. Original model quickly replaced by stretched version, which flew on 8 August 1967. Total delivered: 1,144.

VARIANTS

737-100: Original production version. Only 30 built
737-200: Standard model with small fuselage stretch
737-200C: Convertible passenger/cargo with forward side door
737-200 Advanced: Improved technology
737-200C Advanced: Convertible alternative
737-200QC Advanced: Quick-change version with palletised seats

SPECIFICATIONS: 737-200A

Accommodation: 2 + 130
Cargo/baggage: 24.8 m³ (875 cu.ft)
Max speed: M0.84 (481 kt; 890 km/h)
Range: 2,530 nm (4,688 km)

DIMENSIONS

Wingspan: 28.4 m (93 ft 0 in)
Length: 30.5 m (100 ft 2 in)
Height: 11.3 m (37 ft 0 in)

FEATURES

Low/swept wing; twin underwing P&W JT8D turbofans in slim engine Nacelles; swept tailfin and low-set tailplane

Boeing 737-300/400/500 USA

Twin-turbofan short-haul airliner

Stretched development of popular twin, incorporating advanced technology CFM56 engines and other improvements. First flown on 24 February 1984 and put into service by launch customer Southwest Airlines on 7 December that year. Longer and shorter derivatives added. Models now replaced by next-generation 737s. Total delivered: 1,988.

VARIANTS
737-300: Initial baseline model
77-33: Corporate model
737-400: Longer variant with strengthened structure
737-500: Short-fuselage variant
Some aircraft, especially the 737-300, operated in all cargo or quick-change configuration with suffix C

SPECIFICATIONS: 737-400
Accommodation: 2 +170
Cargo/baggage: 30.2 m^3 (1,070 cu.ft)
Max speed: M0.84 (481 kt; 890 km/h)
Range: 2,500 nm (4,633 km)

DIMENSIONS
Wingspan: 28.9 m (94 ft 9 in)
Length: 36.5 m (119 ft 7 in)
Height: 11.1 m (36 ft 6 in)
FEATURES
Low/swept wing; large twin underwing CFM56-3 turbofans; swept tailfin with dorsal fin and low-set tailplane

Boeing 737-600/700/800/900 USA

Twin-turbofan short-haul airliner

'Current 'next generation' family, initially referred to as the 737X, with increased wing, new high-lift devices, and greater range and speed. Maiden flight was made on 9 February 1997, and the 737-700 was the first to enter service with launch customer Southwest Airlines in October that year. Total delivered: 1,420.

VARIANTS

737-600: Smallest version equivalent to 737-500
737-700: Mid-size model equivalent to 737-300
737-700C: Quick-change version with palletised seats
737-800: More powerful engines, roughly equivalent to 737-400
737-900: Largest 737 version for up to 189 passengers
BBJ: Boeing Business Jet based on the 737-700
BBJ 2: Boeing Business Jet based on the 737-800

SPECIFICATIONS: 737-700

Accommodation: 2 + 149
Cargo/baggage: 27.4 m³ (966 cu.ft)
Max speed: M0.82 (470 kt; 870 km/h)
Range: 1,540 nm (2,852 km)

DIMENSIONS

Wingspan: 34.3 m (112 ft 7 in)
Length: 33.6 m (110 ft 4 in)
Height: 12.6 m (41 ft 3 in)

FEATURES

Low/swept wing (blended winglets on BBJ and some -800s); twin underwing CFM56-7 turbofans; swept tailfin with dorsal fin and low-set tailplane

Boeing 747-100/200/SP USA

Four-turbofan long-haul airliner

First widebody airliner developed as a by-product of work done by Boeing on CH-X military transport requirement. Officially launched into production on 25 July 1966 and made first flight on 9 February 1969. Put into service by launch customer Pan American on the North Atlantic on 21 January 1970. Total delivered: 643.

VARIANTS
747SP: Longer-range short-body derivative
747-100: Original production model
747-100B: Higher gross weight and strengthened structure
747-100SF: Cargo conversion with main deck cargo door
747-100SR: Short-range version optimised for high T-O/landing cycles
747-200B: Increased fuel capacity and uprated engines
747-200C: Passenger/cargo model with upward-hinged nose
747-200F: Pure freighter with upward-hinged nose.
747-200M: Combi with large port side cargo door aft of wing

SPECIFICATIONS: 747-200B
Accommodation: 3 + 516
Cargo/baggage: 90,720 kg (200,000 lb)
Max speed: M0.92 (525 kt; 973 km/h)
Range: 6,600 nm (12,223 km)

DIMENSIONS
Wingspan: 59.6 m (195 ft 8 in)
Length: 70.7 m (231 ft 10 in)
Height: 19.3 m (63 ft 5 in)

FEATURES
Low/swept wings; four underwing GE CF6, P&W JT9D or Rolls-Royce RB 211 turbofans; short upper deck; swept tailfin and low-set tailplane; widebody fuselage

Boeing 747-300/400 USA

Four-turbofan long-haul airliner

Extended upper-deck development announced on 12 June 1980. Initially known as 747SUD (stretched upper deck) and 747EUD (extended upper deck), but first flown as 747-300 on 5 October 1982. Extensive changes, including a two-crew flight deck resulted in the –400 model, first flown on 29 April 1988. Total delivered 81 (-300) 81; 614 (-400).

VARIANTS

747-300: Initial upper deck model
747-300M: Combi with rear port-side cargo door
747-300SR: Short-range version with extra windows
747-400: Extended wingtips with winglets, two-crew flight deck and low fuel-burn engines
747-400ER: Extended range with additional fuel tankage
747-400F: 747-200F fuselage with short upper deck combined with larger –400 wing, improved cargo handling system
747-400M: Combi with port-side rear cargo door
747-400 Domestic: Special high-density version with five additional upper deck windows, no winglets
747-400SF: Freighter conversion

SPECIFICATIONS: 747-400

Accommodation: 2 + 568
Cargo/baggage: 113,000 kg (249,125 lb)
Max speed: M0.88 (507 kt; 938 km/h)
Range: 7,260 nm (13,445 km)

DIMENSIONS

Wingspan: 64.4 m (211 ft 5 in)

Length: 70.7 m (231 ft 10 in)
Height: 19.4 m (63 ft 8 in)

FEATURES

Low/swept wing with large winglets (not on -300); four underwing GE CF6-80, P&W PW4000 or Rolls-Royce RB 211 turbofan engines; extended upper deck; swept tailfin and low-set tailplane; widebody fuselage

Boeing 757 USA

Twin-turbofan medium-haul airliner

New-technology twin-engined 757/767/777 family announced in mid-1978, of which the 757 was the second to fly on 19 February 1982.

Revenue services began by launch customers Eastern Air Lines on 1 January and British Airways on 9 February 1983. Total delivered: 1,036.

VARIANTS

757-200: Initial production version
757-200ER: Extended-range with increased fuel
757-200M: Combi with forward upward-opening cargo door on port side
757-200PF: Package freighter with large forward cargo door, no windows
757-200SF: Special Freighter conversion for DHL
757-300: Stretched derivative

SPECIFICATIONS: 757-200

Accommodation: 2 + 289
Cargo/baggage: 47.3 m3 (1,670 cu.ft)
Max speed: M0.86 (493 kt; 912 km/h)
Range: 3,930 nm (7,278 km)

DIMENSIONS

Wingspan: 38.1 m (124 ft 10 in)
Length: 47.3 m (155 ft 3 in)
Height: 13.6 m (44 ft 6 in)

FEATURES

Low/swept wing; twin underwing P&W PW2000 or Rolls-Royce RB 211 turbofans; swept tailfin with low-set tailplane; long, narrow fuselage

Boeing 767 USA

Twin-turbofan medium-haul airliner

Launched on receipt of United Air Lines order on 14 July 1978 and made its maiden flight 26 September 1981. Initial service of P&W JT9D-powered aircraft with United Airlines on 8 September 1982, followed by GE CF6-80A-powered variant with Delta Air Lines on 25 October 1982. Total delivered: 916.

VARIANTS

767-200: Basic model
767-200ER: Extended-range with centre-section fuel tanks
767-300: Stretched model with strengthened landing gear
767-300ER: Extended-range with further increase in centre tankage
767-300F: Pure freighter with forward port cargo door, no windows
767-400ER: Stretched version with improved flight deck
KC-767: Aerial tanker/transport

SPECIFICATIONS: 767-300ER

Accommodation: 2 + 350
Cargo/baggage: 147.0 m^3 (5,190 cu.ft)
Max speed: M0.86 (493 kt; 912 km/h)
Range: 5,875 nm (10,880 km)

DIMENSIONS

Wingspan: 47.6 m (156 ft 1 in)
Length: 54.9 m (180 ft 3 in)
Height: 15.9 m (52 ft 0 in)

FEATURES

Low/swept wing; twin underwing GE CF6-80C2, P&W PW4000 or Rolls-Royce RB 211 turbofans; swept tailfin and low-set tailplane; widebody fuselage; blended winglets available for retrofit on 767-300ER

Boeing 777 USA

Twin-turbofan long-haul airliner

Designed to fit between the 767 and the 747, and initially known as the 767-X, the fly-by-wire 777 was launched in October 1990 and made its maiden flight on 12 June 1994. First revenue service with United Airlines between London and Washington DC took place on 7 June 1995. Total delivered: 463.

VARIANTS

777-200: Baseline aircraft
777-200ER: Longer-range variant, formerly known as the 777-200IGW (increased gross weight)
777-200LR: Ultra long-range proposal, optional auxiliary fuel tank
777-300: Stretched derivative with strengthened fuselage, inboard wing and landing gear
777-300ER: Ultra long-range, strengthened tail surfaces and wing, added wingtips

SPECIFICATIONS: 777-300

Accommodation: 2 + 550
Cargo/baggage: 200.5 m^3 (7,080 cu.ft)
Max speed: M0.89 (510 kt; 944 km/h)
Range: 5,720 nm (10,593 km)

DIMENSIONS

Wingspan: 60.9 m (199 ft 11 in)
Length: 73.9 m (242 ft 4 in)
Height: 18.5 m (60 ft 9 in)

FEATURES

Low/swept wing (folding optional); twin underwing GE90, P&W PW4000 or Rolls-Royce Trent 800 turbofans; swept tailfin and low-set tailplane; widebody fuselage

Boeing (McDonnell Douglas) MD-11 USA

Three-turbofan medium-haul airliner

Sokol Ymeri

Follow-on design to DC-10, similar in configuration but slightly larger and distinguished by the addition of wingtips, revealed at Paris Air Show in June 1985. Launched on 30 December 1986 and first flown on 10 January 1990. Went into service with Finnair on 20 December 1990. Total delivered: 200.

VARIANTS

MD-11: Standard passenger version
MD-11C: Combi with main deck cargo door on rear port-side
MD-11CF: Convertible passenger/freight model with main deck cargo door at front on port side
MD-11ER: Extended-range version with removable auxiliary fuel tank in lower cargo hold
MD-11F: All-cargo model with no cabin windows
Most passenger aircraft are being converted to freighters

SPECIFICATIONS: MD-11ER

Accommodation: 2 + 410
Cargo/baggage: 633.7 m^3 (22,380 cu.ft)
Max speed: M0.945 (542 kt; 1,003 km/h)
Range: 7,240 nm (13,408km)

DIMENSIONS

Wingspan: 51.6 m (169 ft 5 in)
Length: 61.6 m (202 ft 2 in)
Height: 17.6 m (57 ft 8 in)

FEATURES

Low/swept wing with winglets; three GE CF6-80C2 or P&W PW4000 turbofans, one near base of tailfin, the others on underwing pylons; swept tailfin and low-set tailplane; widebody fuselage

Boeing (McDonnell Douglas) MD-80 USA

Twin-turbofan short-haul airliner

Development of the McDonnell Douglas DC-9 with refanned engines and other refinements, initially known as the DC-9 Super 80 Series. First flight on 18 October 1979, followed by the first

revenue service with Swissair on 5 October 1980. Total delivered: 1,191.

VARIANTS

MD-81: Baseline model, formerly the DC-9 Super 81

MD-82: Uprated engines with emergency thrust reverse, formerly DC-9 Super 82

MD-83: Further thrust increase and more fuel in cargo compartments, formerly DC-9 Super 83

MD-87: Shorter fuselage version with extended tailfin

MD-88: Enhanced relative of MD-82 with EFIS, FMS and IRS

SPECIFICATIONS: MD-82

Accommodation: 2 + 172
Cargo/baggage: 35.5 m^3 (1,255 cu.ft)
Max speed: M0.87 (500 kt; 925 km/h)
Range: 1,877 nm (3,476 km)

DIMENSIONS

Wingspan: 32.8 m (107 ft 8 in)
Length: 45.0 m (147 ft 8 in)
Height: 9.00 m (29 ft 6 in)

FEATURES

Low/swept wings; twin, rear side fuselage-mounted P&W JT8D turbofans; swept T-tail and tailplane

Boeing (McDonnell Douglas) MD-90 USA

Twin-turbofan short-haul airliner

Tsen Tsan Tung

Stretched, high-technology MD-80 follow-on with IAE V2500 engines, improved cabin and enlarged tailfin, launched on 14 November 1989. First flight on 22 February 1993 and service entry with Delta Air Lines on 1 April 1995. Total delivered: 114.

VARIANTS
MD-90-30: Baseline model
MD-90-30ER: Extended-range model with auxiliary fuel tank

SPECIFICATIONS: MD-90-30ER
Accommodation: 2 + 172
Cargo/baggage: 36.8 m³ (1,300 cu.ft)
Max speed: M0.76 (437 kt; 809 km/h)
Range: 2,172 nm (4,023 km)

DIMENSIONS
Wingspan: 32.8 m (107 ft 8 in)
Length: 46.5 m (152 ft 6 in)
Height: 9.3 m (30 ft 6 in)

FEATURES
Low/swept wings; twin, rear side fuselage-mounted IAE V2500 turbofans; swept T-tail and tailplane

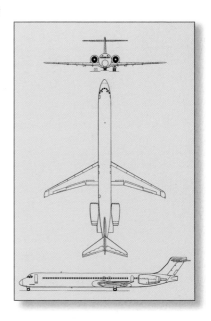

Bombardier Canadair CRJ100/200 Canada

Twin-turbofan regional airliner

Developed from Challenger business jet with extended fuselage for regional airline operations. Formal go-ahead given on 31 March 1989, first flight on 10 May 1991. Initial delivery to Lufthansa CityLine on 29 October 1992. Total delivered: 881.

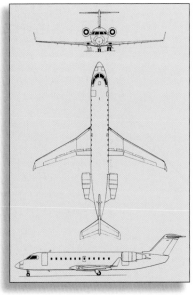

VARIANTS

CRJ100: Original standard aircraft
CRJ100ER: Extended-range derivative with additional fuel capacity
CRJ100LR: Long-range model with further fuel increase
CRJ200: Standard production aircraft
CRJ200ER: Extended-range with optional increase in fuel capacity
CRJ200LR: Long-range variant
CRJ440: Version with 44 seats for US market
Corporate Jetliner: Company shuttle with 18-30 seats
Challenger 800: Executive transport for 5-19 passengers

SPECIFICATIONS: CRJ200ER

Accommodation: 2 + 50
Cargo/baggage: 13.7 m3 (484 cu.ft)
Max speed: M0.81 (465 kt; 860 km/h)
Range: 1,645 nm (3,046 km)

DIMENSIONS

Wingspan: 21.2 m (69 ft 7 in)
Length: 26.8 m (87 ft 10 in)
Height: 6.2 m (20 ft 5 in)

FEATURES

Low/swept wings with winglets; high rear fuselage-mounted GE CF34 twin turbofans; swept T-tail and tailplane

Bombardier Canadair CRJ700/900 Canada

Twin-turbofan regional airliner

Developed as 70-seat stretched derivative of CRJ200. First flown on 27 May 1999, with initial delivery to French regional Brit Air in February 2001. Further capacity increase to 90 seats in CRJ900, which made its maiden flight on 21 February 2001 and entered service with launch customer Mesa Air in January 2003. Total delivered: 124 (700), 10 (900).

VARIANTS
CRJ700 Series 701: Standard 68-seat model
CRJ700 Series 705: Reduced capacity for US market
CRJ700ER: Extended-range model with increased weight and fuel
CRJ900: Minimum stretch for 86-90 passengers
CRJ900ER: Heavier extended range model
CRJ900LR: Longer range capability

SPECIFICATIONS: CRJ700ER
Accommodation: 2 + 78
Cargo/baggage: 23.3 m^3 (824 cu.ft)
Max speed: M0.83 (475 kt; 879 km/h)
Range: 1,984 nm (3,674 km)

DIMENSIONS
Wingspan: 23.2 m (76 ft 3 in)
Length: 32.5 m (106 ft 8 in)
Height: 7.6 m (24 ft 10 in)

FEATURES
Low/swept wing with winglets; high rear fuselage-mounted GE CF34 twin turbofans; swept T-tail and tailplane

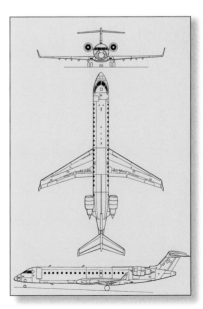

Embraer ERJ135/140/145 Brazil

Twin-turbofan regional airliner

Original development plans for regional twin-jet revealed at Paris Air Show in June 1989, but aircraft subsequently completely redesigned. First flight of ERJ145 on 11 August 1995 and first deliveries to US launch customer Continental Express on 19 December 1996. Total delivered: 105 (ERJ135); 74 (ERJ140), 531 (ERJ145).

VARIANTS
ERJ135: Short-fuselage version
Legacy: Corporate variant of ERJ135
ERJ140: Mid-size version, primarily for US market
ERJ145: Baseline model
ERJ145ER: Extended range with increased fuel
ERJ145EU: Customised for European operations
ERJ145LR: Long-range model with uprated engines and increased fuel
ERJ145XR: Extra long-range with other improvements
EMB-145SA: AEW version for Brazilian Air Force, designated R-99A
EMB-145RS: Remote sensing version for Brazilian Air Force as R-99B

SPECIFICATIONS: ERJ145ER
Accommodation: 2 + 50
Cargo/baggage: 14.8 m^3 (521 cu.ft)
Max speed: M0.78 (450 kt; 833 km/h)
Range: 1,600 nm (2,963 km)

DIMENSIONS
Wingspan: 20.0 m (65 ft 9 in)
Length: 29.9 m (98 ft 0 in)
Height: 6.8 m (22 ft 2 in)

FEATURES
Low/swept wing; twin rear fuselage-mounted Rolls-Royce Allison AE 3007A turbofans; swept T-tail with dorsal fin and swept tailplane

Embraer 170/190 Brazil

Twin-turbofan regional airliner

Higher-capacity development of baseline ERJ145, announced in February 1999. New design with podded wing-mounted turbofans and clean tail. First 170 (formerly ERJ170) rolled out on 28 October 2001, with first flight on 19 February 2002. Service entry immediately following FAA certification on 20 February 2004. Embraer 175 flew on 14 June 2003, followed by Embraer 190 on 12 March 2004 and 190 on 7 December 2004. Total ordered: 149 (170), 110 (190), 15 (195). Total delivered: 25 (170).

VARIANTS

170: Baseline version for 70 passengers
175: Stretch proposal for 78-86 passengers, reinforced wing, higher gross weight and, enhanced management system
190: Further stretch for 98 passengers, strengthened landing gear
195: Lengthened fuselage for up to 108 passengers
Longer range (LR) variants with additional fuel will also be offered

SPECIFICATIONS: 170

Accommodation: 2 + 70
Max speed: M0.80 (461 kt; 851 km/h)
Range: 1,800 nm (3,333 km)

DIMENSIONS

Wingspan: 26.0 m (83 ft 4 in)
Length: 29.9 m (98 ft 1 in)

Height: 9.7 m (31 ft 9 in)

FEATURES

Low/swept wing; twin underwing podded GE CFE34-8 turbofans; swept tailfin with small dorsal fin and swept tailplane

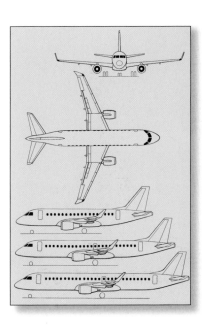

Fairchild Dornier 328JET Germany/USA

Twin-turbofan regional airliner

Jet-powered development of 328 turboprop aircraft, originally designated 328-300. Announced on 5 February 1997 and formally launched at Paris Air Show in June that year. First flight on 20 January 1998; first delivery to Skyway Airlines in June 1999. Production being restarted by Avcraft Aerospace following bankruptcy of Fairchild-Dornier. Total delivered: 86.

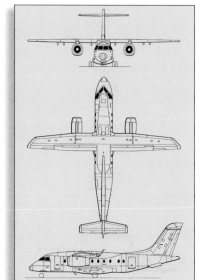

VARIANTS

328JET: Baseline regional transport for up to 34 passengers
Corporate Shuttle: High-density version for corporate transport
Envoy 3: Corporate version for up to 19 passengers

SPECIFICATIONS: 328JET

Accommodation: 2 + 34
Cargo/baggage: 6.4 m^3 (226 cu.ft)
Max speed: M0.70 (405 kt; 750 km/h)
Range: 900 nm (1,666 km)

DIMENSIONS

Wingspan: 21.0 m (68 ft 10 in)
Length: 21.3 m (69 ft 10 in)
Height: 7.2 m (23 ft 9 in)

FEATURES

High/straight wing with tapered leading edge; twin underwing P&WC PW300 turbofans; swept T-tail with dorsal fin and tapered tailplane

Fokker F28 Fellowship The Netherlands

Twin-turbofan regional airliner

Developed as a jet transport partner for the F27 turboprop, with first details published in April 1962. Made its maiden flight on 9 May 1967 and entered service with launch customer LTU of Germany on 24 February 1969. Total delivered: 241.

VARIANTS

F28 Mk 1000: Initial short-fuselage version for up to 65 passengers
F28 Mk 1000C: Convertible passenger/cargo model with large cargo door at front port side
F28 Mk 2000: Lengthened fuselage for up to 79 passengers
F28 Mk 3000: Short-fuselage model with new engines and increased span
F28 Mk 4000: Long-fuselage derivative for up to 85 passengers

SPECIFICATIONS: F28 MK 4000

Accommodation: 2 + 85
Cargo/baggage: 15.8 m^3 (560 cu.ft)
Max speed: M0.75 (430 kt; 795 km/h)
Range: 1,025 nm (1,900 km)

DIMENSIONS

Wingspan: 25.1 m (82 ft 3 in)
Length: 29.6 m (97 ft 2 in)
Height: 8.5 m (27 ft 10 in)

FEATURES

Low/swept wing; twin rear fuselage-mounted Rolls-Royce Spey turbofans; swept T-tail with dorsal fin and swept tailplane

Fokker 70/100 The Netherlands

Twin-turbofan short-haul regional airliner

New technology derivatives of F28, first announced on 24 November 1984, including new aerofoil, digital avionics and greater use of composites. Prototype of Fokker 100 flew on 30 November 1986 with first delivery to Swissair on 29 February 1988. Smaller Fokker 70 made its first flight on 2 April 1993. Total delivered: 48 (70), 283 (100).

VARIANTS

Fokker 70: Short-fuselage version for up to 79 passengers
Executive Jet 70: VIP/corporate shuttle version
Executive Jet 70ER: VIP/corporate shuttle with extended-range
Fokker 100: Standard model for up to 109 passengers
Fokker 100EJ: Executive conversion by Stork Aerospace with auxiliary fuel tank

SPECIFICATIONS: FOKKER 100

Accommodation: 2 + 109
Cargo/baggage: 19.7 m3 (695 cu.ft)
Max speed: M0.77 (441 kt; 816 km/h)
Range: 1,550 nm (2,870 km)

DIMENSIONS

Wingspan: 28.1 m (92 ft 2 in)
Length: 35.5 m (116 ft 6 in)
Height: 8.5 m (27 ft 10 in)

FEATURES

Low/swept wing; twin rear fuselage-mounted Rolls-Royce Tay turbofans; swept T-Tail with dorsal fin and swept tailplane

Ilyushin Il-62 'Classic' Russia

Four-turbofan long-haul airliner

Developed to provide Aeroflot with long-haul jet airliner and unveiled on 24 September 1962, featuring four rear-mounted turbofan engines and high-tail layout. First flight on 3 January 1963, but did not enter service until 15 September 1967. Total delivered: 289.

VARIANTS

IL-62: Initial production model with Kuznetsov NK-8 engines
IL-62M: Improved variant with Soloviev D-30KU engines
IL-62MK: Strengthened to permit operations at higher weights

SPECIFICATIONS: Il-62M

Accommodation: 3 + 186
Cargo/baggage: 48.0 m^3 (1,695 cu.ft)
Max speed: M0.85 (486 kt; 900 km/h)
Range: 4,210 nm (7,800 km)

DIMENSIONS

Wingspan: 43.2 m (141 ft 9 in)
Length: 53.1 m (174 ft 3 in)
Height: 12.4 m (40 ft 7 in)

FEATURES

Low/swept wing; four rear-mounted NK-8 or D-30 turbofans, two on each side of the fuselage; swept T-tail and tailplane; prominent bullet fin fairing

Ilyushin Il-76 'Candid' Russia

Four-turbofan medium/long-haul freighter

Developed in late 1960s to replace turboprop Antonov An-12 and made its first flight on 25 March 1971. Originally designed for and delivered to military customers, but many since converted

for civil use. Low rate production continues. Total built to date: c. 920.

VARIANTS

IL-76MD: Incorporates improvements of IL-76TD
IL-76T: Civil conversion with additional fuel tankage
IL-76TD: Strengthened wings and centre fuselage
IL-76TF: Civil production version available from 1996; none sold
+ several military models (which see)

SPECIFICATIONS: IL-76TD

Passengers 7 + 140 (troops)
Cargo 50,000 kg (110,230 lb)
Max speed: M0.77 (441 kt; 817 km/h)
Range: 1,970 nm (3,650 km)

DIMENSIONS

Wingspan: 50.5 m (165 ft 8 in)
Length: 46.6 m (152 ft 11 in)
Height: 14.8 m (48 ft 6 in)

FEATURES

High/swept wing with slight anhedral; four Aviadvigatel D-30 turbofans; rear loading ramp/door; T-tail with sweptback tail surfaces; tricycle landing gear retracting into large side fairings

Ilyushin Il-86 'Camber' Russia

Four-turbofan medium-haul airliner

Rainer Eixenberger

First Soviet-built widebody airliner intended as successor to IL-62, and first to have wing-mounted engines. Made first flight on 22 December 1976 and entered Aeroflot service on 26 December 1980. Performance shortfall resulted in curtailed production run. Total delivered: 103.

86 turbofans; swept tailfin and swept low-set tailplane; widebody fuselage

VARIANTS

IL-86: Standard production model continuously updated but not redesignated

IL-87 'Maxdome': Airborne strategic command post version with large boat-shaped fairing above forward fuselage and large pod with ram air intake under each inner wing

SPECIFICATIONS

Accommodation: 3 + 350
Max speed: M0.89 (512 kt; 950 km/h)
Range: 1,944 nm (3,600 km)

DIMENSIONS

Wingspan: 48.1 m (157 ft 9 in)
Length: 59.5 m (195 ft 4 in)
Height: 15.8 m (51 ft 10 in)

FEATURES

Low/swept wing; four underwing Kuznetsov NK-

Ilyushin Il-96 Russia

Four-turbofan long-haul airliner

Rainer Eixenberger

Developed from the IL-86 to provide improved performance and increased range, featuring a new supercritical wing and large winglets. Made its first flight on 28 September 1988 and entered Aeroflot service in early 1993. Programme dogged by lack of funding and only 18 delivered to date.

VARIANTS

IL-96-300: Initial production version
IL-96PU: VIP model built for Russian President
IL-96-400: Stretched and extended range passenger model
IL-96-400T: Freighter with cargo door forward of wing on port side

SPECIFICATIONS: IL-96M

Accommodation: 3 + 386
Cargo/baggage: 115.9 m^3 (4,094 cu.ft)
Max speed: M0.86 (493 kt; 912 km/h)
Range: 6,195 nm (11,482 km)

DIMENSIONS

Wingspan: 60.1 m (197 ft 3 in)
Length: 64.7 m (212 ft 3 in)
Height: 15.7 m (51 ft 7 in)

FEATURES

Low/swept wing with large winglets; four underwing PS-90A turbofans; swept tailfin and low-set tailplane; widebody fuselage

Lockheed L1011 TriStar USA

Three-turbofan medium-haul airliner

Toni Marimon

Developed to an American Airlines requirement for a high capacity aircraft with transcontinental range and able to take off from comparatively short runways. First flown on 17 November 1970, the TriStar entered revenue service with Eastern Air Lines on 26 April 1972. Total delivered: 250.

VARIANTS

L1011-1: Initial production version
L1011-50: Conversion of TriStar 1 with higher operating weight
L1011-100: Higher gross weight and fuel capacity
L1011-150: Conversion of TriStar 1 to increase range capability
L1011-200: Uprated engines and higher gross weight
L1011-250: Converted TriStar 1 with same engines as Model 500
L1011-500: Shorter fuselage, long-range with aerodynamic improvements

SPECIFICATIONS: L1011-500

Accommodation: 3 + 330
Cargo/baggage: 118.9 m³ (4,200 cu.ft)
Max speed: M0.84 (481 kt; 890 km/h)
Range: 5,297 nm (9,815 km)

DIMENSIONS

Wingspan: 47.3 m (155 ft 4 in)
Length: 50.1 m (164 ft 3 in)
Height: 16.9 m (55 ft 4 in)

FEATURES

Low/swept wings; three Rolls-Royce RB 211 turbofans, two on pylons under wing, the third at base of and integrated with swept tailfin; low-set swept tailplane; widebody fuselage

McDonnell Douglas DC-8 USA

Four-engined medium/long-haul airliner

First Douglas commercial jet launched in June 1955, featuring, like the Boeing 707, four turbojets under the wing. Made maiden flight on 30 May 1958 and entered service simultaneously with Delta Air Lines and United on 18 September 1959. Total delivered: 293.

VARIANTS

DC-8-10: Initial production version for domestic routes
DC-8-20: Long-range with more powerful P&W JT4A turbojets
DC-8-30: Intercontinental range with uprated engines
DC-8-40: Similar to Series 30 but with Rolls-Royce Conway engines
DC-8-50: Similar to Series 30 but with P&W JT3D turbofans
DC-8F-55: Freighter with cargo door and strengthened floor

SPECIFICATIONS: DC-8-50

Accommodation: 3 + 179
Cargo/baggage: 39.4 m3 (1,390 cu.ft)
Max speed: M0.88 (505 kt; 934 km/h)
Range: 6,078 nm (11,260 km)

DIMENSIONS

Wingspan: 43.4 m (142 ft 5 in)
Length: 45.9 m (150 ft 6 in)
Height: 12.9 m (42 ft 4 in)

FEATURES

Low/swept wing; four underwing P&W JT3C or JT4A or Rolls-Royce Conway turbojets, or P&W JT3D turbofans; Swept tailfin and low-set tailplane; auxiliary chin intakes

McDonnell Douglas DC-8 'Super Sixty' USA

Four-turbofan long-haul airliner

Launched in April 1965 as follow-on from one-size initial DC-8 series with considerably lengthened fuselage and various aerodynamic improvements. First flight made on 14 March 1966, with service entry on 25 February the following year. Total delivered: 263.

VARIANTS

DC-8-61: First stretched variant for 259 passengers
DC-8-62: Shorter fuselage than -61, ultra long-range capability
DC-8-63: Combines long fuselage of –61 with powerplant of –62
Convertible (CF) and all-freighters (AF) available in all three models
DC-8-71: Re-engined Series 61 with new CFM56-2 turbofans
DC-8-72: Re-engined Series 62 with new CFM56-2 turbofans
DC-8-73: Re-engined Series 63 with new CFM56-2 turbofans

SPECIFICATIONS: DC-8-63

Accommodation: 2 + 259
Cargo/baggage: 70.8 m³ (2,500 cu.ft)
Max speed: M0.91 (521 kt; 965 km/h)
Range: 4,000 nm (7,400 km)

DIMENSIONS

Wingspan: 45.2 m (148 ft 5 in)
Length: 57.1 m (187 ft 5 in)
Height: 12.9 m (42 ft 5 in)

FEATURES

Low/swept wing; four underwing P&W JT3D or CFM56-2 turbofans; swept tailfin and low-set tailplane; auxiliary chin intakes; long slim fuselage

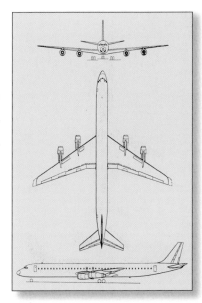

McDonnell Douglas DC-9 USA

Twin-turbofan short/medium-haul airliner

Design studies of a short/medium-range aircraft with twin rear-mounted turbofans as partner to the DC-8 were released in 1962, leading to the official launch on 8 April 1963. First flight on 25 February 1965, with service entry with Delta following on 8 December that year. Total delivered: 976.

VARIANTS

DC-9-10: Initial production version with two engine options
DC-9-15MC: Multiple-change convertible with forward port cargo door
DC-9-15RC: Rapid-change with roller floor and cargo door
DC-9-20: Hot-and-high model combining wings of Series 30 and short-fuselage of Series 10
DC-9-30: Longer fuselage, uprated engines and high-lift devices
DC-9-30CF: Convertible freighter, no cargo door, for small packages
DC-9-30F: Freighter with no windows, formerly DC-9-30AF
DC-9-40: Further stretch, uprated engines and increased fuel
DC-9-50: Longest model with new interior
+ military models under **C9A, C-9B** and **VC-9C** designation (which see)

SPECIFICATIONS: DC-9-50

Accommodation: 2 + 139
Cargo/baggage: 29.3 m³ (1,034 cu.ft)
Max speed: M0.87 (500 kt; 926 km/h)
Range: 1,795 nm (3,326 km)

DIMENSIONS: DC-9-50

Wingspan: 28.5 m (93 ft 5 in)
Length: 40.7 m (133 ft 7 in)
Height: 8.5 m (28 ft 0 in)

FEATURES

Low/swept wing; twin rear fuselage-mounted P&W JT8D turbofans; swept T-tail and tailplane

McDonnell Douglas DC-10 USA

Three-turbofan medium/long-haul airliner

Thomas Posch

Developed from an American Airlines specification of March 1966 for a so-called 'jumbo twin', but eventually became a larger capacity tri-jet. Launched in April 1968 and made its first flew 29 August 1970. Entered service with launch customer American Airlines on 5 August 1971. Total delivered (including military): 446.

VARIANTS

DC-10-10: Initial GE CF6-powered US domestic
DC-10-10CF: Convertible with forward side cargo door
DC-10-15: Hot-and-high model with uprated engines
DC-10-30: Heavier and more powerful long-range model
DC-10-30CF: Convertible with forward side cargo door
DC-10-30ER: Extended-range with higher weights and fuel capacity
DC-10-30F: Pure freighter without cabin windows
DC-10-40: Version with P&W JT9D turbofans, formerly Series 20
MD-10: Advanced freighter conversion with two-crew cockpit
+ military **KC-10A** tankers (which see)

SPECIFICATIONS: DC-10-30

Accommodation: 3 + 380
Cargo/baggage: 103 m³ (3,655 cu.ft)
Max speed: M0.88 (505 kt; 934 km/h)
Range: 4,000 nm (7,413 km)

DIMENSIONS

Wingspan: 50.4 m (165 ft 5 in)

Length: 55.5 m (182 ft 1 in)
Height: 17.7 m (58 ft 1 in)

FEATURES

Low/swept wing; three GE CF6 or P&W JT9D turbofans, two on underwing pylons, the third above rear fuselage near base of swept tailfin; swept low-set tailplane; widebody fuselage; additional two-wheel landing gear on centreline of Series 30 only

SATIC Super Transporter (Beluga)

France/Germany/Spain/UK

Twin-turboprop outsize freight transport

Announced in December 1990 as replacement for Super Guppy to carry Airbus assemblies between manufacturing plants. Based on Airbus A300-600 with enlarged unpressurised upper fuselage and upward-hinged door above flight deck. First flown 13 September 1994 and entered service with Airbus in January 1996. Military cargolifter also proposed but future uncertain.
Total built to date: 5.

VARIANTS

A300-600ST: Basic and only model built to date

SPECIFICATIONS:

Crew: 4
Cargo: 47,300 kg (104,279 lb)
Max speed: M0.70 (401 kt; 742 km/h)
Range: 900 nm (1,666 km)

DIMENSIONS

Wingspan: 44.8 m (147 ft 0 in)
Length: 56.2 m (184 ft 4 in)
Height: 17.2 m (56 ft 6 in)

FEATURES

Low/swept wing; twin GE CF6-80C2 turbofans; large cargo compartment with upward-opening nose section for front loading; flight deck below main cargo deck; raised fin and tailplane with large endplate fins

Tupolev Tu-134 'Crusty' Russia

Twin-turbofan short-haul airliner

Rear-engined twin-turbofan development of the Tu-124, initially known as Tu-124A, started in early 1960s. Believed to have made its first flight in December 1963. Commercial services with Aeroflot began in September 1967. Total delivered: 850+.

VARIANTS

Tu-134: Initial production version with Soloviev D-30 turbofans
Tu-134A: Small stretch, uprated engines and improved avionics
Tu-134A-3: Improved engines and new lightweight seats
Tu-134B: Spoilers for direct lift and forward-facing crew compartment
Tu-134B-1: Minor internal improvements
Tu-134B-3: Further internal revisions to increase seating
+ various military models (which see)

SPECIFICATIONS: TU-134A

Accommodation: 3 + 96
Max speed: M0.85 (485 kt; 897 km/h)
Range: 1,630 nm (3,020 km)

DIMENSIONS: TU-134A

Wingspan: 29.0 m (95 ft 2 in)
Length: 37.1 m (121 ft 7 in)
Height: 9.1 m (30 ft 0 in)

FEATURES

Low/swept wing; twin rear fuselage-mounted Soloviev D-30 turbofans; Swept T-tail with dorsal fin and swept tailplane; early models have glazed nose

Tupolev Tu-154 'Careless' Russia

Three-turbofan medium-haul airliner

Gerd Beilfuss

Announced in spring 1966, the Tu-154 was designed to operate from poorly-surfaced airfields. It made its first flight on 4 October 1968 and, after many proving and ad-hoc flights entered commercial service with Aeroflot on 9 February 1972. Still in limited production. Total delivered: 950+.

VARIANTS
Tu-154: Initial production version
Tu-154A: Uprated engine, higher gross weight and increased fuel
Tu-154B: Improved version with new avionics and cabin interior
Tu-154B-2: Western flight control and navigation system
Tu-154C: Freighter with forward port side cargo door and roller tracks
Tu-154M-LK-1: Head-of-state use
Tu-154M: More powerful D-30KU engines, redesigned lifting devices
Tu-156M: Cryogenic-fuel development

SPECIFICATIONS: TU-154M
Accommodation: 3 + 180
Cargo/baggage: 43.0 m^3 (1,519 cu.ft)
Max speed: M0.90 (515 kt; 953 km/h)
Range: 3,723 nm (6,900 km)

DIMENSIONS
Wingspan: 37.6 m (123 ft 3 in)
Length: 47.9 m (157 ft 2 in)
Height: 11.4 m (37 ft 5 in)

FEATURES
Low/swept anhedral wing; three Soloviev D-30 rear-mounted turbofans, one each side of rear fuselage, third atop fuselage in base of tailfin; swept T-tail with bullet fin fairing and swept tailplane

Tupolev Tu-204/214 Russia

Twin-turbofan medium-haul airliner

Andy Graf

Developed to replace the Tu-154 and IL-62 and first announced in 1983. Conventionally designed aircraft with twin underwing turbofans and winglets, the Tu-204 made its maiden flight with PS-90AT engines on 2 January 1989. Initially used for freight, but first passenger flight operated by Vnukovo Airlines on 23 February 1996. Total delivered: 17.

VARIANTS

Tu-204: Basic model with PS-90A turbofans
Tu-204C: Basic freighter model
Tu-204-100: Extended-range version with additional fuel in wing
Tu-204-120: As –100, but with Rolls-Royce RB 211-535 turbofans
Tu-204-300: Shortened, longer range derivative, formerly Tu-234
Tu-204-500: Enhanced version with smaller wing and higher MTOW under development
Tu-214: As –100, higher gross-weight, formerly Tu-204-200
All models are available as freighters with C suffix

SPECIFICATIONS: TU-214

Accommodation: 2 + 212
Cargo/baggage: 26.4 m³ (932 cu.ft)
Max speed: M0.80 (459 kt; 850 km/h)
Range: 2,591 nm (4,800 km)

DIMENSIONS

Wingspan: 41.8 m (137 ft 2 in)

Length: 46.1 m (151 ft 3 in)
Height: 13.9 m (45 ft 7 in)

FEATURES

Low/swept wing with large winglets; twin underwing Aviadvigatel PS-90A or R-R RB 211-535 turbofans; swept tailfin and low-set tailplane

Tupolev Tu-334 Russia

Twin-turbofan short/medium-haul regional jet

Launched in 1986 as replacement for Tu-134, but funding shortages delayed first flight to 8 February 1999. Much commonality with Tu-204, including identical cockpit. Certification was expected by end of 2001, with service entry late 2002/early 2003 but this has been further delayed to 2004/2005. Total ordered: 24.

VARIANTS
Tu-334-100: Basic version with Ivchenko Progress D-436T1 engines
Tu-334-100C: Combi version
Tu-334-100D: Extended-range, increased wingspan and uprated engines
Tu-334-120: As –100 but R-R Deutschland BR710 turbofans
Tu-334-120D: As –100D but R-R Deutschland BR710 turbofans
Tu-334-200: Extended fuselage and increased span; also known as Tu-354
Tu-334-200C: Freighter

SPECIFICATIONS: TU-334-100D
Accommodation: 2 + 102
Cargo/baggage: 16.2 m^3 (572 cu.ft)
Max speed: M0.77 (442 kt; 820 km/h)
Range: 2,213 nm (4,100 km)

DIMENSIONS
Wingspan: 32.6 m (107 ft 0 in)
Length: 31.8 m (104 ft 4 in)
Height: 9.4 m (30 ft 9 in)

FEATURES
Low/swept wing with winglets; twin rear fuselage-mounted Ivchenko Progress D-436 or R-R Deutschland BR710 turbofans; Swept T-tail with dorsal fin and swept tailplane

Yakovlev Yak-40 'Codling' Russia

Three-turbofan short-haul regional jet

Designed to replace the Lisunov Li-2 and to operate from grass airfields. Made first flight on 21 October 1966 and entered passenger service with Aeroflot on 30 September 1968. Clam-shell thrust reverser added on centre engine during production run. Total delivered: 1,000+.

VARIANTS

Yak-40: Basic production model
Yak-40EC: Export version with westernised avionics
Yak-40K: Passenger/cargo model
Yak-40V: Export version with AI-25T engines and higher gross weight

SPECIFICATIONS:

Accommodation: 2 + 32
Max speed: M0.70 (401 kt; 742 km/h)
Range: 971 nm (1,800 km)

DIMENSIONS

Wingspan: 25.0 m (82 ft 0 in)
Length: 20.4 m (66 ft 10 in)
Height: 6.5 m (21 ft 4 in)

FEATURES

Low/straight wing; three Ivchenko (Lotarev) AI-25 turbofans, two on side of rear fuselage, one atop at base of and integrated with tailfin; swept T-tail and tailplane; ventral access

Yakovlev Yak-42 'Clobber' Russia

Three turbofan short/medium-haul airliner

Tony Marimon

Developed as medium-capacity aircraft for Aeroflot. Closely resembling in configuration the smaller Yak-40, the new type made its first flight on 7 March 1975 and began passenger flights in late 1980. Total delivered: 200+.

VARIANTS

Yak-42: Initial standard production model
Yak-42A: Improved version with increased fuel and new Russian avionics
Yak-42D: Current production with increased range and forward passenger door
Yak-42D-100: Western avionics
Yak-42-200: Projected stretch for 150 passengers
Yak-42T: Projected freighter with cargo door

SPECIFICATIONS: YAK-42D

Accommodation: 2 + 120
Cargo/baggage: 29.3 m^3 (1,035 cu.ft)
Max speed: M0.76 (437 kt; 810 km/h)
Range: 1,240 nm (2,300 km)

DIMENSIONS

Wingspan: 34.9 m (114 ft 6 in)
Length: 36.2 m (118 ft 10 in)
Height: 9.8 m (32 ft 3 in)

FEATURES

Low/swept wing; three Ivchenko Progress D-36 turbofans, one each on side of rear fuselage, the third atop at base of and integrated with tailfin; swept T-tail and tailplane

CIVIL
PROP
AIRLINERS

Airtech (EADS CASA/Indonesian Aerospace)
CN-235 Spain/Indonesia

Twin-turboprop short-haul airliner

Preliminary design began in January 1980, with one prototype built by each country. The Spanish-built model flew on 11 November 1983, followed by the Indonesian aircraft on 30 December that year. Merpati Nusantara Airlines put the type into commercial service on 1 March 1988. Total delivered (including military): 213.

VARIANTS

CN-235-10: Initial production aircraft with CT7-7A engines
CN-235-100: Improved CT7-9C with composite nacelles and enhanced systems; built in Spain
CN-235-110: As –100, but built in Indonesia
CN-235-200: Higher weight and increased range; built in Spain
CN-235-220: As –200, but built in Indonesia
CN-235-300: More powerful GE CT7-9C3 engines for improved hot-and-high performance
Civil versions are available in passenger, cargo, or Quick-Change (QC) layouts
+ various military models (which see)

SPECIFICATIONS: CN-235-200

Accommodation: 2 + 44
Cargo/baggage: 5.3 m³ (187 cu.ft)
Max speed: 240 kt (445 km/h)
Range: 860 nm (1,593 km)

DIMENSIONS

Wingspan: 25.8 m (84 ft 8 in)
Length: 21.4 m (70 ft 3 in)
Height: 8.20 m (26 ft 10 in)

FEATURES

High/straight wing; twin wing-mounted GE CT7 turboprops with four-bladed propeller; rear ramp/cargo door; swept tail unit with dorsal fin; straight low-set tailplane

Antonov An-24 'Coke' Ukraine

Twin-turboprop short-haul airliner

Lothar Müller

First developed in 1958 to replace large numbers of piston-engined twins used on internal routes in the Soviet Union, and made its maiden flight in April 1960. Service entry with Aeroflot took place in September 1963. Type later licence-produced in China as the Y-7. Total delivered: 1,100+.

FEATURES
High/straight wing; twin Ivchenko AI-24 turboprops with four-blade propellers; swept dorsal fin; slight dihedral on low-set tailplane

VARIANTS
An-24P: Firefighting version
An-24RT: As An-24T, but with auxiliary turbojets in starboard engine nacelle
An-24V: Initial production version with Ivchenko AI-24 engines
An-24V Series 2: Improved AI-24A engines, increased chord on wing centre section and larger flaps
An-24RV: As An-24V, but with auxiliary turbojet
An-30: Optimised for aerial survey work
+ many military derivatives under **An-24**, **An-26** and **An-32** designations (which see)

SPECIFICATIONS: AN-24V
Accommodation: 3 + 52
Cargo/baggage: 61.0 m³ (2,150 cu.ft)
Max speed: 243 kt (450 km/h)
Range: 1,297 nm (2,400 km)

DIMENSIONS
Wingspan: 29.2 m (95 ft 10 in)
Length: 23.5 m (77 ft 2 in)
Height: 8.3 m (27 ft 3 in)

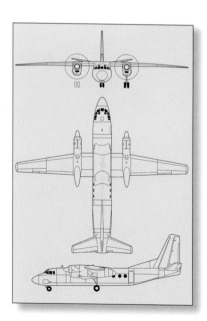

Antonov An-140 Ukraine

Twin-turboprop short-haul transport

David McIntosh

UR-14006

Announced at Paris Air Show in June 1993 as An-24 replacement and designed to operate from unprepared runways at all altitudes and in all weathers, with airline style comfort. Conventional high-wing layout. First flight on 17 September 1997, with first deliveries to Odessa Airlines in March 2002. Built in Russia, Ukraine and Iran. Total delivered: 12.

VARIANTS

An-140A: Basic regional airline version
An-140T: Proposed freighter with large port side cargo door
An-140TK: Convertible, similar to An-140T
An-140-100: Improved model with small increase in wingspan and MTOW
IrAn-140: Model being built under licence in Iran by HESA
+ several military models proposed

SPECIFICATIONS

Accommodation: 2 + 52
Cargo/baggage: 9.0 m^3 (318 cu.ft)
Max speed: 310 kt (575 km/h)
Range: 1,349 nm (2,500 km)

DIMENSIONS

Wingspan: 24.5 m (80 ft 5 in)
Length: 22.6 m (74 ft 2 in)
Height: 8.2 m (26 ft 11 in)

FEATURES

High/straight wing; twin AI-30 turboprops with six-blade propellers; swept tailfin with large dorsal fin; low-set straight tailplane

Avions de Transport Régional ATR 42 France/Italy

Twin-turboprop short-haul regional airliner

Jointly launched by Aerospatiale and Aeritalia in October 1981, the ATR 42 made its maiden flight on 16 August 1984. Deliveries began on 3 December 1985 to French regional Air Littoral, which began revenue service with the type on 9 December. Command Airways became the first US operator in March 1986. Total delivered: 375.

VARIANTS

ATR 42-300: Initial production version with PW120 turboprops
ATR 42-320: Optional PW121 engines for improved hot/high performance
ATR 42-400: Improved PW121As and six-blade propellers
ATR 42-500: More powerful PW127E engines, reinforced wings and higher weights
ATR 42L: Freighter with lateral cargo door
ATR 42 Tube: Quick-change interior
ATR 42 Large Cargo Door: Upward-opening cargo door in front port fuselage
+ *several military derivatives*

SPECIFICATIONS: ATR 42-500

Accommodation: 2 + 50
Cargo/baggage: 9.6 m^3 (340 cu.ft)
Max speed: 300 kt (556 km/h)
Range: 840 nm (1,555 km)

DIMENSIONS

Wingspan: 24.6 m (80 ft 8 in)
Length: 22.7 m (74 ft 5 in)

Height: 7.6 m (24 ft 11 in)

FEATURES

High/straight wing; twin wing-mounted PW127E turboprops with four-bladed propeller; swept double-cranked fin and T-tail with straight tailplane

Avions de Transport Régional ATR 72 France/Italy

Twin-turboprop short-haul regional airliner

Stretched version of ATR 42 announced at 1985 Paris Air Show and launched on 15 January 1986. First flight was made on 27 October 1988 and Finnish airline Karair received the first of the new type on 27 October 1989. Total delivered: 290.

VARIANTS
ATR 72-200: Original production version with PW124B turboprops
ATR 72-210: Improved hot/high performance with uprated PW127s
ATR 72-500: Higher weights and improved airfield performance. Previously referred to as ATR 72-210A.

SPECIFICATIONS: ATR 72-500
Accommodation: 2 + 74
Cargo/baggage: 10.6 m³ (375 cu.ft)
Max speed: 275 kt (509 km/h)
Range: 910 nm (1,685 km)

DIMENSIONS
Wingspan: 27.1 m (88 ft 9 in)
Length: 27.2 m (89 ft 2 in)
Height: 7.7 m (25 ft 2 in)

FEATURES
High/straight wing; twin wing-mounted PW127F turboprops with six-bladed propeller; swept double-cranked fin and T-tail with straight tailplane

BAe (Hawker Siddeley) 748 UK

Twin-turboprop short-haul transport

Developed from the Avro 748 high-wing design of mid-1950s, but had adopted a low-wing configuration and Rolls-Royce Dart turboprops by the time of the first flight on 24 June 1960. Entered service with British airline Skyways in 1962. Total delivered: 379.

VARIANTS

748 Srs 1: Initial production version with Rolls-Royce RDa6 Dart engines
748 Srs 2: Uprated Rolls-Royce RDa7 Dart engines
748 Srs 2A: More powerful RDa7 Darts, a few with RDa8s
748 Srs 2B: Improved and refined model with increased span, new engines and hushkit option
748 Srs 2C: Srs 2A with large cargo door port side of rear fuselage
Super 748: Improved version wit new cockpit and cabin interior
+ military derivatives known as *Andover* and *Coastguarder*

SPECIFICATIONS

Accommodation: 2 + 58
Cargo/baggage: 9.55 m^3 (337 cu.ft)
Max speed: 244 kt (452 km/h)
Range: 926 nm (1,715 km)

DIMENSIONS

Wingspan: 31.2 m (102 ft 5 in)
Length: 20.4 m (67 ft 0 in)
Height: 7.6 m (24 ft 10 in)

FEATURES

Low/straight wing; twin wing-mounted Rolls-Royce Dart turboprop engines with four-bladed propeller; stepped engine nacelles; tailfin with large dorsal fin; low-set tailplane

BAe ATP UK

Twin-turboprop short-haul regional airliner

Conceived as a stretched and modernised 748, the ATP (Advanced Turboprop) used the basic wing of the 748 with a longer fuselage of the same cross-section and new PW124 engines. It was announced in September 1982 and made its first flight on 6 August 1986. British Midland flew the first service on 9 August 1988. First converted freighter flew on 10 July 2002. Total delivered: 64.

VARIANTS
ATP: Only production version
ATPF: Freighter conversion with large sliding cargo door in port rear fuselage
Jetstream 61: Improved version certificated on 16 June 1995 but never put into production.

SPECIFICATIONS
Accommodation: 2 + 68
Cargo/baggage: 13.8 m^3 (485 cu.ft)
Max speed: 271 kt (502 km/h)
Range: 619 nm (1,146 km)

DIMENSIONS
Wingspan: 30.6 m (100 ft 6 in)
Length: 26.0 m (85 ft 4 in)
Height: 7.6 m (24 ft 11 in)

FEATURES
Low/straight wing; twin wing-mounted PW127D turboprops with six-bladed propellers; swept tailfin with large dorsal fin; low-set tailplane

BAe Jetstream 31 UK

Twin-turboprop short-haul commuter

History goes back to 1965 when it was a Handley Page product, but major update initiated by British Aerospace in December 1978. Although externally similar, BAe introduced new technology propellers, revised cockpit and new interiors and systems. First Jetstream 31 flew on 28 March 1980. German airline Contact Air took delivery on 15 December 1982. Total delivered: 381.

VARIANTS

Jetstream 31: Basic production model
Jetstream 32: Significant improvements in performance and passenger comfort. Also known as Jetstream Super 31.
Jetstream 32EP: Enhanced performance upgrade package
Jetstream 31EZ: EEZ patrol version
Corporate: Executive version for 9/10 passengers
Executive Shuttle: Executive company transport for 12 passengers
+ QC (Quick-Change) and military trainers

SPECIFICATIONS

Accommodation: 2 + 19
Cargo/baggage: 2.5 m3 (89 cu.ft)
Max speed: 263 kt (488 km/h)
Range: 680 nm (1,260 km)

DIMENSIONS

Wingspan: 15.9 m (52 ft 0 in)
Length: 14.4 m (47 ft 2 in)
Height: 5.4 m (17 ft 8 in)

FEATURES

Low/straight wing; twin wing-mounted Garrett TPE331 turboprops with four-blade propellers; swept fin with mid-mounted tailplane

BAe Jetstream 41 UK

Twin-turboprop short-haul commuter

A stretched adaptation of the Jetstream 31 for up to 29 passengers, the Jetstream 41, was announced on 24 May 1989 and launched on a risk-sharing basis. It features uprated engines, EFIS, rear baggage door and aerodynamic improvements. First flown on 25 September 1991, it entered service with Loganair and Manx Airlines, both of which took delivery on 25 November 1992. Total delivered: 106.

VARIANTS

Jetstream 41: Basic airliner model
Corporate Shuttle: Executive version for 8-14 passengers
+ *Combi, QC (Quick-Change) and Special Role models*

SPECIFICATIONS

Accommodation: 2 + 29
Cargo/baggage: 6.2 m^3 (218 cu.ft)
Max speed: 295 kt (547 km/h)
Range: 775 nm (1,434 km)

DIMENSIONS

Wingspan: 18.4 m (60 ft 5 in)
Length: 19.3 m (63 ft 2 in)
Height: 5.7 m (18 ft 10 in)

FEATURES

Low/straight wing; twin wing-mounted Garrett TPE331 turboprops with five-blade propellers; swept fin with mid-mounted tailplane

Beech 99 USA

Twin-turboprop short-haul commuter

Developed from the twin-piston Queen Air to enter the commuter airline market. With a fuselage lengthened to accommodate 15 passengers, the Beech 99 made its first flight in December 1965 and entered service with the aptly-named Commuter Airlines in May 1968. Total delivered: 239.

VARIANTS

Beech 99: Initial production model with P&WC PT6A-20 engines
Beech A99: More powerful PT6A-27 engines
Beech B99: Higher gross weight
Beech C99 Airliner: Improved version for dedicated commuter airline operations
+ executive versions

SPECIFICATIONS

Accommodation: 2 + 15
Cargo/baggage: 1.7 m^3 (60 cu.ft)
Max speed: 268 kt (496 km/h)
Range: 578 nm (1,072 km)

DIMENSIONS

Wingspan: 14.0 m (45 ft 11 in)
Length: 13.6 m (44 ft 7 in)
Height: 4.4 m (14 ft 5 in)

FEATURES

Low/straight wing; twin, wing-mounted PT6A turboprops with three-blade propellers; swept tailfin and low-set swept tailplane

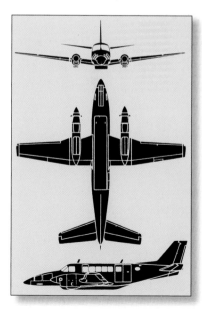

Beech 1900 USA

Twin-turboprop short-haul commuter

Developed for commuter market as successor to Beech 99. Two versions built, including the 13-seat Beech 1300, followed by the 19-seat 1900, based on the Super King Air, but with a lengthened fuselage. The 1900 made its maiden flight on 3 September 1982 and entered service with Bar Harbor Airlines in February 1984. Total delivered: 248 (1900C); 690 (1900D).

VARIANTS

1900C: Initial production version with passenger door forward and upward-hinged cargo door at portside rear
1900 Exec-Liner: Corporate model
1900C-1: Increased fuel and redesigned fuel system
1900D: More powerful engines, stand-up cabin, and ventral strakes for improved stability
1900D Executive: Custom-designed executive interior
C-12J: 1900C-1 for Air National Guard mission support

SPECIFICATIONS: 1900D

Accommodation: 2 + 19
Cargo/baggage: 6.25 m³ (224 cu.ft)
Max speed: 283 kt (524 km/h)
Range: 1,476 nm 92,733 km)

DIMENSIONS

Wingspan: 17.7 m (58 ft 0 in)
Length: 17.6 m (57 ft 10 in)
Height: 4.7 m (15 ft 6 in)

FEATURES

Low/straight wing; twin P&WC PT6A turboprops with four-blade propellers; swept fin and tailplane with taillets on underside near tip; stabilon each side of rear fuselage; ventral strake (1900D only)

Bombardier (DHC) Dash 7 Canada

Four-turboprop short-haul STOL airliner

Developed by de Havilland Canada with the backing of the Canadian Government, targeted primarily at serving downtown STOLports, and featured a high-wing layout and high-lift system. The aircraft took off on its first flight on 27 March 1975 and entered service with US carrier Rocky Mountain Airways on 3 February 1978. Total delivered: 111.

VARIANTS

Srs 100: Basic production model
Srs 101: All-cargo or mixed version with large forward freight door in port side
Srs 150: Higher weights and fuel increase for extended range
Srs 151: All-cargo or mixed passenger/cargo derivative
IR Ranger: Ice reconnaissance model for Canadian Government

SPECIFICATIONS

Accommodation: 2 + 54
Cargo/baggage: 6.8 m³ (240 cu.ft)
Max speed: 213 kt (427 km/h)
Range: 1,170 nm (2,168 km)

DIMENSIONS

Wingspan: 28.4 m (93 ft 0 in)
Length: 24.5 m (80 ft 6 in)
Height: 8.0 m (26 ft 2 in)

FEATURES

High/straight wing; four wing-mounted P&WC PT6A turboprops with four-bladed propellers; swept T-tail with large dorsal fin and straight tailplane

Bombardier (DHC) Dash 8 Canada

Twin-turboprop short-haul regional airliner

Follow-on to the Dash 7 with similar external configuration, but only two powerful new P&WC PW100 engines. Launched in 1980, the Dash 8 first flew on 20 June 1983 and entered revenue service with NorOntair on 19 December 1984. Total delivered: 674.

VARIANTS

Srs 100: Initial production version with either PW120A or PW121 engines
Srs 100A: Restyled interior with more headroom
Srs 100B: PW121 standard for enhanced take-off/climb performance
Srs 200A: Faster and more powerful engines
Srs 200B: Improved engine for better hot/high performance
Srs 300: Extended wingtips and longer fuselage
Srs 300A: improved payload/range performance
Srs 300B: Optional higher gross weight
Srs 300E: Further increase in performance at high temperatures
Srs 400: Final stretch for up to 78 passengers
Aircraft with Noise and Vibration Suppression System (NVS) have Suffix Q

SPECIFICATIONS: SRS 300

Accommodation: 2 + 56
Cargo/baggage: 8.0 m³ (280 cu.ft)
Max speed: 285 kt (528 km/h)
Range: 700 nm (1.2397 km)

DIMENSIONS

Wingspan: 27.4 m (90 ft 0 in)
Length: 25.7 m (84 ft 3 in)
Height: 7.5 m (24 ft 7 in)

FEATURES

High/straight wing; twin wing-mounted PW120 engines; swept T-tail with large dorsal fin and straight tailplane

Convair 580 USA

Twin-turboprop short-haul transport

Dmitry Kudryn

During the late 1950s/early 1960s, many of the famous Convair 240/340/440 piston-engined airliners were converted to turboprop power. The most successful was the Convair 580, which first flew with Allison 501 engines on 19 January 1960, and entered airline service in June 1964. Total converted: 130.

VARIANTS
Model 580: Conversion of CV-340 and CV-440 with Allison 501D turboprops
Model 5800: Stretched conversion by Kelowna Flightcraft in Canada
Model 600: Conversion of CV-240 with Rolls-Royce Dart turboprops
Model 640: Conversion of CV-340 and CV-440 with Rolls-Royce Dart turboprops

SPECIFICATIONS
Accommodation: 2 + 56
Cargo/baggage: 14.6 m^3 (514 cu.ft)
Max speed: 297 kt (550 km/h)
Range: 1,970 nm (3,650 km)

DIMENSIONS
Wingspan: 32.1 m (105 ft 4 in)
Length: 24.8 m (81 ft 6 in)
Height: 8.9 m (29 ft 2 in)

FEATURES
Low/straight wing; twin Allison 501 turboprops with four-blade propellers; curved tailfin with low-set straight tailplane

Douglas DC-3 USA

Twin-piston short-haul airliner

Unequalled among aircraft, design of this ubiquitous twin-engined airliner began in 1932, and led via the DC-1 and DC-2 to the DC-3, which first flew on 17 December 1935. Some 430 were built for airliner use before WW2, when Douglas proceeded to build more than 10,000 for military use. After the end of the war, many found their way to commercial operators and several hundreds remain in service. Also built in USSR as the Lisunov Li-2.

VARIANTS
DC-3C: General designation for commercially operated versions
Super DC-3: Turboprop conversion
+ many military variants under *C-47, C-53, C-117* and *R4D* designations (which see)

SPECIFICATIONS
Accommodation: 2 + 32
Cargo/baggage: 3.5 m^3 (123 cu.ft)
Max speed: 187 kt (346 km/h)
Range: 305 nm (563 km)

DIMENSIONS
Wingspan: 29.0 m (95 ft 0 in)
Length: 19.7 m (64 ft 6 in)
Height: 5.2 m (17 ft 0 in)

FEATURES
Low/tapered wing; twin wing-mounted P&W Twin Wasp piston engines; rounded tailfin with low-set tailplane; semi-retractable landing gear with tailwheel

Douglas DC-4 USA

Four-piston medium-haul airliner

Thomas Posch

Larger and more advanced follow-up to the DC-3 with four engines and intercontinental range. It first flew in its definitive form on 14 February 1942, but was initially built for the US forces as the C-54, before a dedicated civil version was produced after the war. Many war surplus aircraft later found their way into commercial service.

VARIANTS

DC-4-1009: Civil version with accommodation for 44 passengers
DC-4-1037: Incorporated cargo door of C-54
DC-4M-1 North Star: Developed by Canadair with Rolls-Royce Merlin engines for RCAF
DC-4M-2 North Star: Pressurised fuselage and square cabin windows
+ more than 1,000 built for the US armed forces designated *C-54* (which see)

SPECIFICATIONS

Accommodation: 3 + 86
Max speed: 244 kt (451 km/h)
Range: 1,897 nm (3,510 km)

DIMENSIONS

Wingspan: 35 .8 m (117 ft 6 in)
Length: 28.6 m (93 ft 10 in)
Height: 8.4 m (27 ft 6 in)

FEATURES

Low/tapered wing; four wing-mounted P&W Twin Wasp piston engines; curved tailfin with large dorsal fin and low-set tailplane

Douglas DC-6 USA

Four-piston medium-haul airliner

Sokol Ymeri

Successor to the DC-4 with substantially the same wing, but a lengthened fuselage, more powerful engines and improved systems. The aircraft, as the XC-112, first flew on 15 February 1946 and entered airline service on 27 April 1947. Total delivered: 536.

VARIANTS

DC-6: Initial passenger version
DC-6A: Cargo model with lengthened and strengthened fuselage, two port side cargo doors, no cabin windows
DC-6B: Passenger equivalent of DC-6A
DC-6C: Convertible passenger/cargo model
Many passenger models later converted to cargo use with suffix F

SPECIFICATIONS: DC-6B

Accommodation: 4 + 102
Cargo/baggage: 25.1 m^3 (886 cu.ft)
Max speed: 275 kt (509 km/h)
Range: 1,650 nm (3,058 km)

DIMENSIONS

Wingspan: 35.8 m (117 ft 6 in)
Length: 32.2 m (105 ft 7 in)
Height: 9.0 m (29 ft 3 in)

FEATURES

Low/tapered wing; four wing-mounted P&W Double Wasp piston engines; tall rounded tailfin with dorsal fin and low-set tailplane

Embraer EMB-110 Bandeirante Brazil

Twin-turboprop short-haul commuter

Developed in the 1960s to meet a requirement for the Brazilian Air Force, but later aimed at domestic commuter market. Built by Embraer, the first production Bandeirante (pioneer) with PT6A-20 engines flew on 9 August 1972, entering civil revenue service with Transbrasil on 16 April 1973. Total delivered: 494, including military versions.

VARIANTS

EMB-110C: First version for 15 passengers
EMB-110E/J: Seven-seat corporate transport
EMB-110P: Optimised for export with PT6A-27s and accommodation for 18 passengers
EMB-110P1: Mixed passenger/cargo model with aft freight-loading door and longer fuselage
EMB-110P1/41: Higher T-O weight to meet US SFAR Pt 41
EMB-110P2: Airliner alternative for up to 21 passengers
EMB-110P2/41: Optimised for US SFAR Pt 41
Late changes to passenger comfort and handling resulted in the addition of suffix A to production models.
EMB-110S1: Geophysical survey version with wing-tip tanks
+ a number of military version under the *EMB-110* and *EMB-111* designations

SPECIFICATIONS: EMB-110P2

Accommodation: 2 + 21
Cargo/baggage: 2.0 m^3 (71 cu.ft)
Max speed: 248 kt (459 km/h)
Range: 1,060 nm (1,964 km)

DIMENSIONS

Wingspan: 15.3 m (50 ft 3 in)
Length: 15.1 m (49 ft 7 in)
Height: 4.9 m (16 ft 2 in)

FEATURES

Low/straight wing; twin wing-mounted PT6A turboprops with three-bladed propellers; swept tailfin and low-set tailplane; ventral tailfin

Embraer EMB-120 Brasilia Brazil

Twin-turboprop short-haul commuter

Developed as a pressurised version of the Bandeirante for 30 passengers and officially launched in September 1979. The most notable external difference, apart from the lengthened fuselage, was a new T-tail. First flight was made on 27 July 1983 and the first production aircraft went into service in October 1985. Total delivered: 352.

VARIANTS

EMB-120: Initial production model P&WC PW115 engines
EMB-120RT: More powerful PW118s for reduced take-off
EMB-120ER: Aerodynamic improvements, re-designed cockpit and higher cabin comfort levels
Also available in all-cargo, Combi and QC (Quick-Change) versions, and two military derivatives for AEW and remote sensing as the *EMB-120SA* and *EMB-120RS* respectively

SPECIFICATIONS

Accommodation: 2 + 30
Cargo/baggage: 6.4 m³ (226 cu.ft)
Max speed: 327 kt (606 km/h)
Range: 850 nm (1,575 km)

DIMENSIONS

Wingspan: 19.8 m (64 ft 11 in)
Length: 20.1 m (65 ft 11 in)
Height: 6.4 m (20 ft 10 in)

FEATURES

Low/straight wing; twin PW100 turboprops with four-blade propellers; all-swept T-tail with large dorsal fin

Fairchild F-27/FH-227 USA

Twin-turboprop short-haul airliner

Licence-built Fokker design intended as a DC-3 replacement. First US-built production aircraft flew at Hagerstown, Maryland, on 12 April 1958 and entered service with West Coast Airlines on 27 November 1958. Total delivered: 207.

VARIANTS

F-27: Initial production model with Rolls-Royce Dart RDa6 engines
F-27A: Higher gross weight and uprated RDa7s
F-27B: Combi with forward side-loading cargo door, RDa6s
F-27F: As F-27A, for corporate use with more powerful RDa7s
F-27J: More powerful Dart RDa7 Mk 532-7
F-27M: Dart Mk 532-7N engines, higher weight
FH-227: Stretched fuselage
FH-227B: Higher gross weight and strengthened structure

SPECIFICATIONS: F-27J

Accommodation: 2 + 48
Cargo/baggage: 8.4 m³ (297 cu.ft)
Max speed: 280 kt (520 km/h)
Range: 792 nm (1,465 km)

DIMENSIONS

Wingspan: 29.0 m (95 ft 2 in)
Length: 23.5 m (77 ft 2 in)
Height: 8.4 m (27 ft 6 in)

FEATURES

High/straight wing; twin Rolls-Royce Dart turboprops with four-blade propellers; tailfin with large dorsal fin and low-set tailplane

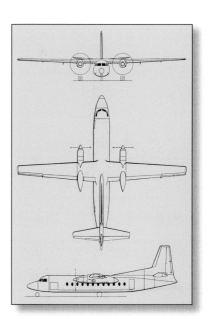

Fairchild (Swearingen) Metro/Merlin USA

Twin-turboprop short-haul commuter

Lothar Müller

Initially developed as a series of business aircraft by Ed Swearingen. Further refinements led to the Metro commuter aircraft, which first flew on 26 August 1969 and entered service in early 1971. In November that year, the Swearingen company was taken over by Fairchild, which continued to improve the aircraft until ceasing production in 1999. Total delivered (including military and corporate): 1,053.

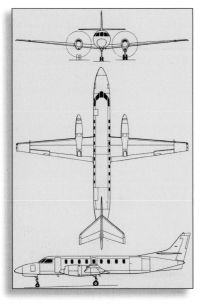

VARIANTS
SA-226TC Metro: Initial production version
SA-226TC Metro II: Squared-off windows and optional rocket in tail for better hot-and-high performance
SA-226TC Metro IIA: Higher gross weight
SA-227AC Metro III: Uprated engines, increased wingspan with small wingtips, four-blade propellers
SA-227AC Metro IIIA: P&WC PT6A engines
Expediter: Large door in rear, reinforced floor
Metro 23: Improved final production model. Each Metro version also produced in *Merlin* corporate configuration
C-26A: Transport for the US National Guard
C-26B: Transport for the US National Guard

SPECIFICATIONS: METRO 23
Accommodation: 2 + 20
Cargo/baggage: 5.05m^3 (179 sq.ft)
Max speed: 290 kt (537 km/h)
Range: 540 nm (1,000 km)

DIMENSIONS
Wingspan: 17.4 m (57 ft 0 in)
Length: 18.1 m (59 ft 5 in)
Height: 5.1 m (16 ft 8 in)

FEATURES
Low/straight wing; twin Honeywell (AlliedSignal) TPE331 or P&WC PT6A turboprops; three- or four-blade propellers; swept tailfin with large dorsal fin; mid-mounted swept tailplane

Fairchild Dornier 328 Germany

Twin-turboprop short-haul regional airliner

Growth version of 228 approved in late 1986, combining the TNT supercritical wing of the 228 with a new pressurised circular fuselage with stand-up cabin and T-tail; extensive use made of composites. First flight on 6 December 1991 and first delivery to Swiss regional Air Engiadina on 21 October 1993. Production halted; 2011 in favour of 328 JET. Total delivered: 112.

VARIANTS

328-100: Initial production version
328-110: Increased weight and range, enlarged dorsal fin
328-120: Improved short-field performance, enlarged dorsal and ventral fins

SPECIFICATIONS

Accommodation: 2 + 33
Cargo/baggage: 6.3 m^3 (223 cu.ft)
Max speed: 335 kt (620 km/h)
Range: 900 nm (1,666 km)

DIMENSIONS

Wingspan: 21.0 m (68 ft 10 in)
Length: 21.3 m (69 ft 10 in)
Height: 7.2 m (23 ft 9 in)

FEATURES

High/straight wing; twin wing-mounted P&WC PW119 turboprops with six-blade propellers; T-tail

Fokker F27 Friendship The Netherlands

Twin-turboprop short-haul airliner

First post-war Fokker design intended as a DC-3 replacement. Prototype first flew on 24 November 1955, but progressively stretched to eventually provide seating for 50 passengers. Aircraft also built under licence by Fairchild (which see). First Fokker- built F27 went into service with Aer Lingus in December 1958. Total delivered: 579.

VARIANTS

F27 Mk 100: Initial production model with Rolls-Royce Dart RDa6 engines
F27 Mk 200: Higher gross weight and uprated RDa7 engines
F27 Mk 300: Combi with forward side-loading cargo door, RDa6s
F27 Mk 400: Combined cargo door with RDa7s
F27 Mk 500: Large cargo door and lengthened fuselage
F27 Mk 600: Quick-change with roller tracks and palletised seats
Military versions include the *F27Mk 400M Troopship* for 46 troops with enlarged parachute door on each side, and *F27 Maritime* and *F27 Maritime Enforcer*, respectively unarmed and armed

SPECIFICATIONS: MK 500

Accommodation: 2 + 60
Cargo/baggage: 8.4 m³ (297 cu.ft)
Max speed: 259 kt (480 km/h)
Range: 935 nm (1,741 km)

DIMENSIONS

Wingspan: 29.0 m (95 ft 2 in)
Length: 25.1 m (82 ft 3 in)
Height: 8.7 m (28 ft 7 in)

FEATURES

High/straight wing; twin Rolls-Royce Dart turboprops with four-blade propellers; tailfin with large dorsal fin and low-set tailplane

Fokker 50/60 The Netherlands

Twin-turboprop short-haul airliner

Follow-on development of the F27 announced on 24 November 1983. Substantial application of new technology structure and systems; more than 80% of components new or modified. Rolls-Royce Darts replaced by modern P&WC PW120 engines. Fokker 50 first flew on 28 December 1985 and entered service on 7 August 1987. Stretched Fokker 60 launched in February 1994. Total delivered: 212.

VARIANTS
Fokker 50: Baseline model with PW125B turboprops, three or four doors
Fokker 50 High Performance: Uprated PW127B engines for improved hot-and-high performance
Fokker 50 Utility: Three-door model with additional multi-purpose door and heavy-duty floor
Fokker 60: Stretched baseline version, none ordered
Fokker 60 Utility: As Fokker 50 Utility, but additional upward opening starboard front cargo door. Ordered only by RNethAF

SPECIFICATIONS: FOKKER 50
Accommodation: 2 + 58
Cargo/baggage: 8.4 m^3 (297 cu.ft)
Max speed: 290 kt (537 km/h)
Range: 1,216 nm (2,252 km)

DIMENSIONS
Wingspan: 29.0 m (95 ft 2 in)

Length: 25.3 m (82 ft 10 in)
Height: 8.3 m (27 ft 3 in)

FEATURES
High/straight wing; twin PW120 turboprops with six-blade composite propellers; tailfin with large dorsal fin and low-set tailplane

HAMC Y-12 China

Twin-turboprop short-haul commuter

David McIntosh

Developed from the Y-11 utility aircraft. Main changes in the Y-12 (Y for **Yunshuji** or Transport Aircraft) included the installation of P&WC PT6A turboprops, new aerofoil sections, bonded construction and integral fuel tanks. First of three prototypes flew on 14 July 1982 and entered service with local airlines sometime in 1986. Total delivered: 100+.

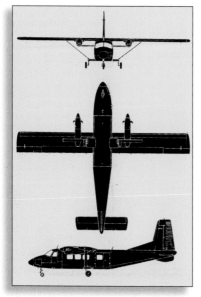

VARIANTS

Y-12 (I): Initial production version with PT6A-11 engines

Y-12 (II): Higher rated engines, no leading-edge slats and smaller ventral fin

Y-12 (IV): Improved version with sweptback wingtips, starboard rear baggage door, western avionics and cabin enhancements

Y-12E: More powerful engines, four-bladed propeller and new avionics

Y-12F: Pressurised proposal

Y-12G: Proposed freighter with side cargo door

Twin Panda: Y-12 (IV) with uprated PT6A-34 engines, marketed in North America by Canadian Aerospace Group

SPECIFICATIONS: Y-12 (IV)

Accommodation: 2 + 19
Cargo/baggage: 2.7 m3 (95 cu.ft)
Max speed: 162 kt (300 km/h)
Range: 707 kt (1,310 km)

DIMENSIONS

Wingspan: 19.2 m (63 ft 0 in)
Length: 14.9 m (48 ft 9 in)
Height: 5.6 m (18 ft 4 in)

FEATURES

High/straight and braced wing with small stub wings at cabin floor level; twin P&WC PT6A turboprops with three-blade propeller; upswept rear fuselage; large dorsal fin; ventral fin under tailcone

Ilyushin Il-18 'Coot' Russia

Four-turboprop medium-haul airliner

David McIntosh

New generation turboprop airliner developed to meet the needs of Aeroflot. The prototype first flew in July 1957, then named **Moskva**, and the new type entered Aeroflot service on 20 April 1959. It was first available with either Kuznetsov NK-4 or Ivchenko AI-20 turboprops, but the latter was adopted as standard from the 21st production aircraft. Total delivered: 800+.

VARIANTS

IL-18: Initial version with either NK-4 or AI-20 engines
IL-18D: Additional fuel in centre bag tanks for increased range
IL-18E: More powerful AI-20M engine and redesigned cabin for 110 passengers
IL-18V: Major production version with AI-20K engines.
Also used as military and VIP transport. After retirement from frontline passenger service, many IL-18s were converted for cargo use with a large freight door in the rear fuselage

SPECIFICATIONS: Il-18D

Accommodation: 5 + 122
Cargo/baggage: 29.3 m^3 (1,035 cu.ft)
Max speed: 364 kt (675 km/h)
Range: 1,997 nm (3,700 km)

DIMENSIONS

Wingspan: 37.4 m (122 ft 9 in)
Length: 35.9 m (117 ft 9 in)

Height: 10.2 m (33 ft 4 in)

FEATURES

Low/straight wing; four AI-20 turboprop engines with four-blade propellers; deeper inner engine nacelles; tailfin with large dorsal fin and low-set tailplane

Ilyushin Il-114 Russia

Twin-turboprop short-haul regional airliner

Designed as successor to the An-24. Design finalised in 1986 and prototype made its first flight at Khodinka on 29 March 1990. Accidents and withdrawal of government funding delayed programme, and first commercial service by Uzbekistan Airways not until 27 August 1998. Total delivered: 15.

VARIANTS

IL-114: Baseline aircraft with Klimov TV7-117 engines
IL-114FK: Military reconnaissance, elint and cartographic version under development
IL-114M: Increased T-O weight, TV7M-117s
IL-114MA: As IL-114M but proposed with P&WC engines
IL-114P: Maritime patrol version, large cargo door at portside rear, slightly reshaped nose for radar
IL-114PR: SIGINT model announced October 2000
IL-114T: Cargo version with portside rear cargo door and removable roller floor
IL-114-100: P&WC PW127H turboprops and six-blade propellers

SPECIFICATIONS

Accommodation: 2 + 64
Cargo/baggage: 76.0 m3 (2,684 cu.ft, IL-114T)
Max speed: 270 kt (500 km/h)
Range: 540 nm (1,000 km)

DIMENSIONS

Wingspan: 30.0 m (98 ft 5 in)
Length: 26.9 m (88 ft 2 in)
Height: 9.2 m (30 ft 2 in)

FEATURES

Low/straight wing; twin TV7-117 turboprops with six-blade propellers; swept fin and low-set tailplane

Lockheed L188 Electra USA

Four-turboprop short/medium-haul airliner

Gerd Beilfuss

Designed to an American Airlines specification
for a 100-seater with a range of some 2,000nm.
First of four prototypes flew on 6 December 1957
and the Electra entered service with launch
customers Eastern Air Lines on 12 January 1959
and with American Airlines on 23 January. Electra
later developed into the successful P-3 Orion
(which see). Total delivered: 170 (civil).

VARIANTS

L188A: Initial production model
L188C: Higher fuel capacity for longer range
L188AF: Freighter or combi conversion of L188A
with large port cargo door forward of the wing
and strengthened floor
L188CF: Freighter or combi conversion of L188C
with large port cargo door forward of the wing
and strengthened floor

SPECIFICATIONS: L188A

Accommodation: 3 + 98
Cargo/baggage: 15.0m³ (530 cu.ft)
Max speed: 352 kt (652 km/h)
Range: 1,910 nm (3,534 km)

DIMENSIONS

Wingspan: 30.2 m (99 ft 0 in)
Length: 31.8 m (104 ft 6 in)
Height: 10.0 m (32 ft 10 in)

FEATURES

Low/straight wing; four Allison 501 turboprops
with four-blade propellers; curved tail with dorsal
fin and low-set dihedral tailplane

NAMC YS-11 Japan

Twin-turboprop short-haul regional airliner

Harima Yoshihiro

Japan's first indigenous civil airliner built by Nihon Aircraft Manufacturing Co (NAMC), a joint venture between six airframers, primarily for domestic airlines. The prototype first flew on 30 August 1962, with deliveries to airlines starting in March 1965. Total delivered: 182.

VARIANTS

YS-11: Initial production version, later known as YS-11-100

YS-11A-200: Higher operating weights and increased payload

YS-11A-300: Mixed passenger/cargo model with forward side-loading cargo door

YS-11A-400: All-cargo aircraft. Used mostly by military

YS-11A-500: As YS-11A-200 but increased T-O weight

YS-11A-600: As YS-11A-300 but increased T-O weight

SPECIFICATIONS: YS-11A-200

Accommodation: 2 + 60
Cargo/baggage: 10.7 m³ (378 cu.ft)
Max speed: 253 kt (469 km/h)
Range: 590 nm (1,092 km)

DIMENSIONS

Wingspan: 32.0 m (105 ft 0 in)
Length: 26.3 m (86 ft 4 in)
Height: 9.0 m (29 ft 6 in)

FEATURES

Low/straight wing; twin Rolls-Royce Dart turboprops; tailfin with large dorsal fin and low-set tailplane

Saab 340 Sweden

Twin-turboprop short-haul regional airliner

Gerd Beilfuss

Developed as a 34-seat regional aircraft jointly by Saab and Fairchild, initially known as the SF-340. The SF designation was dropped when Fairchild pulled out. First of three test aircraft flew on 25 January 1983 and entered service with launch customer Crossair on 15 June 1984. Total delivered: 459.

Height: 7.0 m (22 ft 11 in)

FEATURES

Low/straight wing; twin GE CT7 turboprops with four-blade propellers; swept tailfin with large dorsal fin and dihedral tailplane

VARIANTS

340A: Initial production model with GE CT7-5A engines
340B: Higher weights and increased tailspan, CT7-9Bs
340BPlus: New interior, active noise control and wing extensions for improved performance. Quick-change (QC) and corporate versions have also been produced
340AEW&C: Reconnaissance version for the Swedish Air Force with dorsal-mounted Erieye side-looking radar
SAR-200: 340BPlus rescue version for the Japan Maritime Safety Agency.

SPECIFICATIONS: 340B

Accommodation: 2 + 37
Cargo/baggage: 8.3 m^3 (293 cu.ft)
Max speed: 282 kt (522 km/h)
Range: 870 nm (1,611 km)

DIMENSIONS

Wingspan: 22.8 m (74 ft 8 in)
Length: 19.7 m (64 ft 8 in)

Saab 2000 Sweden

Twin-turboprop short/medium-haul regional airliner

Design definition for a larger regional aircraft to complement the 340 began in 1988, although against the general trend, Saab persisted with a turboprop rather than jet configuration, but providing high-speed with low operating costs. It proved the wrong decision, and the 2000 sold only in small numbers until production ended in 1998. First flown on 26 March 1992, it entered service with launch customer Crossair in September 1994. Total delivered: 63.

VARIANTS

2000: Only version built for airline and corporate customers with stretched fuselage and greater wingspan than the 340.

SPECIFICATIONS

Accommodation: 2 + 58
Cargo/baggage: 10.2 m^3 (360 cu.ft)
Max speed: 368 kt (682 km/h)
Range: 1,200 nm (2,222 km)

DIMENSIONS

Wingspan: 24.8 m (81 ft 3 in)
Length: 27.3 m (89 ft 6 in)
Height: 7.7 m (25 ft 4 in)

FEATURES

Low/straight wing; twin Rolls-Royce (Allison) AE 2100A turboprops with six-blade propellers; swept tailfin with large dorsal fin; low-set straight, dihedral tailplane

Shorts 330 UK

Twin-turboprop short-haul regional airliner

Andy Graf

Developed from the Skyvan to tackle the emerging market of the 30-seat commuter airliner, the Shorts 330, initially referred to as the SD3-30, received its formal go-ahead on 23 May 1973. The first prototype flew on 22 August 1974 and entered revenue service with Time Air in Canada on 24 August 1976. Total delivered: 139.

VARIANTS

330-100: Initial production version continuously updated with various models of the PT6A turboprop

330-200: Increase fuel capacity for greater range

330-UTT: Utility tactical transport with strengthened floor, structural reinforcements and rear inward-opening cabin doors for paradropping

C-23A Sherpa: Military freighter for US Air Force with full width rear ramp loading door, no cabin windows

C-23B: Utility version for US Army National Guard, 11 cabin windows on each side

SPECIFICATIONS: 330-200

Accommodation: 2 + 30
Cargo/baggage: 4.1 m3 (145 cu.ft)
Max speed: 190 kt (352 km/h0)
Range: 473 nm (876 km)

DIMENSIONS

Wingspan: 22.8 m (74 ft 8 in)
Length: 17.7 m (58 ft 0 in)
Height: 5.0 m (16 ft 3 in)

FEATURES

High/straight braced wing; twin P&WC PT6A turboprops with five-blade propellers; square-section tapering fuselage; ramp in upswept rear fuselage in military versions; twin tail unit

Shorts 360 UK

Twin-turboprop short-haul regional airliner

Thomas Posch

Developed from the 330 and stretched to take advantage of increased capacity allowed following deregulation in the US. Most notable difference from the 330 is the replacement of the twin tail with a conventional single fin. First flown on 1 June 1981, the 360 began revenue service with Suburban Airlines in the US on 1 December 1982. Total delivered: 164.

VARIANTS

360-100: Initial production model first known simply as 360
360-200: First referred to as 360 Advanced, introduced more powerful PT6A-65AR engines
360-300: New PT6A-67ARs, autopilot and enhanced passenger comfort
360-300F: Freighter adaptation
C-23B+ Sherpa: Structural conversion for US Army National Guard, basically to 330 configuration with twin tail unit

SPECIFICATIONS: 360-300

Accommodation: 2 + 39
Cargo/baggage: 6.1 m³ (215 cu.ft)
Max speed: 216 kt (400 km/h)
Range: 402 nm (745 km)

DIMENSIONS

Wingspan: 22.8 m (74 ft 10 in)
Length: 21.6 m (70 ft 10 in)
Height: 7.3 m (23 ft 11 in)

FEATURES

High/straight braced wing; twin P&WC PT6A turboprops with six-blade propellers; square-section, tapering fuselage; swept tailfin with dorsal fin and low-set straight tailplane

XAC Y7/MA60 China

Twin-turboprop transport aircraft

David McIntosh

Westernised version of Y7, which has been built in China since first flown on 25 December 1970 as a reversed engineered model of the Antonov An-24. MA60 (Modern Ark 60) first flown, as Y7-200A on 26 December 1993, and shown as MA60 for first time outside China at Asian Aerospace 2002 in Singapore. Total delivered: 100+ (Y7); 12 (MA60).

VARIANTS

Y7: Initial production version
Y7-100: Improved with winglets, new interior and systems
Y7-200: New four-blade propellers, new avionics; winglets deleted
Y7H: Military cargo model with underfuselage ramp/door; rough field landing gear; derived from An-26
Y7H-500: Equivalent civil cargo version
MA40: Proposed shorter 40-seat variant of MA60
MA60: Development of Y7-200A, PW127 turboprops, Rockwell Collins avionics, APU, renovated cabin
MA60-MPA: Proposed military patrol aircraft, named *Fearless Albatross*

SPECIFICATIONS

Accommodation: 2 + 60
Cargo/baggage: 11.2 m3 (395 cu.ft)
Max speed: 248 kt (460 km/h)
Range: 1,325 nm (2,450 km)

DIMENSIONS

Wingspan: 29.2 m (95 ft 10 in)
Length: 24.7 m (81 ft 0 in)

Height: 8.9 m (29 ft 1 in)

FEATURES

High straight wing with tapered leading edge; twin Pratt & Whitney PW127 turboprops with four-blade propellers; sweptback vertical tail with large dorsal fin; slight dihedral horizontal tailplane; retractable tricycle landing gear

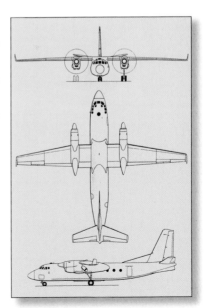

CIVIL
UTILITY
AIRCRAFT

Aeroprogress/ROKS-Aero T-101 Grach Russia

Single-turbine utility aircraft

Designed as monoplane successor to Antonov An-2 and first flown on 7 December 1994. In limited series production.

VARIANTS

T-101: Basic passenger/cargo transport with Mars TVD-10B turboprop engine

T-101E: As T-101, but with P&WC PT6A turboprop

T-101L: Ski landing gear

T-101P: Firefighting version, non-amphibious floats

T-101S: Military version with small stub wings with weapon pylons, two stores pylons under each wing

T-101SKh: Major redesign for agricultural work, strut-braced low wings and with spraybars under

SPECIFICATIONS

Accommodation: 1 + 9
Cargo/baggage: 1,400 kg (3,086 lb)
Max speed: 162 kt (300 km/h)
Range: 685 nm (1,270 km)

DIMENSIONS

Wingspan: 18.2 m (59 ft 9 in)
Length: 15.1 m (49 ft 5 in)
Height: 4.9 m (16 ft 0 in)

FEATURES

Braced high/straight wing (low wing in T-101SKh);

single Mars TVD-10 or P&WC PT6T turboshaft engine with three-blade propeller; non-retractable landing gear; sweptback fin with dorsal fin and low-set tailplane

Antonov An-2 'Colt' Ukraine

Single-piston utility aircraft

Biplane designed to USSR Ministry specification for agricultural aircraft and first flown in 1947. Became all round general purpose aircraft and more than 5,000 built before production moved to PZL-Mielec in Poland. Also licence-built in China as the Shijiazhuang Y-5B. Total delivered: 17,000+

VARIANTS

An-2L: Water-bombing version
An-2M: Agricultural version
An-2P: Basic general purpose aircraft with bulged side windows
An-2R: Polish designation of An-2S
An-2S: Agricultural version with long-stroke landing gear
An-2T: Polish-built mixed passenger/cargo version, equivalent to An-2P
An-2V: Floatplane version of An-2P
+ many other specialist variants for both civil and military use

SPECIFICATIONS

Accommodation: 2 + 12
Cargo/baggage: 1,500 kg (3,307 lb)
Max speed: 139 kt (258 km/h)
Range: 485 nm (897 km)

DIMENSIONS

Wingspan (upper): 18.2 m (59 ft 8 in)
Wingspan (lower): 14.2 m (46 ft 8 in)
Length: 13.0 m (42 ft 6 in)
Height: 4.2 m (13 ft 9 in)

FEATURES

Straight unequal span biplane; single Shvetsov Ash-62 or PZL ASz-621 piston engine with four-blade propeller; non-retractable landing gear; round cabin windows; large rounded or squared-off tailfin with low-set tailplane

Antonov An-12 'Cub' Ukraine

Four-turboprop cargo aircraft

David McIntosh

Developed from the earlier passenger Antonov An-10, using the same airframe but with full-section rear doors. The An-12 flew for the first time in 1958 and entered service in 1959 with the Soviet armed forces, before also being used by Aeroflot and later sold to 'friendly' airlines. Many now operated for commercial freight transport. Also built in China as the Y-8.
Total delivered: 900+

AI-20K turboprops with four-blade propellers; upswept rear fuselage with ramp/door for direct loading; large tailfin and dorsal fin with low-set tailplane; gun turret at rear of ex-military machines, otherwise faired over

VARIANTS
An-12BP: Original military version with twin gun turret at rear
An-12B: Dedicated civil version with turret removed
+ other specialised military versions (which see)

SPECIFICATIONS
Accommodation: 5 + 100 (troops)
Cargo/baggage: 20,000 kg (44,090 lb)
Max speed: 361 kt (670 km/h)
Range: 1,940 nm (3,600 km)

DIMENSIONS
Wingspan: 38.0 m (124 ft 8 in)
Length: 33.1 m (108 ft 7 in)
Height: 10.5 m (34 ft 6 in)

FEATURES
High/straight wing; four wing-mounted Ivchenko

Antonov An-38 Ukraine

Twin-turboprop general purpose aircraft

Details of high wing light turboprop transport announced and model displayed at Paris Air Show in June 1991. Prototype made first flight on 23 June 1994 with Honeywell (AlliedSignal) TPE331 engines. Type entered service with Vostok Airlines following certification in April 1997. Only produced in small numbers to date.

VARIANTS

An-38-100: Basic production model with Honeywell TPE331 turboprops
An-38-110: Reduced avionics fit
An-38-120: Enhanced avionics fit
An-38-200: With Omsk TVD-20 engines
An-38K: Convertible An-38-100 with large upward-hinged on port side at rear
+ other options available including forest patrol (*An-38D*), aerial photography (*An-38F*), survey (*An-38GF*), aerial ambulance (*An-38S*) and fishery/ice patrol (*An-38LR*)

SPECIFICATIONS

Accommodation: 2 + 27
Cargo/baggage: 2,500 kg (5,510 lb)
Max speed: 219 kt (405 km/h)
Range: 324 nm (600 km)

DIMENSIONS

Wingspan: 22.1 m (72 ft 5 in)
Length: 15.7 m (51 ft 5 in)
Height: 4.6 m (15 ft 1in)

FEATURES

High/braced straight wing; twin wing-mounted Honeywell TPE-331 or Omsk TVD-20 turboprops with five-blade propellers; optional cargo door under upswept rear fuselage; twin tailfins

Beech 18 USA

Light utility transport

Henry Tenby

Development of this eight-seat commercial transport began in 1935. First flown on 15 January 1937, its production run was boosted by war requirements, with some 5,000 built for the military. Production ceased in 1969. Total built: 9,000+.

VARIANTS (MAJOR)
C18S: P&W Wasp Junior engines
D18S: Post-war civil model with streamlined nacelles
E18S: Roomier cabin with four enlarged windows, pointed nose, also known as Super 18
G18S: Panoramic centre window, new cockpit
H18: Fully retracting mainwheels, optional tricycle undercarriage
Beech C-45: Major military designation, but many others used
Float and ski landing gear used frequently. Many later conversions undertaken, producing among others the Volpar Turboliner, Dumod, PAC Tradewind and Hamilton Westwind.

SPECIFICATIONS
Accommodation: 2 + 6
Max speed: 243 kt (450 km/h)
Range: 300 nm (555 km)

DIMENSIONS
Wingspan: 15.1 m (49 ft 8 in)
Length: 10.7 m (35 ft 3 in)
Height: 2.8 m (9 ft 4 in)

FEATURES
Low/straight wing tapered for most part; twin wing-mounted piston engines; cantilever tail unit with twin vertical fins; retractable tailwheel landing gear

Beech 65 Queen Air USA

Twin-piston light utility/commuter aircraft

Tomás Coelho

Design of this large piston-twin started in April 1958, with first flight just four months later on 28 August. The Queen Air combined the wing, tail, engines and landing gear of the Twin Bonanza with a substantially larger fuselage. Total delivered (including military): 1,001.

VARIANTS
65 Queen Air: Initial production model with up to nine seats

A65 Queen Air: Fourth starboard cabin window, swept tail
A65-8200 Queen Air: A65 certificated at 8,200 lb TOGW
70 Queen Air: Longer wingspan and seating for 11
65-80 Queen Air: Swept tail and more powerful engines
65-A80 Queen Air: Longer span wing, increased weight, 11 seats
65-B80 Queen Air: Extra starboard window, higher weight, 13 seats
65-88 Queen Air: 10-seat pressurised cabin, porthole windows
65-A80-8800 Queen Airliner: Optimised for commuter operations
Also delivered to the US Army as the *U-8 Seminole*, and to the JMSDF as navigation trainer

SPECIFICATIONS: 65-B80
Accommodation: 1 + 12
Cargo/baggage: 160 kg (350 lb)
Max speed: 195 kt (362 km/h)
Range: 1,055 nm (1,950 km)

DIMENSIONS
Wingspan: 15.3 m (50 ft 3 in)
Length: 10.8 m (35 ft 6 in)
Height: 4.3 m (14 ft 3 in)

FEATURES
Low/straight wing; twin Lycoming piston engines with three-blade propellers; three/four cabin windows; swept tailfin (except 65) and low-set tailplane; retractable tricycle landing gear

Beriev Be-103 Russia

Six-seat twin-turboprop utility amphibian

Design of this light utility amphibian started in 1992, with first flight taking place at Taganrog on 15 July 1997. Prototype destroyed a month later, as was second prototype on 29 April 1999. Certificated to AP-23 Russian airworthiness standards in 2001, followed by US FAR 23 in summer 2003. Production underway at KnAAPO at Komsomolsk-on-Amur. Total delivered: 10.

VARIANTS:
Be-103: Basic twin-engined production version for five passengers.
SA-20P: Eight-seat single-engine derivative for local Russian market.

SPECIFICATIONS: BE-103
Accommodation: 1+ 5
Max speed: 154 kt (285 km/h)
Range: 600 nm (1,110 km)

DIMENSIONS
Wingspan: 12.7 m (41 ft 9 in)
Length: 10.7 m (35 ft 0 in)
Height: 3.8 m (12 ft 4 in)

FEATURES
Low-mounted displacement wing of moderate sweep with large wingroot extensions; two-step boat hull but no stabilizing floats; horizontal strake each side of nose and vertical strake ahead of second hull step; Teledyne Continental engines mounted on horizontal pylons above and behind the wing; sweptback fin and rudder with mid-set tailplane

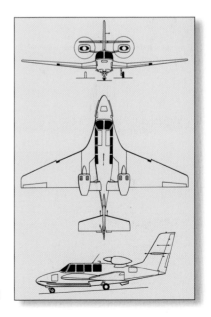

Beriev Be-200 Altair Russia

Large twin-jet utility amphibian

Design of this multirole twin-jet amphibian initiated in 1989, but first flight from land not achieved until 24 September 1998; first water take-offs and landings on 10 September 1999. In small-scale production.

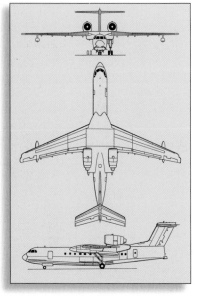

VARIANTS

Be-200: basic version available in passenger, cargo, ambulance and patrol configurations
Be-200ChS: Firefighting version with tanks under cabin floor, retractable water scoops; jump door at rear of cabin on starboard side
Be-200P: Projected anti-submarine version
BE-200PS: Search and rescue derivative with loudspeaker, searchlights, inflatable rafts and motorboats.
Be-210: Development for airline use with seating for 72 passengers. Formerly known as Be-200M

SPECIFICATIONS

Accommodation: 2 + 72
Cargo/baggage: 84 m³ (2,966 cu.ft)
Max speed: 388 kt (720 km/h)
Range: 1,000 nm (1,850 km)

DIMENSIONS

Wingspan: 32.8 m (107 ft 7 in)
Length: 31.4 m (103 ft 1 in)
Height: 8.9 m (29 ft 2 in)

FEATURES

Swept wings with high lift devices; single-step hull; all-swept T-tail; high-mounted ZMKB Progress D-436TP turbofan engines above the rearportion of centre wing; strakes on each side of nose and by wings; large underwing pod each side of hull

Bombardier Canadair 415 Canada

Twin-turboprop amphibian aircraft

Introduced as a follow-on to piston-engined CL-215 amphibious aircraft intended mainly for firefighting Turboprop CL-415 officially launched on 16 October 1991. First flight on 6 December 1993 was followed by first deliveries in January 1995. Total delivered: 57.

VARIANTS

415: Standard produc7tion model in firefighting configuration
415GR: In service in Greece with boat handling and cargo hoist provisions
415M: Available for maritime, SAR and special missions
415MP: Multipurpose verion with FLIR, SLAR and nose-mounted search radar
215T: Turboprop retrofit of original piston-engined model; also some new-build aircraft

SPECIFICATIONS

Accommodation: 2 + 14
Cargo/baggage: 6,132 kg (13,500 lb)
Max speed: 203 kt (376 km/h)
Range: 1,310 nm (2,426 km)

DIMENSIONS

Wingspan: 28.6 m (93 ft 11 in)
Length: 19.8 m (65 ft 0 in)
Height: 9.0 m (29 ft 6 in)

FEATURES

High/straight wing with endplates; high-mounted twin P&WC PW123 turboprops with four-blade propeller; boat-hull fuselage; finlets and tailplane/fin bullet

Britten-Norman BN-2A Islander UK

Twin-piston or -turboprop light aircraft

Conceived by John Britten and Desmond Norman in early 1960s as rugged, low-cost general purpose and commuter aircraft and first flown on 13 June 1965. First deliveries made to Glosair and Loganair in August 1967. Subsequently underwent several ownership changes. Total delivered: 1,240.

VARIANTS
BN-2 Islander: Initial production version
BN-2A Islander: Several product improvements
BN-2B Islander: Higher landing weight, extended span wingtips, improved interior and various engine options
BN-2S: Islander: Long-nose variant with two more seats
BN-2T Turbine Islander: Allison 250 replacing Lycoming pistons
BN-2T-4R Defender: Military variant with four underwing hardpoints
BN-2T-4S Defender 4000: Enlarged wing and lengthened fuselage

SPECIFICATIONS: BN-2T
Accommodation: 1 + 11
Cargo/baggage: 692 kg (1,526 lb)
Max speed: 170 kt (315 km/h)
Range: 1,006 nm (1,863 km)

DIMENSIONS
Wingspan: 14.9 m (49 ft 0 in)
Length: 10.9 m (35 ft 8 in)
Height: 4.2 m (13 ft 9 in)

FEATURES
Straight/high wing with flared-up wingtips; twin Textron Lycoming piston or R-R (Allison) 250 turboprop engines with two-blade or three-blade propellers; swept tail fin with small dorsal fin and low-set tailplane; non-retractable tricycle landing gear with main leg mounted aft of rear wing spar.

Britten-Norman BN-2A Mk III Trislander UK

Three-piston light aircraft

Design to 'stretch' Islander began in 1968 and prototype flew on 14 July 1968. Additional power was needed and a third engine was then fitted at top of tailfin. It flew under the new configuration on 11 September 1970 and Aurigny Air Services took delivery of the first production aircraft on 29 June 1971. The Channel Islands-based airline remains the world's largest operator of the type. Total delivered: 85.

VARIANTS

BN-2A Mk III Trislander: Initial production model
BN-2A Mk III-1 Trislander: Higher gross weight
BN-2A Mk III-2 Trislander: Long-nose version with additional baggage space
BN-2A Mk III-3 Trislander: Auto feather system
Tri-Commutair: Trislander built under licence by IAC in the US; 12 completed

SPECIFICATIONS

Accommodation: 2 + 16
Cargo/baggage: 1,610 kg (3,550 lb)
Max speed: 156 kt (290 km/h)
Range: 868 nm (1,610 km)

DIMENSIONS

Wingspan: 16.2 m (53 ft 0 in)
Length: 15.0 m (49 ft 3 in)
Height: 4.3 m (14 ft 2 in)

FEATURES

High/straight wing with flared-up wingtips; three Textron Lycoming O-540 piston engines with two-blade propellers; third engine mounted high on tailfin together with tailplane; non-retractable tricycle landing gear

CASA C-212 Aviocar Spain

Twin-turboprop light aircraft

Developed in 1960s to meet Spanish Air Force requirement for tactical transport and first flown on 26 March 1971. Entered production for the Spanish Air Force, but CASA then designed 19-seat commuter aircraft for civil market. Also built under licence by IPTN in Indonesia. Total delivered: 475.

VARIANTS
C-212 CA: Initial civil variant with TPE331 turboprops
C-212 CB: Higher gross weight version
C-212 Series 100: TPE331-5 engines
C-212 Series 200: More powerful TPE331-10R and Dowty Rotol propellers; higher gross weight
C-212 Series 300: Updated engines, redesigned wingtips and more baggage space in nose
C-212-400: Improved model for hot/high conditions; higher payload
+ military models for transport, ASW, maritime patrol and Elint/ECM (which see)

SPECIFICATIONS: SERIES 200:
Accommodation: 2 + 24
Cargo/baggage: 2,770 kg (6,107 lb)
Max speed: 202 kt (374 km/h)
Range: 750 nm (1,388 km)

DIMENSIONS
Wingspan: 19.0 m (62 ft 4 in)
Length: 15.2 m (49 ft 9 in)
Height: 6.3 m (20 ft 8 in)

FEATURES
High/straight wing; twin wing-mounted TPE331 turboprops with four-blade propellers; ramp/door in upswept rear fuselage; tailfin with large dorsal fin and low-set tailplane; non-retractable tricycle landing gear

Cessna 208 Caravan/Grand Caravan USA

Single-turboprop light aircraft

Launched in 1981 for passenger/cargo transport, but also aimed at a multitude of other roles. First flight of prototype was made on 9 December 1982, leading to full production from 1985, with early aircraft all delivered to Federal Express. Total delivered: 1,300+.

VARIANTS

208 Caravan I: Basic utility version for passengers and cargo
208 Caravan Amphibian: Floats and tailplane finlets
208A Cargomaster: No windows and starboard door; underfuselage cargo pannier; extended tailfin
208B Super Cargomaster: Similar to 208A, but stretched fuselage and more powerful engine
Grand Caravan: 208B passenger version
Caravan 675: Combines 208-airframe with fully-rated engine of 208B
Soloy Pathfinder 21: Dual-engine conversion
UC-27A: Military utility/special mission derivative of Model 208A

SPECIFICATIONS: GRAND CARAVAN

Accommodation: 1 + 13
Cargo/baggage: 1,360 kg (3,000 lb)
Max speed: 175 kt (325 km/h)
Range: 960 nm (1,776 km)

DIMENSIONS

Wingspan: 15.9 m (52 ft 1 in)
Length: 12.7 m (41 ft 8 in)
Height: 4.5 m (14 ft 10 in)

FEATURES

Braced high/straight wing; single P&WC PT6A turboprop engine with three-blade propeller; swept tailfin with dorsal fillet; auxiliary fins on floatplane only; non-retractable tricycle landing gear or floats with or without retractable land wheels

de Havilland Canada DHC-2 Beaver/Turbo Beaver Canada

Single-piston/turboprop light STOL aircraft

Henry Tenby

First of a family of rugged STOL aircraft, the Beaver was designed for the Canadian bush. Work began in 1946 and the prototype first flew on 16 August 1947. Deliveries started to both civil and military customers following certification in March 1948. Turboprop development flew for the first time on 30 December 1963. Total built (including some 60 Turbo Beavers): 1,692.

VARIANTS

Mk I Beaver: Standard production model available with wheeled, ski and float landing gear
MK I Beaver Amphibian: Edo floats accommodating retractable main and nose wheels
Mk III Turbo Beaver: Turboprop version powered by the P&W PT6A
+ military derivatives for US Army as *U-6A* and British Army as *AL.Mk I*

SPECIFICATIONS: MK I

Accommodation: 1 + 7
Cargo/baggage: 3.4 m³ (120 cu.ft)
Max speed: 121 kt (225 km/h)
Range: 676 nm (1,252 km)

DIMENSIONS

Wingspan: 14.6 m (48 ft 0 in)
Length: 9.2 m (30 ft 4 in), floatplane 10.0 m (32 ft 9 in)
Height: 2.8 m (9 ft 0 in), floatplane 3.2 m (10 ft 5 in)

FEATURES

Braced high/straight wing; single P&W Wasp Junior piston or PT6A turboprop engine; rounded tail with large dorsal fin; non-retractable tailwheel type as standard, plus skis and floats (ventral strake under rear fuselage in amphibious version)

de Havilland Canada DHC-3 Otter Canada

Single-piston light STOL aircraft

Henry Tenby

Larger development of successful Beaver with lengthened fuselage and greater wingspan. Design work on the Otter, originally known as the King Beaver, started in January 1951, culminating in the first flight on 12 December that year. The Otter went into commercial service a year later and was also used by the US Army and other forces around the world. Total delivered: 460.

FEATURES
Braced high/straight wing; single P&W piston engine; rounded tail with large dorsal fin; non-retractable tailwheel type as standard, plus skis and floats

VARIANTS
DHC-3 Otter: Standard production model available with wheeled, ski and float landing gear
DHC-3 Otter Amphibian: Edo floats accommodating retractable main and nose wheels
Cox Turbo Single Otter: Small numbers of turboprop conversions by Cox Air Services with P&WC PT6A
+ military derivatives for US Army (as *U-1A*) and other customers simply with DHC-3 Otter designation

SPECIFICATIONS
Accommodation: 1 + 11
Cargo/baggage: 3.8 m^3 (134 cu.ft)
Max speed: 140 kt (247 km/h)
Range: 760 nm (1,410 km)

DIMENSIONS
Wingspan: 17.7 m (58 ft 0 in)
Length: 12.8 m (41 ft 10 in)
Height: 3.8 m (12 ft 7 in), floatplane 4.6 m (15 ft 0 in)

Twin-turboprop light aircraft

Design of this twin-engined development of the Otter began in January 1964, aimed specifically at the commercial operator requiring short take-off and landing (STOL) capabilities. First flight was on 20 May 1965 and first customer deliveries in July 1966. Total delivered: 842.

VARIANTS

Series 100: Initial production model
Series 200: Lengthened nose fairing with increased baggage space
Series 300: Uprated engines and improved payload/range
Series 300M: Basic military version available in transport and counter-insurgency roles, the latter with cabin-mounted machine gun and external ordnance on four underwing hardpoints
Series 300MR: Maritime reconnaissance model with chin mounted radome and searchlight pod
Series 300S: Enhanced aerodynamics to operate from city-centre STOLports

SPECIFICATIONS: SERIES 300

Accommodation: 2 + 20
Cargo/baggage: 3.6 m³ (126 cu.ft)
Max speed: 182 kt (338 km/h)
Range: 700 nm (1,297 km)

DIMENSIONS

Wingspan: 19.8 m (65 ft 0 in)
Length: 15.8 m (51 ft 9 in)
Height: 5.9 m (19 ft 6 in)

FEATURES

Braced high/straight wing; twin wing-mounted P&WC PT6A turboprop engines with three-bladed propellers; swept tailfin with low-set tailplane; non-retractable tricycle landing gear

Dornier 228 Germany

Twin-turboprop light utility and commuter aircraft

Successor to the Do 28/128 with new technology wing, turboprop engines and generous use of composites in structure. Two versions with different lengths were developed in parallel and made their first flights on 28 March and 9 May 1981. Deliveries began in February 1982. Also built under licence by Hindustan Aeronautics in India. Total delivered: 308.

VARIANTS

228-100: Basic version with seating for 15 passengers
228-101: Reinforced fuselage and new mainwheel tyres to permit higher operating weights
228-200: Lengthened fuselage for 19 passengers
228-201: As -101, but lengthened fuselage
228-202: Further improvements in payload/range performance
228-212: Uprated engines, stronger landing gear and new avionics
228 Maritime Patrol: Surveillance, SAR and border and fisheries protection, with radar and bubble window for observer

SPECIFICATIONS: 228-212

Accommodation: 2 + 19
Cargo/baggage: 3.5 m³ (124 cu.ft)
Max speed: 231 kt (428 km/h)
Range: 560 nm (1,038 km)

DIMENSIONS

Wingspan: 17.0 m (55 ft 8 in)
Length: 16.6 m (54 ft 4 in)

Height: 4.9 m (16 ft 0 in)

FEATURES

High/straight wing with tapered outer section and raked tips; twin wing-mounted Honeywell (AlliedSignal) TPE331 turboprops with four-blade propellers; long, pointed nose; swept tailfin with dorsal fin and low-set tailplane; retractable tricycle landing gear

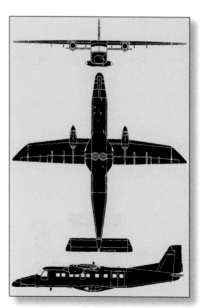

GAF Nomad Australia

Twin-turboprop light STOL aircraft

Development of small utility aircraft for civil and military roles began at the Government Aircraft Factories (GAF) in the mid-1960s. The high-wing monoplane flew for the first time on 23 July 1971 and went into service on 18 December 1975 with local commuter airline Aero Pelican. Total delivered: 170.

VARIANTS

N22 Nomad: Initial production version
N22B Nomad: Standard short-fuselage version with higher gross weight
N24 Nomad: Lengthened for 17 passengers
N24A Nomad: Definitive version with increased gross weight
Floatmaster: Twin floats or amphibious gear
Medicmaster: Air ambulance version
Missionmaster: Short-fuselage military version with four underwing pylons and drop doors in cabin floor
Searchmaster: Coastal patrol versions with search radar and scanner nose radome or undernose 'guppy' radome
Surveymaster: geological and geophysical research platform

SPECIFICATIONS: N24A

Accommodation: 2 + 17
Cargo/baggage: 1.13 m^3 (40 cu.ft)
Max speed: 169 kt (313 km/h)
Range: 580 nm (1,074 km)

DIMENSIONS

Wingspan: 16.5 m (54 ft 2 in)
Length: 14.4 m (47 ft 2 in)
Height: 5.5 m (18 ft 2 in)

FEATURES

Braced high/straight wing; twin wing-mounted R-R (Allison) 250 turboprops with three-blade propellers; slab-sided fuselage upswept at rear; cranked tailfin with low-set tailplane

Gippsland GA8 Airvan Australia

Single-piston light aircraft

Robust utility aircraft with short take-off and landing capability. Prototype construction started in early 1994, with first flight taking place on 3 March 1995, but destroyed during spinning trials on 7 February 1996. Two further prototypes completed leading to FAR Pt 23 certification on 18 December 2000. First delivery to Fraser Island Air four days later. Total deliveries: 37.

VARIANTS

GA8 Airvan: Initial production model for passenger or freight use, or combination of the two

SPECIFICATIONS

Accommodation: 1 + 7
Cargo/baggage: 90 kg (200 lb)
Max speed: 130 kt (241 km/h)
Range: 730 nm (1,350 km)

DIMENSIONS

Wingspan: 12.4 m (40 ft 9 in)
Length: 8.9 m (29 ft 3 in)
Height: 3.9 m (12 ft 9 in)

FEATURES

Strut-braced high straight wing; single Textron Lycoming IO-540 piston engine with two-blade propeller; sweptback vertical tailfin with dorsal fillet and straight rectangular tailplane; ventral finlet; non-retractable tricycle landing gear

Helio Courier USA

Single-piston light STOL aircraft

Shawn Miller

The Helio Courier, initially known as the Helioplane Four, first flew during 1953, with deliveries starting the following year. Continuous development resulted in many variants, all powered by Lycoming engines. Total delivered: 501.

VARIANTS

H-391B Courier: Initial production model with GO-435 engine

H-392 Strato Courier: High-altitude version with GO-480 engine
H-395 Super Courier: Similar to H-391B, but more powerful engine
H-250 Courier II: Stretched fuselage with O-540
H-295 Super Courier: Similar to H-395
H-500 Helio Twin: Six-seat model, engines mounted on high wing
HST-550A Stallion: Turboprop version with PT6A
H-700 Courier: H-295 with new undercarriage and upturned wingtips
+ various others built in small numbers and military derivatives under *U-10* designation

SPECIFICATIONS: H-250
Accommodation: 1 + 5
Cargo/baggage: 0.4 m³ (15 cu.ft)
Max speed: 140kt (257 km/h)
Range: 575 nm (1,060 km/h)

DIMENSIONS
Wingspan: 11.9 m (39 ft 0 in)
Length: 9.5 m (31 ft 0 in)
Height: 2.7 m (18 ft 10 in)

FEATURES
High/straight wing; single Lycoming piston engine with three-bladed propeller; swept tailfin with dorsal fin and low-set tailplane; non-retractable tailwheel type landing gear

IAI Arava Israel

Twin-turboprop light STOL aircraft

Design work began in 1966, with the objective to carry 25 troops into and out of short unprepared airstrips. The result was a high-wing, short fuselage aircraft with twin booms and tailfins. First flight was on 27 November 1969, and the type went into production in both civil and military versions. Total delivered: 90+.

VARIANTS

Arava 101B: Modified civil version with enhanced performance. Marketed in the US as the *Cargo Commuterliner*
Arava 102: Initial civil model with P&WC PT6A turboprops
Arava 201: Initial military transport, sold in greatest numbers
Arava 202: Upgraded and longer military derivative with 'wet' wing and winglets; armed or unarmed; 24 troops

SPECIFICATIONS: ARAVA 102

Accommodation: 2 + 20
Cargo/baggage: 5.8 m3 (205 cu.ft)
Max speed: 176 kt (325 km/h)
Range: 540 nm (1,000 km)

DIMENSIONS

Wingspan: 21.0 m (68 ft 9 in)
Length: 13.1 m (42 ft 9 in)
Height: 5.2 m (17 ft 1 in)

FEATURES

Braced high/straight wing (endplate winglets on 202); twin wing-mounted P&WC PT6A turboprops with three-blade propellers; high mounted twin booms with twin fins and rudders; non-retractable tricycle landing gear

Ibis Aerospace Ae270 Ibis Czech Republic/Taiwan

Single-turboprop light transport

Announced by Aero Vodochody in Czechoslovakia in the early 1990s, initially designated as L-270. Designed by Jan Mikula, the 9/10-passenger utility Ibis underwent several design changes prior to its first flight in July 2000. By that time, Ibis Aerospace had been set up as a joint venture between Aero Vodochody and AIDC of Taiwan. Service entry planned for early 2005. Total ordered: 73.

VARIANTS
Ae 270P: Basic production model with a 634 kW (850 shp) P&WC PT6A turboprop engine
Ae 270HP: High performance variant with more powerful engine
Ae 270W: Walter M601F turboprop and Czech avionics
Ae 270 Spirit: Executive version

SPECIFICATIONS: AE270P
Accommodation: 2 + 8
Cargo/baggage: 1,200 kg (2,645 lb)
Max speed: 206 kt (381 km/h)
Range: 1,231 nm (2,280 km)

DIMENSIONS
Wingspan: 13.8 m (45 ft 3 in)
Length: 12.2 m (40 ft 1 in)
Height: 4.8 m (15 ft 9 in)

FEATURES
Low/straight dihedral wing with leading edge taper; single P&WC PT6A turboprop engine with four-blade propeller; swept tailfin and low-set tailplane; retractable tricycle landing gear (wheeled floats optional)

Let L-410 Turbolet Czech Republic

Twin-turboprop short-haul commuter and utility aircraft

After licence production of Soviet types, the Let Kunovice works began design of a twin-engined transport to meet the needs of the Soviet Union and East European satellite countries. The prototype first flew 16 April 1969, initially powered by PT6A engines, replaced by Walter turboprops in production aircraft. The L-410 entered service with Slov-Air in late 1971. Total delivered: 1,001.

VARIANTS

L-410A: Initial version with P&WC PT6A-27s
L-410AF: Aerial survey model with glazed nose
L-410AS: Soviet avionics fit
L-410M: First production aircraft with the Walter M 601A
L-410MA: More powerful M 601B engines
L-410MU: Special equipment fit for Aeroflot
L-410UVP: Increased wingspan and aerodynamic changes
L-410UVP-E: Five-blade propellers, tip tanks and more powerful engines
L-420: Upgraded version with more powerful Walter engines

SPECIFICATIONS: L410UVP-E

Accommodation: 2 +19
Cargo/baggage: 1.4 m3 (49 cu.ft)
Max speed: 194 kt (360 km/h)
Range: 294 nm (546 km)

DIMENSIONS

Wingspan: 20.0 m (65 ft 7 in)
Length: 14.4 m (47 ft 4 in)

Height: 5.8 m (19 ft 1 in)

FEATURES

High/straight wing; twin wing-mounted PT6A or M 601 turboprops with three- or five-blade propellers; shallow dorsal fin and deeper ventral fin; tip tanks in UVP-E

Lockheed L100 Hercules USA

Four-turboprop freight transport

Toni Marimon

The commercial Hercules originated as a civilianised version of the C-130 military tactical transport, which can be dated back to a USAF specification of 1951. A civil company demonstrator was first flown on 21 April 1964, and the L100 was put into production in 1965. It is used mostly for freight flights, although one customer used it in passenger configuration. Total built (civil only): 110.

VARIANTS
L100-20: Similar to military C-130B, but uprated Allison D22A engines and lengthened fuselage
L100-30: Further fuselage stretch
+ numerous military models (which see)

SPECIFICATIONS: L100-30
Accommodation: 3 + 128
Cargo/baggage: 23,158 kg (51,054 lb)
Max speed: 315 kt (583 km/h)
Range: 1,363 kg (2,526 km)

DIMENSIONS
Wingspan: 40.4 m (132 ft 7 in)
Length: 34.4 m (112 ft 9 in)
Height: 11.7 m (38 ft 3 in)

FEATURES
High/straight wing; four wing-mounted Allison 501-D22A turboprops with four-blade propellers; upswept rear fuselage with loading ramp; tailfin with dorsal fillet and low-set tailplane; retractable tricycle landing gear

Pacific Aerospace 750XL New Zealand

Single-turboprop light utility aircraft

Developed from the Cresco agricultural and utility turboprop, work on this wide-body version powered by a single Pratt & Whitney Canada PT6A-34 engine began in January 2000. The prototype first flew on 5 September 2001. Certification from the New Zealand CAA obtained on 20 August 2003 and from the FAA in March 2004, the 750XL becoming the first NZ designed and built aircraft to be accepted in the US. First customer delivery September 2003. Total delivered: 10.

VARIANTS
750XL: Initial production version

SPECIFICATIONS
Accommodation: 2 + 9
Cargo: 3.8 m^3 (134 cu.ft)
Max speed: 155 kt (287 km/h)
Range: 595 nm (1,100 km)

DIMENSIONS
Wingspan: 12.8 m (42 ft 0 in)
Length: 11.5 m (37 ft 7 in)
Height: 3.8 m (12 ft 7 in)

FEATURES
Low/straight broad wing with outer dihedral; single PWAC PT6A turboprop engine with three-

blade propeller; upright tapered tailfin with dorsal fillet; tailplane set low into rear fuselage; port freight door at rear; non-retractable tricycle landing gear

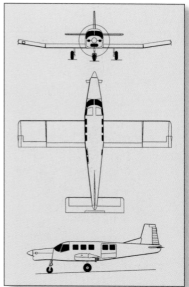

Pilatus PC-6 Porter/Turbo Porter Switzerland

Single-piston/turboprop light STOL aircraft

Design of a single piston-engined general utility aircraft with STOL capability began in 1957. This resulted in the Porter braced high-wing taildragger, which first flew on 4 May 1959. Some 45 were built before being replaced by the Turbo Porter, which offered considerably improved performance. Some produced under licence by Fairchild in the US. Total delivered: 550+

VARIANTS
PC-6: Basic Porter with Lycoming piston engine
PC-6/A-H1: Initial turboprop model with Turbomeca Astazou IIE
PC-6/A1-H2: More powerful Astazou XIIE engine
PC-6/B1-H2: First variant with P&WC PT6A turboprop
PC-6/B2-H2: Improved PT6A engine
PC-6/B2-H4: Strengthened airframe, enlarged dorsal fin, extended wingtips
PC-6/C1-H2: Licence-built with Garrett TPE331 turboprops

SPECIFICATIONS: PC-6/B2-H4
Accommodation: 1 + 10
Cargo/baggage: 945 kg (2,083 lb)
Max speed: 151 kt (280 km/h)
Range: 560 nm (1,036 km)

DIMENSIONS
Wingspan: 15.9 m (52 ft 1 in)
Length: 11.0 m (35 ft 11 in)
Height: 3.2 m (10 ft 6 in)

FEATURES
Braced high/straight wing; single P&WC PT6A turboprop with three-blade propeller; rectangular upright tailfin with dorsal fin and low-set tailplane; non-retractable tailwheel type or floats with ground wheels

Pilatus **PC-12** Switzerland

Single-turbine light aircraft

Launched in October 1989 for executive use, its envelope was soon extended to cover the general utility market. The PC-12 (initially referred to as the PC-XII) made its maiden flight on 31 May 1991 and entered service in April 1994. Total delivered: 520.

VARIANTS

PC-12 Standard: Basic commuter or passenger/cargo combi
PC-12/45: Higher gross weight version
PC-12 Executive: Customised interior for up to six people
PC-12 Spectre: Surveillance and special mission version with ventral pannier carrying EO sensors (formerly Eagle)
PC-12M: Multi-mission development with enhanced equipment package

SPECIFICATIONS

Accommodation: 1 or 2 + 9
Cargo/baggage: 1.13 m^3 (40 cu.ft)
Max speed: 240 kt (444 km/h)
Range: 2,261 nm (4,187 km)

DIMENSIONS

Wingspan: 16.2 m (53 ft 3 in)
Length: 14.4 m (47 ft 3 in)
Height: 4.3 m (14 ft 0 in)

FEATURES

Low/tapered wing with tiplets; single P&WC PT6A turboprop with four-blade propeller; T-tail with fin bullet fairing, enlarged dorsal fin and ventral strakes; retractable tricycle landing gear

PZL (Antonov) An-28 Poland

Twin-turboprop utility and commuter aircraft

Developed by Antonov in the former Soviet Union for Aeroflot and made its first flight as the An-28M in September 1969. A first pre-production aircraft did not fly until April 1978, after which sole production was assigned to PZL in Poland. The first Polish-built aircraft flew on 22 July 1984. Total delivered: 100+.

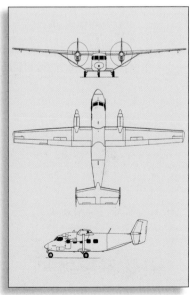

VARIANTS

An-28: Basic commercial production version
An-28TD Bryza 1TD: Paradrop/transport version with rear clamshell doors replaced by a single door sliding under fuselage
M-28B Bryza 1R: Maritime reconnaissance, formerly An-28RM
M-28 Skytruck: Westernised development with P&WC PT6A turboprops and Honeywell avionics
M-28 Skytruck Plus: Stretched development with raised ceiling for both passenger and freight roles

SPECIFICATIONS: SKYTRUCK

Accommodation: 2 + 18
Cargo/baggage: 2,000 kg (4,409 lb)
Max speed: 178 kt (330 km/h)
Range: 736 nm (1,365 km)

DIMENSIONS

Wingspan: 22.1 m (72 ft 5 in)
Length: 13.1 m (43 ft 0 in)
Height: 4.9 m (16 ft 1 in)

FEATURES

Braced high/straight wing with optional winglets; twin TVD-10 or P&WC PT6A turboprops with three-blade and five-blade propellers respectively; upswept rear fuselage incorporating clamshell doors; twin fins and rudder; short stub wing extending from lower fuselage to carry wing bracing and non-retractable tricycle landing gear

Reims F406 Caravan II France

Twin-turboprop light multirole aircraft

Extrapolated from the Cessna Titan airframe and Conqest II wings and announced in mid-1982. Made its first flight in France on 22 September 1983 and entered service in 1985. Operated by a mix of commercial operators and government agencies. Total delivered: 100+.

VARIANTS

F406 Caravan II: Basic passenger, freight and utility version
F406 Mk II Caravan: New avionics and interior
Vigilant: Surveillance version with radar and FLIR
Vigilant Comint/Imint: Dedicated comms and imaging intelligence
Vigilant Frontier: Border patrol and anti-drug version
Vigilant Polmar I, II and III: Pollution surveillance with scanner and SLAR
Vigilant Surmar: Armed or unarmed maritime surveillance version
Vigilant Surpolmar: Maritime surveillance version for Hellenic Coast Guard

SPECIFICATIONS: CARAVAN II

Accommodation: 2 + 12
Cargo/baggage: 1,563 kg (3,445 lb)
Max speed: 229 kt (424 km/h)
Range: 1,153 nm (2,135 km)

DIMENSIONS

Wingspan: 15.1 m (49 ft 6 in)
Length: 11.9 m (39 ft 1 in)
Height: 4.0 m (13 ft 2 in)

FEATURES

Low/straight wing; twin wing-mounted P&WC PT6A turboprops with three- or four-blade (Mk II) propellers; swept tailfin with dorsal fin and dihedral tailplane; retractable tricycle landing gear

Rockwell (Aero Commander) Commander 500/560/580 USA

Twin-piston light corporate/utility aircraft

Nigel Steele

Prolific series of high-wing twin-piston aircraft originating from the L-3085 prototype, which first flew as long ago as 23 April 1948. The first production model was the 520, which led to many improved and more powerful models with both normally-aspirated and turbocharged engines. Total delivered: 710.

VARIANTS

500 Commander: As 560E, but with 250 hp engines

500U Shrike Commander: Pointed nose and squared-off fin
520 Commander: Initial model with two 290 hp engines
560 Commander: Swept tail, strengthened structure, seven seats
680F Commander: Fuel-injected engines, new landing gear
680FL Grand Commander: Stretched fuselage for 11 passengers, four square cabin windows
720 Alti Cruiser: 680 with pressurised cabin, extended wing
+ many other variants and subvariants with suffixes *E* denoting extended wing, *P* for pressurised models, and *L* with long fuselage. Also used by US Army and USAF with designation *U-4*.

SPECIFICATIONS: 680FL
Accommodation: 1 + 10
Cargo/baggage: 1.7 m^3 (60 cu.ft)
Max speed: 212 kt (393 km/h)
Range: 1,250 nm (2,313 km)

DIMENSIONS: 680FL
Wingspan: 15.0 m (49 ft 1 in)
Length: 12.6 m (41 ft 3 in)
Height: 4.4 m (14 ft 6 in)

FEATURES
High/straight wing with slight dihedral; twin Lycoming engines with two- or three-blade propellers; swept tailfin with dorsal fillet and low-set dihedral tailplane; retractable tricycle landing gear

Rockwell (Aero Commander) Turbo Commander/Jetprop USA

Twin-turboprop corporate/utility aircraft

John Olafson

Based on the piston-engined pressurised 680FLP Grand Commander, but substituting twin Garrett TPE331 turboprops, the Turbo Commander first flew on 31 December 1964 and entered production the following year. This model also spawned many variants, which were eventually built under different ownerships. Total delivered: 1,290.

VARIANTS

680T Turbo Commander: Initial production model
680W Turbo II Commander: Pointed nose, squared-off fin, one panoramic and two small cabin windows
681 Hawk Commander: Improved systems, redesigned nose
690 Commander: New wing centre section, engines moved outwards
690C Jetprop 840: Increased wingspan and winglets
695A Jetprop 1000: More powerful engines, revised interior
+ other variants differing mainly in fitted engines

SPECIFICATIONS: JETPROP 1000
Accommodation: 1 + 10
Cargo/baggage: 318 kg (700 lb)
Max speed: 308 kt (571 km/h)
Range: 2,080 nm (3,855 km)

DIMENSIONS
Wingspan: 15.9 m (52 ft 2 in)
Length: 13.1 m (43 ft 0 in)

Height: 4.6 m (15 ft 0 in)

FEATURES
High/straight wing with or without winglets; twin Garrett TPE331 turboprops with three-blade propellers; swept tailfin with long slim dorsal fillet and low-set dihedral tailplane; retractable tricycle landing gear

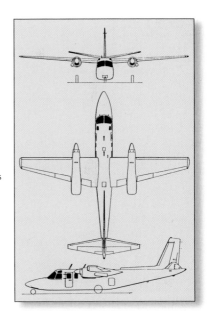

Socata **TBM 700** France

Single-turbine light multirole aircraft

Originally developed in partnership with Mooney in the US. It first flew on 14 July 1988, with first delivery taking place on 21 December 1990. Although optimised for business flying, the TBM 700 has also found application in a variety of other roles. Total delivered: 300+.

VARIANTS

TBM 700: Basic transport also offered in a variety of multi-mission versions, both civil and military

TBM 700 Freighter: Cargo version with reinforced floor, port side cargo door and separate cockpit door

TBM 700C1: Improved version with strengthened airframe and other modifications

TBM 700C2: Increased payload/range capability

SPECIFICATIONS: TBM 700C2

Accommodation: 1 + 5
Cargo/baggage: 150 kg (330 lb)
Max speed: 300 kt (555 km/h)
Range: 1,075 nm (1,990 km)

DIMENSIONS

Wingspan: 12.7 m (41 ft 8 in)
Length: 10.6 m (34 ft 11 in)
Height: 4.4 m (14 ft 4 in)

FEATURES

Low/straight wing; single P&WC PT6A turboprop with four-blade propeller; conventional swept tailfin with extended dorsal fin and twin strakes under rear fuselage; retractable tricycle landing gear

Shorts SC.7 Skyvan UK

Twin-turboprop light STOL aircraft

Development for a small multi-role transport with good STOL characteristics began in 1959, making use of the Miles high aspect ratio wing used on the Aerovan. The square-sided SC.7, later dubbed Skyvan, flew on 17 January 1963 with Continental piston engines, but these were replaced by Turbomeca Astazou turboprops prior to the aircraft entering service in 1966. Total built (including military versions): 150.

VARIANTS

Skyvan 2: Initial production version with Astazou engines
Skyvan 3: Switch to Garrett TPE331 turboprop engines
Skyliner: Higher standard furnishings for airline use
Skyvan 3A: Increased take-off weight
Skyvan 3M: Designation of military transport
Skyvan 3M-200: Higher gross weight military version

SPECIFICATIONS

Accommodation: 2 + 19
Cargo/baggage: 2,086 kg (4,600 lb)
Max speed: 175 kt (324 km/h)
Range: 162 nm (300 km)

DIMENSIONS

Wingspan: 19.8 m (64 ft 11 in)
Length: 12.2 m (40 ft 1 in)
Height: 4.6 m (15 ft 1 in)

FEATURES

Braced high/straight wing; twin wing-mounted Garrett TPE331 turboprops with three-blade propellers; square-sided fuselage upswept at rear with loading ramp; twin square-sided tail units; fixed tricycle landing gear

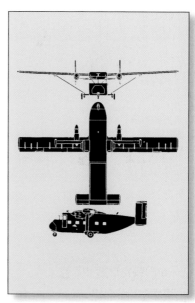

Technoavia SM-92 Finist Russian Federation

Single-piston light STOL aircraft

Design of this rugged STOL transport began started in July 1992 by Interavia. Initially known as the I-5, it was redesignated the SM-92 Finist by the time of the first flight on 28 December 1993. Production disrupted and only 15 built.

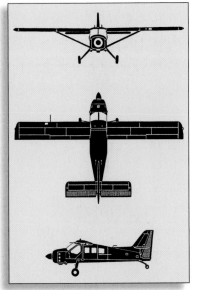

VARIANTS

SM-92: Basic production version available for passenger/freight transport and for other aerial work missions
SM-92P: Armed border patrol version with removable outrigger pylons for rockets and machine gun, and two underbelly hardpoints for 100kg bombs or auxiliary tanks
SM-92T: Tip tanks for increased range
SMG-92 Turbo Finist: Development with Walter M601D turboprop
Z 400 Rhino: Licence-production by Zlin with Orenda OE-600A piston diesel engine

SPECIFICATIONS

Accommodation: 1 + 6
Cargo/baggage: 600 kg (1,323 lb)
Max speed: 140 kt (260 km/h)
Range: 594 nm (1,100 km)

DIMENSIONS

Wingspan: 14.6 m (47 ft 11 in)
Length: 9.3 m (30 ft 6 in)
Height: 3.1 m (10 ft 2 in)

FEATURES

Braced high/straight wing; single VOKBM M-14 piston engine with three-blade propeller; tapering fuselage ending in sweptback fin with small dorsal fin; tailplane with bracing strut each side; fixed tailwheel type landing gear

Vulcanair (Partenavia) P68 Observer Italy

Twin-piston light utility aircraft

Originally designed by Prof Ing Luigi Pascale in 1968, the P68 Victor first flew on 25 May 1970. Various improved versions followed until 1994, when Partenavia assets bought by Vulcanair. Total delivered (including licence production in India): 420+.

VARIANTS

P68 Victor: Original production model with Lycoming piston engine
P68B Victor: Enhanced development
P68C: Improved with lengthened nose and other refinements
P68C-TC: Turbocharged version for better hot-and-high performance
P68 Observer: Largely transparent nose section and underfloor hatch for various sensors
P68 Observer 2: Current model with further improvements
P68TC Observer: Turbocharged version for better hot-and-high performance
P68 Diesel: SMA SR305-230 diesel engine

SPECIFICATIONS

Accommodation: 1 + 6
Cargo/baggage: 0.6 m³ (20 cu.ft)
Max speed: 173 kt (320 km/h)
Range: 590 nm (1,093 km)

DIMENSIONS

Wingspan: 12.0 m (39 ft 5 in)
Length: 9.4 m (30 ft 11 in)
Height: 3.4 m (11 ft 2 in)

FEATURES

High/straight wing; twin wing-mounted Textron Lycoming piston engines with two-blade propellers; extensively glazed nose in Observer; swept tailfin and dorsal fin with low-seat tailplane; non-retractable landing gear, streamlined wheel fairings optional

Vulcanair (Partenavia) AP68TP Viator Italy

Twin-turboprop light utility aircraft

Developed from the P68R, basically a P68B with retractable landing gear, but with Allison 250 turboprops, lengthened fuselage and larger fuel tanks. First flown on 11 September 1978.

Produced by Partenavia until programme taken over by Vulcanair. Total delivered: 23.

VARIANTS
P68T: Initial version, but only four built
AP68TP-300 Spartacus: Improved version with fixed landing gear, better soundproofing and upturned wingtips
AP68TP-600 Viator: Stretched and retractable landing gear
VA 300: New version with twin diesel engines expected to enter service in 2005

SPECIFICATIONS: VIATOR
Accommodation: 1 + 10
Cargo/baggage: 0.55 m^3 (20 cu.ft)
Max speed: 200 kt (370 km/h)
Range: 777 nm (1,440 km)

DIMENSIONS: VIATOR
Wingspan: 12.0 m (39 ft 5 in)
Length: 11.3 m (37 ft 0 in)
Height: 3.6 m (11 ft 11 in)

FEATURES
High/straight wing; twin wing-mounted R-R (Allison) 250 turboprop engines with three-blade propellers; swept tailfin and dorsal fin with low-seat tailplane; retractable tricycle landing gear

Vulcanair (SIAI-Marchetti) SF.600 Canguro/ VF 600 Mission Italy

Twin-turboprop light utility aircraft

Originally designed by Stelio Frati and built by General Avia. The CF.600 Canguro prototype flew on 30 December 1978 with piston engines, but these were replaced by Allison 250 turboprops in production. Programme then transferred to SIAI-Marchetti, before passing on to Vulcanair, which intends to revive this model. New single-engine VF 600W Mission first flown 30 January 2003. Total delivered: 11.

VARIANTS

SF.600A: Basic current production model available in several specialised versions for passenger/cargo transport, paratrooping, air ambulance, maritime and electronic surveillance and agricultural work

SF.600TP: Original production version with choice of non-retractable and retractable landing gear

VF 600W Mission: Single-engined version with Walter M 601 turboprop fitted into nose; P&WC PT6A optional

SPECIFICATIONS

Accommodation: 1 + 10
Max speed: 165 kt (306 km/h)
Range: 929 nm (1,722 km)

DIMENSIONS

Wingspan: 15.0 m (49 ft 3 in)
Length: 12.2 m (40 ft 1 in)
Height: 4.3 m (14 ft 1 in)

FEATURES

High/straight wing; twin wing-mounted R-R Allison 250 turboprop engines with three-blade propellers; swept tailfin and dorsal fin with low-seat tailplane; non-retractable tricycle landing gear

BUSINESS JETS
AND
TURBOPROPS

Adam Aircraft A500 USA

Twin-turboprop light business aircraft

Designed by Burt Rutan, development of this lightweight centerline-thrust piston twin built of graphite carbon composites started in September 1999, leading to first flight of proof-of-concept aircraft on 21 March 2000. Production-configuration A500 flew on 11 July 2002. FAA certification received in 2004. Total ordered: 100+.

connected by high-set tailplane; retractable tricycle landing gear

VARIANTS
A500: Initial production version

SPECIFICATIONS
Accommodation: 1 + 5
Max speed: 250 kt (460 km/h)
Range: 1,050 nm (1,940 km)

DIMENSIONS
Wingspan: 13.4 m (44 ft 0 in)
Length: 11.2 m (36 ft 8 in)
Height: 2.9 m (9 ft 6 in)

FEATURES
Straight low wings with slight dihedral on outboard panels; two Teledyne Continental flat-six piston engines in centerline-thrust configuration; three cabin windows each side; twin-boom configuration with swept fins

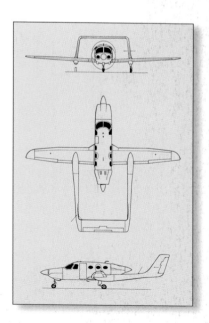

Adam Aircraft A700 USA

Twin-turbofan light business jet

Jet development of A500 light piston business aircraft, powered by two Williams International FJ33 turbofans pylon-mounted on rear fuselage. Announced on 21 October 2002 and first flown on 27 July 2003. First deliveries were anticipated in December 2004.

VARIANTS
A700: Initial production version

SPECIFICATIONS
Accommodation: 2 + 4
Max speed: 340 kt (630 km/h)
Range: 1,100 nm (2,040 km)

DIMENSIONS
Wingspan: 13.4 m (44 ft 0 in)
Length: 12.4 m (40 ft 9 in)
Height: 2.9 m (9 ft 6 in)

FEATURES
Straight low wings with dihedral for full length; two Williams International FJ33 turbofan engines at rear fuselage; four cabin windows each side; twin-boom configuration with swept fins connected by high-set tailplane; retractable tricycle landing gear

Aerospatiale SN 601 Corvette France

Twin-turbofan light executive jet

Designed primarily as a corporate transport, it was also targeted at a variety of utility roles, including commuter, air taxi, aerial photography, trainer, ambulance and others. First flown on 16 July 1970, the Corvette entered service in September 1974. Total delivered: 40.

VARIANTS

Corvette 100: Standard production model
Corvette 200: Stretch proposal, never built.

SPECIFICATIONS

Accommodation: 2 + 14
Cargo/baggage: 1,000 kg (2,205 lb)
Max speed: M0.72 (410 kt; 759 km/h)
Range: 800 nm (1,480 km)

DIMENSIONS

Wingspan: 12.9 m (42 ft 3 in)
Length: 13.8 m (45 ft 5 in)
Height: 4.2 m (13 ft 11 in)

FEATURES

Low/swept wing with or without tip tanks; twin rear fuselage-mounted P&WC JT15D turbofans; highly-swept tailfin with mid-mounted tailplane

British Aerospace (HS) BAe 125 UK

Twin-turbojet/turbofan light business jet

Developed as a private venture by de Havilland and first flew on 13 August 1962, by which time DH had become part of Hawker Siddeley. Early models, which entered service on 10 October 1964, were powered by the Viper turbojet. Total delivered: 572.

VARIANTS

125 Series 1: Initial production model
125 Series 1A: More powerful engines, for US market

125 Series 1B: Similar, but for non-US markets
125 Series 2: Dominie T.1 crew trainer for RAF
125 Series 3A: Higher gross weight, for US market
125 Series 3B: Similar, but for non-US markets
125 Series 3A/RA: As 3A, but with ventral long-range fuel tank
125 Series 3B/RA: As 3B, but with ventral long-range fuel tank
125 Series 400A: Improved flight deck, for US
125 Series 400B: Similar, for non-US markets
125 Series 600A: Stretched, lengthened nose, sixth window
125 Series 600B: Similar, but for non-US markets
125 Series 700A: Series 600A with Garrett TFE731 turbofans
125 Series 700B: Series 600B with Garrett TFE731 turbofans

SPECIFICATIONS: SERIES 700
Accommodation: 2 + 14
Max speed: M0.76 (437 kt;808 km/h)
Range: 2,420 nm (4,480 km)

DIMENSIONS
Wingspan: 14.3 m (47 ft 0 in)
Length: 15.4 m (15 ft 6 in)
Height: 5.3 m (17 ft 3 in)

FEATURES
Low/swept wing; twin Rolls-Royce Viper turbojets or Garrett TFE731 turbofans; five or six cabin windows each side; highly-swept tailfin with dorsal fin and high-mounted swept tailplane

Beech King Air 90/100 USA

Twin-turboprop business aircraft

Derived from the Queen Air, the pressurised King Air prototype first flew on 20 January 1964. Deliveries began later that year. The type has been continuously developed since and remains in production. Total built: 2,890+.

VARIANTS

King Air 90: Initial production model
King Air A90: Slight increase in engine power
King Air B90: Same engine as B90 with further enhancements
King Air C90: Improved engines and cabin refinements
King Air C90B: Current production model available since 1991
King Air C90SE: Customised Special Edition
King Air E90: Combines airframe of C90 with PT6A-28 engines
King Air F90: Short-span wings of King Air 100 and T-tail of 200
King Air 100: Lengthened fuselage for 13 passengers
King Air A100: Refined development
King Air B100: Garrett TPE331 truboprops

SPECIFICATIONS: KING AIR C90B

Accommodation: 2 + 6
Cargo/baggage: 1.5 m^3 (54 cu.ft)
Max speed: 247 kt (457 km/h)
Range: 1,039 nm (1,924 km)

DIMENSIONS

Wingspan: 15.3 m (15 ft 3 in)

Length: 10.8 m (35 ft 6 in)
Height: 4.3 m (14 ft 3 in)

FEATURES

Low/straight wing; twin wing-mounted P&WC PT6A turboprops with four-blade propellers; four cabin windows; swept tailfin and low-set tailplane

Beech King Air B200 USA

Twin-turboprop light business and multirole transport

Design of pressurised Super King Air 200 (the Super was deleted in 1996) began in October 1970. First flown on 27 October 1972 and entered service the following year. Higher performance B200 sold from March 1981. Total delivered: 2,400.

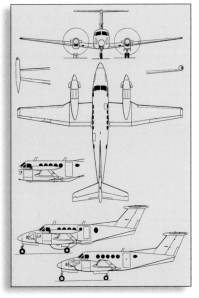

VARIANTS
King Air 200: Initial production version
King Air B200: Improved version from 1981
King Air B200C: As B200, but with cargo door
King Air B200CT: Combines tip tanks and cargo door. Only 9 built
King Air B200SE: Improved avionics and three-blade propellers
King Air B200T: Provision for removable tip tanks
200 HISAR: Radar surveillance platform + various military models under *C-12*, *RC-12*, *TC-12* and *UC-12* designations
King Air 300: Improved model with more powerful engines
King Air 300LW: Leightweight model for European market

SPECIFICATIONS
Accommodation: 2 + 9
Cargo/baggage: 1.5 m^3 (54 cu.ft)
Max speed: 292 kt (541 km/h)
Range: 1,477 nm (2,735 km)

DIMENSIONS
Wingspan: 16.6 m (54 ft 6 in)
Length: 13.4 m (43 ft 10 in)
Height: 4.5 m (14 ft 10 in)

FEATURES
Low/straight wing; twin wing-mounted P&WC PT6A turboprops with four-blade propellers; five cabin windows; swept T-tail with dorsal fin and swept tailplane

Beech King Air 350 USA

Twin-turboprop business aircraft

Stretched development of King Air 300, first flown in September 1988 and introduced at the NBAA convention in 1989. Certified in commuter category, with initial delivery on 6 March 1990. Total delivered: 400.

VARIANTS

King Air 350: Baseline version
King Air 350C: Incorporates cargo door with built-in airstair passenger door
C-12S: Quick-change US Army version
RC-350 Guardian: Elint version with wingtip pods and underfuselage bulge
LR-2: JGSDF liaison and reconnaissance version

SPECIFICATIONS

Accommodation: 2 + 11
Cargo/baggage: 1.5 m³ (54 cu.ft)
Max speed: 315 kt (584 km/h)
Range: 1,358 nm (2,515 km)

DIMENSIONS

Wingspan: 17.7 m (57 ft 11 in)
Length: 14.2 m (46 ft 8 in)
Height: 4.4 m (14 ft 4 in)

FEATURES

Low/straight wing with winglets; twin wing-mounted P&WC PT6A turboprops with four-blade propellers; seven cabin windows; swept T-tail with dorsal fin and swept tailplane

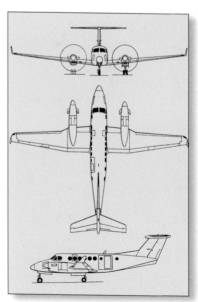

Beech 390 Premier USA

Twin-turbofan light business jet

Design started at Beechcraft in early 1994 under the designation PD374 (later PD390) and brief

details first revealed in June 1995, prior to launch at the NBAA convention the following September. First flight was made on 22 December 1998 and the new type, the first to carry only the Raytheon name, entered service in March 2001. Reverted to Beech name in 2002. Total delivered: 110.

VARIANTS
Premier I: Initial production version
Premier II: Proposed stretched development

SPECIFICATIONS
Accommodation: 2 + 6
Cargo/baggage: 68 kg (150 lb)
Max speed: M0.80 (461 kt; 854 km/h)
Range: 1,500 nm (2,778 km)

DIMENSIONS
Wingspan: 13.6 m (44 ft 6 in)
Length: 14.0 m (46 ft 0 in)
Height: 4.7 m (15 ft 4 in)

FEATURES
Low/swept wing mounted below fuselage; twin rear-mounted Williams FJ44 turbofans; three cabin windows; swept T-tail and swept tailplane

Beech Beechjet 400 USA

Twin-turbofan business jet and military trainer

Started life as the Mitsubishi MU-300 Diamond, which first flew on 29 August 1978. Beech acquired rights from Mitsubishi in December 1985 and renamed the improved aircraft the Beechjet 400. Deliveries of the Beechjet began in June 1986. Total delivered: 630.

VARIANTS

Beechjet 400: Initial production version
Beechjet 400A: Enhanced performance model with new EFIS
Beechjet 400T: Military trainer for JASDF designated *T-400*
Beechjet T-1A Jayhawk: USAF tanker and transport trainer

SPECIFICATIONS: 400A

Accommodation: 2 + 8
Cargo/baggage: 0.75 m^3 (26.4 cu.ft)
Max speed: M0.82 (470 kt; 870 km/h)
Range: 1,673 nm (1,925 km)

DIMENSIONS

Wingspan: 13.3 m (43 ft 6 in)
Length: 14.8 m (48 ft 5 in)
Height: 4.2 m (13 ft 11 in)

FEATURES

Low/swept wing; twin rear fuselage-mounted P&WC JT15D turbofans; six cabin windows; swept T-tail and tailplane, with small ventral fin

151

Bombardier BD-100 Challenger 300 Canada

Twin-turbofan super mid-size business jet

Design study into super mid-size business jet with transcontinental range and high long-range cruise speed first revealed at Paris Air Show in June 1997, then known as the Model 70. Officially launched at the same show two years later. Maiden flight took place on 14 August 2001, when designated BD-100 Contnental. Total delivered: 15.

VARIANTS

BD-100 Challenger 300: Initial production model

SPECIFICATIONS

Accommodation: 2 + 8
Cargo/baggage: 3.0 m^3 (106 cu.ft)
Max speed: M0.82 (470 kt; 870 km/h
Range: 3,100 nm (5,741 km)

DIMENSIONS

Wingspan: 19.5 m (63 ft 10 in)
Length: 20.9 m (68 ft 8 in)
Height: 6.2 m (20 ft 3 in)

FEATURES

Low/swept wing with winglets; rear fuselage-mounted twin Honeywell AS907 turbofans; swept T-tail with swept tailplane

Bombardier BD-700 Global Express Canada

Twin-turbofan long-range business jet

Developed to meet perceived requirement for ultra long-range business jet and announced at the NBAA convention in October 1991. Combines fuselage cross-section of Challenger with cabin length of CRJ, mated to a new supercritical wing. First flown on 13 October 1996, followed by initial delivery on 8 July 1999. Total delivered: 140.

VARIANTS

Global Express: Basic corporate transport
Global Express XRS: Updated model with additional windows available from end of 2004
Global 5000: Shortened version launched in February 2002
Sentinel R.1 (ASTOR): Modified platform for UK airborne stand-off radar programme in service in 2004

SPECIFICATIONS

Accommodation: 2 + 19
Cargo/baggage: 4.95 m^3 (175 cu.ft)
Max speed: M0.88 (505 kt; 935 km/h)
Range: 5,320 nm (9,852 km)

DIMENSIONS

Wingspan: 28.7 m (94 ft 0 in)
Length: 30.3 m (99 ft 5 in)
Height: 7.6 m (24 ft 10 in)

FEATURES

Low/swept wing with winglets; twin rear fuselage-mounted Rolls-Royce Deutschland BR710 turbofans; swept T-tail with swept anhedral tailplane

Bombardier Canadair CL-600 Challenger Canada

Twin-turbofan mid-size business jet

Evolved from a design by Bill Lear for a fast 14-seat business jet dubbed the LearStar 600. Canadair acquired exclusive rights and launched the aircraft on 29 October 1976, leading to the first flight on 8 November 1978. By that time aircraft had been renamed the Challenger. First delivered on 30 December 1980. Total delivered: 625.

VARIANTS

Challenger 600: Initial production model with ALF502 turbofans
Challenger 601-1A: Replacement version with GE CF34 turbofans
Challenger 601-3A: Advanced 'glass' cockpit and improved CF34s
Challenger 601-3R: Extended range option with conformal tailcone fuel tank, which increased fuselage length
Challenger 604: Further range increase and other improvements
+ military models for Canadian Department of National Defence for coastal patrol and general transport, designated *CC-144*.

SPECIFICATIONS 604

Accommodation: 2 + 19
Cargo/baggage: 3.25 m^3 (115 cu.ft)
Max speed: M0.82 (470 kt; 870 km/h)
Range: 3,769 nm (6,980 km)

DIMENSIONS

Wingspan: 19.6 m (64 ft 4 in)
Length: 20.9 m (68 ft 5 in)
Height: 6.3 m (20 ft 8 in)

FEATURES

Low/swept wing with winglets; twin GE CF34 turbofans (ALF502s in Model 600) rear fuselage-mounted; swept T-tail with swept tailplane

Cessna 401/402/411 USA

Twin-piston business aircraft and commuterliner

Launched in the mid 1950s as a five/six-seat business transport, with both Model 401 and 402 developed simultaneously with identical airframe and engines. First flown on 26 August 1965. Total delivered: 546 (401); 1,645 (402); 302 (411).

VARIANTS

401: Baseline model, similar to 411 but broader tail
402: As 401, but with seating for nine passengers or utility interior
411: Retractable undercarriage, oval windows, airstair doors and tip tanks
Suffix A on all three models denotes increased baggage space in lengthened nose
402B: Larger cabin and five square windows, available in *Utiliner* and *Businessliner* versions, the latter having additional deluxe cabin trim
402C: Increased T-O weight and longer span wing without tip tanks, also available in *Utiliner* and *Businessliner* versions

SPECIFICATIONS 402C

Accommodation: 1 + 8
Cargo/baggage: 0.75 m³ (26 cu.ft)
Max speed: 213 kt (394 km/h)
Range: 1,273 nm (2,379 km)

DIMENSIONS

Wingspan: 13.5 m (44 ft 2 in)
Length: 11.1 m (36 ft 5 in)
Height: 3.5 m (11 ft 6 in)

FEATURES

Low/straight wing; twin wing-mounted Continental piston engines with three-blade propellers; swept tailfin with dorsal fin and low-set tailplane; four cabin portholes (five square windows in 402B/C); retractable tricycle landing gear

Cessna 404 Titan USA

Twin-piston business aircraft and commuterliner

Essentially a stretched 402B with enlarged vertical tail, dihedral tailplane, more powerful Continental engines and higher gross weight. Made its first flight on 26 February 1975, followed by first deliveries in October 1976. Total delivered: 396.

VARIANTS
404 Titan: Baseline model
404 Titan Courier: Cargo interior
404 Titan Ambassador: Accommodation for 10 passengers
Suffixes II and III for each model denote improved versions with mainly equipment changes

SPECIFICATIONS: 404 TITAN
Accommodation: 2 + 10
Cargo/baggage: 680 kg (1,500 lb)
Max speed: 232 kt (430 km/h)
Range: 1,843 nm (3,410 km)

DIMENSIONS
Wingspan: 14.2 m (46 ft 8 in)
Length: 12.0 m (39 ft 5 in)
Height: 4.0 m (13 ft 2 in)

FEATURES
Low/straight wing; twin wing-mounted Continental piston engines with three-blade propellers; swept tailfin and low-set dihedral tailplane; six square cabin windows; retractable tricycle landing gear

Cessna 414 Chancellor USA

Twin-piston business aircraft

Introduced on 10 December 1969 as a 'step-up' pressurised model, combining the basic fuselage and tail unit of the Model 421 with the wing of the Model 402, and was powered by turbocharged Continental engines. It made its maiden flight on 1 November 1968. Total delivered: 1,070.

VARIANTS

414: Baseline model
414 Chancellor: Narrower tail, longer wingspan without tip tanks, lengthened nose
414 Chancellor II: Improved avionics as standard
414 Chancellor III: Air conditioning and all-weather avionics package

SPECIFICATIONS

Accommodation: 1 + 7
Cargo/baggage: 494 kg (1,000 lb)
Max speed: 235 kt (436 km/h)
Range: 1,099 nm (2,036 km)

DIMENSIONS

Wingspan: 13.5 m (44 ft 2 in)
Length: 11.1 m (36 ft 5 in)
Height: 3.5 m (11 ft 6 in)

FEATURES

Low/straight wing with or without tip tanks; twin wing-mounted Continental piston engines with three-blade propellers; swept tailfin with dorsal fin and low-set tailplane; five round cabin windows; retractable tricycle landing gear

Cessna 421 Golden Eagle USA

Twin-piston business aircraft

Similar to Model 411A with pressurised cabin, higher T-O weight, broader vertical tail and smaller side windows. It first flew on 14 October 1965 and entered service the following year. Total built: 1,916.

VARIANTS

421: Baseline model
421A: Minor improvements
421B Golden Eagle: Longer span wings, longer cabin with toilet area, and lengthened nose for more baggage space
421C Golden Eagle: Narrower tailfin, longer span wing without tip tanks, new engines with larger propellers
Both models B and C were available in Executive Commuter versions with more luxurious interior, and with suffixes II and III denoting equipment and systems changes

SPECIFICATION: 421C

Accommodation: 1 + 7
Cargo/baggage: 680 kg (1,500 lb)
Max speed: 258 kt (478 km/h)
Range: 1,197 nm (2,218 km)

DIMENSIONS

Wingspan: 12.5 m (41 ft 1 in)
Length: 11.1 m (36 ft 5 in)
Height: 3.5 m (11 ft 6 in)

FEATURES

Low/straight wing; twin wing-mounted Continental GTSIO-520 piston engines with three-blade propellers; swept tailfin and low-set tailplane; five round cabin windows; retractable tricycle landing gear

Cessna 425 Corsair/Conquest I USA

Twin-turboprop business aircraft

Based on the Model 421C airframe, design of the Corsair began in November 1977, and a prototype flew for the first time on 12 September 1978. Customer deliveries started in November 1980. The name was changed to Conquest I in late 1982. Total delivered: 236.

VARIANTS
425 Corsair/Conquest I: Only production model

SPECIFICATIONS
Accommodation: 1 + 7
Cargo/baggage: 499 kg (1,100 lb)
Max speed: 264 kt (489 km/h)
Range: 1,339 nm (2,480 km)

DIMENSIONS
Wingspan: 13.5 m (44 ft 2 in)
Length: 10.9 m (35 ft 10 in)
Height: 3.8 m (12 ft 7 in)

FEATURES
Low/straight wing with slight dihedral; twin P&WC PT6A turboprops with three-blade propellers; five cabin windows; highly-swept tailfin with dorsal fin and low-set dihedral tailplane; retractable tricycle landing gear

Cessna 441 Conquest II USA

Twin-turboprop business aircraft

Announced at the same time as the Model 404 Titan, the 441 was intended purely as a business aircraft, introducing for the first time turboprop engines in place of turbocharged piston engines. Flown on 26 August 1975. Total delivered: 362.

VARIANTS
441 Conquest II: Only production model, available with a number of different options

SPECIFICATIONS
Accommodation: 1 + 10
Cargo/baggage: 680 kg (1,500 lb)
Max speed: 295 kt (547 km/h)
Range: 2,063 nm (3,820 km)

DIMENSIONS
Wingspan: 15.0 m (49 ft 4 in)
Length: 11.9 m (39 ft 1 in)
Height: 4.0 m (13 ft 2 in)

FEATURES
Low/straight wing; twin wing-mounted Garrett TPE331 turboprop engines with three-blade propellers; swept tailfin and low-set dihedral tailplane; six semi-square cabin windows; retractable tricycle landing gear

Cessna 500 Citation I USA

Twin-turbofan mid-size business jet

Pressurised executive Fanjet 500 turbofan aircraft able to operate from most airfields announced on 7 October 1968. Name changed to Citation following first flight on 15 September 1969. Many changes and improvements incorporated subsequently and first delivery made on 21 December 1976. Total delivered: 691.

VARIANTS

500 Citation I: Basic production version
501 Citation I/SP: Similar, but certificated for single pilot operation

SPECIFICATIONS

Accommodation: 2 + 7
Cargo/baggage: 454 kg (1,000 lb)
Max speed: M0.70 (402 kt; 745 km/h)
Range: 1,328 nm (2,459 km)

DIMENSIONS

Wingspan: 14.4 m (47 ft 1 in)
Length: 13.3 m (43 ft 6 in)
Height: 4.4 m (14 ft 4 in)

FEATURES

Low/straight wing; twin P&WC JT15D turbofans mid-mounted on rear fuselage; four cabin windows each side; swept T-tail and large dorsal fin; low-set swept tailplane

Cessna 525 CitationJet USA

Twin-turbofan small business jet

Developed as a small, affordable entry level jet to replace the earlier Citation I. Launched at the 1989 NBAA convention, the CitationJet made its first flight on 29 April 1991. First customer delivery took place on 30 March 1993. Replaced by improved CJ1 and CJ2 from 2000/2001. Total delivered: 735.

VARIANTS

525 CitationJet: Initial production version
525 Citation CJ1: Increased take-off weight and new avionics suite
525A Citation CJ2: Stretched CJ1 with more powerful engines and improved performance, more comfortable cabin
525B Citation CJ3: Stretched development with uprated engines

SPECIFICATIONS: CJ2

Accommodation: 2 + 6
Cargo/baggage: 306 kg (675 lb)
Max speed: M0.72 (413 kt; 764 km/h)
Range: 1,475 nm (2,731 km)

DIMENSIONS

Wingspan: 15.1 m (49 ft 6 in)
Length: 14.3 m (46 ft 11 in)
Height: 4.2 m (13 ft 10 in)

FEATURES

Low/straight wing; twin Williams FJ44 turbofans mounted high on rear fuselage; four cabin windows (six on CJ2, seven on CJ3); swept T-tail with straight tailplane

Cessna 550 Citation II USA

Twin-turbofan mid-size business jet

Stretched version of the Citation I for up to 10 passengers built in parallel. Announced on 14 September 1976, the Citation II made its first flight on 31 January 1977 and entered service in March 1978. Total built (including 15 T-47As for the US Navy): 733. Replaced by Citation Bravo, which first flew on 25 April 1995. Total delivered: 183.

VARIANTS

550 Citation II: Initial production version
551 Citation II/SP: Certificated for single pilot operation
S550 Citation S/II: Improved model introduced in July 1984
550 Citation Bravo: More efficient wing, new PW530 turbofans, substantial performance improvements
T-47A: Acquired by US Navy for the radar training role

SPECIFICATIONS: CITATION BRAVO

Accommodation: 2 + 8
Cargo/baggage: 522 kg (1,150 lb)
Max speed: 403 kt (746 km/h)
Range: 1,780 nm (3,295 km)

DIMENSIONS

Wingspan: 15.9 m (52 ft 2 in)
Length: 14.4 m (47 ft 3 in)
Height: 4.6 m (15 ft 0 in)

FEATURES

Low/straight tapered wing; twin P&WC JT15D (or PW530 in Bravo) turbofans mid-mounted on rear fuselage; six cabin windows each side; swept tailfin with tapered mid-set tailplane

Cessna 560 Citation V USA

Twin-turbofan mid-size business jet

Stretched and internally restyled development of the Citation II/SP announced at the 1987 NBAA convention. Most notable external feature was a seventh cabin window. Engineering prototype made its first flight in August 1987, and customer deliveries started in April 1989. Total delivered: 260. Replaced by Ultra and Encore. Total delivered: 650.

VARIANTS

560 Citation V: Initial production model with JT15Ds
560 Citation Ultra: Improved version with EFIS and increased payload/range performance
560 Citation Encore: More powerful PW535 turbofans
OT-47B: Radar-equipped tracker aircraft for USAF based on Ultra
UC-35A and UC-35B: Transport for US Army and USMC
UC-35D: USMC model based on Ultra Encore

SPECIFICATIONS: ENCORE

Accommodation: 2 + 7
Cargo/baggage: 272 kg (600 lb)
Max speed: M0.75 (430 kt; 796 km/h)
Range: 2,000 nm (3,704 km)

DIMENSIONS

Wingspan: 16.6 m (54 ft 6 in)
Length: 14.9 m (48 ft 11 in)
Height: 4.6 m (15 ft 0 in)

FEATURES

Low/straight wing; twin P&WC JT15D or PW500 turbofans mid-mounted on rear fuselage; seven cabin windows; swept tailfin with large dorsal fin

Cessna 560XL Citation Excel USA

Twin-turbofan mid-size business jet

Announced at NBAA convention in October 1994 and made its first flight on 29 February 1996. Combines systems and wing and tail surfaces of the Citation Ultra (Encore) with shortened Citation X fuselage, providing 10-seat cabin with stand-up headroom. First delivery to Swift Transportation of Phoenix, Arizona on 2 July 1998. Total delivered: 505.

VARIANTS

Citation Excel: Initial production version
Citation XLS: Upgraded model available from 2004

SPECIFICATIONS: CITATION EXCEL

Accommodation: 2 + 9
Cargo/baggage: 317 kg (700 lb)
Max speed: 429 kt (795 km/h)
Range: 2,165 nm (4,010 km)

DIMENSIONS

Wingspan: 17.9 m (55 ft 9 in)
Length: 15.8 m (51 ft 10 in)
Height: 5.2 m (17 ft 2 in)

FEATURES

Low/straight wing cranked at front and tapered at rear; rear fuselage-mounted PWAC PW545A turbofans; six cabin windows on right side and five on left; moderately swept tailfin with large dorsal fillet and low-set tailplane; dual ventral strakes

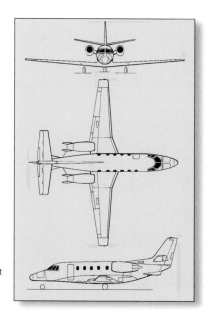

Cessna 650 Citation III/VI/VII USA

Twin-turbofan mid-size business jet

All-new high-performance aircraft designed to extend Cessna's portfolio to attract more prosperous customers. Notable features were a new supercritical wing, swept T-tail and much longer fuselage. First flown on 30 May 1979, the Citation III entered service in spring 1983. Total delivered: 187 (III), 37 (VI), 120 (VII).

VARIANTS

650 Citation III: Initial production model
650 Citation VI: Low-cost version with new avionics
650 Citation VII: More powerful engines for better hot-and-high performance
650 Citation Magnum: Choice of flight management systems

SPECIFICATIONS: CITATION VII

Accommodation: 2 + 13
Cargo/baggage: 1.4 m³ (51 cu.ft)
Max speed: M0.83 (476 kt (881 km/h)
Range: 2,180 nm (4,037 km)

DIMENSIONS

Wingspan: 16.3 m (53 ft 6 in)
Length: 16.9 m (55 ft 6 in)
Height: 5.1 m (16 ft 9 in)

FEATURES

Low/swept wing; twin Honeywell TFE731 turbofans mounted on side of rear fuselage; six cabin windows; swept T-tail with swept tailplane

Cessna 680 Citation Sovereign USA

Twin-turbofan mid-size business jet

Design of this super midsize twin-jet with US coast-to-coast range was initiated in 1998 and first announced at NBAA on 18 October that same year. Prototype first flew on 27 February 2002 and FAA certification was obtained on 24 December 2003. First delivered in early 2004. Total delivered: 10.

VARIANTS
Citation Sovereign: Initial production model

SPECIFICATIONS
Accommodation: 2 + 9
Cargo/baggage: 2.83 m³ (100 cu.ft)
Max speed: 429 kt (795 km/h)
Range: 2,680 nm (4,965 km)

DIMENSIONS
Wingspan: 16.5 m (54 ft 1 in)
Length: 14.9 m (48 ft 10 in)
Height: 4.6 m (15 ft 0 in)

FEATURES
Low/straight wing with swept back leading edge; PWAC PW306C podded turbofans on rear fuselage shoulders; eight cabin windows on right side and seven on left; swept tailfin with mid-set swept tailplane

Cessna 750 Citation X USA

Twin-turbofan long-range mid-size business jet

Largest and fastest Cessna jet optimised for non-stop US transcontinental and transatlantic operations. Announced at the NBAA convention in October 1990, the Citation X first flew on 21 December 1993. Golfer Arnold Palmer accepted the first aircraft in July 1996. Total delivered: 225.

VARIANTS

Citation X: Initial production model with Rolls-Royce AE 3007 turbofans

SPECIFICATIONS

Accommodation: 2 + 12
Cargo/baggage: 2.32 m^3 (82 cu.ft)
Max speed: M0.91 (521 kt; 965 km/h)
Range: 3,430 nm (6,352 km)

DIMENSIONS

Wingspan: 19.4 m (63 ft 7 in)
Length: 22.1 m (72 ft 4 in)
Height: 5.8 m (19 ft 2 in)

FEATURES

Low/swept wing; twin Rolls-Royce (Allison) AE3007C turbofans mounted high on sides of rear fuselage; seven cabin windows; highly-swept T-tail and tailplane

Dassault Falcon 10/100 France

Twin-turbofan small business jet

Smallest of Dassault's business jet line-up, the Falcon 10 (originally referred to as the Mini-Falcon) was a scaled-down version of the Falcon 20. Conceived in the late 1960s, it originally flew on 1 December 1970 with GE CJ610 turbojets. These were replaced by Garrett TFE731 turbofans, with which it flew for the first time on 15 October 1971. Customer deliveries started in November 1973. Known as Mystère in France. Total delivered: 195 (10); 31 (100).

VARIANTS

Falcon 10: Initial production version
Falcon 100: Improved version with optional EFIS
Mystère 10 MER: Pilot trainer sold to French Navy

SPECIFICATIONS

Accommodation: 2 + 7
Cargo/baggage: 1,305 kg (2,414 lb)
Max speed: M0.86 (492 kt; 912 km/h)
Range: 1,880 nm (3,480 km)

DIMENSIONS

Wingspan: 13.1 m (40 ft 11 in)
Length: 13. 9 m (45 ft 6 in)
Height: 4.6 m (15 ft 2 in)

FEATURES

Low/swept wings; twin Garrett TFE731 turbofans

mounted on sides of rear fuselage; four cabin windows each side; highly swept tailfin with swept mid-mounted tailplane

Dassault Falcon 20/200 France

Twin-turbofan corporate and utility aircraft

Developed in a collaboration with Sud-Aviation in the late 1950s and made its first flight on 4 May 1963. The first prototype was fitted with the P&W JT12A turbojet, but production aircraft had GE CF700 turbofans, the first of which flew on 1 January 1965. First delivery, to Pan American, was made in June that year. Known as Mystère in France. Total delivered: 473 (20), 35 (200).

VARIANTS

Falcon 20C: Baseline aircraft

Falcon 20D: Uprated engine and greater fuel capacity
Falcon 20E: Higher take-off weight and revised rudder
Falcon 20F: Full leading edge slats and further fuel increase
Falcon 20G: Maritime surveillance version
Falcon 200: New Garrett ATF3 turbofans and larger integral fuel tank. Initially known as Falcon 20H
Falcon 20NA: French Air Force navigation system trainer
Falcon 20NR: French Air Force navigation/reconnaissance trainer
HU-25A/B/C Guardian: Three models for SAR, offshore surveillance, identification and tracking
+ many other Falcon/Mystère 20s used for target towing, medevac, ECM and remote sensing

SPECIFICATIONS

Accommodation: 2 + 12
Cargo/baggage: 1.45 m3 (52 cu.ft)
Max speed: M0.82 (470 kt; 870 km/h)
Range: 2,510 nm (4.650 km)
DIMENSIONS
Wingspan: 16.3 m (53 ft 6 in)
Length: 17.2 m (56 ft 3 in)
Height: 5.3 m (17 ft 5 in)

FEATURES

Low/swept wings; twin GE CF700 or Garrett ATF3 turbofans mounted on sides of rear fuselage; five cabin windows each side; highly swept tailfin with swept mid-mounted tailplane

Dassault Falcon 50 France

Three-turbofan long-range business jet

Developed to cover the emerging US transcontinental and transatlantic business jet market, the Falcon 50 used the fuselage cross-section of the Falcon 20/200, married to a new supercritical wing, and the addition of a third engine. First flown on 7 November 1976, the Falcon 50 entered service in early 1979. Total delivered: 335.

VARIANTS
Falcon 50: Initial production model
Falcon 50EX: Uprated turbofans and increased range
Falcon 50 Surmar: Maritime surveillance version with search radar and FLIR

SPECIFICATIONS: 50EX
Accommodation: 2 + 19
Cargo/baggage: 3.97 m^3 (140 cu.ft)
Max speed: M0.86 (493 kt; 912 km/h)
Range: 3,285 nm (6,083 km)

DIMENSIONS
Wingspan: 18.9 m (61 ft 11 in)
Length: 18.5 m (60 ft 9 in)
Height: 7.0 m (22 ft 11 in)

FEATURES
Low/swept and tapered wing; three Honeywell TFE731 turbofans, two mounted on sides of rear fuselage, the third atop and at base of tail at centreline; seven cabin windows each side; tall swept tailfin and low-mounted tailplane

Dassault Falcon 900 France

Three-turbofan long-range business jet

Development of intercontinental business jet announced at Paris Air Show on 27 May 1983. Derived from the Falcon 50, but substantially revised, the prototype Falcon 900 powered by Garrett TFE731 turbofan engines first flew on 21 September 1984. First customer deliveries took place in December 1986. Total delivered: 340.

VARIANTS

Falcon 900: Initial production model
Falcon 900B: Increased power and range, able to operate from unprepared airstrips
Falcon 900C: Enhanced avionics from 900EX model
Falcon 900EX: Longer range, further increase in engine thrust
JMSA: Long-range surveillance aircraft with US search radar, in service in Japan

SPECIFICATIONS: 900EX

Accommodation: 2 + 19
Cargo/baggage: 3.6 m³ (127 cu.ft)
Max speed: M0.84 (481 kt; 891 km/h)
Range: 3,810 nm (7,056 km)

DIMENSIONS

Wingspan: 19.3 m (63 ft 5 in)
Length: 20.2 m (66 ft 3 in)
Height: 7.6 m (24 ft 10 in)

FEATURES

Low/swept and tapered wing; three Honeywell TFE731 turbofans, two mounted on sides of rear fuselage, the third atop and at base of tail; 12 cabin windows; tall swept tailfin and mid-mounted swept tailplane

Dassault Falcon 2000 France

Twin-turbofan long-range widebody business jet

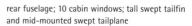

Direct descendant from the Falcon 900, with a two-engine configuration and area ruled rear fuselage the obvious external changes. Announced at the Paris air show in 1989 as the Falcon X, it was launched as the Falcon 2000 on 4 October 1990 and first flew on 4 March 1993. First delivery on 16 February 1995. Total delivered: 245.

VARIANTS

Falcon 2000: Basic production version
Falcon 2000EX: Increased range, new PW308C turbofans and new avionics

SPECIFICATIONS: 2000EX

Accommodation: 2 + 19
Cargo/baggage: 3.8 m³ (134 cu.ft)
Max speed: M0.84 (481 kt; 891 km/h)
Range: 3,800 nm (7,030 km)

DIMENSIONS

Wingspan: 19.3 m (63 ft 5 in)
Length: 20.2 m (66 ft 4 in)
Height: 7.1 m (23 ft 2 in)

FEATURES

Low/swept wing; two Honeywell TFE731 or PW308C (2000EX) turbofans mounted on sides of rear fuselage; 10 cabin windows; tall swept tailfin and mid-mounted swept tailplane

Embraer EMB-121 Xingu Brazil

Twin-turboprop corporate transport

Combining the wing and engines of the Bandeirante with an all-new fuselage, the 10-seat Xingu made its maiden flight on 10 October 1976 and entered service the following year with both civil and military customers. An improved version flew on 4 September 1981. Total delivered: 105.

VARIANTS
Xingu I: Initial production model
Xingu II: More powerful PT6A engine, increased seating and fuel
+ military derivatives for France, used for training and liaison, and to the Brazilian Air Force under designation *VU-9*

SPECIFICATIONS: XINGU II
Accommodation: 2 + 9
Cargo/baggage: 1.0 m³ (35.3 cu.ft)
Max speed: 251 kt (465 km/h)
Range: 1,230 nm (2,278 km)

DIMENSIONS
Wingspan: 14.1 m (46 ft 2 in)
Length: 12.3 m (40 ft 3 in)
Height: 4.8 m (15 ft 10 in)

FEATURES
Low/straight wing; twin wing-mounted P&WC PT6A turboprops with three- or four-blade propellers; swept T-tail with large dorsal fin and tapered tailplane

Grumman G-159 Gulfstream I USA

Twin-turboprop executive transport

Work started in 1956 on a new design to replace war surplus piston twins then used for executive transport, incorporating a generous cabin cross section and Rolls-Royce Dart turboprops for a high speed cruise. The first Gulfstream I flew on 14 August 1958, and customer deliveries followed from June 1959. Total delivered: 200 (including five G-IC conversions).

VARIANTS

Gulfstream I: Basic production version
Gulfstream I-C: Stretched airliner conversion seating 38 passengers
TC-4C: Navigator trainer for US Navy with A-6A radome nose
VC-4A: VIP transport for US Coast Guard

SPECIFICATIONS: G-I

Accommodation: 2 + 24
Cargo/baggage: 3.62 m³ (128 cu.ft)
Max speed: 302 kt (560 km/h)
Range: 2,206 nm (4,087 km)

DIMENSIONS

Wingspan: 23.9 m (78 ft 6 in)
Length: 19.4 m (63 ft 9 in)
Height: 6.9 m (22 ft 9 in)

FEATURES

Low/straight wing with front and rear taper; twin wing-mounted Rolls-Royce Dart turboprops with four-blade propeller; five cabin windows; swept tailfin with low-set tailplane

Grumman G-1159 Gulfstream II/III USA

Twin-turbofan large long-range business jet

Jet-powered development of the Gulfstream I announced on 17 May 1965. Apart from the engines, other significant differences were a new swept wing and T-tail. It first flew on 2 October 1966 and entered service in December 1967. The improved G-III followed the purchase of Grumman's GA aircraft line by Gulfstream American in 1978. The G-III flew on 2 December 1979. Total delivered: 258 (G-II), 206 (G-III).

VARIANTS

Gulfstream II: Initial jet-powered model
Gulfstream IIB: Retrofit with G-III wing
Gulfstream III: Stretched version; redesigned wing with winglets and increased fuel capacity
Gulfstream Maritime: Used on fishery patrols by Royal Danish AF
Gulfstream SRA-1: Special missions variant
C-20A: Modified for USAF airlift under C-SAM

SPECIFICATIONS: G-III
Accommodation: 2 + 21
Cargo/baggage: 907 kg (2,000 lb)
Max speed: M0.88 (505 kt; 936 km/h)
Range: 4,100 nm (7,598 km

DIMENSIONS
Wingspan: 23.7 m (77 ft 10 in)
Length: 25.3 m (83 ft 1 in)
Height: 7.4 m (24 ft 4 in)

FEATURES
Low/swept wing with winglets; twin Rolls-Royce157 Spey turbofans mounted on sides of rear fuselage; five cabin windows; swept T-tail with swept tailplane

Gulfstream Aerospace Gulfstream IV/G300/ G400/G450 USA

Twin-turbofan large long-range business jet

Significantly improved and advanced development of G-III with new Rolls-Royce Tay engines, stretched fuselage, revised wing and 'glass' cockpit. Design was initiated in April 1982 and the G-IV flew for the first time on 19 September 1985. Customer deliveries commenced in spring 1987. Total delivered: 535.

VARIANTS

Gulfstream IV: Initial production model
Gulfstream IV-SP: Higher weight and improved payload/range
Gulfstream IV-MPA: Quick-change multi-purpose
G300: Mid-range version of IV-SP
G400: New; similar to IV-SP
G450: Upgraded, with G550 avionics
Gulfstream SRA-4: Special missions versions, including ASW, electronic surveillance, maritime patrol, medevac and others. Designations *C-20F/G/H* applied to US Army, US Navy and USAF aircraft respectively; electronic intelligence gathering as *S 102B Korpen* and military transport as *Tp 102* for Swedish Air Force; and multi-mission aircraft for JASDF as *UC-4*.

SPECIFICATIONS: IV-SP

Accommodation: 2 + 19
Cargo/baggage: 907 kg (2,000 lb)
Max speed: M0.80 (459 kt; 851 km/h)
Range: 4,220 nm (7,805 km)

DIMENSIONS

Wingspan: 23.7 m (77 ft 11 in)

Length: 26.9 m (88 ft 4 in)
Height: 7.4 m (24 ft 5 in)

FEATURES

Low/swept wing with winglets; twin Rolls-Royce157 Tay turbofans mounted on sides of rear fuselage; six cabin windows; swept T-tail with swept tailplane

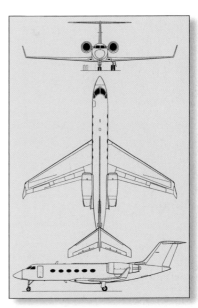

Gulfstream Aerospace Gulfstream V/G500/ G550 USA

Twin-turbofan large ultra long-range business jet

Study into very long-range business jet was announced at the NBAA convention in October 1991. Based on a lengthened and re-engineered G-IV fuselage, but with more efficient wing and new Rolls-Royce157 Deutschland BR710 turbofans, the G-V made its first flight on 28

November 1995 and subsequently set many world records. First customer delivery on 1 July 1997. Total delivered: 240.

VARIANTS
Gulfstream V: Standard production version
Gulfstream V-SP: Enhanced performance, more usable cabin space
G500: Reduced-range version of V
G550: New; similar to V-SP
C-37A: Military transport version operated by the USAF

SPECIFICATIONS
Accommodation: 2 + 19
Cargo/baggage: 6.4 m³ (226 cu.ft)
Max speed: M0.85 (488 kt; 903 km/h)
Range: 6,500 nm (12,038 km)

DIMENSIONS
Wingspan: 28.5 m (93 ft 6 in)
Length: 29.4 m (96 ft 5 in)
Height: 7.9 m (25 ft 10 in)

FEATURES
Low/swept wing with winglets; twin Rolls-Royce157 Deutschland BR710 turbofans mounted on sides of rear fuselage; six cabin windows each side (seven in V-SP); swept T-tail with swept tailplane

Gulfstream Aerospace (IAI) G100 USA

Twin-turbofan mid-size business jet

Descendant of Aero Commander 1121 Jet Commander, acquired by Israel Aircraft Industries in 1968 and developed successively as the Commodore Jet and Westwind. The Model 1125 was launched at NBAA in October 1979 and named Astra in 1981. First flown on 19 March 1984, deliveries of the Astra started on 30 June 1986. Astra line sold to Gulfstream Aerospace in June 2001 and re-designated. Total delivered: 152.

VARIANTS
Astra: Initial production version
Astra SP: Improved with new avionics and revised cabin interior
Astra SPX: More powerful engine, winglets and advanced avionics
C-38A: Transport and medevac aircraft operated by US Air National Guard
G100: Current production model

SPECIFICATIONS: G100
Accommodation: 2 + 9
Cargo/baggage: 1.4 m³ (51 cu.ft)
Max speed: M0.81 (465 kt; 861 km/h)
Range: 2,949 nm (5,461 km)

DIMENSIONS
Wingspan: 16.6 m (54 ft 7 in)
Length: 16.9 m (55 ft 7 in)
Height: 5.5 m (18 ft 2 in)

FEATURES
Low/swept wing with winglets (SPX only); twin Honeywell TFE731 turbofans; six cabin windows; swept tailfin with low-mounted swept tailplane

Gulfstream Aerospace (IAI) G200 USA

Twin-turbofan super mid-size business jet

Initiated by Israel Aircraft Industries as a derivative of the Astra SP with a new widebody fuselage and more headroom, new engines, and transatlantic range. Formally announced on 20 September 1993 and first flown on 25 December 1997. First customer delivery made in January 2000. Astra/Galaxy line sold to Gulfstream Aerospace in June 2001 and redesignated. Total delivered: 90.

VARIANTS

Galaxy: Original production model of Israel Aircraft Industries
G200: Current production version

SPECIFICATIONS

Accommodation: 2 + 18
Cargo/baggage: 3.7 m³ (130 cu.ft)
Max speed: M0.82 (470 kt; 870 km/h)
Range: 3,620 nm (6,704 km)

DIMENSIONS

Wingspan: 17.7 m (58 ft 1 in)
Length: 19.0 m (62 ft 3 in)
Height: 6.5 m (21 ft 5 in)

FEATURES

Low/swept wing with winglets; twin P&WC PW306 turbofans; eight cabin windows; swept tailfin with mid-mounted swept tailplane

Hawker 800 UK/USA

Twin-turbofan mid-size business jet

Derived from the BAe 125 built in the UK and introducing a number of improvements, including the introduction of an EFIS cockpit, the first in a business jet. First Srs 800 flew on 26 May 1983 and entered service in spring 1984. Adopted the Hawker 800 name when programme purchased by Raytheon in 1993. Total delivered: 665.

VARIANTS

125-800/Hawker 800: Initial production model
Hawker 800SP: Modification with winglets
Hawker 800XP: Extended range version introduced in 1995
Hawker 800FI: Flight calibration model sold to USAF as *C-29A*, Brazilian Air Force as *EU-93*, and JASDF as *U-125*
Hawker 800RA: Surveillance version of XP with radar, defensive aids and military communications
Hawker 800SIG: Signals intelligence version of XP operated by RoKAF
Hawker 800SM: SAR version operated by JASDF as *U-125A*

SPECIFICATIONS: XP

Accommodation: 2 + 14
Cargo/baggage: 1.67 m^3 (59 cu.ft)
Max speed: M0.80 (461 kt; 854 km/h)
Range: 2,955 nm (5,472 km)

DIMENSIONS

Wingspan: 15.7 m (51 ft 5 in)
Length: 15.6 m (51 ft 2 in)

Height: 5.4 m (17 ft 7 in)

FEATURES

Low/swept wing; twin Honeywell TFE731 turbofans mounted on sides of rear fuselage; six cabin windows; highly-swept tailfin with high-mounted swept tailplane

Hawker 1000 UK/USA

Twin-turbofan long-range mid-size business jet

Based on the Hawker 800, but with a stretched fuselage and new P&W PW305 turbofans replacing the TFE731s used in the smaller aircraft. Launched by British Aerospace in October 1989, the BAe 1000 made its maiden flight on 16 June 1990 and entered service in December 1991. Re-designated Hawker 1000 when programme purchased by Raytheon in 1993. Total delivered: 51.

VARIANTS
125-1000/Hawker 1000: Basic production model

SPECIFICATIONS
Accommodation: 2 + 15
Cargo/baggage: 1,043 kg (2,300 lb)
Max speed: M0.82 (470 kt; 870 km/h)
Range: 3,635 nm (6.736 km)

DIMENSIONS
Wingspan: 15.7 m (51 ft 4 in)
Length: 16.4 m (53 ft 10 in)
Height: 5.2 m (17 ft 1 in)

FEATURES
Low/swept wing; twin P&WC PW305 turbofans mounted on sides of rear fuselage; seven cabin windows; highly-swept tailfin with high-mounted swept tailplane

Hawker Horizon USA

Twin-turbofan mid-size business jet

All-new design under PD376 started in 1993, but model not announced until NBAA convention in November 1996. Generally conventional layout, but with flat-floor stand-up cabin. First flown on 11 August 2001, the Hawker Horizon entered service in summer 2004. Total ordered: 150+.

VARIANTS

Hawker Horizon: Initial production model

SPECIFICATIONS

Accommodation: 2 + 12
Cargo/baggage: 2.83 m³ (100 cu.ft)
Max speed: M0.84 (481 kt; 890 km/h)
Range: 4,200 nm (6,297 km)

DIMENSIONS

Wingspan: 18.8 m (61 ft 9 in)
Length: 21.1 m (69 ft 2 in)
Height: 6.0 m (19 ft 7 in)

FEATURES

Low/swept wing; twin P&WC PW308A turbofans mounted on sides of rear fuselage; swept T-tail with swept tailplane

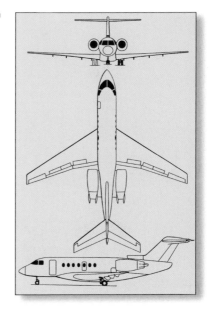

IAI Westwind Israel

Twin-turbojet/turbofan mid-size business jet

Origins in Jet Commander first flown in USA on 27 January 1963. Production transferred in 1968 to IAI in Israel, which later developed the Commodore Jet and Westwind derivatives. The first stretched 1123 Westwind, powered by GE CJ610 turbojets, flew in September 1970. Production soon transferred to the new 1124 model with Garrett TFE731 turbofans, introduced in 1975. Total delivered: 36 (1123), 256 (1124).

VARIANTS

1123 Westwind: Initial production model with GE turbojets
1124 Westwind: Initial turbofan-powered production model
1124 Westwind I: Increased fuel and various enhancements
1124A Westwind 2: New wing and improved hot-and-high performance
1124N Sea Scan: Maritime version with search radar and bubble windows delivered to the Israeli Navy

SPECIFICATIONS

Accommodation: 2 + 10
Cargo/baggage: 476 kg (1,050 lb)
Max speed: M0.82 (470 kt; 870 km/h)
Range: 2,905 nm (5,385 km)

DIMENSIONS

Wingspan: 13.7 m (44 ft 10 in)
Length: 15.9 m (52 ft 3 in)
Height: 4.8 m (15 ft 9 in)

FEATURES

Mid/straight wing with front and rear taper and tip-mounted fuel tanks (winglets on Westwind 2); twin GE CJ610 turbojets or Garrett TFE731 turbofans mounted on sides of rear fuselage; swept tailfin and low-mounted tailplane

Learjet 23/24/25/28/29 USA

Twin-turbojet light business jet

Designed by Bill Lear in Switzerland as the SAAC-23, but production moved to the USA, where the Learjet 23, powered by a pair of GE CF610 turbojets, made its first flight on 7 October 1963. Replaced by a number of improved models. Total delivered: 105 (23), 258 (24); 368 (25), 5 (28), 2 (29) = 738.

VARIANTS

Learjet 23: Initial production version
Learjet 24: Improved cruise performance
Learjet 24B: Increased thrust
Learjet 24D: Longer range and square windows
Learjet 24E: Refined interiors and enhanced aerodynamics
Learjet 24F: Increased weight and range
Learjet 25: Stretched for up to eight passengers
Learjet 25B: No bullet fin fairing and four rectangular windows
Learjet 25C: Long-range model with additional fuel tank
Learjet 25D: Improved engines and new wing
Learjet 25F: Further increases in fuel and range
Learjet 25G: 25D with increased weight and wing modifications
Learjet 28: Supercritical wing with winglets, no tip tanks
Learjet 29 Longhorn: Long-range variant of Model 28

SPECIFICATIONS: 25D

Accommodation: 2 + 8
Cargo/baggage: 1.13 m3 (40 cu.ft)
Max speed: 464 kt (859 km/h)
Range: 1,437 nm (2,660 km)

DIMENSIONS

Wingspan: 10.8 m (35 ft 7 in)
Length: 14.5 m (47 ft 4 in)
Height: 3.7 m (12 ft 3 in)

FEATURES

Low/straight wing with tapered leading edge and tip tanks (tip tanks replaced by wingtips on 28/29); twin rear fuselage-mounted GE CJ610 turbojets; T-tail (bullet fin fairing on earlier models); three or four round or square windows

Learjet 31 USA

Twin-turbofan light business jet

Combines the fuselage and powerplant of the Model 35/36 with the more modern wing of the Learjet 55. Delta fins were added to the rear to stabilise the aircraft at high speeds. An aerodynamic prototype first flew on 11 May 1987, and the new type was officially introduced the following September. Deliveries started in summer 1988. Total delivered: 250.

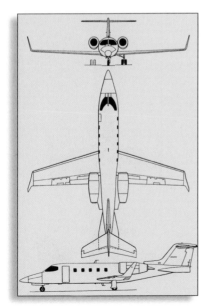

VARIANTS

Learjet 31: Initial production model
Learjet 31A: New integrated avionics and increase in speed
Learjet 31A/ER: Optional extended range with more fuel

SPECIFICATIONS: 31A

Accommodation: 2 + 7
Cargo/baggage: 1.76 m³ (62 cu.ft)
Max speed: M0.81 (465 kt; 860 km/h)
Range: 1,455 nm (2,691 km)

DIMENSIONS

Wingspan: 13.36 m (43 ft 10 in)
Length: 14.83 m (48 ft 8 in)
Height: 3.75 m (12 ft 4 in)

FEATURES

Low/straight wing with tapered leading edge and winglets; twin rear fuselage-mounted Honeywell TFE731 turbofans; swept T-tail and tailplane, delta fin (strake) each side below tail; six cabin windows on right side

Learjet 35/36 USA

Twin-turbofan light business jet and special missions aircraft

Larger and turbofan-powered development of Learjet 25, featuring Garrett TFE731 engines, a slightly bigger wing and additional window on right side of fuselage. Prototype (originally known as the Learjet 26) flew on 4 January 1973 and customer deliveries started in summer 1974. Total delivered: 710.

VARIANTS

Learjet 35: Initial production version
Learjet 35A: Redesigned wing for better short-field performance
Learjet 36: Longe-range variant with increased fuel
Learjet 36A: Same wing modifications as Model 35A
C-21A: Operational support aircraft of USAF (Model 35A)
U-36A: Liaison/training aircraft operated by the JASDF + many special missions 35A/36A variants operated by a number of other military forces

SPECIFICATIONS: 35A

Accommodation: 2 + 8
Cargo/baggage: 1.13 m^3 (40 cu.ft)
Max speed: M0.82 (470 kt; 870 km/h)
Range: 2,289 nm (4,239 km)

DIMENSIONS

Wingspan: 12.0 m (39 ft 6 in)
Length: 14.8 m (48 ft 8 in)
Height: 3.7 m (12 ft 3 in)

FEATURES

Low/straight wing with tapered leading edge and tip tanks; twin rear fuselage-mounted Garrett TFE731 turbofans; Swept T-tail and tailplane; five cabin windows on right side; four on left

Learjet 40/45 USA

Twin-turbofan mid-size business jet

All-new design unveiled at the NBAA Convention in September 1992. Although generally similar to the Model 31, it is marked by larger fuselage, wing and tail unit, and increased head and shoulder room. First flown on 7 October 1995, first customer delivery was made on 28 July 1998. deliveries of Learjet 40 started in January 2004. Total delivered: 240.

VARIANTS
Learjet 45: Initial production version
Learjet 45XR: Longer range and improved hot-and-high performance
Learjet 40: Slightly shorter, high performance derivative

SPECIFICATIONS: LEARJET 45
Accommodation: 2 + 9
Cargo/baggage: 1.45 m³ (51 cu.ft)
Max speed: M0.81 (465 kt; 860 km/h)
Range: 2,120 nm (3,922 km)

DIMENSIONS
Wingspan: 14.5 m (47 ft 9 in)
Length: 17.6 m (57 ft 9 in)
Height: 4.3 m (14 ft 2 in)

FEATURES
Low/straight wing with tapered leading edge and winglets; twin Honeywell TFE731 turbofans, mounted high on rear fuselage; eight cabin windows; swept T-tail and tailplane; delta fin (strake) each side under tail

Learjet 55/60 USA

Twin-turbofan mid-size business jet

New series of business jets announced at Paris Air Show in June 1977, known as the Longhorn 50 series, providing a stand-up 'widebody' cabin and accommodation for 10 passengers. The name Longhorn was subsequently dropped. The prototype Model 55 made its first flight on 15 November 1979, and deliveries started on 30 April 1981. Replaced by the stretched Learjet 60 in January 1993. Total delivered: 147 (55); 270 (60).

Height: 4.47 m (14 ft 8 in)

FEATURES

Low/straight wing with tapered leading edge and winglets; twin Honeywell TFE731 or P&WC PW305A turbofans, mounted high on rear fuselage; six cabin windows on right and five on left; swept T-tail and tailplane; delta fin (strake) each side under tail

VARIANTS

Learjet 55: Initial production model
Learjet 55B: Improved performance and digital flight deck
Learjet 55C: Delta fins and redesigned engine pylons
Learjet 55C/ER: Additional fuel tank in tailcone
Learjet 55C/LR: Further increase in range with optional fuel tank
Learjet 55LR: Seven-passenger cabin and increased fuel
Learjet 55XLR: Six-passenger cabin and further fuel increase
Learjet 60: Stretched fuselage and new PW305A turbofans

SPECIFICATIONS: LEARJET 60

Accommodation: 2 + 9
Cargo/baggage: 1.39 m^3 (49 cu.ft)
Max speed: M0.81 (465 kt; 860 km/h)
Range: 2,735 nm (5,065 km)

DIMENSIONS

Wingspan: 13.34 m (43 ft 9 in)
Length: 17.88 m (58 ft 8 in)

Lockheed L.1329 JetStar USA

Four-turbojet/turbofan mid-size corporate transport

Designed initially to fulfill a USAF requirement for a multi-engined light transport and first announced in March 1957. The four-engined JetStar first flew on 4 September that year and entered service with the USAF in 1960. The first civil customer took delivery in early 1961. Total delivered: 204.

VARIANTS

JetStar: Initial production version with P&W JT12A turbojets
JetStar II: Enhanced turbofan-powered development
C-140A: Navaid calibration aircraft operated by USAF
VC-140B: VIP transport operated by USAF

SPECIFICATIONS

Accommodation: 2 + 10
Cargo/baggage: 1,280 kg (2,822 lb)
Max speed: M0.86 (493 kt (912 km/h)
Range: 2,220 nm (3,573 km)

DIMENSIONS

Wingspan: 16.6 m (54 ft 5 in)
Length: 18.4 m (60 ft 5 in)
Height: 6.2 m (20 ft 5 in)

FEATURES

Low/swept wings with fuel tanks set into mid-wing; four P&W JT12A turbojets or Garrett TFE731 turbofans in pairs on sides of rear fuselage; five cabin windows; swept tailfin and mid-mounted swept tailplane

Piaggio P.180 Avanti Italy

Twin-turboprop high-speed corporate transport

Designed to provide jet speed with turboprop economics and launched in 1982. Gates Learjet became a partner in the programme, but withdrew in January 1986 and Piaggio continued development on its own. First flight was made on 23 September 1986, followed by first customer delivery on 30 September 1990. Total delivered: 75.

VARIANTS
P.180 Avanti: Standard production model for corporate market
P.180 AM Avanti: Italian Air Force variant
P.180 E/ACTL-2 Avanti: Italian Army variant

SPECIFICATIONS
Accommodation: 2 + 9
Cargo/baggage: 1.25 m3 (44 cu.ft)
Max speed: 395 kt (732 km/h)
Range: 1,850 nm (3,426 km)

DIMENSIONS
Wingspan: 14.0 m (46 ft 0 in)
Length: 14.4 m (47 ft 4 in)
Height: 4.0 m (13 ft 1 in)

FEATURES
Mid/straight wing towards rear of fuselage; nose-mounted canard foreplane; twin wing-mounted

P&WC PT6A turboprops with five-blade pusher propeller; swept T-tail and swept tailplane; two delta fin strakes under tail

Piper PA-31 Navajo/Mojave USA

Twin-piston business aircraft and commuterliner

Series of light six/eight seat business twins with Lycoming piston engines, first flown as the original Navajo on 30 September 1964. Progressively improved and also targeted at the air taxi and commuter market. Total built: 4,318.

VARIANTS:

PA-31 Navajo: Baseline model with Lycoming IO-470 engines

PA-31 Navajo B: Turbocharged TIO-540 engines
PA-31 Navajo C: Minor improvements
PA-31-325 Navajo C/R: Counter-rotating propellers
PA-31-350 Chieftain: Stretched fuselage and 10-seat interior
PA-31-350 T-1020: Chieftain for commuter use with special interior
PA-31P-425 Pressurised Navajo: Pressurised fuselage, one less window on port side
PA-31P-350 Mojave: Combines Cheyenne I fuselage and Chieftain wings and tail
GM-17 Viper: Russian modification with single Walter M601E turboprop

SPECIFICATIONS: CHIEFTAIN
Accommodation: 1 + 9
Cargo/baggage: 318 kg (700 lb)
Max speed: 231 kt (428 km/h)
Range: 1,210 nm (2,240 km)

DIMENSIONS
Wingspan: 12.4 m (40 ft 8 in)
Length: 10.6 m (34 ft 8 in)
Height: 4.0 m (13 ft 2 in)

FEATURES
Low/straight and cranked wing with slight dihedral; twin wing-mounted Lycoming TIO-540 piston engines with three-blade propellers; three or four cabin windows; swept tailfin with low-set tailplane

Piper PA-31T Cheyenne USA

Twin-piston business aircraft and commuterliner

Essentially a P-31P pressurised Navajo fitted with P&WC PT6A turboprop engines, wingtip fuel tanks and new flight control system. It first flew on 22 October 1969 and was superseded by several improved models in subsequent years. Total delivered: 819.

VARIANTS

PA-31T Cheyenne: Baseline model with PT6A-28 engines, later designated Cheyenne II

PA-31T1 Cheyenne I: Lighter and less powerful PT6A-11 engines

PA-31T1 Cheyenne IA: More powerful engines and improved interior and cockpit layout

PA-31T2 Cheyenne IIXL: Stretched fuselage and extra cabin window

PA-31T3 T-1040: Combines Chieftain fuselage with wings and landing gear of Cheyenne IIXL and engines of Cheyenne I

SPECIFICATIONS: T-1040

Accommodation: 1 + 9
Cargo/baggage: 227 kg (500 lb)
Max speed: 236 kt (437 km/h)
Range: 1,400 nm (2,592 km)

DIMENSIONS

Wingspan: 12.5 m (41 ft 1 in)
Length: 11.2 m (36 ft 8 in)
Height: 4.0 m (13 ft 2 in)

FEATURES

Low/straight and cranked wing with slight dihedral; twin wing-mounted P&WC PT6A turboprops with three-blade propellers; three four rectangular cabin windows; swept tailfin with low-set tailplane

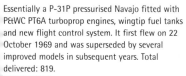

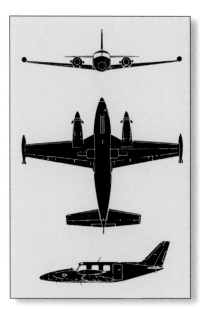

Piper PA-42 Cheyenne III USA

Twin-turboprop business aircraft

Announced on 26 September 1977, the Cheyenne III differed from earlier Cheyenne models primarily by having increased wingspan, a lengthened fuselage, T-tail and more powerful engines. The production prototype first flew on 18 May 1979 and deliveries began on 30 June 1980. Total delivered: 178.

VARIANTS
PA-42 Cheyenne III: Initial production model
PA-42-720 Cheyenne IIIA: Improved engines, increased weight and extra cabin window on each side
PA-42-1000 Cheyenne 400LS: More powerful Garrett TPE331 turboprops, increased T-O weight and updated systems

SPECIFICATIONS: 400LS
Accommodation: 2 + 6
Cargo/baggage: 136 kg (300 lb)
Max speed: 246 kt (455 km/h)
Range: 1,400 nm (2,592 km)

DIMENSIONS
Wingspan: 14.5 m (47 ft 8 in)
Length: 13.2 m (43 ft 4 in)
Height: 5.0 m (16 ft 5 in)

FEATURES
Low/straight wing with slight dihedral and wingtip tanks; twin wing-mounted P&WC PT6A or Garrett TPE331 turboprops with three-blade and four-blade propellers respectively; four cabin windows; swept T-tail

Piper PA-46 Malibu Mirage/Meridian USA

Twin-piston/turboprop light business and private aircraft

Light six-seat business aircraft, which made its first flight on 30 November 1979. Replaced by improved Mirage from October 1988. New Meridian launched at 1997 NBAA convention and made its first flight on 21 August 1998 and entered service in mid-2000. Total delivered: 265 (Malibu); 85 (Mirage); 180 (Meridian).

VARIANTS

PA-46-310P Malibu: Initial production model
PA-46-350P Malibu Mirage: New Lycoming engine replacing the Continental piston engine, increased gross weight
PA-46-500TP Malibu Meridian: New PT6A turboprop engine, strengthened wing and enlarged and strengthened tail

SPECIFICATIONS: MERIDIAN

Accommodation: 1 + 6
Cargo/baggage: 0.94 m³ (33 cu.ft)
Max speed: 262 kt (485 km/h)
Range: 1,070 nm (1.981 km)

DIMENSIONS

Wingspan: 13.1 m (43 ft 0 in)
Length: 9.0 m (29 ft 7 in)
Height: 3.5 m (11 ft 4 in)

FEATURES

Low/straight wing with dihedral (cranked leading edge on Meridian); twin wing-mounted Continental or Lycoming piston engine, or P&WC turboprop with three-blade propellers; three cabin windows; swept tailfin and low-set tailplane

Piper (Ted Smith) 600 Aerostar USA

Twin-piston light business aircraft

Mid-wing six-seat cabin monoplane with circular fuselage and swept tailfin designed by Ted Smith and first flown in production form on 20 December 1967. The Aerostar line was purchased by Piper Aircraft in March 1978 and continued in production until 1984. Total delivered: 1,076.

VARIANTS

Model 600: Initial production model with Lycoming IO-540 engines
Model 600A: Minor changes
Model 601: Addition of turbocharged TIO-540 engines
Model 601B: Increased wingspan and higher gross weight
Model 601P: Pressurised version
Model 602P: Piper development of 601P, initially named *Sequoia*
Suffix E applied to various models for the European market
PA-60-700P: Model 602P with counter-rotating Lycoming engines

SPECIFICATIONS: 700P

Accommodation: 1 + 5
Cargo/baggage: 109 kg (240 lb)
Max speed: 266 kt (492 km/h)
Range: 890 nm (1,648 km)

DIMENSIONS

Wingspan: 11.2 m (36 ft 8 in)
Length: 10.6 m (34 ft 10 in)
Height: 3.7 m (12 ft 1 in)

FEATURES

Mid/straight wing; twin wing-mounted Lycoming IO-540 piston engines with three-blade propellers; three cabin windows; swept tailfin and low-set tailplane

Rockwell Sabreliner USA

Twin-turbojet/turbofan executive jet

Started life in 1952 with North American Aviation (NAA) as the NA.286 Sabreliner, which first flew on 16 September 1958 and entered service with the USAF. The first civil model was certificated in April 1963. NAA later became part of Rockwell International, which itself sold the line to a new company Sabreliner. Total delivered (including military T-39s): 631.

VARIANTS

Sabreliner 40: First civil model similar to the T-39 and powered by P&W JT12A turbojets
Sabreliner 60: Lengthened fuselage for 10 passengers
Sabreliner 60A: Aerodynamic improvements
Sabreliner 65A: More efficient Garrett TFE731 turbofans
Sabreliner 75: Stand-up cabin and square windows, JT12As
Sabreliner 75A: JT12As replaced by GE CF700 turbofans
T-39 Sabre: Trainer and utility aircraft for US forces, including the *T-39A* support aircraft; *T-39B* and *T-39D* radar and radar interception trainers; *CT-39E* rapid response airlifter; *CT-39G* tactical support aircraft; and *T-39N* navigation trainer

SPECIFICATIONS: 75A

Accommodation: 2 + 10
Cargo/baggage: 1,135 kg (2,500 lb)
Max speed: M0.85 (487 kt (901 km/h)
Range: 1,713 nm (3,174 km)

DIMENSIONS

Wingspan: 13.6 m (44 ft 8 in)

Length: 14.4 m (47 ft 2 in)
Height: 5.3 m (17 ft 3 in)

FEATURES

Low/swept wing; twin rear-mounted P&W JT12A turbojets or Garrett TFE731 or GE CF700 turbofans; squat fuselage with rounded triangular windows (square in 75A); swept tail with low-mounted tailplane

Sino Swearingen SJ30 USA/Taiwan

Twin-turbofan light business jet

Announced on 30 October 1986 as the SA-30

Fanjet. Underwent several ownership changes prior to making its first flight on 13 February 1991. Aircraft continuously revised with stretched fuselage, more powerful engines and aerodynamic improvements, which made for long development programme. Certification expected in late 2005. Total ordered: 176.

VARIANTS
SJ30-2: Initial production version

SPECIFICATIONS
Accommodation: 2 + 6
Cargo/baggage: 1.7 m^3 (60 cu.ft)
Max speed: M 0.80 (459 kt; 849 km/h)
Range: 2,500 nm (4,630 km)

DIMENSIONS
Wingspan: 12.9 m (42 ft 4 in)
Length: 14.3 m (46 ft 11 in)
Height: 4.3 m (14 ft 3 in)

FEATURES
Low/swept wing; twin rear fuselage-mounted Williams FJ44 turbofans; five cabin windows; highly-swept tailfin and high tailplane

PRIVATE
LIGHT
AIRCRAFT

Aero Boero AB.95/115/180 Argentina

Single-piston light aircraft

Design of conventional braced high-wing monoplane series began in the late 1950s, and the AB.95 was first flown on 12 March 1959. It entered service in 1961. Subsequent models were distinguished by increases in power and specialist applications. Total delivered: 600+.

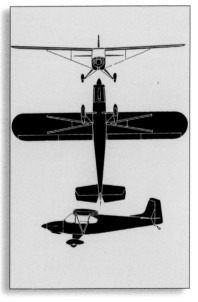

VARIANTS

AB.95: Initial version with 95 hp Continental C-90 engine
AB.95A: More powerful 100 hp Continental O-200 engine
AB.95-115: 115 hp Lycoming O-235 engine
AB.115: Refined version with metal ailerons and modified landing gear, later fitted with larger wing and swept tail
AB.115/150RV: Rear vision window for training, 150 hp Lycoming
AB.180 Condor: Enlarged version with four seats, more powerful engine
Several models were produced in ambulance configuration with suffix BS, agricultural (AG), with rear view window (RV), and glider tug (RVR)

SPECIFICATIONS: AB.180
Accommodation: 1 + 3
Cargo/baggage: 100 kg (220 lb)
Max speed: 108 kt (201 km/h)
Range: 635 nm (1,175 km)

DIMENSIONS
Wingspan 10.8 m (35 ft 5 in)
Length: 7.1 m (23 ft 3 in)
Height: 2.1 m (6 ft 9 in)

FEATURES
High/braced straight wing with rounded tips; single Continental or Lycoming piston engine with two-blade propeller; swept tailfin (AB.115/180) and low-set tailplane; tailwheel type landing gear and wheel fairings on some models

Beech 23/24 Musketeer/Sierra/Sundowner USA

Single-piston light aircraft

Developed as lower cost, lower performance complement to the Debonair/Bonanza range. First flown on 23 October 1961, the all-metal Musketeer differed in having less powerful engines and a fixed tricycle landing gear. Continual product upgrades resulted in a number of variants very different to the original. The Musketeer name was dropped in 1971, when existing production models were renamed Sundowner and Sierra. Total delivered: 4,455.

VARIANTS

23 Musketeer: Initial production model
A23 Musketeer II: Fuel injected engine, third window each side
A23A Musketeer Custom III: Higher TOGW and minor system changes
A23-19 Musketeer Sport III: Trainer version with two windows
A23-24 Musketeer Super III: Fuel injection, higher payload
C23 Sundowner 180: Standard port and starboard doors, deeper side windows
B24R Sierra 200: Retractable landing gear, extra port side door
C24R Sierra: Increased fuel capacity, larger propeller
Minor detail changes produced several other subvariants

SPECIFICATIONS: C23

Accommodation: 1 + 3
Cargo/baggage: 122 kg (270 lb)
Max speed 123 kt (228 km/h)
Range: 641 nm (1,187 km)

DIMENSIONS

Wingspan 10.0 m (32 ft 9 in)
Length: 7.9 m (25 ft 11 in)
Height: 2.5 m (8 ft 3 in)

FEATURES

Low/straight wing; single Continental or Lycoming piston engine with two-blade propeller; two or three windows; swept tailfin with dorsal fillet and low-set tailplane; fixed or retractable landing gear

Beech 33 Debonair/Bonanza USA

Single-piston light aircraft

Similar in configuration to the Model 35 Bonanza, but distinguished by a conventional tail unit and swept vertical tail surfaces. The prototype first flew on 14 September 1959, and production models were known as Debonairs until 1967. Total delivered: 3,210+.

VARIANTS

33 Debonair: Initial production model with utility interior
A33 Debonair: Rear side windows
C33 Debonair: Teardrop rear side windows, enlarged dorsal fillet
C33A Debonair: Optional fifth seat
E33 Bonanza: Less powerful engine, but improved trim
F33 Bonanza: Minor improvements, deeper rear side windows
Plus a number of other models and subtypes with minor detail changes and various engine models, including the *B33, D33, E33A, E33B, E33C, F33A, F33C* and *G33*

SPECIFICATIONS: F33A
Accommodation: 1 + 4
Cargo/baggage: 122 kg (270 lb)
Max speed: 182 kt (338 km/h)
Range: 838 nm (1,553 km)

DIMENSIONS
Wingspan: 10.2 m (33 ft 6 in)
Length: 8.1 m (26 ft 7 in)
Height: 2.5 m (8 ft 3 in)

FEATURES
Low/straight wing; single Continental piston engine with two-blade propeller; three windows each side; swept tailfin with small dorsal fillet and low tailplane; retractable tricycle landing gear

Beech V35 Bonanza USA

Single-piston light aircraft

The prototype all-metal, high-performance Bonanza flew for the first time on 22 December 1945 and the type went into production in 1947. It featured a distinctive V-tail and retractable landing gear, and was powered by a 165 hp Continental piston engine. Total delivered: 10,404.

VARIANTS

35: Initial production version
C35: Metal propeller and larger tail surfaces
F35: Additional rear window each side, auxiliary fuel tanks
H35: New propeller and structural strengthening
M35: Optional fifth seat
N35: Teardrop rear side windows, increased fuel capacity
S35: Longer cabin with optional fifth and sixth seats
V35: Single-piece and streamlined widshield
V35-TC: Turbocharged engine
Plus many other models and subtypes with progressive increase in power and weight, but minimal external changes, including *B35, D35, E35, G35, J35, K35, P35, V35A* and *V35B*

SPECIFICATIONS: V35B

Accommodation: 1 + 4
Cargo/baggage: 122 kg (270 lb)
Max speed: 182 kt (338 km/h)
Range: 838 nm (1,553 km)

DIMENSIONS

Wingspan: 10.2 m (33 ft 6 in)
Length: 8.1 m (26 ft 7 in)
Height: 2.3 m (7 ft 6 in)

FEATURES

Low/straight wing with or without tip tanks; single Continental piston engine with two-blade propeller; three windows each side; V-tail; retractable tricycle landing gear

Beech 36 Bonanza/T36 Turbo Bonanza USA

Single-piston light aircraft

Developed from the V35B Bonanza, the A36 differs in having a fuselage stretch for a full six-seat capacity, swept tailfin, large double doors on the starboard side and increased baggage capacity. It first flew on 4 January 1968 and remains in production: Total delivered: 4,000+.

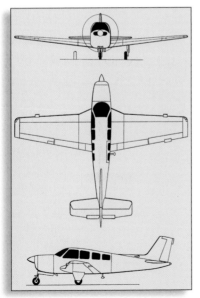

VARIANTS
36 Bonanza: Initial production model with 285 hp engine
A36 Bonanza: Deluxe interior
A36AT Bonanza: Dedicated airline trainer, three-blade propeller
A36TC Bonanza: 300 hp turbocharged Continental engine
B36TC Bonanza: Longer span wing, increased range
T36TC Bonanza: T-tail version

SPECIFICATIONS: B36TC
Accommodation: 1 + 5
Cargo/baggage: 181 kg (400 lb)
Max speed: 213 kt (394 km/h)
Range: 1,022 nm (1,893 km)

DIMENSIONS
Wingspan: 11.5 m (37 ft 10 in)
Length: 8.4 m (27 ft 6 in)
Height: 2.6 m (8 ft 6 in)

FEATURES
Low/straight tapered wings; single Continental piston engine with two- or three-blade propeller; four windows each side; swept tailfin and low-set swept tailplane (T-tail on T36TC); retractable tricycle landing gear

Beech 55/56/58 Baron/Turbo Baron USA

Twin-piston light aircraft

Essentially a re-engineered and re-engined B95 Travel Air with sweptback tailfin and longer side windows, the 95-55 Baron made its first flight on 29 February 1960, with deliveries starting during 1961. Several model improvements led to the 58 Baron, which remains in production. Total delivered: 3,728 (55); 94 (56); 2,700 (58).

VARIANTS

95-55 Baron: Initial production model
A55 Baron: Optional sixth seat, narrower fin/rudder
B55 Baron: Full six-seat cabin
B55B Cochise: B55 for US Army as *T-42A*
C55/D55/E55 Baron: Minor changes
56TC Turbo Baron: Turbocharged Lycoming
A56TC Turbo Baron: Minor system changes
58 Baron: Longer cabin, dual starboard rear doors
58P Pressurised Baron: Pressurised cabin, turbocharged Continental engines; three-blade propellers
58TC Baron: Unpressurised version of 58P

SPECIFICATIONS: 58

Accommodation: 1 + 5
Cargo/baggage: 181 kg (400 lb)
Max speed: 203 kt (376 km/h)
Range: 860 nm (1,593 km)

DIMENSIONS: 58

Wingspan: 11.5 m (37 ft 9 in)
Length: 9.1 m (29 ft 9 in)
Height: 3.0 m (9 ft 11 in)

FEATURES

Low/straight tapered wing with leading edge gloves; twin Lycoming or Continental piston engines with two-blade or three-blade propellers; four windows each side; swept tailfin with dorsal fillet and low-set tailplane; retractable tricycle landing gear

Beech 60 Duke USA

Twin-piston light touring aircraft

Designed in early 1965 to slot in between the Queen Air and Baron in size, the pressurised, turbocharged and high-performance six-seat

Duke first flew on 29 December that year. Initial deliveries followed in July 1968. Total delivered: 596.

VARIANTS

60 Duke: Initial production model with turbocharged Lycoming engines and rear port side entry door
A60 Duke: Increased T-O weight and improved turbocharger
B60 Duke: Larger cabin and enhanced pressurisation system

SPECIFICATIONS: B60

Accommodation: 1 + 4
Max speed: 239 kt (433 km/h)
Range: 1,020 nm (1,887 km)

DIMENSIONS

Wingspan: 12.0 m (39 ft 3 in)
Length: 10.3 m (33 ft 10 in)
Height: 3.8 m (12 ft 5 in)

FEATURES

Low/straight wing; twin Lycoming piston engines with three-blade propeller; three cabin windows; swept tailfin with dorsal fillet and low-set tailplane; retractable tricycle landing gear

Beech 76 Duchess USA

Twin-piston light aircraft

Developed in the mid-1970s, the Duchess featured a T-tail, entry doors on each side of the cabin and electric trim and flap controls. A prototype, designated PD289, flew in September 1974, but the definitive aircraft did not take to the skies until 24 May 1977. Deliveries commenced in May 1978. Total delivered: 437.

VARIANTS

76 Duchess: Only version built, but several factory-installed optional equipment packages were available, including *Weekender* incorporating sun visor and tinted windscreen, cabin boarding steps and more; *Holiday* with coat hook and garment hanger and enhanced avionics; and *Professional,* with two-seat headrests, true airspeed indicator and wing-mounted taxi lights

SPECIFICATIONS

Accommodation: 1 + 3
Cargo/baggage: 91 kg (200 lb)
Max speed: 166 kt (308 km/h)
Range: 711 nm (1,317 km)

DIMENSIONS

Wingspan: 11.6 m (38 ft 1 in)
Length: 8.9 m (29 ft 2 in)
Height: 2.9 m (9 ft 6 in)

FEATURES

Low/straight wing with leading edge wing gloves; twin wing-mounted Lycoming piston engines with two-blade propeller; three windows each side; swept T-tail; retractable tricycle landing gear

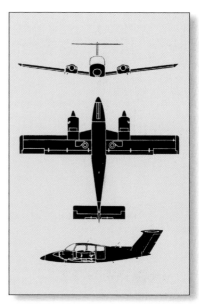

Bellanca 17 Viking USA

Single-piston light touring aircraft

Developed from the Bellanca 260 series with improved engines and minor airframe changes, replacing the former in 1967. The Viking proved a capable and successful aircraft, but production was halted in April 1980. Total delivered (including the Aries): 1,383.

VARIANTS
17-30 Viking 300: Initial production model with 300 hp engine
17-30A Super Viking: New airframe and enlarged wing tanks
17-30B Super Viking: Minor internal changes
17-31 Viking 300: 290 hp engine
17-31A Super Viking: Improved Lycoming engine
17-31TC Turbo Viking: Rayjay-supercharged engine
17-31ATC Turbo Super Viking: Improved supercharged engine
T-250 Aries 250: Improved performance, retractable landing gear

SPECIFICATIONS
Accommodation: 1 + 3
Cargo/baggage: 84 kg (186 lb)
Max speed: 181 kt (335 km/h)
Range: 929 nm (1,722 km)

DIMENSIONS
Wingspan: 10.4 m (34 ft 2 in)
Length: 8.0 m (26 ft 3 in)
Height: 2.2 m (7 ft 3 in)

FEATURES
Low/straight tapered wing; single Continental or Lycoming engine with two-blade propeller; swept tailfin with dorsal fillet and low-set tailplane; fixed tricycle landing gear (retractable in Aries)

Cessna 172 Skyhawk/Cutlass/175 Skylark USA

Single-piston light aircraft

Started initially as a tricycle development of the Model 170 and went on to become the most successful general aviation aircraft. The high-wing Model 172 first flew on 12 June 1955 and remained in production for 30 years. Total built of all models: 41,000+ (172); 2,118 (175).

VARIANTS

172: Initial production model
172A: Sweptback fin and rudder
172B Skyhawk: External streamlining and new avionics, spats optional
172RG Cutlass: Retractable landing gear and three-blade prop
172S Skyhawk SP: Special performance version
FR172E Reims Rocket: Built in France by Reims Aviation
R172E: More powerful engines, also used by USAF as *T-41 Mescalero*
R172K Hawk XP: Luxury interior
175 Skylark: Uprated engine and redesigned engine cowlings
+ many other variants within the *Skyhawk*, *Cutlass* and *Skylark* series

SPECIFICATIONS: 172RG

Accommodation: 1 + 3
Cargo/baggage: 54 kg (120 lb)
Max speed: 140 kt (259 km/h)
Range: 840 nm (1,554 km)

DIMENSIONS

Wingspan: 10.9 m (35 ft 10 in)
Length: 8.2 m (26 ft 11 in)

Height: 2.6 m (8 ft 6 in)

FEATURES

High/braced straight wing; single Continental or Lycoming piston engine with two-blade propeller; swept tailfin with dorsal fillet and low-set tailplane; fixed or retractable tricycle landing gear (wheel fairing on some models)

Cessna 177 Cardinal USA

Single-piston light aircraft

All-new replacement for the Model 172 family, featuring more spacious cabin and other external and internal refinements. First flown on 15 July 1966. Total delivered: 4,240.

VARIANTS

177: Basic production version with fixed landing gear
177A: More powerful engine and new tailcone.
177B: Redesigned wing with cambered wingtips Deluxe models of *177* and *177A* with main wheel fairings, overall paint scheme and refined interior are named *Cardinal*, with deluxe *177B* named *Cardinal Classic*
177RG Cardinal RG: Uprated engine and retractable landing gear
F177RG: Reims-built model

SPECIFICATIONS: 177RG

Accommodation: 1 + 3
Cargo/baggage:
Max speed: 156 kt (289 km/h)
Range: 895 nm (1,656 km)

DIMENSIONS

Wingspan: 10.8 m (35 ft 6 in)
Length: 8.3 m (27 ft 3 in)
Height: 2.6 m (8 ft 6 in)

FEATURES

High/braced straight wing; single Lycoming engine with two-blade propeller; swept tailfin with dorsal fillet and swept low-set tailplane; fixed or retractable tricycle landing gear

Cessna 180/185 Skywagon USA

Single-piston light utility aircraft

More powerful development of the Model 170B with rectangular tailfin with dorsal fairing and reshaped side windows. It first flew on 26 May 1952 and spawned numerous variants with engine upgrades and minor detail changes. The larger, six-seat Model 185 was first flown in July 1960. Total delivered: 6,210 (180); 4,339 (185), including military U-17 versions.

VARIANTS

180: Initial production version
180G: Six-seat capacity and extra side windows
180H Skywagon: Detail changes
185 Skywagon: Strengthened airframe, enlarged dorsal fin, optional utility interior, cargo pod, skis & floats
A185E Skywagon: Increased weight and more powerful engine
A185F Skywagon: Three-blade propeller and minor improvements
+ many other models with minor changes in engine power and external and internal details, including the *180A, 180B, 180C, 180E, 180F, 180J, 180K, 185A, 185B. 185C, 185D, 185E* and special *AgCarryall* agricultural model. Also used by USAF as *U-17A, U-17B* and *U-17C*.

SPECIFICATIONS: A185F

Accommodation: 1 + 5
Cargo/baggage: 160 kg (350 lb)
Max speed: 147 kt (272 km/h)
Range: 850 nm (1,573 km)

DIMENSIONS

Wingspan: 11.0 m (36 ft 1 in)
Length: 7.9 m (25 ft 9 in)
Height: 2.4 m (7 ft 10 in)

FEATURES

Low/straight wing; single Continental piston engine with two- or three-blade propeller; tailfin with large dorsal fillet and low-set tailplane; tailwheel type landing gear

Cessna 182 Skylane USA

Single-piston light aircraft

Essentially a Model 180 with a fixed tricycle landing gear, the Model 182 first flew in 1956 was went into service in January 1958. Final versions had retractable landing gear. Total delivered: 21,864.

VARIANTS:
182: Initial basic production version
182C: Swept tailfin and third cabin window
182E: Cut-down rear fuselage and omni-vision rear windows

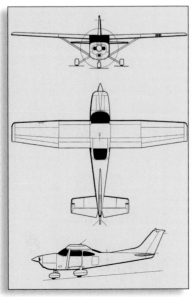

182P: Tubular steel landing gear legs, larger dorsal fin
182R: Optional turbocharged engine
182S Skylane: New production from 1995
182T Skylane: Improved model from 2001
T182T Turbo Skylane: Turbocharged model
182R Skylane: Optional turbocharged engine
R182 Skylane RG: Retractable landing gear and optional turbocharger
FR182 Skylane RG: Reims-built Model R182
+ many other variants with minor changes, including *182A, 182B, 182D, 182F, 182G, 182H, 182J, 182K, 182L, 182M, 182N* and *182Q*. DINFIA-built models have prefix *A*
Deluxe versions with overall paintscheme and wheel fairings named Skylane

SPECIFICATIONS: 182R
Accommodation: 1 + 3
Cargo/baggage: 91 kg (200 lb)
Max speed: 150 kt (278 km/h)
Range: 1,025 nm (1,896 km)

DIMENSIONS
Wingspan: 10.9 m (35 ft 10 in)
Length: 8.5 m (27 ft 11 in)
Height: 2.8 m (9 ft 3 in)

FEATURES
High/braced straight wing; single Continental or Lycoming piston engine with two-blade propeller; swept tailfin with dorsal fillet and low-set tailplane; fixed or retractable landing gear (wheel fairings on some models)

Cessna 205/206/207 Super Skywagon/Stationair USA

Single-piston light utility aircraft

Fixed undercarriage derivative of the Model 210 Centurion optimised for cargo/utility roles, featuring an additional small cargo door on the port side of the fuselage. Deliveries began in August 1962, leading to a multitude of developments until production ceased in 1985. Total built: 574 (205); 8,200+ (206); 790 (207).

VARIANTS

205: Initial production model
206 Super Skywagon: Uprated engine, starboard double cargo door
P206 Super Skylane: Deluxe interior, wheel fairings, two main doors
U206A Super Skywagon: Optional belly cargo pod and turbocharger
U206F Stationair: Cambered wing, new instrument panel, three-blade propeller
U206G Stationair 6: Turbocharged engine
206H Stationair 6: Re-designed wingtips, fuel-injected engine
207 Skywagon: Stretched 206D with seven seats
207A Stationair 8: Fitted with eight seats
+ many other variants with minor changes, including *205A, U206, and 206A, 206B, 206C, 206D, 206E*, each model with *U, P* and *TU* (turbocharged) prefixes

SPECIFICATIONS: U206G

Accommodation: 1 + 5
Cargo/baggage: 109 kg (240 lb)
Max speed: 147 kt (272 km/h)
Range: 680 nm (1,259 km)

DIMENSIONS

Wingspan: 10.9 m (35 ft 10 in)
Length: 8.6 m (28 ft 3 in)
Height: 2.8 m (9 ft 3 in)

FEATURES

High/braced straight wing; single Continental or Lycoming piston engine with two- or three-blade propeller; swept tailfin with dorsal fillet and low-set tailplane; fixed tricycle landing gear with optional wheel fairings; optional floats

Cessna 210 Centurion USA

Single-piston light utility aircraft

First Cessna model to have retractable tricycle landing gear, but otherwise followed the usual braced high-wing and swept tailfin formula. First flown in January 1957, the Model 210 entered service in late 1959. Total delivered: 9,240.

VARIANTS

210: Initial production model

210A: Third window on each side, higher rear roof
210B: Cut-down rear fuselage, rear vision window
210D Centurion: Increased weight and more powerful engine
210G Centurion: Cantilever wing and wraparound rear window
210K Centurion: Enlarged cabin with six seats
P210N Pressurised Centurion: 210N with pressurised cabin and four windows each side
P210R Centurion: Cambered wingtips, more powerful engine
+ other versions with minor changes, including *210C, 210E, 210F, 210H, 210J, 210L, 210M, 210N* and *210R*. Models with turbocharged engines are prefixed T and are known as *Turbo Centurion*

SPECIFICATIONS: T210M

Accommodation: 1 + 5
Cargo/baggage: 109 kg (240 lb)
Max speed: 193 kt (357 km/h)
Range: 900 nm (1,667 km)

DIMENSIONS

Wingspan: 11.2 m (36 ft 9 in)
Length: 8.6 m (28 ft 3 in)
Height: 2.9 m (9 ft 6 in)

FEATURES

High/ braced or cantilever straight wing; single Continental piston engine with two- or three-blade propeller; swept tailfin with dorsal fillet and low-set tailplane; retractable tricycle landing gear

Cessna T303 Crusader USA

Twin-piston light corporate aircraft

Originally developed as a four-seat aircraft, but re-designed for six seats and with turbocharged engines and counter-rotating propellers, with which it first flew on 17 October 1979. First deliveries were made in October 1981, but production ceased four years later.
Total delivered: 297.

VARIANTS

T303 Crusader: Only production model. Initially named *Clipper*

SPECIFICATIONS

Accommodation: 1 + 5
Cargo/baggage: 267 kg (590 lb)
Max speed: 196 kt (363 km/h)
Range: 895 nm (1,658 km)

DIMENSIONS

Wingspan: 11.9 m (39 ft 0 in)
Length: 9.3 m (30 ft 5 in)
Height: 4.1 m (13 ft 4 in)

FEATURES

Low/straight dihedral wing; twin turbocharged Continental piston engine with three-blade counter-rotating propellers; swept tailfin with dorsal fillet and mid-mounted tailplane; retractable tricycle landing gear

Cessna 310/320 Skyknight USA

Twin-piston light aircraft

First twin-engined Cessna design to enter production after the war, including fuel storage in tip tanks and thrust augmentation from engine exhausts. The model 310 first flew on 3 January 1953 and went into production in 1954. The enlarged turbocharged 320 Skyknight followed. Total delivered: 5,438 including military models (310); 575 (320).

VARIANTS

310: Initial production version

310F: Extra cabin window, pointed nose, reshaped tip tanks
310K: Higher weight, 'vista view' side windows
310Q: Bulged rear roof and rear-view windows in later models
310R: Lengthened nose with baggage compartment, three-blade propellers
320 Skyknight: Enlarged 310F with six seats and extra window
320E Executive Skyknight: Pointed nose, single piece windscreen
+ many other variants with minor changes, including *310B, 310C, 310D. 310E, 310G, 310H, 310I, 310J, 310L, 310M, 310N, 310P, 320A, 320B, 320C* and *320D.* USAF acquired the *310A Blue Canoe* designated *U-3A,* and the *310E Blue Canoe* as the *U-3B.*

SPECIFICATIONS: 310L
Accommodation: 1 + 5
Cargo/baggage: 163 kg (360 lb)
Max speed: 193 kt (357 km/h)
Range: 676 nm (1,250 km)

DIMENSIONS
Wingspan: 11.3 m (37 ft 1 in)
Length: 9.0 m (29 ft 6 in)
Height: 3.0 m (9 ft 10 in)

FEATURES
Low/straight wing with tip tanks; twin Continental piston engines with two- or three-blade propellers; swept tailfin with small dorsal fillet and low-set tailplane; retractable tricycle landing gear

Cessna 336 Skymaster/337 Super Skymaster USA

Twin-piston light corporate/utility aircraft

The Skymaster represented a major departure for Cessna, in that it used a push-pull engine configuration to eliminate asymetric handling characteristics in one engine out situations, combined with a twin-boom tail layout. The Model 336 first flew on 18 February 1961 and entered service in mid-1963, but was quickly replaced by the improved 337 Super Skymaster. Total delivered: 195 (336); 2,798 (337, including military).

VARIANTS
336 Skymaster: Initial production model
337 Super Skymaster: Redesigned nose, retractable landing gear, revised rear engine intake
337B Super Skymaster: Optional belly cargo pack and optional turbocharged engines
337G Super Skymaster: Split airstair door, smaller rear windows, larger propeller
T337G Pressurised Skymaster: Pressurised cabin, dual front seat windows, turbocharged engines + many other variants with minor changes, including *337A, 337C, 337D, 337E, 337F* and *337H.* Reims-built models are prefixed **F,** pressurised models *P.* Also *M337* operated by USAF as *O-2A,* and *MC337* operated as *O-2B.*

SPECIFICATIONS: T337G
Accommodation: 1 + 5
Cargo/baggage: 165 kg (364 lb)
Max speed: 205 kt (380 km/h)
Range: 1,308 nm (2,422 km)

DIMENSIONS
Wingspan: 11.6 m (38 ft 1 in)

Length: 9.1 m (29 ft 9 in)
Height: 2.8 m (9 ft 3 in)

FEATURES
High/braced straight wing; twin Continental piston engines with two-blade push/pull propellers; twin slim metal tailboom with swept tailfins and connecting tailplanes; retractable tricycle landing gear

Cessna 335/340 USA

Twin-piston corporate aircraft

Development of the pressurised Model 340 with retractable undercarriage, tip tanks, turbocharged engines and port side rear entry door began in 1969, leading to service entry on 8 December 1971. Total delivered: 64 (335); 1,287 (340).

VARIANTS
335: Low-cost, non-pressurised version of Model 340
340: Initial pressurised production version
340A: More powerful engines, improved air conditioning, prop synchrophasers, new seats
340A II: Enhanced avionics package
340A III: Higher level of avionics

SPECIFICATIONS: 340A
Accommodation: 1 + 5
Cargo/baggage: 422 kg (930 lb)
Max speed: 229 kt (425 km/h)
Range: 1,106 nm (2,049 km)

DIMENSIONS
Wingspan: 11.6 m (38 ft 1 in)
Length: 10.5 m (34 ft 4 in)
Height: 3.8 m (12 ft 5 in)

FEATURES
Low/straight wing with tip tanks; twin Continental turbocharged piston engines with three-blade propellers; four round porthole type cabin windows; swept tailfin and low-set tailplane; retractable tricycle landing gear

Cirrus Design SR20 USA

Single-piston light personal/business aircraft

Development of this low-wing composites aircraft began in 1990, with mockup first revealed at Oshkosh in 1994. First flight was made on 31 March 1995, but deliveries did not start until 22 March 1999. Total delivered: 385 (SR20); 800 (SR22).

VARIANTS

SR20: Initial production model
SR20A: Increased T-O weight and higher spec avionics
SR21tdi: SR22 airframe with SMA SR-305 turbocharged diesel engine
SR22: Modified wing and more pwoerful engine

SPECIFICATIONS

Accommodation: 1 + 3
Max speed: 160 kt (296 km/h)
Range: 800 nm (1,481 km)

DIMENSIONS

Wingspan: 10.8 m (35 ft 6 in)
Length: 7.9 m (25 ft 11 in)
Height: 2.8 m (9 ft 3 in)

FEATURES

Low/straight wing with slight dihedral and upturned wingtips; single Teledyne Continental piston engine with two-blade propeller; swept and curved tailfin with dorsal fillet and low-set tailplane; fixed tricycle landing gear

Diamond DA 40 Star Austria/Canada

Four-seat turbo diesel-powered light touring/utility aircraft

Four-seat development of DA 20-C1, launched on 23 April 1997 at Aero 97 in Friedrichshafen, initially named Katana. Proof-of-concept prototype first flown 5 November 1997, with JAR certification 25 October 2000. First deliveries to US customers during EAA Air-Venture, July 2001. Turbo-diesel prototype first flew 22 November 2001. Total delivered: 425.

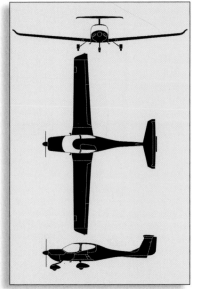

VARIANTS
DA 40-180: Original version with Lycoming IO-360 engines. Now produced in Canada.
DA 40 TDI: Thielert TAE 125 turbo-diesel variant. Built in Austria.

SPECIFICATIONS: DA 40 TDI
Accommodation: 1 + 3
Max speed: 154 kt (285 km/h)
Range: 750 nm (1,390 km)

DIMENSIONS
Wingspan: 11.9 m (39 ft 2 in)
Length: 8.0 m (26 ft 3 in)
Height: 2.0 m (6 ft 7 in)

FEATURES
Low/straight wing; single turbo-diesel with three-blade propeller; streamlined fuselage with integral T-tail with dorsal fillet and downturned tips; single strake/tail bumper; fixed tricycle landing gear; speed fairings on all three wheels

Diamond DA 42 Twinstar Austria

Four-seat twin turbo-diesel light touring/utility aircraft

Twin-engined version of DA 40 Star. Decision to built was taken in September and the aircraft was formally launched on 7 May 2002 with letter of intent from Lufthansa training school for 40 aircraft. Prototype first flew on 9 December 2002. First deliveries were due at end of 2004.

VARIANTS

DA 42 Twinstar: Initial production version with Thielert TAE 125 turbo-charged diesel engines.

SPECIFICATIONS:

Accommodation: 1 + 3
Max speed: 203 kt (376 km/h)
Range: 1,060 nm (1,965 km)

DIMENSIONS

Wingspan: 13.2 m (44 ft 0 in)
Length: 8.5 m (27 ft 11 in)
Height: 2.6 m (8 ft 6 in)

FEATURES

Low/straight wing with large winglets; twin turbo-diesel engines with three-blade propeller; streamlined fuselage with integral T-tail with dorsal fillet and downturned tips; single strake/ tail bumper; retractable tricycle landing gear

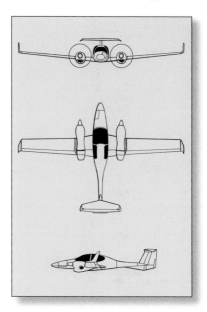

Extra EA-400 Germany

Single-piston light touring/business aircraft

Announced in February 1993 and designed in collaboration with Delft University, the high-wing,

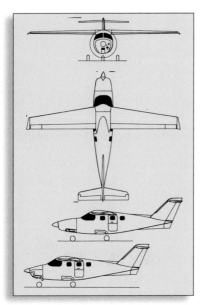

high-performance, composites Extra 400 first flew on 4 April 1996. Turboprop EA-500 first flew on 26 April 2002. First customer delivery followed on 21 August 1998. Total delivered: 25.

VARIANTS
Extra EA-400: Initial production model with Teledyne Continental Voyager TSIOL engine
EA-500: Turboprop version

SPECIFICATIONS
Accommodation: 1 + 5
Max speed: 243 kt (450 km/h)
Range: 1,403 nm (2,600 km)

DIMENSIONS
Wingspan: 11.5 m (37 ft 9 in)
Length: 9.6 m (31 ft 5 in)
Height: 3.1 m (10 ft 2 in)

FEATURES
High/cantilever straight wing with dihedral; single Teledyne Continental engine with four-blade propeller (three-blade optional); highly-swept T-tail; retractable tricycle landing gear

Fuji FA-200 Aero Subaru Japan

Single-piston light touring aircraft

First indigenous light aircraft to enter series production in Japan. Design of this conventional low-wing aircraft started in 1964, followed by the first flight on 12 August 1965, with deliveries starting a year later. Total delivered: 299.

VARIANTS

FA-200-160: Basic production aircraft with a 160 hp engine
FA-200-180: More powerful 180 hp fuel injected engine
FA-200-180AO: Low-cost reduced specification model

SPECIFICATIONS: FA-200-180

Accommodation: 1 + 3
Cargo/baggage: 20 kg (44 lb)
Max speed: 126 kt (233 km/h)
Range: 755 nm (1,400 km)

DIMENSIONS

Wingspan: 9.4 m (30 ft 11 in)
Length: 8.0 m (26 ft 3 in)
Height: 2.0 m (6 ft 8 in)

FEATURES

Low/straight dihedral wing; single Lycoming piston engine with two-blade propeller; swept tailfin and straight horizontal tailplane; fixed tricycle landing gear

Grumman American AA-5
Traveller/Cheetah/Tiger USA

Single-piston light touring aircraft

Larger four-seat development of the two-seat American Aviation AA-1, with which it shares some 60% commonality. It first flew on 21 August 1970, followed by initial customer deliveries in December 1971. Total delivered: 3,225+.

VARIANTS

AA-5 Traveller: Initial four-seat model with 150 hp engine

AA-5A Cheetah: Aerodynamic changes, longer rear windows

AA-5B Tiger: More powerful 180 hp engine, increased weight

AG-5B Tiger: Refined Tiger built by American General

SPECIFICATIONS: AA-5B

Accommodation: 1 + 3
Cargo/baggage: 54 kg (120 lb)
Max speed: 143 kt (265 km/h)
Range: 550 nm (1,018 km)

DIMENSIONS

Wingspan: 9.6 m (31 ft 5 in)
Length: 6.7 m (22 ft 0 in)
Height: 2.4 m (7 ft 10 in)

FEATURES

Low/straight wing; single Lycoming engine with two-blade propeller; tailfin with dorsal fillet and low-set tailplane; fixed tricycle landing gear with optional wheel fairings

Gulfstream Aerospace (Grumman American) GA-7 Cougar USA

Twin-piston light touring aircraft

Grumman American design to complement its AA-1 and AA-5 single-engine line, first flown on 20 December 1974. Over subsequent years, many design changes were made, including replacing the sliding canopy by a conventional fixed arrangement, and adding a third window on each side. Deliveries finally started in February 1978, by which time Grumman's light aircraft division had been acquired by Gulfstream. The production run was short-lived as Gulfstream opted out of light aircraft manufacture the following year. Total delivered: 115.

VARIANTS

GA-7 Cougar: Only production model with twin 160hp Lycoming engines. A higher specification model was also available, but with same model number

SPECIFICATIONS

Accommodation: 1 + 3
Max speed: 160 kt 9296 km/h)
Range: 1,170 nm (2,165 km)

DIMENSIONS

Wingspan: 11.2 m (36 ft 9 in)
Length: 9.1 m (29 ft 9 in)
Height: 3.2 m (10 ft 4 in)

FEATURES

Low/straight wing with leading edge wing gloves; twin Lycoming engines with two-blade propeller; swept tailfin and low-set tailplane; retractable tricycle landing gear

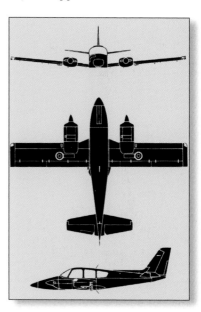

Ilyushin Il-103 Russia

Four-seat single piston engine light aircraft

Exhibited in model form in Moscow in 1990 and made its first flight on 17 May 1994. Definitive Russian certification not achieved until 4 December 1997, followed a year later by FAR Pt 23 certification. Local deliveries believed to have begun in 1998. Total delivered: 25.

VARIANTS
IL-103-01: Baseline version for Russian market
IL-103-10: Export version with upgraded avionics
IL-103-11: Export version with partly upgraded avionics
IL-103P: Surveillance version with sensors and possible armament
IL-103SKh: Crop-sprayer, first flown on 29 March 2000.

SPECIFICATIONS
Accommodation: 1 + 3
Max speed: 119 kt (220 km/h)
Range: 432 nm (800 km)

DIMENSIONS
Wingspan: 10.6 m (34 ft 8 in)
Length: 8.0 m (26 ft 3 in)
Height: 3.1 m (10 ft 3 in)

FEATURES
Low/straight dihedral wing tapered front and rear; single Teledyne Continental or Lycoming piston engine PT6A turboprop engine with two-blade propeller; moderately swept tailfin with low-set tailplane port freight door at rear; non-retractable tricycle landing gear

Lake LA-4 Buccaneer/Renegade/Seafury/Seawolf USA

Single-piston light amphibious aircraft

Development of the Colonial C-2 Skimmer IV with greater wingspan, strengthened structure and higher weights, the LA-4 made its first flight in November 1959 and entered production in August 1960. Several more and improved variants built for both civil and military markets. Total delivered: 1,200+.

VARIANTS

LA-4-180: Initial production model with 180 hp engine

LA-4-200 Buccaneer: More powerful 200 hp engine, extra fuel

LA-4-200EP: Extended prop shaft, redesigned cowling

LA-4-200EPR: Reversible propeller

LA-250 Renegade: Six-seat stretched fuselage, swept tail, 250 hp engine and starboard entry hatch

LA-250 Turbo: Renegade with turbocharged 250 hp engine

LA-270 Turbo: Turbo Renegade with uprated 270hp engine

LA-250 Seawolf: Military derivative with four hardpoints, engine nacelle-mounted radar, 290 hp engine

LA-270 Seafury: Improved corrosion proofing for salt water ops

SPECIFICATIONS: RENEGADE

Accommodation: 1 + 5
Cargo/baggage: 90 kg (200 lb)
Max speed: 139 kt (258 km/h)
Range: 900 nm (1,668 km)

DIMENSIONS

Wingspan: 11.6 m (38 ft 1 in)
Length: 8.6 m (28 ft 3 in)
Height: 2.8 m (9 ft 3 in)

FEATURES

Mid/straight dihedral wing with balancer floats; single Lycoming engine mounted on pylon above hull with two-blade propeller; swept tailfin with high-mounted tailplane; retractable tricycle landing gear

Lancair Columbia USA

Single-piston light touring aircraft and trainer

Announced in 1996 as the LC-40, this low-wing monoplane made its first flight in July 1996 and made its public depot at Oshkosh in August 1997. First production aircraft was delivered on 24 February 2000. Total delivered: 80+.

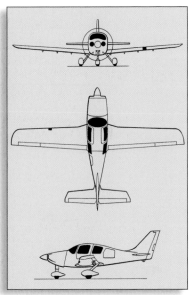

VARIANTS

Columbia 300: Basic production aircraft with 300 hp engine; also available as trainer with derated 155hp engine
Columbia Turbo 400: Turbocharged 310 hp engine
Columbia IV: Proposed pressurised version with retractable landing gear
Columbia 350: All-electric systems, more powerful engine

SPECIFICATIONS: COLUMBIA 300
Accommodation: 1 + 3
Cargo/baggage: 54 kg (120 lb)
Max speed: 190 kt (352 km/h)
Range: 1,385 nm (2,565 km)

DIMENSIONS
Wingspan: 11.0 m (36 ft 1 in)
Length: 7.7 m (25 ft 3 in)
Height: 2.7 m (8 ft 10 in)

FEATURES
Low/straight wing; single Teledyne Continental engine with three-blade propeller; swept tailfin with curved leading edge and low-set tailplane; fixed tricycle landing gear

Let L-200 **Morava** Czechoslovakia

Twin-piston light touring/business aircraft

Designed by Ladislav Smrcek, the all-metal L-200 was first flown on 8 April 1957. It was distinguised by its clean lines, twin tail, retractable landing gear, and wingtip tanks. Production was undertaken both by the National Aircraft Works in Kunovice, and by LIBIS in the then Yugoslavia. Total delivered: 1,000+.

VARIANTS

L-200 Morava: Initial version with two 160 hp Walter engines

L-200A Morava: Higher powered 210 hp M337 fuel-injected engines driving electrically-operated propellers, reprofiled cabin and hydraulically-operated landing gear

L-200D Morava: Three-blade propeller, strengthened landing gear, improved electronics and equipment

SPECIFICATIONS: L-200D

Accommodation: 1 + 4
Cargo/baggage: 135 kg (297 lb)
Max speed: 157 kt (290 km/h)
Range: 923 nm (1,710 km)

DIMENSIONS

Wingspan: 12.3 (40 ft 5 in)
Length: 8.6 (28 ft 3 in)
Height: 2.3 m (7 ft 6 in)

FEATURES

Low/straight wing with wingtip fuel tanks; twin wing-mounted Walter engines; twin rounded triangular tailfins; retractable tricycle landing gear

Maule M-4/M-7 Rocket/Comet/Orion USA

Single-piston light STOL aircraft

Originally intended as a kitbuilt aircraft, the M-4, first flown on 8 September 1960, spawned a prolific series of rugged high-wing STOL taildragger aircraft, which remains in production. Total delivered of all series: 2,070.

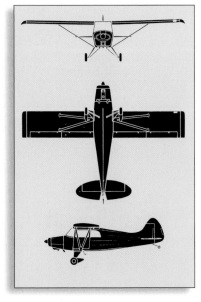

VARIANTS

M-4 Jetasen/Rocket/Astro Rocket/Strata Rocket: Seven other variants and subvariants differing primarily in engine make and power, with or without cargo door

M-5 Strata Rocket/Lunar Rocket: Six variants with enlarged swept tail, drooped wingtips, four cabin doors, and different engines

M-6 Super Rocket: Longer wingspan, increased T-O weight, optional extra children's seats and windows

M-7 Super Rocket/Star Rocket/Comet/Orion: Enlarged cabin, various engine and landing gear combinations. Current production models.

SPECIFICATIONS: M-7-235B
Accommodation: 1 + 4
Cargo/baggage: 349 kg (770 lb)
Max speed: 130 kt (241 km/h)
Range: 829 nm (1,537 km)

DIMENSIONS
Wingspan: 10.3 m (33 ft 10 in)
Length: 7.2 m (23 ft 6 in)
Height: 1.9 m (6 ft 4 in)

FEATURES
High/braced straight dihedral wing; single Continental, Franklin or Lycoming engine; swept tailfin and low-set tailplane; tailwheel type or fixed tricycle landing gear

Mooney M.20A/G Ranger/Chaparral/ Executive/Master/Statesman USA

Single-piston light touring aircraft

Based on an original single-seat design by Al Mooney, the new improved and high performance four-seater M.20 with a distinctive forward swept tail flew on 10 August 1953 and was put into production in 1955. Several variants were produced and for a short time in early 1970s were known as Aerostar when company was bought by Aerostar Aircraft Corporation. Production ceased in 1972. Total delivered: 6,235.

VARIANTS

M.20: Initial production model with 150 hp engine
M.20A: More powerful 180 hp engine
M.20B Mk.21: Re-engineered to all-metal construction
M.20C Ranger: Squared-off windows and new windshield
M.20D Master: Low-spec model with fixed landing gear
M.20E Super 21: Increased T-O weight and 200 hp engine
M.20E Chaparral: Squared-off windows and new windshield
M.20F Executive: Longer fuselage with three windows each side
M.20G Statesman: Reduced power

SPECIFICATIONS: M.20F

Accommodation: 1 + 3
Cargo/baggage: 54 kg (120 lb)
Max speed: 152 kt (283 km/h)
Range: 997 nm (1,845 km)

DIMENSIONS

Wingspan: 10.7 m (35 ft 1 in)

Length: 7.4 m (24 ft 3 in)
Height: 2.5 m (8 ft 3 in)

FEATURES

Low/straight dihedral wing with wing glove; single continental or Lycoming engine with two-blade propeller; forward swept tailfin and low-set tailplane; two or three cabin windows each side; retractable landing gear (fixed in M.20D)

Mooney M.20J/S Allegro/Encore/ Bravo/Eagle/Ovation USA

Single-piston light touring aircraft

Improved Mooney range put into production following the acquisition of Mooney by the Republic Steel Company in late 1973. Initially, the Ranger, Chaparral and Executive were produced before a new line emerged in 1976 with a more streamlined exterior, new windscreen and rounded off window. Several models remain in production. Total delivered: 3,985.

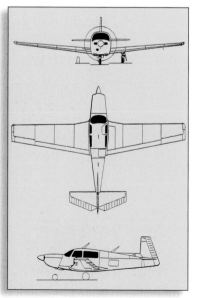

VARIANTS

M.20J 201: Cleaned-up exterior, two windows each side, produced in *LM* (Lean Machine), **SE** (Special Edition), *205* with rounded side windows, *ATS* reduced spec, and *MSE* modified IFR versions. MSE named *Allegro* from 1990.
M.20K 231: Turbocharged 210 hp engine, increased fuel. Also in **SE**, and **252TSE** turbocharged SE variants, named *Encore* from 1997
M.20L PFM: Longer fuselage and 217 hp Porsche
M.20M TLS: Turbocharged 270 hp engine, three-blade propeller. Named Bravo from 1996
M.20R Ovation: Luxury interior and 280 hp Continental engine
M.20S Eagle: Lower-cost entry level version, derated engine
Ovation 2 and Eagle 2 are latest models

SPECIFICATIONS: M.20M
Accommodation: 1 + 3
Cargo/baggage: 54 kg (120 lb)
Max speed: 220 kt (407 km/h)
Range: 1,070 nm (1,982 km)

DIMENSIONS
Wingspan: 11.0 m (36 ft 1 in)
Length: 8.2 m (26 ft 11 in)
Height: 2.5 m (8 ft 3 in)

FEATURES
Low/straight dihedral wing with wing glove; single Continental, Lycoming or Porsche engine with two- or three-blade propeller; two cabin windows each side; forward swept tailfin with dorsal fillet and low-set tailplane; retractable tricycle landing gear

Piper PA-23 Apache/Aztec USA

Twin-piston light aircraft

Based on a Stinson design for a four-seat light twin, the PA-23 Apache, an all-metal monoplane with retractable landing gear, first took to the skies on 2 March 1952 and entered production in March 1954. Enlarged and more powerful Aztec was available from the end of 1959. Total delivered: 2,047 (Apache); 4,929 (Aztec).

VARIANTS

PA-23-150 Apache: Initial production model with 150 hp engine
PA-23-160 Apache G: Longer internal cabin and extra rear window
PA-23-250 Aztec: Enlarged and more powerful 250 hp engine, swept tailfin
PA-23-250 Aztec B: Longer nose with baggage compartment
PA-23-250 Aztec C: Improved engine, optional turbocharger
PA-23-250 Aztec E: More pointed nose, single piece windscreen
PA-23-250 Aztec F: System improvements, cambered wingtips
+ other variants, including the *PA-23-160 Apache E* and *H*, and the *PA-23-235 Apache*. Also Aztec operated by US Navy with designation *U-11A*.

SPECIFICATIONS: AZTEC C
Accommodation: 1 + 5
Cargo/baggage: 136 kg (300 lb)
Max speed: 179 kt (331 km/h)
Range: 970 nm (1,779 km)

DIMENSIONS
Wingspan: 11.3 m (37 ft 1 in)
Length: 9.2 m (30 ft 2 in)
Height: 3.1 m (10 ft 2 in)

FEATURES
Low/straight wing; twin Lycoming piston engines with two-blade propellers; three or four cabin windows; swept tailfin and low-set tailplane; retractable tricycle landing gear

Piper PA-24 Comanche USA

Single-piston light aircraft

High performance all-metal design with retractable landing gear, swept fin and laminar flow wing. First flown on 24 May 1956, with deliveries starting in late 1957. Total delivered: 4,856.

VARIANTS
PA-24-180 Comanche: Initial production version
PA-24-250 Comanche: More powerful 250 hp engine
PA-24-260 Comanche B: Increased weight and engine power
PA-24-260 Comanche C: Various improvements including 'Tiger Shark' cowling, optional turbocharged Engine
PA-24-400 Comanche 400: 400 hp engine, three-blade propeller, modified engine cowling, enlarged tailplane

SPECIFICATIONS: COMANCHE B
Accommodation: 1 + 3
Cargo/baggage: 113 kg (250 lb)
Max speed: 158 kt (293 km/h)
Range: 964 nm (1,783 km)

DIMENSIONS
Wingspan: 11.0 m (36 ft 1 in)
Length: 7.7 m (25 ft 3 in)
Height: 2.3 m (7 ft 6 in)

FEATURES
Low/straight wing; single Lycoming piston engine with two- or three-blade propeller; swept tailfin and low-set tailplane; retractable tricycle landing gear

Piper PA-28 Cherokee USA

Single-piston light touring aircraft and trainer

A low-wing metal replacement for Piper's PA-22 series, the Cherokee made its first flight on 14 January 1960 and was the forerunner of numerous variants with more powerful engines and performance improvements. Deliveries started in 1961. Total delivered: 30,000+.

VARIANTS

PA-28-140 Cherokee: Basic two-seat model with 150 hp engine
PA-28-150 Cherokee: Four-seater with choice of trim
PA-28-151 Warrior: New wing with tapered outer panels
PA-28-161 Warrior II: Uprated 160 hp engine
PA-28-161 Warrior III: Refined development with new wing
PA-28-161 Cadet: 2+2 seat trainer
PA-28-180 Challenger: Fuselage stretch and increase in wingspan
PA-28-180 Archer: Minor changes
PA-28-235 Cherokee: Longer wings and 235 hp engine, extra fuel
PA-28-235 Charger: Enlarged windows and door, increased TOGW
PA-28-235 Pathfinder: Minor changes
PA-28-236 Dakota: Pathfinder with semi-tapered Warrior wing
PA-28-201T Turbo Dakota: Turbocharged 200 hp engine
+ numerous other variants suffixed **B, C, D, E** and **F** denoting minor changes

SPECIFICATIONS: PA-28-235B

Accommodation: 1 + 3
Cargo/baggage: 91 kg (200 lb)
Max speed: 135 kt (251 km/h)

Range: 984 nm (1,820 km)

DIMENSIONS

Wingspan: 9.8 m (32 ft 1 in)
Length: 7.2 m (23 ft 6 in)
Height: 2.2 m (7 ft 4 in)

FEATURES

Low/straight wing, some with semi-tapers; single Lycoming engine with two-blade propeller; swept tailfin with low-set tailplane; non-retractable landing gear (optional wheel fairings)

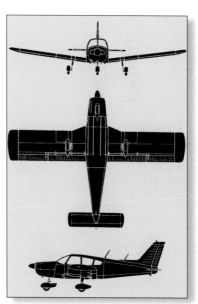

Piper PA-28R Cherokee Arrow USA

Single-piston light tourer

Derived from the Cherokee Archer II, but with more powerful engine, retractable landing gear with automatic extension and untapered wings. First flown on 1 February 1967.
Total delivered: 7,000+.

VARIANTS

PA-28R-180 Cherokee Arrow: Initial production model
PA-28R-200 Cherokee Arrow: 200 hp engine
PA-28R-200 Cherokee Arrow B: New fuel system
PA-28R-200 Cherokee Arrow II: Small fuselage stretch, larger door
PA-28R-201 Arrow III: Longer semi-tapered wing
PA-28R-201 Arrow IV: redesigned rear fuselage and new T-tail Arrow III and IV also built as *PA-28RT-201T* with turbocharged engine

SPECIFICATIONS: ARROW III

Accommodation: 1 + 3
Cargo/baggage: 90 kg (200 lb)
Max speed: 145 kt (268 km/h)
Range: 880 nm (1,630 km)

DIMENSIONS

Wingspan: 10.8 m (35 ft 6 in)
Length: 7.5 m (24 ft 8 in)
Height: 2.4 m (7 ft 10 in)

FEATURES

Low/straight tapered wing with leading edge wing gloves; single Lycoming engine with two-blade propeller; swept tailfin with dorsal fillet and low-set tailplane (T-tail in Arrow IV); retractable landing gear

Piper PA-30/39 Twin Comanche USA

Twin-piston light aircraft

A twin-engined development of the PA-24 Comanche, the PA-30 made its maiden flight on 7 November 1962 and was first delivered in summer 1963. The PA-39 introduced counter-rotating propellers. Total delivered; 2,001 (PA-30); 155 (PA-39).

Lycoming piston engines with two-blade propellers; two or three windows each side; swept tailfin and low-set tailplane; retractable tricycle landing gear

VARIANTS

PA-30 Twin Comanche: Initial production version
PA-30 Twin Comanche B: Third cabin window each side and optional turbocharged engines
PA-30 Twin Comanche C: Improved engine, new instrument panel, optional tip tanks and turbocharged engine
PA-39 Twin Comanche C/R: Counter-rotating propellers and optional turbocharged engine

SPECIFICATIONS: TWIN COMANCHE B

Accommodation: 1 + 3
Cargo/baggage: 113 kg (250 lb)
Max speed: 167 kt (312 km/h)
Range: 892 nm (1,650 km)

DIMENSIONS

Wingspan: 11.0 m (36 ft 1 in)
Length: 7.7 m (25 ft 3 in)
Height: 2.5 m (8 ft 3 in)

FEATURES

Low/straight wing with optional tip tanks; twin

Piper PA-32 Cherokee Six/Lance/Saratoga USA

Single-piston light tourer/business aircraft

Higher capacity six-seat stretched model developed from the PA-28-235 and incorporating strengthened landing gear and larger tail unit. The Cherokee Six was first flown on 6 December 1963, with deliveries from mid-1965. Also built in Brazil as EMB-720 Minuano. A new wing and fuel injected engine produced the Saratoga, while the Lance was fitted with a T-tail. Total delivered: 7,200+.

VARIANTS

PA-32 Cherokee Six: Initial production model with 250 hp engine
PA-32-260 Cherokee Six: 260 hp engine
PA-32-300 Cherokee Six: 300 hp engine
PA-32-301 Saratoga: New semi-tapered wing
PA-32-301T Turbo Saratoga: Turbocharged
PA-32R-300 Cherokee Lance: PA-32-300 with retractable landing gear
PA-32RT-300 Lance II: Fitted with T-tail
PA-32R-301 Saratoga SP: Lance retractable landing gear, no T-tail
PA-32RT-301 Saratoga II HP: High performance model, reduced depth side windows
PA-32R-301T Saratoga II TC: New interior
Some models also built with turbocharged engines; Cherokee Six also with *B, C, D* and *E* suffixes denoting minor changes
6XT: Turbocharged fixed-gear version of Saratoga II

SPECIFICATIONS: SARATOGA II HP

Accommodation: 1 + 5
Cargo/baggage: 90 kg (200 lb)
Max speed: 175 kt (324 km/h)
Range: 859 nm (1,590 km)
DIMENSIONS
Wingspan: 11.0 m (36 ft 1 in)
Length: 8.5 m (27 ft 11 in)
Height: 2.6 m (8 ft 6 in)

FEATURES

Low/straight wing with leading edge wing gloves; single Lycoming piston engine with two-blade propeller; swept tailfin with small dorsal fillet and low-set tailplane (T-tail in Lance II)

Piper PA-34 Seneca USA

Twin-piston light aircraft

Twin-engined development of the Cherokee Six, first flown in definitive form in October 1969. Production deliveries began on 23 September 1971 and latest model remains in service. Also built in Poland under licence by PZL-Mielec as the M-20 Mewa and in Brazil. Total delivered: 4,700+.

VARIANTS

PA-34-200 Seneca: Initial production model with 200 hp engines

PA-34-200T Seneca II: Turbocharged engines

PA-34-220T Seneca III: 220 hp turbocharged engine, single piece windshield, increased MGTOW, new instrument panel

PA-34-220T Seneca IV: Upgraded interior, reduced depth side windows

PA-34-220T Seneca V: Upgraded interior, new turbocharged Teledyne Continental engine

SPECIFICATIONS: SENECA IV

Accommodation: 1 + 5
Cargo/baggage: 84 kg (185 lb)
Max speed: 193 kt (358 km/h)
Range: 826 nm (1,529 km)

DIMENSIONS

Wingspan: 11.9 m (38 ft 11 in)
Length: 8.7 m (28 ft 7 in)
Height: 3.0 m (9 ft 10 in)

FEATURES

Low/straight wing with leading edge wing gloves; twin Continental or Lycoming piston engines with three- or two-blade propellers respectively; swept tailfin and low-set tailplane; retractable tricycle landing gear

Piper PA-44 Seminole USA

Twin-piston light aircraft

Conceived in 1970s as a Twin Comanche replacement and as a twin-engined trainer. Developed from the PA-28R Archer, it featured a T-tail and swept fin, and first flew in May 1976. Turbocharged model introduced from 1980. Total delivered: 650.

VARIANTS
PA-44-180 Seminole: Initial production model with 180 hp engine
PA-44-180T Turbo Seminole: Turbocharged engine

SPECIFICATIONS: PA-44-180T
Accommodation: 1 + 3
Cargo/baggage: 91 kg (200 lb)
Max speed: 168 kt (311 km/h)
Range: 820 nm (1,517 km)

DIMENSIONS
Wingspan: 11.8 m (38 ft 7 in)
Length: 8.4 m (27 ft 7 in)
Height: 2.6 m (8 ft 6 in)

FEATURES
Low/straight tapered wing with leading edge wing gloves; twin Lycoming piston engine with three- or two-blade (turbocharged model) propellers; swept T-tail; retractable tricycle landing gear

PZL Warszawa PZL-104 Wilga Poland

Single-piston light general-purpose aircraft

Development of this rugged high-wing aircraft began in the early 1960s, with the prototype Wilga 1 making its maiden flight on 24 April 1962. Substantial redesign followed and the Wilga 2 flew in August 1963. Some early models also built in Indonesia by Lipnur Gelatik. The latest Wilga 2000 remains in production: Total delivered: 1,120+.

VARIANTS

PZL-104 Wilga 3: Initial production model in *3A* utility and *3S* ambulance versions

PZL-104 Wilga 32: Indonesian-built and modified Wilga 35

PZL-104 Wilga 35: Reconfigured cabin and landing gear

PZL-104 Wilga 80: Minor changes to air intake

PZL-104M Wilga 2000: Westernised version flown on 21 August 1996

PZL-104 MW Wilga 2000 Hydro: Floatplane

+ several subvariants of Wilga 35 and 80 models suffixed *A* for flying club use with glider towing hook, *H* floatplane, *P* ambulance with two stretchers, and *R* agricultural with underfuselage hooper and spraybars

SPECIFICATIONS: WILGA 2000

Accommodation: 1 + 3
Cargo/baggage: 35 kg (77 lb)
Max speed: 112 kt (208 km/h)
Range: 750 nm (1,390 km)

DIMENSIONS

Wingspan: 11.3 m (37 ft 1 in)
Length: 8.1 m (26 ft 7 in)

Height: 3.0 m (9 ft 11 in)

FEATURES

High/straight wing; single PZL AI-14 or Textron Lycoming IO-540 engine with two- or three-blade propeller respectively; swept wing with dorsal fillet and low-set tailplane; non-retractable tailwheel type landing gear

Robin DR 400 Petit Prince/Dauphin/ Major/Regent France

Single-piston light touring and training aircraft

Evolved from the Jodel taildraggers, combining the wing with a four-seat cabin and tricycle landing gear, the DR 400 Petit Prince first flew on 15 May 1972. It was subsequently developed into a number of improved models and for different roles, and remains in production as a tourer and gliding tug. Total delivered: 1,700+.

VARIANTS

DR.400-120 Petit Prince: 120 hp engine, forward sliding canopy

DR 400/120 Dauphin 2+2: Extra cabin windows and 2+2 seating

DR 400/140B Dauphin 4: Full four-seater, previously known as *Major 80*

DR 400/160 Major: Additional rear cabin window on each side, external baggage compartment door on port side

DR 400/180 Regent: 180 hp engine

DR 400/180R Remo 180: Glider tug, formerly named *Remorqueur*

+ several other earlier models distinguished largely through engine power

SPECIFICATIONS: REGENT

Accommodation: 1 + 3
Cargo/baggage: 60 kg (132 lb)
Max speed: 140 kt (260 km/h)
Range: 785 nm (1,453 km)

DIMENSIONS

Wingspan: 8.7 m (28 ft 7 in)
Length: 7.0 m (22 ft 10 in)
Height: 2.2 m (7 ft 3 in)

FEATURES

Low/straight tapered wing with upturned outer section; single Textron Lycoming engine with two-blade propeller; swept tailfin with low-set tailplane; fixed tricycle landing gear with wheel fairings; tail skid

Robin HR.100 Royal/Safari/R.1180 Aiglon France

Single-piston light aircraft

Low-wing all-metal design with spatted fixed tricycle landing gear and enclosed cabin for four people, the HR.100 first flew on 3 April 1969 and entered production in 1971. Unlike previous Robin Jodel designs, the HR.100 abandoned the traditional cranked wing shape. Total delivered: 174.

VARIANTS

HR.100-200B Royal: Initial production model with 200 hp engine
HR.100-210 Safari: 210 hp Continental engine, increased TOGW
HR.100-210D: Special designation German version
HR.100-250TR Tiara: 250 hp Continental Tiara engine, increased HGTOW
HR.100-285TR Tiara: More powerful 285 hp Continental Tiara
R.1180 Aiglon: Modified HR.100 with lighter airframe
R.1180T Aiglon: Longer cabin windows, more fuel
R.1180TD Aiglon II: New interior

SPECIFICATIONS

Accommodation: 1 + 4
Max speed: 135 kt (251 km/h)
Range: 878 nm (1,624 km)

DIMENSIONS

Wingspan: 9.1 m (29 ft 9 in)
Length: 7.6 m (24 ft 11 in)

Height: 2.7 m (8 ft 10 in)

FEATURES

Low/straight wing; single Continental or Lycoming engine with two-blade propeller; swept tailfin and low-set tailplane; fixed tricycle landing gear

Rockwell (Aero Commander) Commander 112/114 USA

Single-piston light touring aircraft

Designed by Rockwell's Aero Commander division, the low-wing four-seater with a retractable tricycle landing gear made its first flight on 4 December 1970. The first production aircraft was delivered in August 1972. More powerful versions followed, but production ceased in 1979. Total delivered: 1,310.

VARIANTS

112: Basic production model with 200 hp engine
112A: Strengthened airframe, metal cabin doors
112B: Increased wingspan, higher payload, new propeller and larger wheels
112TC: Turbocharged engine
112TC-A Alpine Commander: Similar improvements to 112B
114: More powerful 260 hp fuel-injected engine
114A Grand Turismo Commander: Similar airframe mods as 112B
114B: New propeller and external detail changes, interior restyling

SPECIFICATIONS: 114

Accommodation: 1 + 3
Cargo/baggage:
Max speed: 157 kt (290 km/h)
Range: 730 nm (1,350 km)

DIMENSIONS

Wingspan: 10.0 m (32 ft 9 in)
Length: 7.6 m (24 ft 11 in)
Height: 2.6 m (8 ft 6 in)

FEATURES

Low/straight dihedral wing; single Lycoming engine with two- or three-blade propeller; swept tailfin with dorsal fillet and mid-mounted tailplane; retractable tricycle landing gear

SIAI-Marchetti S.205/S.208 Italy

Single-piston light touring aircraft

Work on a four-seat, all-metal aircraft was started in March 1964, designed to form the basis of several models with different engine options and either fixed or retractable landing gear. The S.205 made its first flight in 1965, with the larger S.208 following in 1968. Total delivered: 620.

VARIANTS

S.205/18F: Initial production model with 180 hp engine and fixed landing gear
S.205/18R: Similar but retractable landing gear
S.205/20F: 200 hp engine
S.205/20R: 20F with retractable landing gear
S.205/22R: 220 hp Franklin engine, known as *Sirius* or *Vela* in the US
S.208: Five-seat versions, 260 hp engine
S.208M: Military derivative sold to Italian Air Force

SPECIFICATIONS: S.208

Accommodation: 1 + 4
Max speed: 162 kt (300 km/h)
Range: 973 nm (1,800 km)

DIMENSIONS

Wingspan: 11.2 m (36 ft 9 in)
Length: 8.1 m (26 ft 7 in)
Height: 2.9 m (9 ft 6 in)

FEATURES

Low/straight wing; single Lycoming or Franklin engine with two-blade propeller; tailfin with large dorsal fin and low-set tailplane; fixed or retractable tricycle landing gear

Socata GY Horizon/ST Diplomate France

Single-piston light aircraft

The original low-wing Horizon began life as a private design by Yves Gardan, who flew a prototype on 21 July 1960. Sud-Aviation acquired the manufacturing rights on 10 July 1962 and put the type into production in 1963. Transferred in 1966 to the new Socata works at Tarbes-Ossun.

An improved version, initially called the Super Horizon 200, flew on 7 November 1967. It later became the Provence and then the Diplomate. Total delivered: 267 (Horizon); 55 (Diplomate).

VARIANTS

GY-80-150 Horizon: Basic production version with 150 hp engine
GY-80-160 Horizon: Alternative higher-powered 160 hp model
GY-80-180 Horizon: More powerful 180 hp engine
ST-10 Diplomate: Stretched cabin and 200 hp fuel-injected engine

SPECIFICATIONS: HORIZON

Accommodation: 1 + 3
Cargo/baggage: 40 kg (88 lb)
Max speed: 126 kt (234 km/h)
Range: 515 nm (953 km)

DIMENSIONS

Wingspan: 9.7 m (31 ft 10 in)
Length: 6.6 m (21 ft 9 in)
Height: 2.6 m (8 ft 6 in)

FEATURES

Low/straight wing with outer dihedral; single Lycoming piston engine with two-bladed propeller; swept tailfin with small dorsal fillet and low-set tailplane; semi-retractable tricycle landing gear

Socata MS Rallye Club/Commodore France

Single-piston light touring and training aircraft

Originally designed by Moraine Saulnier, the first three-seater Rallye with tricycle landing gear and various aerodynamic innovations flew on 10 June 1959. Deliveries started at the end of 1961, leading to the production of a prolific family of light three/four-seat aircraft. Also built in Poland as the Koliber. Total delivered: 3,500+.

VARIANTS

MS.880B Rallye Club: Initial production version with 100 hp engine
MS.883 Rallye 115: Large dorsal fin and 115 hp engine
MS.885 Super Rallye: More powerful engine and increased weight
MS.892A Commodore: 145 hp engine, heavier airframe and enlarged tail unit, enhanced equipment fit
MS.893A Commodore 180: 180 hp engine and streamlined body
MS.894A Minerva 220: 220 hp Franklin engine, sold in US
Rallye 235GT Gabier: More powerful 235 hp engine
+ many other variants and subvariants too numerous to detail here

SPECIFICATIONS: MS.880B
Accommodation: 1 + 3
Cargo/baggage: 40 kg (88 lb)
Max speed: 105 kt (194 km/h)
Range: 460 nm (853 km)

DIMENSIONS
Wingspan: 9.6 m (31 ft 5 in)

Length: 7.0 m (22 ft 11 in)
Height: 2.7 m (8 ft 10 in)

FEATURES
Low/straight wing; single Continental, Lycoming or Franklin engine with two- or three-blade propeller; swept tailfin and low-set tailplane; fixed tricycle landing gear (skis or floats also used)

Socata TB Tampico/Tobago/Trinidad France

Single-piston light touring aircraft

Design work began in 1975 on a new aircraft intended to replace the successful Rallye series. Of conventional low-wing configuration, the prototype first flew on 23 February 1977, with initial deliveries commencing in September 1979. Similar but more powerful addition to the line followed in quick succession. Total delivered: 1,950+.

VARIANTS

TB 9 Tampico: Initial production model with 160 hp engine

TB 10 Tobago: More powerful 180 hp engine, faired undercarriage and higher gross weight

TB 200 Tobago XL: Fuel injected engine

TB 20 Trinidad: More powerful 250 hp engine, retractable gear

TB 20 Trinidad GT Premium: Limited edition deluxe version

TB 21 Trinidad: Turbocharged variant of TB 20 Tobago also built with fixed-pitch propeller suffixed *FP*, and with constant speed propeller suffixed *CS*; various improvements produced the *Tampico Club* and *Tampico Sprint* models. New, improved models from 2000 carry suffix *GT* (Generation Two).

SPECIFICATIONS: TB 200 TOBAGO GT

Accommodation: 1 + 4
Cargo/baggage: 45 kg (100 lb)
Max speed: 130 kt (241 km/h)
Range: 637 nm (1,180 km)

DIMENSIONS

Wingspan: 10.0 m (32 ft 9 in)
Length: 7.7 m (25 ft 3 in)
Height: 3.0 m (9 ft 11 in)

FEATURES

Low/straight dihedral wing with upturned wingtips; single Textron Lycoming engine with two-blade propeller; swept tailfin and low-set tailplane; fixed tricycle landing gear (retractable in Trinidad models)

CIVIL
HELICOPTERS

Aerospatiale SA 316B/319B Alouette III France

Single-turboshaft utility helicopter

Developed from the Alouette II, with larger cabin, greater power, improved equipment and higher performance. The prototype flew for the first time on 28 February 1958 and the type entered service in 1960. Total delivered: 1,523 (346 civil, 1,097 military). Hindustan Aeronautics continues to build small numbers under the name of Chetak.

VARIANTS

SE 3160: Initial production model
SA 316B: Artouste-powered version with strengthened transmission, higher gross weight and increased payload
IAR-316B: Built under licence by IAR in Romania
SA 319B: Similar to 316B but with Astazou XIV turboshaft
HAL Chetak: SA 316B built under licence in India

SPECIFICATIONS: SA 316B

Accommodation: 1 + 6
Cargo/baggage: 750 kg (1,653 lb)
Max speed: 113 kt (210 km/h)
Range: 257 nm (477 km)

DIMENSIONS

Main rotor diameter: 11.0 m (36 ft 1 in)
Length (rotors turning): 12.8 m (42 ft 1 in)
Height: 3.0 m (9 ft 9 in)

FEATURES

Three-blade rotor; single exposed Turbomeca Artouste or Astazou turboshaft; tricycle landing gear; enclosed cabin and tailboom; tricycle landing gear or fixed skids

Aerospatiale SA 315B Lama France

Single-turboshaft utility helicopter

Design of the Lama began in late 1968, initially to meet a requirement of the Indian armed forces. It combined the airframe of the Alouette II and the dynamic systems and engine of the Alouette III. A prototype was first flown on 17 March 1969, and the type went into service the following year. Total delivered: 418 (in France and Brazil). 245 in India where production continues.

VARIANTS

SA 315B Lama: French-built production model
SA 315B Gaviao: Small number built under licence by Helibras
HAL Cheetah: Licence-built by Hindustan Aeronautics in India

SPECIFICATIONS

Accommodation: 1 + 4
Cargo/baggage: 450 kg (992 lb)
Max speed: 113 kt (210 km/h)
Range: 296 nm (550 km)

DIMENSIONS

Main rotor diameter: 11.0 m (36 ft 1 in)
Length (rotors turning): 12.9 m (42 ft 4 in)
Height: 3.1 m (10 ft 2 in)

FEATURES

Three-blade main rotor/single exposed Turbomeca Artouste turboshaft; glazed bubble canopy; lattice tailboom; fixed skid landing gear with removable ground handling wheels

Agusta A 109 Italy

Twin-turbine light utility helicopter

Feasibility studies for medium-capacity twin-turbine model, began in 1969, led to the start of construction in summer 1970. Five prototypes were used in certification work, the first of which flew on 4 August 1971. Deliveries commenced in early 1976. Latest A 109 Power first flew in October 1994. Total delivered: 700+.

VARIANTS

A 109A: Initial production model with Allison 250 engines

A 109A MkII: Extensive improvements in equipment and systems fit

A 109A MkII Plus: Special law enforcement model

A 109C: More powerful engines and 'widebody' interior

A 109K2: SAR and police version with special equipment

A 109MAX: Medevac model with upward-opening 'bulged' doors

A 109 Power: Extensively upgraded version based on K2 airframe, but wider, new FADEC-equipped P&WC engines and new landing gear

SPECIFICATIONS: A 109 POWER

Accommodation: 1 + 7
Cargo/baggage: 1,000 kg (2,204 lb)
Max speed: 154 kt (285 km/h)
Range: 528 nm (977 km)

DIMENSIONS

Main rotor diameter 11.0 m (36 ft 1 in)
Length (rotors turning): 13.0 m (42 ft 9 in)
Height: 3.5 m (11 ft 6 in)

FEATURES

Four-blade main rotor and two-blade tail rotor; twin Rolls-Royce 250 or P&WC PW206C turboshafts; swept upper and lower vertical fin; retractable tricycle landing gear

Agusta A 119 Koala Italy

Single-turbine light helicopter

Go-ahead for single engine version based on the
A 109 given in August 1994, with first flight early
in 1995. Initially flown with Turbomeca Arriel, but
Pratt & Whitney Canada PT6B adopted for
production model. First delivered in summer 1999.
Total delivered: 32.

VARIANTS

A 119 Koala: Only production model to date

SPECIFICATIONS

Accommodation: 1 + 7
Cargo/baggage: 1,420 kg (3,130 lb)
Max speed: 150 kt (278 km/h)
Range: 479 nm (886 km)

DIMENSIONS

Main rotor diameter: 10.8 m (36 ft 6 in)
Length (rotors turning): 13.0 m (42 ft 9 in)
Height: 3.8 m (12 ft 5 in)

FEATURES

Four-blade main rotor and two-blade tail rotor;
twin P&WC PT6B turboshafts; swept upper
vertical fin and horizontal stabilisers at rear of tail
boom; fixed skid landing gear; large tail skid

Bell 47 USA

Single-piston general utility helicopter

Made its first flight on 8 December 1945 and granted first helicopter type certificate in the USA on 8 March 1946. Produced in many versions, and also under licence by Agusta as the AB-47; Kawasaki as the KH-4; and Westland in the UK for the army. Total delivered: 5,048.

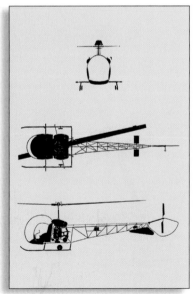

VARIANTS

47G-2: Initial production version with Lycoming engine

47G-3: More powerful and later turbocharged engine

47G-4A: Basic three-seat utility version from December 1965

47G-5: Low-cost models with non-essential removed

47H-1: De-luxe version with enclosed and soundproofed cabin

47J Ranger: Redesigned with fully enclosed cabin and bench-seat

H-13: US military designation (which see)

SPECIFICATIONS: 47G-4A

Accommodation: 1 + 2
Cargo/baggage: 454 kg (1,000 lb)
Max speed: 91 kt 9169 km/h)
Range: 225 nm (416 km)

DIMENSIONS

Main rotor diameter: 11.3 m (37 ft 1 in)
Length (rotors turning): 13.2 m (43 ft 3 in)
Height: 2.8 m (9 ft 3 in)

FEATURES

Twin-blade main rotor; single Franklin or Lycoming piston engine; bubble canopy; lattice tail boom with twin-blade tail rotor; fixed skid landing gear with small ground handling wheels

Bell 206 JetRanger USA

Single-turbine light helicopter

Developed from a losing design for a Light Observation Helicopter (LOH) for the US Army and targeted at civil market. First flight was made on 10 January 1966 and first deliveries in same month a year later. Also built under licence by Agusta as the AB 206. Total delivered: 5,000+.

250 turboshaft; swept upper and lower vertical fins; horizonta stabilisers at mid-section tail boom; fixed skid landing gear; two side windows

VARIANTS

206A JetRanger: Initial production model with Allison 250-C18
206B JetRanger II: More powerful 250-C20 engine
206B JetRanger III: Current model with greater power
TH-57 SeaRanger: US Navy primary trainer
TH-67 Creek: US Army pilot trainer
OH-58 Kiowa: Military version (which see)

SPECIFICATIONS: 206B JETRANGER III
Accommodation: 1 + 5
Cargo/baggage: 680 kg (1,500 lb)
Max speed: 115 kt (214 km/h)
Range: 365 nm (676 km)

DIMENSIONS
Main rotor diameter: 10.2 m (33 ft 4 in)
Length (rotors turning): 11.8 m (38 ft 9 in)
Height: 3.2 m (10 ft 5 in)

FEATURES
Twin-blade main and tail rotor; single Rolls-Royce

Bell 206L LongRanger USA

Single-turbine light helicopter

Stretched derivative of JetRanger to increase seating capacity from five to seven, announced on 25 September 1973. Made its first flight on 11 September 1974, with first deliveries early 1976. Total delivered to date: 1,700.

VARIANTS

206L LongRanger: Initial model powered by 250-C20B

206L-1 LongRanger II: Higher-powered version from 1978

206L-3 LongRanger III: Improved performance from 1982

206L-4 LongRanger IV: Improved current standard available from December 1992

206LT TwinRanger: Small number twin-engine versions built from new, others converted from L-3 and L-4 models by Tridair as the Gemini ST.

SPECIFICATIONS:
206L-4 LONGRANGER IV

Accommodation: 1 + 7
Cargo/baggage: 907 kg (2,000 lb)
Max speed: 112 kt (207 km/h)
Range: 321 nm (595 km)

DIMENSIONS

Main rotor diameter: 11.3 m (37 ft 0 in)
Length (rotors turning): 13. 0 m (42 ft 7 in)
Height: 3.1 m (10 ft 3 in)

FEATURES

Twin-blade main and tail rotor; single Rolls-Royce 250 turboshaft (two in 206LT); swept upper and lower vertical fins; horizontal stabilisers at mid-section tailboom; fixed skid landing gear; three side windows

Bell 214 USA

Twin-turboshaft intermediate helicopter

Developed from the Huey and first delivered as military models to Iran from 26 April 1975. Commercial variant announced on 4 January 1974 as 214B, and later stretched as the 214ST, which first flew in February 1977. Total civil delivered: 65 (214B), 96 (214ST).

vertical tailfin with top-mounted two-blade tail rotor; large horizontal stabilser at rear; non-retractable skid or wheeled landing gear

VARIANTS

214A: Initial model delivered to the Iranian Imperial Forces
214B BigLifter: Commercial version with Lycoming T5508Ds
214B-1: As 214B, but with restricted internal gross weight
214ST: Stretched derivative, also known as Super Transporter

SPECIFICATIONS: 214ST

Accommodation: 2 + 18
Cargo/baggage: 3,628 kg (8,000 lb)
Max speed: 140 kt (259 km/h)
Range: 463 nm (858 km)

DIMENSIONS

Main rotor diameter: 15.9 m (52 ft 0 in)
Length (rotors turning): 19.0 m (62 ft 3 in)
Height: 4.8 m (15 ft 10 in)

FEATURES

Two-blade main rotor; twin Lycoming T5508D (214B) or GE CT7 (214ST) turboshafts; large swept

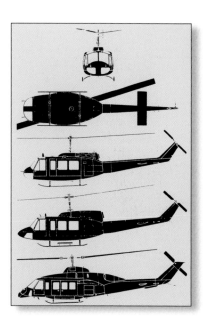

Bell 222 USA

Twin-turboshaft intermediate helicopter

First commercial light twin helicopter in the USA, making its maiden flight on 13 August 1976. First delivery, to Petroleum Helicopters, made on 16 January 1980. Production ceased in 1989. Total delivered: 188.

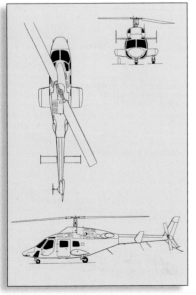

VARIANTS

222A: Initial production model with Lycoming LTS 101 turboshafts
222B: More powerful LTS 101 engines and larger main rotor
222B Executive: Improved systems and luxury interior
222UT: Utility version; skid gear with lock-on ground handling wheels

SPECIFICATIONS: 222B

Accommodation: 1 + 7
Cargo/baggage: 1,134 kg (2,500 lb)
Max speed: 150 kt (278 km/h)
Range: 255 nm (472 km)

DIMENSIONS

Main rotor diameter: 12.8 m (42 ft 0 in)
Length (rotors turning): 15.4 m (50 ft 5 in)
Height: 3.5 m (11 ft 6 in)

FEATURES

Two-blade main rotor; twin LTS 101 turboshafts; swept upper and lower vertical fins with two-blade tail rotor; mid-section horizontal stabilisers with swept endplate fins; retractable tricycle or skid type gear with ground wheels

Bell 230 USA

Twin-turbine intermediate helicopter

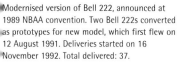

Modernised version of Bell 222, announced at 1989 NBAA convention. Two Bell 222s converted as prototypes for new model, which first flew on 12 August 1991. Deliveries started on 16 November 1992. Total delivered: 37.

with two-blade tail rotor and tail skid; mid-section horizontal stabiliser with swept endplate fins; retractable tricycle or skid type landing gear; short span sponsons on fuselage sides

VARIANTS

230 Executive: Basic production aircraft for corporate use
230 Utility: Model for general transport applications
230 EMS: Air ambulance version with one or two stretchers and three or four medical attendants

SPECIFICATIONS

Accommodation: 2 + 7
Cargo/baggage: 1,270 kg (2,800 lb)
Max speed: 141 kt (261 km/h)
Range: 385 nm (713 km)

DIMENSIONS

Main rotor diameter: 12.8 m (42 ft 0 in)
Length (rotors turning): 15.3 m (50 ft 2 in)
Height: 3.7 m (12 ft 2 in)

FEATURES

Two-blade main rotor; twin Rolls-Royce 250-C30 turboshafts; swept upper and lower vertical fins

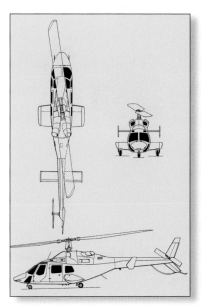

Bell 407 USA/Canada

Single-turbine light helicopter

Design definition launched in 1993 and concept demonstrator (modified 206L-4) first flown on 21 April 1994. Officially launched at Heli-Expo in Las Vegas in January 1995, leading to first flight of prototype on 1 June that same year. First delivery in February 1996. Total delivered: 600.

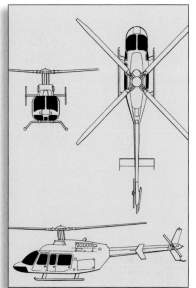

VARIANTS
407: Initial production model

SPECIFICATIONS
Accommodation: 2 + 5
Cargo/baggage: 1,200 kg (2,646 lb)
Max speed: 128 kt (237 km/h)
Range: 312 nm (577 km)

DIMENSIONS
Main rotor diameter: 10.7 m (35 ft 0 in)
Length (rotors turning): 12.7 m (41 ft 9 in)
Height: 3.6 m (11 ft 10 in)

FEATURES
Four-blade main rotor; single Rolls-Royce209 250-C47B turboshaft; swept upper and lower vertical fins with two-blade tail rotor and tail skid; mid-section horizontal stabiliser with swept endplate fins; fixed skid landing gear; tail skid

Bell 412 USA/Canada

Twin-turboshaft intermediate helicopter

Development of Bell Model 212 announced on 8 September 1978, featuring an advanced four-blade rotor design. Two new 212s were modified for certification programme, with flight trials starting on 4 August 1979. First delivery made on 18 January 1981. Also licence-built in Indonesia by ITPN as *NBell-412* and in Italy by Agusta as *AB412EP*. Total delivered to date (civil only) 525.

VARIANTS

412: Initial model powered by P&WC PT6T-3b turboshafts
412EP: Enhanced Performance version
412HP: Improved transmission
412SP: Special Performance version with increased T-O weight and better seating
Griffon: Military variants (which see)

SPECIFICATIONS: 412EP

Accommodation: 2 + 14
Cargo/baggage: 2,041 kg (4,800 lb)
Max speed: 122 kt (226 km/h)
Range: 402 nm (745 km)

DIMENSIONS

Main rotor diameter: 14.0 m (46 ft 0 in)
Length (rotors turning): 17.1 m (56 ft 2 in)
Height: 4.6 m (15 ft 0 in)

FEATURES

Four-blade main rotor; twin P&WC PT6T

turboshafts; swept vertical fin with top-mounted two-blade tail rotor; horizontal stabilisers at rear; high skid, emergency pop-out float or non-retractable tricycle landing gear; fixed stabilisers

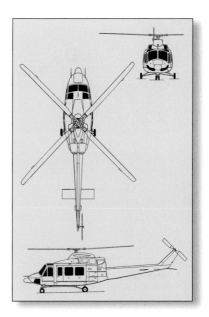

Bell 427 USA

Twin-turboshaft light helicopter

Collaborative programme between Bell and Samsung announced at Heli Expo 96. Based on Bell 407 but slightly longer, the Model 427 made its first flight on 11 December 1997 and entered service in early 2000. Final assembly by Bell at Mirabel, Canada, and by Samsung at Sachon plant for China and Korea. Total delivered: 35.

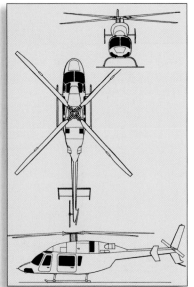

VARIANTS
427: Initial production model

SPECIFICATIONS
Accommodation: 1 + 6
Cargo/baggage: 1,361 kg (3,000 lb)
Max speed: 140 kt (259 km/h)
Range: 390 nm (722 km)

DIMENSIONS
Main rotor diameter: 11.3 m (37 ft 0 in)
Length (rotors turning): 13.1 m (42 ft 11 in)
Height: 3.5 m (11 ft 6 in)

FEATURES
Four-blade main rotor; twin P&WC PW207 turboshafts; fixed high or low skids or emergency floats; swept upper and lower vertical fins; midway mounted horizontal stabilisers with endplate fins

Bell 430 USA/Canada

Twin-turboshaft intermediate helicopter

Stretched, four-blade rotor and higher-powered variant of Bell 230. Prototype modified from Bell 230 first flew on 25 October 1994. Deliveries began on 25 June 1996. Total delivered: 100.

VARIANTS

430: Initial production model with Rolls-Royce209 250-C40B turboshafts

SPECIFICATIONS

Accommodation: 2 + 9
Cargo/baggage: 1,587 kg (3,500 lb)
Max speed: 138 kt (256 km/h)
Range: 272 nm (503 km)

DIMENSIONS

Main rotor diameter: 12.8 m (42 ft 0 in)
Length (rotors turning): 15.3 m (50 ft 3 in)
Height: 4.0 m (13 ft 2 in)

FEATURES

Four-blade main rotor; twin Rolls-Royce209 250 turboshafts; fixed skid or retractable tricycle landing gear; swept upper and lower vertical fins; small tail skid; mid-way mounted horizontal stabilisers with endplate fins; short-span sponsons on fuselage side

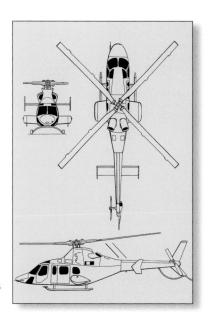

Bell/Agusta AB 139 USA/Italy

Twin-turboshaft intermediate helicopter

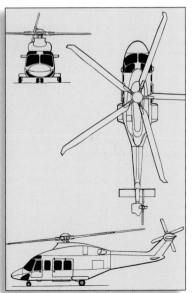

Joint development programme for multirole helicopter announced at the Farnborough Air Show in September 1998. Many risk-sharing partners. First flight on 3 February 2001, with certification and deliveries planned for 2002. Total delivered: 5.

VARIANTS
AB 139: Initial civil version
AB 139 Military: Proposed version for all-weather operations

SPECIFICATIONS
Accommodation: 1 + 15
Cargo/baggage: 2,700 kg (5,952 lb)
Max speed: 157 kt (290 km/h)
Range: 400 nm (740 km)

DIMENSIONS
Main rotor diameter: 13.8 m (45 ft 3 in)
Length overall, rotors turning: 16.7 m (54 ft 8 in)
Height: 5.0 m (16 ft 3 in)

FEATURES
Five-blade main rotor and four-blade tail rotor mounted atop swept tailfin on right; twin P&WC PT6C turboshafts; tricycle landing gear retracting into side sponsons

Brantly B-2B USA

Single-piston light utility helicopter

Developed from the B-1 by N O Brantly and made its maiden flight as long ago as 1953. First deliveries made in 1960. Underwent several ownership changes since, as well as some breaks in production. Presently in production by Brantly International. Total delivered: 336.

VARIANTS

B-2A: Initial production version
B-2B: Improved model with new metal rotor blades and fuel-injected Lycoming piston engine
H-2: Designation of B-2B when produced by Brantly-Hynes between 1976 and 1979

SPECIFICATIONS: B-2B

Accommodation: 1 + 1
Cargo/baggage: 113 kg (250 lb)
Max speed: 87 kt (161 km/h)
Range: 217 nm 9400 km)

DIMENSIONS

Main rotor diameter: 7.2 m (23 ft 9 in)
Length (rotors turning): 8.5 m (28 ft 0 in)
Height: 2.1 m (6 ft 9 in)

FEATURES

Three-blade main rotor; single Textron Lycoming IVO-360 air-cooled engine; slightly swept vertical fin with top-mounted two-blade tail rotor and tail skid; fixed skid or float gear and fixed tailskid; bubble canopy

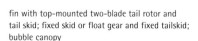

Enstrom F28/280 USA

Single-piston light utility helicopter

Development of this three-seater helicopter started in 1960, leading to the first flight of the F-28 on 27 May 1962. Continuously updated and built side-by-side with aerodynamically refined 280 Shark. Total delivered: 972.

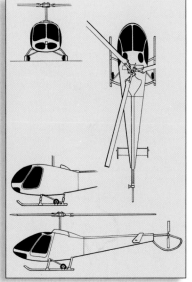

VARIANTS

F28A: Initial production version
F28C: Turbocharged with two-piece windscreen
F28C-2: Similar but single piece windscreen and new console
F28F Falcon: Present much improved model
F28F-P Sentinel: Dedicated police patrol version with searchlight, FLIR and PA systems
280 Shark: Aerodynamic restyling for corporate market
280C Shark: Aerodynamically refined version of F28C-2
280FX Shark: New seats, new tailplane and faired landing gear

SPECIFICATIONS: 280FX

Accommodation: 1 + 2
Cargo/baggage: 49 kg (108 lb)
Max speed: 102 kt (189 km/h)
Range: 260 nm (483 km)

DIMENSIONS

Main rotor diameter: 9.8 m (32 ft 0 in)
Length: 8.9 m (29 ft 3 in)
Height: 2.7 m (9 ft 0 in)

FEATURES

Three-blade main rotor; single Textron Lycoming HIO-360 turbocharged piston engine; fixed skids or floats; tailboom with horizontal stabilisers and swept endplate fins to rear; large tail skid protection for two-blade tail rotor

Enstrom 480 USA

Single-turboshaft light helicopter

Developed to meet US Army training requirement, but lost out to Bell. Definitive wide cabin 480/TH-28 flown for first time in October 1989 and first delivery following FAA certification in 1994. Total delivered 66.

VARIANTS

480: Initial civil version with four staggered seats or convertible to three-seat training/executive layout
480B: Enhanced and more powerful version available since early 2001
TH-28: Military training/light patrol version with crashworthy seats and fuel tanks

SPECIFICATIONS: 480B

Accommodation: 1 + 4
Cargo/baggage: 592 kg (1,305 lb)
Max speed: 125 kt (231 km/h)
Range: 435 nm (806 km)

DIMENSIONS

Main rotor diameter: 9.8 m (32 ft 0 in)
Length: 9.1 m (29 ft 10 in)
Height: 3.0 m (9 ft 10 in)

FEATURES

Three-blade main rotor; single Rolls-Royce 250 turboshaft; fixed skids or popout floats; tailboom with horizontal stabilisers and swept endplate fins to rear; large tail skid protection for two-blade tail rotor

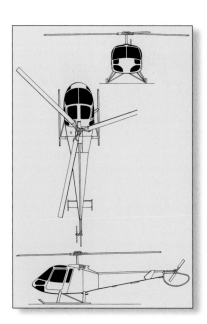

Eurocopter EC 120 Colibri
France/Germany/China/Singapore

Single-turboshaft light helicopter

Multi-national partnership programme launched on 15 February 1990. Similar to EC 135 but new single Turbomeca Arrius 2F turboshaft and new generation fenestron tail rotor. First flight on 9 June 1995, followed by first delivery on 23 January 1998. Total delivered: 340.

VARIANTS
EC 120B: Initial production version, available with mission specific kits for passenger, corporate, police, training and EMS work

SPECIFICATIONS
Accommodation: 1 + 4
Cargo/baggage: 700 kg (1,543 lb)
Max speed: 150 kt (278 km/h)
Range: 395 nm (732 km)

DIMENSIONS
Main rotor diameter: 10.0 m (32 ft 10 in)
Length (blades folded): 11.5 m 937 ft 9 in)
Height: 3.4 m (11 ft 2 in)

FEATURES
Three-blade main rotor and 8-blade shrouded fenestron tail rotor; single Turbomeca Arrius turboshaft; fixed skid landing gear; horizontal stabiliser at rear

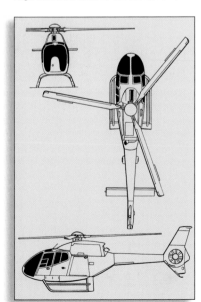

Eurocopter EC 130 France/Germany

Single-turboshaft light helicopter

Derived from the AS 350 B3 Ecureuil, but with fenestron tail rotor and wider cabin. First flown in June 1999, with deliveries starting after the model was revealed at Heli-Expo 01 in Las Vegas in February. Total delivered: 75.

VARIANTS
EC 130 B4: Initial production version

SPECIFICATIONS
Accommodation: 1 + 7
Cargo/baggage: 400 kg (882 lb)
Max speed: 155 kt (287 km/h)
Range: 345 nm (640 km/h)

DIMENSIONS
Main rotor diameter: 10.7 m (35 ft 1 in)
Length (rotors turning): 12.6 m (41 ft 4 in)
Height: 3.6 m 911 ft 10 in)

FEATURES
Three-blade main rotor and 10-blade shrouded fenestron tail rotor; horizontal stabilisers at rear; single Turbomeca Arriel turboshaft; fixed skid landing gear; tail skid

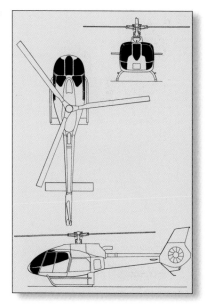

Eurocopter EC 135 France/Germany

Twin-turbine light helicopter

Designed to succeed BO 105 and technology prototype designated BO 108 made first flight on 15 October 1988. Design progressively improved and pre-production model with advanced fenestron tail rotor flown on 15 February 1994.

Deliveries began on 31 July 1996. Total delivered: 330.

VARIANTS

EC 135 P1: Pratt & Whitney-powered production model
EC 135 T1: Turbomeca-powered alternative
EC 635 P1: Multi-mission armed or unarmed, with P&WC engines
EC 635 T1: Multi-mission armed or unarmed version with Turbomeca engines

SPECIFICATIONS

Accommodation: 1 + 7
Cargo/baggage: 1,361 kg (3,000 lb)
Max speed: 150 kt (278 km/h)
Range: 402 nm (745 km)

DIMENSIONS

Main rotor diameter: 10.2 m (33 ft 6 in)
Length (rotors turning): 12.2 m (39 ft 11 in)
Height: 3.6 m (11 ft 10 in)

FEATURES

Four-blade main rotor and 11-blade shrouded fenestron tail rotor; twin P&WC PW206 or Turbomeca Arrius turboshafts; fixed skid landing gear, horizontal stabiliser with swept end plate fins

Eurocopter EC 155 France/Germany

Twin-turboshaft intermediate helicopter

Higher performance development of successful
Dauphin 2 series, first unveiled at Paris Air Show
in June 1997; initially designated AS 365 N4.
Main differences are new five-blade main rotor
and redesigned wide-body cabin. First flight on 17
June 1997, with first deliveries in March 1999.
Total delivered: 50.

VARIANTS

EC 155B: Initial production model
EC 155B1: More powerful Arriel 2C2 engines

SPECIFICATIONS

Accommodation: 2 + 12
Cargo/baggage: 2,000 kg (4,409 lb)
Max speed: 170 kt (315 km/h)
Range: 448 nm (830 km)

DIMENSIONS

Main rotor diameter: 12.6 m (41 ft 4 in)
Length (rotors turning): 14.4 m (47 ft 4 in)
Height: 4.4 m (14 ft 4 in)

FEATURES

Five-blade main rotor and 10-blade shrouded
fenestron tail rotor; tailboom stabilisers with
swept downward endplate fins at rear; retractable
tricycle landing gear

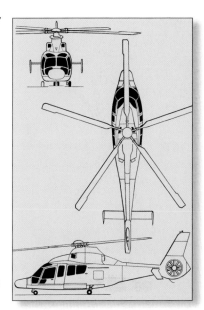

Eurocopter (Aerospatiale)
AS 332 Super Puma France/Germany

Twin-turbine intermediate helicopter

Extensively improved derivative of SA 330 Puma, receiving formal go-ahead from the French Government in June 1975. Prototype flew for the first time on 13 September 1978. First civil model delivered in 1981. Total built to date (civil/paramilitary only): 166.

VARIANTS
AS 332 C: Initial civil version
AS 332 C1: SAR version with search radar and six stretchers
AS 332 L: As 332 C but lengthened fuselage and increased fuel
AS 332 L1: Long fuselage and airline interior
AS 332 L2: Mk II Super Puma with Spheriflex rotor head and EFIS
EC 225: New five-bladed main rotor, new engines, increased gross weight
AS 532 and EC 725 Cougar: Military versions (which see)

SPECIFICATIONS: AS 332 L2
Accommodation: 2 + 24
Cargo/baggage: 5,000 kg (11,023 lb)
Max speed: 177 kt 9327 km/h)
Range: 460 nm (851 km)

DIMENSIONS
Main rotor diameter: 16.2 m (53 ft 2 in)
Length (rotors turning): 19.5 m (63 ft 11 in)
Height: 4.9 m (16 ft 2 in)

FEATURES
Four- or five-blade main rotor and five-blade tail rotor on side of tailboom; twin Turbomeca Makila turboshafts; retractable tricycle landing gear; lateral sponsons

Eurocopter (Aerospatiale)
AS 350 Ecureuil/AStar France/Germany

Single-turboshaft light helicopter

Developed as successor to Alouette, the Ecureuil (Squirrel) embodies Aerospatiale's Starflex-type rotor head. It first flew on 27 June 1974 and entered service early in 1978. Built in France and by Helibras in Brazil. Total delivered (civil/paramilitary only): 2,400.

VARIANTS
AS 350 B: Initial production model with Turbomeca Arriel 1
AS 350 B1: More powerful, higher weight replacement from 1987
AS 350 B2: Further increase in engine power, new rotor blades
AS 350 B3: Improved with Arriel 2 with FADEC
AS 350C AStar: Original Lycoming-powered version for US market
AS 350D AStar: Improved for US market
AS 550 Fennec: Military versions (which see)

SPECIFICATIONS: AS 350 B3
Accommodation: 1 + 5
Cargo/baggage: 550 kg (1,213 lb)
Max speed: 155 kt (287 km/h)
Range: 360 nm (666 km)

DIMENSIONS
Main rotor diameter: 10.7 m (35 ft 1 in)
Length (rotors turning): 12.9 m (42 ft 5 in)
Height: 3.1 m (10 ft 3 in)

FEATURES
Three-blade main rotor and two-blade tail rotor on right; single Turbomeca Arriel or Honeywell (AlliedSignal) LTS101 turboshaft; fixed skid landing gear; swept fins above and below tail; horizontal stabilisers at rear

Eurocopter (Aerospatiale)
AS 355 Ecureuil II France/Germany

Twin-turboshaft light helicopter

Development of this twin-engined version of the AS 350 began in mid-1978. Largely similar, but major changes to rotor blades, power plant, transmission, fuel system and fuselage structure. First flew on 28 September 1979, followed by customer deliveries in January 1981. Total delivered (civil/paramilitary only): 563.

VARIANTS
AS 355 E: Initial production model with Allison 250 turboshafts
AS 355 F: Improved rotor blades and systems
AS 355 F1: Increased power, weight and payload
AS 355 F2: Upgraded transmission and higher gross weight
AS 355 N: Current improved civil production version. Known as *TwinStar* in the US
AS 555 Fennec: Military versions (which see)

SPECIFICATIONS: AS 355 N
Accommodation: 1 + 5
Cargo/baggage: 1,134 kg (2,500 lb)
Max speed: 150 kt (278 km/h)
Range: 389 nm (722 km)

DIMENSIONS
Main rotor diameter: 10.7 m (35 ft 1 in)
Length (rotors turning): 12.9 m (42 ft 5 in)
Height: 3.1 m (10 ft 3 in)

FEATURES
Three-blade main rotor and two-blade tail rotor on right; twin Turbomeca Arrius turboshafts; fixed skid landing gear; swept fins above and below tail; horizontal stabilisers at rear

Eurocopter (Aerospatiale)
AS 365 Dauphin France/Germany

Twin-turboshaft intermediate helicopter

Developed initially as a single-engined replacement for the Alouette III under designation SA 360 Dauphin, but limited success. First twin-engined SA 365 Dauphin 2 flew on 24 January 1975 with Astazou engines and characteristic fenestron tail rotor. Prefix SA (Sud-Aviation) later changed to AS (Aerospatiale). Total delivered (civil/paramilitary only): 550.

VARIANTS
SA 360: Initial single-engined model
AS 365 C: Twin-turboshaft production version
AS 365 N: Improved model with 90 new components
AS 365 N1: Power reserve-margin increase through Turbomeca Arriel 1s
AS 365 N2: Further improvements
AS 365 N3: Improved hot-and-high performance with FADEC- equipped Arriel 2s
AS 565 Panther: Military versions (which see)

SPECIFICATIONS: AS 365 N2
Accommodation: 1 + 12
Cargo/baggage: 1,600 kg (3,527 lb)
Max speed: 155 kt (287 km/h)
Range: 464 nm (859 km)

DIMENSIONS
Main rotor diameter: 11.9 m (39 ft 2 in)
Length (rotors turning): 13.7 m (44 ft 11 in)
Height: 4.0 m (13 ft 1 in)

FEATURES
Four-blade main rotor and 11-blade shrouded fenestron tail rotor; twin Turbomeca Arriel turboshafts; retractable tricycle landing gear; horizontal stabiliser with endplate fins at rear

Eurocopter (MBB) BO 105 Germany

Twin-turboshaft light helicopter

Development began in July 1962 and first flying prototype took to the air in Germany on 16 February 1967. Many design changes undertaken. Full-scale production commenced in 1972. Total delivered (civil/paramilitary only): 680.

VARIANTS

BO 105 C: Initial version with choice of Allison 250 engines

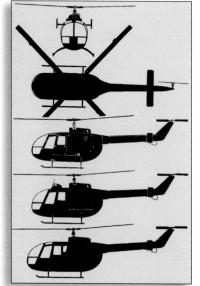

BO 105 CB: Improved engines and better hot-and-high performance
BO 105 CBS-4: Small cabin extension for more leg room. Named Twin Jet II in US
BO 105 D: UK certified offshore version
BO 105 LS: Increased power, built in Canada
BO 105 LSA-3: Hot-and-high version, solely built in Canada
BO 105 LSA-3 Super Lifter: Optimised for external load missions, built in Canada
EC Super Five: High performance version of CBS-4
+ several armed/unarmed military derivatives (which see)

SPECIFICATIONS: CBS-4
Accommodation: 1 + 5
Cargo/baggage: 800 kg (1,764 lb)
Max speed: 131 kt (242 km/h)
Range: 305 nm (565 km)

DIMENSIONS
Main rotor diameter: 9.8 m (32 ft 3 in)
Length (rotors turning): 11.9 m (38 ft 11 in)
Height: 3.0 m (9 ft 11 in)

FEATURES
Four-blade main rotor; twin Rolls-Royce 250 turboshafts; fixed skid landing gear; horizontal stabiliser with small endplate fins at rear of high tailboom; swept tail fin with top-mounted two-blade tail rotor

Eurocopter/Kawasaki BK 117 France/Germany/Japan

Twin-turboshaft intermediate helicopter

Developed under joint agreement signed on 25 February 1977 between MBB and Kawasaki. First of four prototypes flew on 13 June 1979 and deliveries began in early 1983. Built in Germany and Japan. Total delivered: 520.

VARIANTS

BK 117 A: Initial production version with Lycoming LTS101s

BK 117 A-1: Increased T-O weight

BK 117 A-3: Further growth in T-O weight and enlarged tail rotor

BK 117 A-4: Uprated transmission and improved tail rotor head

BK 117 B-1: Further improvements

BK 117 B-1C: UK certified with reduced range and endurance

BK 117 B-2: Production model from 1992, increased T-O weight

BK 117 C-1: New cockpit and Arriel engines

BK 117 C-2: Larger cabin, increased payload

EC 145: European-built version of BK 117 C-2

SPECIFICATIONS: BK 117 C-2

Accommodation: 1 + 9

Cargo/baggage: 1,700 kg (3,748 lb)

Max speed: 145 kt (268 km/h)

Range: 378 nm (700 km)

DIMENSIONS

Main rotor diameter: 11.0 m (36 ft 1 in)

Length (rotors turning): 13.0 m (42 ft 8 in)

Height: 3.8 m (12 ft 7 in)

FEATURES

Four-blade main rotor; twin Honeywell (AlliedSignal) LTS101 or Turbomeca Arriel turboshafts; fixed skid landing gear with ground handling wheels; detachable tailcone with tail rotor and horizontal stabiliser with large offset endplate fins

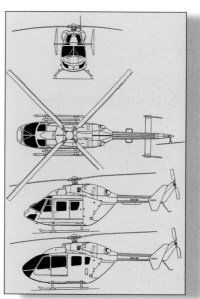

Hiller UH-12 USA

Single-piston light utility helicopter

Designed by Stanley Hiller and derived from the Model 360 of 1948. Initially produced for US military as H-23 Raven. Production ceased in 1983, but few subsequently built first by Rogerson-Hiller, then a newly constituted Hiller Aircraft. Total delivered: 2,595.

VARIANTS

UH-12A: Original model powered by Franklin piston engine

UH-12B: Improved trainer used by US Navy

UH-12C: All-metal rotor blades and 'goldfish bowl' canopy

UH-12D: US Army version; Lycoming V-540

UH-12E: Increased Lycoming power

UH-12ET: Allison 250-powered turbine version

UH-12E3: New three-seat production version

UH-12E3T: Turbine-powered new production version

UH-12E4: Four-seat configuration; anhedral stabiliser

UH-12E4T: Turbine-powered version of four-seat configuration

UH-12L-4: Lengthened and wider cabin doors

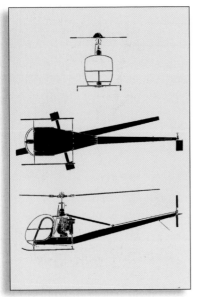

SPECIFICATIONS: UH-12E3

Accommodation: 1 + 2
Cargo/baggage: 600 kg (1,323 lb)
Max speed: 83 kt (154 km/h)
Range: 202 nm 9373 km)

DIMENSIONS

Main rotor diameter: 10.8 m (35 ft 5 in)
Length (rotors turning): 12.4 m (40 ft 8 in)
Height: 3.1 m (10 ft 2 in)

FEATURES

Two-blade main rotor; single Franklin or Lycoming piston engine, or Allison 250 turbine; bubble canopy; thin sloped tailboom with two-blade tail rotor and tail skid

Kaman K-MAX USA

Single-turbine external lift helicopter

Developed for external lift operations and first flown on 23 December 1991. Made public debut in March 1992. First deliveries following certification in August 1994, but small production run. Total delivered: 31.

VARIANTS
K-1200 K-MAX: Basic production version

SPECIFICATIONS
Accommodation: Pilot only
Cargo/baggage: 2,721 kg (6,000 lb)
Max speed: 100 kt (185 km/h)
Range: 300 nm (555 km)

DIMENSIONS
Main rotor diameter: 14.7 m (48 ft 4 in)
Length (rotors turning): 15.9 m (52 ft 1 in)
Height: 4.1 m (13 ft 7 in)

FEATURES
Twin two-blade intermeshing main rotors; no tail rotor; single Lycoming turboshaft; tricycle landing gear; single tailfin and mid-mounted tailplane with endplate fins

Kamov Ka-26/126 'Hoodlum' Russia

Twin-piston light helicopter

Versatile machine developed for agricultural and other aerial work and first flown in 1965. Notable for the interchangeable modules aft of the flight deck for passenger/freight transport, aerial ambulance, firefighting and more. Entered service in the Soviet Union in 1970. Total delivered: 850+.

VARIANTS
Ka-26: Basic production model
Ka-126: Turbine-powered development

SPECIFICATIONS
Accommodation: 1 + 6
Cargo/baggage: 1,100 kg (2,425 lb)
Max speed: 91 kt (170 km/h)
Range: 215 nm (400 km)

DIMENSIONS
Main rotor diameter: 13.0 m (42 ft 8 in)
Length (of fuselage): 7.8 m (25 ft 7 in)
Height: 4.1 m (13 ft 4 in)

FEATURES
Twin four-blade coaxial contrarotating main rotors; twin Vedeneyev air-cooled piston engines mounted in pods on short stub wings at top of fuselage; twin tailboom with horizontal stabiliser and large downward oriented endplate fins

Kamov Ka-32 'Helix-C' Russia

Twin-turbine medium helicopter

Developed jointly with KA-27 naval model and features typical Kamov contrarotating rotors. First Ka-32 flew on 11 January 1980 and exhibited at Minsk in late 1981. Total delivered: 125+.

VARIANTS

Ka-32A: Initial production version
Ka-32A1: Firefighting version equipped with Bambi bucket
Ka-32A2: Police version with two searchlights and loudspeaker
Ka-32A3: Special version for rescue, salvage and evacuation
Ka-32A7: Armed version developed from military Ka-27PS
Ka-32A11BC: Transport Canada-certified version
Ka-32A12: Swiss-registered and approved version
Ka-32K: Flying crane with retractable gondola for second pilot
Ka-32S: Maritime version with undernose radar
Ka-32T: Utility transport

SPECIFICATIONS: KA-32T

Accommodation: 2 + 16
Cargo/baggage: 5,000 kg (11,023 lb)
Max speed: 135 kt (250 km/h)
Range: 432 nm (800 km/h)

DIMENSIONS

Main rotor diameter: 15.9 m (52 ft 2 in)
Length (rotors folded): 12.3 m (40 ft 3 in)
Height: 5.4 m (17 ft 9 in)

FEATURES

Three-blade coaxial contrarotating rotors, no tail rotor; twin Klimov TV3 turboshaft engines; short tailboom with large twin endplate fins; four-wheel landing gear (skis optional)

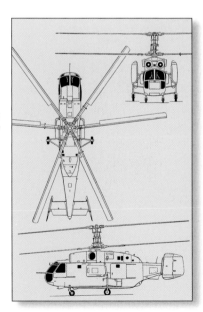

Kamov Ka-226 Russia

Twin-turbine light helicopter

Refined development of the Ka-126 with changes to shape of nose and tailfins, rudder and

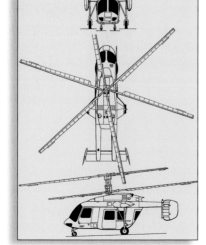

passenger pod. Announced at Heli-Expo in Dallas in 1990, but not flown until 4 September 1997.

VARIANTS

Ka-226A: Basic civil production version
Ka-226A-50: Improved model
Ka-226U: Military training version

SPECIFICATIONS

Accommodation: 1 or 2 + 6
Cargo/baggage: 1,300 kg (2,865 lb)
Max speed: 115 kt (214 km/h)
Range: 324 nm (600 km)

DIMENSIONS

Main rotor diameter: 13.0 m (42 ft 8 in)
Length (fuselage): 8.1 m (26 ft 7 in)
Height: 4.2 m (13 ft 8 in)

FEATURES

Three-blade coaxial contrarotating rotors; no tail rotor; twin Rolls-Royce 250 turboshaft engines; interchangeable accommodation pods; short twin tailboom with large downward endplate fins; four-wheel landing gear

Kazan Ansat Russia

Twin-turboshaft light utility helicopter

Design started in 1993 and fuselage mock-up first displayed at Paris Air Show in June 1995. First hover of prototype made on 17 August 1999, followed by initial forward flight on 6 October. Certification expected in 2005. Total orders (unconfirmed): 312.

horizontal stabilizers with endplate fins at rear tailboom; two P&W Rus PW207K turboshaft engines; fixed skid-type landing gear

VARIANTS

Ansat: Initial production model with PW207K engines
Ansat-AG: Version for Gazprom pipeline inspection
Ansat-U: Proposed variant optimized for training with dual controls and wheeled landing gear.
Ansat Nablyudatel: Proposed military scout version with much modified nose section and tandem seating.

SPECIFICATIONS

Accommodation: 2 + 9
Max speed: 148 kt (275 km/h)
Range: 342 nm (635 km)

DIMENSIONS

Main rotor diameter: 11.5 m (37 ft 9 in)
Length (rotors turning): 13.5 m (44 ft 5 in)
Height: 3.4 m (11 ft 2 in)

FEATURES

Four-blade main rotor and two-blade tail rotor;

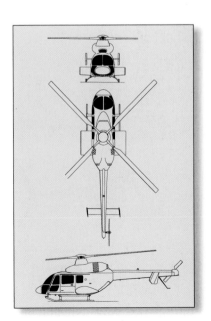

MD Helicopters MD 500/530 USA

Single-turbine light helicopter

Civilian development of the Hughes OH-6A Cayuse military helicopter announced on 21 April 1965. First Model 500 (engineering designation 369) flew in early 1967, with full-scale production commencing in November 1968. Hughes sold out to McDonnell Douglas in January 1984 which became subsidiary of Boeing in August 1997. Light helicopter line then sold to RDM Holdings in January 1999. Total delivered (including military): 4,570.

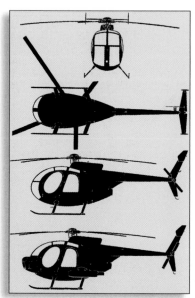

VARIANTS

500: Initial model with Allison 250-C18 turboshaft engine
500C: Improved hot-and-high performance with more powerful engine
500D: New five-blade main rotor; small T-tail
500E/MD 500E: Many cabin improvements and external changes
530F/MD 530F: Increased main rotor and transmission rating
+ military models (which see)

SPECIFICATIONS

Accommodation: 1 + 4
Cargo/baggage: 907 kg (2,000 lb)
Max speed: 152 kt (282 km/h)
Range: 233 nm (431 km)

DIMENSIONS

Main rotor diameter: 8.1m (26 ft 5 in)
Length (rotors turning): 8.6 m (28 ft 3 in)
Height: 2.7 m (8 ft 9 in)

FEATURES

Five-blade main rotor, two-blade tail rotor; single Rolls-Royce 250 turboshaft engine; narrow-chord fin with high-set tailplane and endplate fins (500D and 500E only); fixed-skid landing gear

MD Helicopters MD 520N USA

Single-turboshaft light helicopter

Developed from the Model 500, but with new
NOTAR (no tail rotor) system. Commercial version
announced in February 1988 and officially
launched in January 1999. First flight of MD 530N
on 29 December 1989, but none built to date.
First flight of MD 520N on 1 May 1990 and
delivered to Phoenix Police on 31 October 1991.
Total delivered: 85.

VARIANTS
MD 520N: Basic production version

SPECIFICATIONS
Accommodation: 1 + 4
Cargo/baggage: 1,004 kg (2,214 lb)
Max speed: 152 kt (281 km/h)
Range: 202 nm (375 km)

DIMENSIONS
Main rotor diameter: 8.3 m (27 ft 4 in)
Length (rotors turning): 9.8 m (32 ft 2 in)
Height: 2.7 m (9ft 0 in)

FEATURES
Five-blade main rotor; single Rolls-Royce 250
turboshaft engine; high tailboom with NOTAR and
top-mounted stabiliser with endplate fins; fixed-
skid landing gear

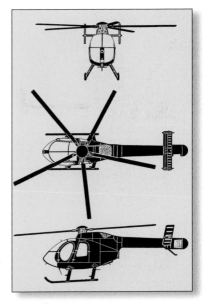

MD Helicopters MD 600N USA

Single-turbine light helicopter

Stretched development of MD 520N with new six-blade main rotor, more powerful engine and

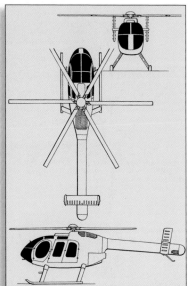

uprated transmission. First flown on 22 November 1994, and first delivery to launch customer AirStar Helicopters on 6 June 1997. Total delivered: 55.

VARIANTS
MD 600N: Basic production model

SPECIFICATIONS
Accommodation: 1 + 7
Cargo/baggage: 1,361 kg (3,000 lb)
Max speed: 135 kt (250 km/h)
Range: 342 nm (633 km)

DIMENSIONS
Main rotor diameter: 8.4 m (27 ft 7 in)
Length (rotors turning): 11.3 m (36 ft 11 in)
Height: 2.7 m (8 ft 9 in)

FEATURES
Six-blade main rotor; single Rolls-Royce 250 turboshaft engine; high tailboom with NOTAR and top-mounted stabiliser with endplate fins; fixed-skid landing gear

MD Helicopters MD Explorer USA

Twin-turbine light helicopter

Twin-engined NOTAR model, formerly known as MDX, announced in February 1988 and launched in January 1989. First flight on 18 December 1992, and first delivery 16 December 1994. Total delivered: 94.

VARIANTS

MD 900 Explorer: Initial utility model powered by P&WC PW206A engines
MD 901 Explorer: Civil utility model with alternative Turbomeca Arrius engines. None ordered
MD 902 Explorer: Higher performance replacement from November 1997
MH-90 Enforcer: Armed variant operated by US Coast Guard
Combat Explorer: Demonstrator displayed at Paris Air Show in June 1995.
+ specially equipped Police and EMS versions

SPECIFICATIONS

Accommodation: 2 + 6
Cargo/baggage: 1,361 kg (3,000 lb)
Max speed: 160 kt (296 km/h)
Range: 293 nm (542 km)

DIMENSIONS

Main rotor diameter: 10.3 m (33 ft 10 in)
Length (rotors turning): 11.8 m (38 ft 10 in)
Height: 3.7 m (12 ft 1 in)

FEATURES

Five-blade main rotor; twin P&WC PW200 turboshaft engines; high tailboom with NOTAR and top-mounted stabiliser with endplate fins; fixed-skid landing gear

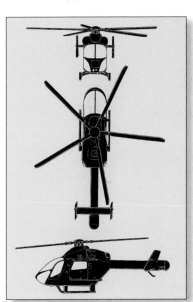

Mil Mi-2 'Hoplite' Russia/Poland

Twin-turbine light helicopter

Designed in the USSR and first flown 22 September 1961. Agreement signed for further development, exclusive production and marketing with Polish industry; first Polish-built example flew 4 November 1965. Total delivered (including military): 5,450.

VARIANTS

Mi-2: Basic civil version
Mi-2B: Improved systems and navigational aids
Mi-2P: Standard passenger/cargo convertible with external sling and electric hoist
Mi-2S: Medevac equipped for up to four litters plus attendant
Kania: Substantially improved model with Rolls-Royce 250-C20B turboshafts
PZL Mi2plus: Improved version with more powerful GTD-350W2 engines, all-composite main rotor blades, new avionics
+ many specialised military versions

SPECIFICATIONS

Accommodation: 1 + 8
Cargo/baggage: 800 kg (1,763 lb)
Max speed: 113 kt (210 km/h)
Range: 237 nm (440 km)

DIMENSIONS

Main rotor diameter: 14.5 m (47 ft 7 in)
Length (rotors turning): 17.4 m (57 ft 2 in)
Height: 3.8 m (12 ft 4 in)

FEATURES

Three-blade main rotor and two-blade tail rotor; twin Isotov GTD-350 turboshaft engines; square cabin windows; fixed skid landing gear, plus tail skid

Mil Mi-8 'Hip' Russia

Twin-turbine medium helicopter

Development started in May 1962 to replace piston-engined Mi-4. First prototype with single AI-24V turboshaft and four-blade rotor flew in June 1961, but replaced by second prototype with twin TV2 engines and five-blade rotor adopted for production. Total delivered (military and civil): 10,000+

VARIANTS

Mi-8AT: Basic civil transport version built at Ulan-Ude
Mi-8ATS: Agricultural helicopter with hoppers and spray bars
Mi-8P: Standard passenger model with square windows
Mi-8S: VIP configuration for 9-11 passengers
Mi-8T: Civil utility version and circular cabin windows
Mi-8TM: Upgraded transport with weather radar
Mi-8 VIP: Current de luxe version by Kazan, 7-9 passengers
+ many military models (which see)

SPECIFICATIONS: Mi-8T

Accommodation: 2 + 32
Cargo/baggage: 3,000 kg (6,614 lb)
Max speed: 140 kt (260 km/h)
Range: 229 nm (425 km)

DIMENSIONS

Main rotor diameter: 21.3 m (69 ft 11 in)
Length (rotors turning): 25.2 m (82 ft 9 in)
Height: 5.7 m (18 ft 7 in)

FEATURES

Five-blade main rotor and three-blade starboard tail rotor; twin Klimov TV2-117 turboshaft engines; horizontal stabiliser near rear of tailboom; rear clamshell doors; rectangular or round cabin windows; tricycle landing gear

Mil Mi-17 'Hip' Russia

Twin-turbine medium helicopter

Improved successor to Mi-8 for civil use and export. Prototype built with basic Mi-8 airframe and powerplant and dynamics of Mi-14, first displayed at Paris Air Show in 1981. First exported in 1983. Production continues at Kazan and Ulan-Ude. Total delivered: 810.

VARIANTS
Mi-17: Basic production model
Mi-17KF: Updated to meet US and Canadian certification
Mi-17-1V: Improved hot-and-high version for export. Designated Mi-8MTV-1 for local use
Mi-171: More powerful turboshafts, improved rates of climb
Mi-17-1VA: Flying hospital
Mi-172: Equipment changes and performance improvements
+ military models under Mi-17 and Mi-8 designations (which see)

SPECIFICATIONS
Accommodation: 2 + 32
Cargo/baggage: 3,000 kg (6,614 lb)
Max speed: 135 kt (250 km/h)
Range: 267 nm (495 km)

DIMENSIONS
Main rotor diameter: 21.3 m (69 ft 11 in)
Length (rotors turning): 25.4 m (83 ft 3 in)
Height: 5.7 m (18 ft 7 in)

FEATURES
Five-blade main rotor and three-blade portside tail rotor; twin Klimov TV3-117 turboshafts with shorter engine nacelles; horizontal stabiliser near rear of tailboom; rear clamshell doors; rectangular or round cabin windows

Mil Mi-26 'Halo' Russia

Twin-turbine heavy helicopter

World's largest helicopter first displayed in the west at the 1981 Paris Air Show. Development started in early 1970s and prototype first flew 14 December 1977. Operational in 1983, with export deliveries starting in June 1986. Total delivered: 300+.

VARIANTS

Mi-26MS: Medical evacuation with fully-equipped medical section
Mi-26P: Civil transport configuration for 63 passengers
Mi-26PK: Flying crane derivative with operator's gondola on port fuselage side
Mi-26T: Basic civil utility transport
Mi-26TC: Cargo version with 6-tonne hoist and electric winches
Mi-26TM: Flying crane derivative with gondola under fuselage, either aft of nose or under rear-loading ramp
Mi-26TP: Firefighting version with belly-mounted water or retardant dump
Mi-26TZ: Flying tanker + several military transport versions

SPECIFICATIONS

Accommodation: 4 + 80
Cargo/baggage: 22,000 kg (48,500 lb)
Max speed: 159 kt (295 km/h)
Range: 270 nm (500 km)

DIMENSIONS

Main rotor diameter: 32.0 m (105 ft 0 in)
Length (rotors turning): 40.0 m (131 ft 3 in)

Height: 8.2 m (26 ft 9 in)

FEATURES

Eight-blade main rotor and five-blade starboard tail rotor; twin ZMKB Progress D-136 turboshafts; clamshell rear doors; swept tail rotor/stabiliser support; tricycle landing gear

Mil Mi-34 'Hermit' Russia

Single-piston or -turbine light helicopter

Multi-purpose light helicopter first flown 17 November 1986 and exhibited at Paris Air Show in mid-1987. Series production started at Progress Plant in Arsenyev in 1993. Total delivered 25+.

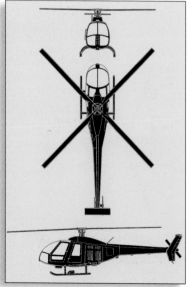

VARIANTS

Mi-34: Basic production version
Mi-34A: Proposal to replace piston engine with Rolls-Royce 250-C20R turboshaft
Mi-34M: Projected twin-turbine 6-seat version
Mi-34P: Police variant in service with Moscow City Police
Mi-34S: As basic Mi-34 but upgraded to meet FAR Pt 27. Also marketed as Mi-34C
Mi-34UT: Dual-control trainer
Mi-234: Proposal with rotary engines; formerly Mi-34VAZ

SPECIFICATIONS

Accommodation: 1 + 3
Cargo/baggage: 550 kg (1,213 lb)
Max speed: 122 kt (225 km/h)
Range: 194 nm (360 km)

DIMENSIONS

Main rotor diameter: 10.0 m 932 ft 10 in)
Length (rotors turning): 11.4 m (37 ft 5 in)
Height: 2.8 m (9 ft 1 in)

FEATURES

Four-blade main rotor and two-blade starboard tail rotor; single VOKBM M-14V piston engine; bubble canopy; sweptback tailfin with small unswept T tailplane; fixed skid landing gear

PZL Šwidnik SW-4 Poland

Single-turbine light helicopter

Development began in 1985, but major redesigns initiated by the time of the first flight on 29 October 1996. Series production to start in 2002.

VARIANTS
SW-4: Initial production version

SPECIFICATIONS
Accommodation: 1 + 4
Cargo/baggage: 750 kg (1,653 lb)
Max speed: 155 kt (88 km/h)
Range: 468 nm (860 km)

DIMENSIONS
Main rotor diameter: 9.0 m (29 ft 6 in)
Length (rotors turning): 10.6 m (34 ft 8 in)
Height: 3.0 in (9 ft 10 in)

FEATURES
Three-blade main rotor and two-blade starboard tail rotor; single Rolls-Royce 250 turboshaft; arrowhead tailfin; narrow tailplane with small endplate fins; fixed skid landing gear

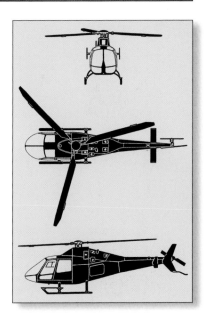

Robinson R22 USA

Single-piston light helicopter

Design began in 1973, leading to the first flight on 28 August 1975. Deliveries started in October 1979. Total delivered: 3,550.

VARIANTS

R22: Initial production model
R22HP: Higher-powered version introduced in 1981

R22 Alpha: Improved and increased gross weight from 1983
R22 Beta: More powerful engines
R22 Mariner: Floats and ground wheels, corrosion-proofed
R22 Beta II: Current production model with significant improvements
R22 Mariner II: Current improved production model
R22 Beta II Police: Equipment inc searchlight, loudspeaker and more
+ other specialist versions available for training and agricultural work

SPECIFICATIONS

Accommodation: 1 + 1
Cargo/baggage: 181 kg (400 lb)
Max speed: 102 kt (190 km/h)
Range: 174 nm (322 km)

DIMENSIONS

Main rotor diameter: 7.7 m (25 ft 2 in)
Length (rotors turning): 8.8 m (28 ft 9 in)
Height: 2.7 m (8 ft 9 in)

FEATURES

Two-blade main rotor and two-blade tail rotor on port side; high-mounted rotorhead; single Textron Lycoming O-360 piston engine; upper and lower tailfin; fixed skid landing gear or floats and ground wheels

Robinson **R44** USA

Single-piston light helicopter

Four-seat development of the R22 began in 1986. First flight of the R44 took place on 31 March 1990 and first deliveries in early 1993. Total delivered: 1,610.

VARIANTS

R44 Astro: Initial production model with fixed skids
R44 Clipper: Float-equipped and lights for night flying
R44 Police: Law enforcement model with specialised equipment
R44 IFR Trainer: Specialised equipment for pilot training
R44 Newscopter: Production-line ENG model with cameras and audio system
R44 Raven: Enhanced version available from April 2000

SPECIFICATIONS

Accommodation: 1 + 3
Cargo/baggage: 445 kg (981 lb)
Max speed: 113 kt (209 km/h)
Range: 347 nm (643 km)

DIMENSIONS

Main rotor diameter: 10.1 m (33 ft 0 in)
Length (rotors turning): 11.7 m (38 ft 3 in)
Height: 3.3 m (10 ft 9 in)

FEATURES

Two-blade main rotor and two-blade tail rotor on port side; high-mounted rotorhead; single Textron Lycoming O-540 piston engine; upper and lower tailfin; fixed skid landing gear or floats and ground wheels

Schweizer (Hughes) 300 USA

Single-piston light helicopter

Design and development of original two-seat Hughes Model 269 began in September 1955, and the first prototype flew in October 1956. Several improved models followed and in July 1983, production was transferred from Hughes to Schweizer. Total delivered (including military): 3,605.

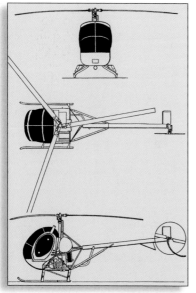

VARIANTS

269A: Original production model
269A-1: Re-engined with fuel injection and larger main rotor
300 (269B): Three-seat follow-up with quiet tail rotor (QTR)
300C (269C): Standard civil production version
300C Sky Knight: Special police version
300CB: 'Bare' version of 300C for training role
300CBi: Improved version with fuel-injected engine
TH-55A: Light primary trainer bought by US Army in 1960s
TH-300C: Current available military training version

SPECIFICATIONS: 300C

Accommodation: 1 + 2
Cargo/baggage: 975 kg (2,150 lb)
Max speed: 91 kt (169 km/h)
Range: 194 nm (360 km)

DIMENSIONS

Main rotor diameter: 8.2 m (26 ft 10 in)
Length (rotors turning): 9.4 m (30 ft 10 in)
Height: 2.7 m (8 ft 9 in)

FEATURES

Three-blade main rotor and two-blade tail rotor; single Textron Lycoming HIO-360 piston engine; braced tubular tailboom with separate dihedral tailplane and fin; bubble canopy; fixed skid landing gear with ground wheels

Schweizer 330 USA

Single-turbine light helicopter

Developed initially for the US Army training helicopter requirement won by Bell. Announced in 1987 and made its first flight in public 14 June 1988. Deliveries started in mid-1993. Total delivered: 41.

VARIANTS

330 (269D): Initial production version
330SP: Improved performance, available as retrofit to earlier aircraft
333: Enhanced derivative of 330SP with better operating performance and 30% more payload

SPECIFICATIONS: 333

Accommodation: 1 + 3
Cargo/baggage: 608 kg (1,340 lb)
Max speed: 105 kt (195 km/h)
Range: 319 nm (590 km)

DIMENSIONS

Main rotor diameter: 8.4 m (27 ft 6 in)
Length (rotors turning): 9.5 m (31 ft 1 in)
Height: 3.4 m (11 ft 10 in)

FEATURES

Three-blade main rotor and two-blade tail rotor on port side; single Rolls-Royce Model 250 turbo shaft engine; upper and lower fin; large tailplane with endplate fins at rear of tail boom; fixed skid landing gear

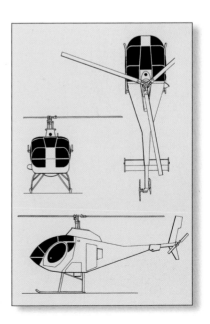

Sikorsky S-58 USA

Single-piston or twin-turbine intermediate helicopter

Developed to a US Navy specification for anti-submarine helicopter and first flown 8 March 1954. Also built under licence by Sud-Aviation in France, and by Westland in the UK as the Wessex. First commercial deliveries made in 1956. First flight of turbine-powered conversion 19 August 1970. Total built (including military): 1,821.

VARIANTS
S-58B: Initial civil passenger/freight version
S-58C: Similar, but with two doors on starboard side
S-58D: Improved model
S-58T: Turbine conversion with P&W PT6T Twin-Pac providing improved performance
Wessex: Licence-produced UK version
H-34: US Army/Navy designation

SPECIFICATIONS: S-58T
Accommodation: 2 + 12
Cargo/baggage: 2,460 kg (5,423 lb)
Max speed: 120 kt (222 km/h)
Range: 260 nm (481 km)

DIMENSIONS
Main rotor diameter: 17.1 m (56 ft 0 in)
Length (rotors turning): 17.3 m (56 ft 8 in)
Height: 4.9 m (15 ft 11 in)

FEATURES
Four-blade main rotor and four-blade portside tail rotor atop swept fin; single Wright R-1820 piston engine or P&W PT6T Twin-Pac turboshaft engines; high-mounted cockpit; three-wheel undercarriage

Sikorsky S-61 USA

Twin-turbine medium helicopter

Developed to meet US Navy requirement for ASW helicopter with boat type hull and retractable landing gear. Prototype first flew 11 March 1959. First commercial version flew 6 December 1960. Also built under licence by Agusta, Mitsubishi and Westland. Total delivered: 794.

VARIANTS

S-61L: Non-amphibious civil model with modified landing gear
S-61L Mk II: Improved version with more powerful CT58 turboshaft engines and individual cargo bins
S-61N: Similar to S-61L, but sealed hull and stabilising floats
S-61N Mk II: Similar to S-61L Mk II, but with sealed hull and stabilising floats
S-61R: Many design changes including rear loading ramp and new landing gear
+ many military versions under *H-3*, *AS-61* and *Sea King/Commando* designations (which see)

SPECIFICATIONS: S-61N
Accommodation: 2 + 30
Cargo/baggage: 3,630 kg (8,000 lb)
Max speed: 144 kt (267 km/h)
Range: 450 nm (833 km)

DIMENSIONS
Main rotor diameter: 18.9 m (62 ft 0 in)
Length overall: 22.2 m (72 ft 8 in)
Height: 5.6 m (18 ft 5 in)

FEATURES

Five-blade main rotor and five-blade portside tail rotor; twin GE CT58 turboshaft engines; boat hull; twin-wheel undercarriage retracting into stabilising floats with fixed tailwheel (non-retractable on S-61L)

Sikorsky S-64 Skycrane/Aircrane USA

Twin-turbine heavylift helicopter

Designed initially for military transport duties and flew for the first time on 9 May 1962. Received civil certification in 1969 as the S-64E for the carriage of external cargo. In 1992, Erickson Air-Crane acquired the type certificate and is now marketing improved versions worldwide for various specialist applications. Total delivered: 100.

VARIANTS

CH-54A: Original model delivered to US Army
CH-54B: Improved US Army version with increased payload, new rotor system with high-lift rotor blades, increased weight
S-64E: New-built civil version, or improved modification of military CH-54A
S-64F: Civil upgrade of military CH-54B
Helitanker: Specialist firefighting version with 10,000 litre water tank
+ military versions under CH-54 designation (which see)

SPECIFICATIONS: S-64E

Accommodation: 3 flight crew
Cargo/baggage: 9,072 kg (20,000 lb)
Max speed: 115 kt (213 km/h)
Range: 200 nm (370 km)

DIMENSIONS

Main rotor diameter: 22.0 m (72 ft 0 in)
Length overall: 27.0 m (88 ft 6 in)
Height: 7.8 m (25 ft 5 in)

FEATURES

Six-blade main rotor and four-blade portside tailrotor; twin P&W JFTD-12 turboshaft engines; non-retractable tricycle landing gear; cockpit pod and beam-type fuselage; starboard stabiliser on top of tail unit

Sikorsky S-76 USA

Twin-turbine intermediate helicopter

Development of executive transport helicopter announced on 19 January 1975 and first flown 13 March 1977. Deliveries started in early 1979. Two military models also offered, but these proved unsuccessful. Total delivered: 533.

VARIANTS

S-76A: Original transport version with P&W PT6Bs
S-76A Mk II: Standard production version from March 1982
S-76A Utility: Basic version with sliding doors and strengthened floor
S-76A+: Retrofit with Turbomeca Arriel 1S turboshafts
S-76A++: Retrofit with Turbomeca Arriel 1S1 turboshafts
S-76B: Powered by P&W PT6B-36A turboshafts
S-76C: Essentially as S-76B, but with Arriel 1S1s
S-76C+: Uprated and improved Arriel 1S1s with FADEC
S-76N: Naval version operated by Royal Thai Navy

SPECIFICATIONS: S-76C+

Accommodation: 2 + 13
Cargo/baggage: 1,497 kg (3,300 lb)
Max speed: 155 kt (287 km/h)
Range: 453 nm (839 km)

DIMENSIONS

Main rotor diameter: 13.4 m (44 ft 0 in)
Length (rotors turning): 16.0 m (52 ft 6 in)
Height: 4.4 m (14 ft 5 in)

FEATURES

Four-blade main rotor and four-blade port side tail rotor; twin P&WC PT6B or Turbomeca Arriel turboshafts; retractable tricycle type landing gear; two large doors on each side; horizontal stabilisers at base of tail unit

Sikorsky S-92 USA

Twin-turbine medium helicopter

First announced as growth development of Black Hawk in March 1992 and launched as international risk-sharing partnership at Paris Air Show in June 1995. Made first flight on 23 December 1998. First delivery made in March 2004.

VARIANTS

S-92A: Transport version for civil market
S-92IU: International civil/military utility version
H-92: Military transport derivative
HV-92: Proposed military VIP version

SPECIFICATIONS

Accommodation: 2 + 22
Cargo/baggage: 4,536 kg (10,000 lb)
Max speed: 165 kt (305 km/h)
Range: 475 nm (879 km)

DIMENSIONS

Main rotor diameter: 17.2 m (56 ft 4 in)
Length (rotors turning): 20.9 m (68 ft 6 in)
Height: 5.4 m (17 ft 9 in)

FEATURES

Four-blade main rotor and four-blade tail rotor on starboard side; large horizontal stabiliser on port side; rear loading ramp; tricycle landing gear retractable into large side sponsons

Whisper Jet (Sikorsky) S-55QT USA

Single-turbine light helicopter conversion

Project initiated in 1992 by Papillon Grand Canyon Helicopters and Vertical Aviation Technologies (VAT) to produce ultra-quiet helicopter for sightseeing flights. Main changes from basic S-55 include new five-blade main rotor and turboshaft engine with acoustically modified engine inlet plenum. Total 100 S-55 airframes available for conversion. Total converted: 5.

engine; quadricycle landing gear; large viewing windows and glass-bottom floor

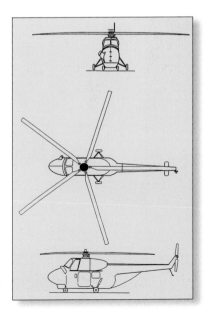

VARIANTS

S-55QT: Initial version with glass-bottom floor and large viewing windows for sightseeing flights

SPECIFICATIONS

Accommodation: 1 + 9
Cargo/baggage: 1,134 kg (2,500 lb)
Max speed: 99 kt (183 km/h)
Range: 215 nm (398 km)

DIMENSIONS

Main rotor diameter: 15.3 m (50 ft 2 in)
Length (rotors turning): 19.0 m (62 ft 4 in)
Height: 4.7 m (15 ft 3 in)

FEATURES

Five-blade main rotor and two-blade tail rotor on port side; single Garrett TSE-331 turboshaft

COMBAT
AIRCRAFT

AIDC F-CK-1 Ching-Kuo Taiwan

Air superiority fighter

First flight of prototype, aka Indigenous Fighter Aircraft (IDF), on 28 May 1989 with production deliveries (of 120 IDFs) from 1994 to January 2000.

VARIANTS & OPERATORS
F-CK-1A: RoCAF
F-CK-1B: RoCAF

SPECIFICATIONS
Crew/accommodation:
    F-CK-1A = pilot,
    F-CK-1B = student and instructor
Max speed: 700kt (1,296km/h)
RoA/range: n/a

ARMAMENT
Internal gun: one 20mm M61 cannon
Hardpoints: six (plus wingtips)
Max weapon load: 3,901kg (8,600 lb)
Representative weapons: AAMs; ASMs; AGMs; PGMs; bombs; FFAR pods

DIMENSIONS
Wingspan: 8.5m (28ft 0in) over missile rails
Length: 13.3m (43ft 6in)
Height: 4.7m (15ft 3in)

FEATURES
Like F-16 but with two underwing air intakes; mid swept wing; twin ITEC TFE1042-70 turbofans; tall fin

AMX International AMX Italy/Brazil

Strike/attack fighter

The AMX International consortium (Alenia and Aermacchi of Italy and EMBRAER of Brazil) was created in 1980 to replace the G91R/Y and F-104G/S in Italy and the MB-326 Xavante in Brazil. First flown on 15 May 1984 and 198 delivered.

VARIANTS & OPERATORS
AMX: Brazil (A-1), Italy
AMX-T: Brazil (AT-1), Italy
AMX-ATA (Super AMX-T): Venezuela (24 ordered)

SPECIFICATIONS
Crew/accommodation:
    AMX = pilot,
    AMX-T = student and instructor
Max speed: M 0.86
Radius of action: 480nm (889km)

ARMAMENT
Internal gun(s): one 20mm M61 (Italy) or two 30mm DEFA cannon (Brazil).
Hardpoints: five (plus wingtips)
Max weapon load: 3,800kg (8,377 lb).
Representative weapons: wingtip AAMs; Paveway II LGBs; AM-39 Exocet or Marte ASMs; bombs; FFAR pods.

DIMENSIONS
Wingspan: 10.0m (32ft 8in)
Length: 13.2m (43ft 5in)
Height: 4.5m (14ft 11in)

FEATURES
Shoulder/swept wing; single Rolls-Royce Spey Mk.807 turbofan; shoulder intakes; wingtip missiles

Avione IAR-93/SOKO J-22 Orao (Eagle)

Romania/Yugoslavia (Bosnia-Herzegovina)

Ground attack and reconnaissance aircraft

Joint Romanian/Yugoslav project initiated in 1970. Prototype flew on 31 October 1974 (one in each country) with two-seater flying on 29 January 1977, with 138 delivered.

VARIANTS & OPERATORS

IAR-93A/93B: Romanian single- and two-seaters fitted with Viper Mk632/633 turbojets.
IJ-22/INJ-22 - Orao 1: Yugoslav tactical recce version, some two-seat conversion trainers.
NJ-22 Orao: Two-seat Yugoslav tactical recce version, some with afterburning Vipers.
J-22 Orao 2: Yugoslav single-seat attack version, some with afterburning Vipers; first flown 20 October 1983.

SPECIFICATIONS

Crew/accommodation: See above
Max speed: 586kt (1,086km/h)
Radius of action: 248nm (460km)

ARMAMENT: IAR-93A/B

Internal gun: two 23mm twin-barrel cannon
Hardpoints: five
Max weapon load: 1,500kg (3,307 lb)
Representative weapons: AAMs; 250kg or 500kg bombs; FFAR pods; external fuel tanks

DIMENSIONS

Length: 14.9m (48ft 11in)
Length (trainer): 15.4m (50ft 6in)

Wingspan: 9.3m (30ft 6in)
Height: 4.5m (14ft 0in)

FEATURES

Shoulder/swept wing; twin Rolls-Royce Viper turbojets; short pointed nose

BAE Systems (British Aerospace) Hawk 200 UK

Light multirole fighter

Derived from the Hawk 100 series advanced jet trainer, the single-seat Hawk 200 series has APG-66 radar of the F-16A/B. First flown on 19 May 1986, 62 have been built.

VARIANTS & OPERATORS
Mk.203: Oman (12)
Mk.208: Malaysia (18)
Mk.209: Indonesia (32)

SPECIFICATIONS
Crew/accommodation: Pilot only
Max speed: 540kt (1,000km/h)
Radius of action: 345nm (638km)

ARMAMENT
No internal gun
Hardpoints: five (plus wingtips)
Max weapon load: 3,000kg (6,614 lb)
Representative weapons: centreline 30mm gun pod; AIM-9 AAM; AGM-65 Maverick AGM; bombs; FFAR pods; CBLS; external fuel tanks

DIMENSIONS
Length: 11.3m (37ft 2in)
Wingspan: 9.4m (30ft 9in)
Height: 4.1m (13ft 7in)

FEATURES
Low swept wing; single Rolls-Royce/Turbomeca Adour Mk.871 turbofan; 'blown' canopy

BAE Systems Sea Harrier FA.2/FRS.51 UK

STOVL Fighter, recce and strike aircraft

Sea Harrier FRS.51

Sea Harrier FA.2 is MLU of FRS.1 (first flown 20 August 1978) with new Blue Vixen, rear fuselage lengthened and LERX added. Development aircraft flown 19 September 1989. Re-deliveries of 33 conversions from April 1993, with 18 new-build aircraft completed by 24 December 1998. One operational unit remains with OSD of 2006. Sea Harrier FRS.51 is export version of RN FRS.1 for India. Deliveries from December 1983 to April 1992.

VARIANTS & OPERATORS
Sea Harrier FA.2: RN (51)
Sea Harrier FRS.51: Indian Navy (23)

SPECIFICATIONS
Crew/accommodation: pilot
Max speed
    FA.2: 640+kt (1,185+km/h)
    FRS.51: 618kt (1,144km/h)
Radius of action: FA.2 = 250nm (463km)
    FRS.51 = 200nm (370km)

ARMAMENT
No internal guns, but two 30mm Aden cannon fuselage pods
Hardpoints: five
Max weapon load: 3,630kg (8,000 lb)
Representative weapons: AAMs; ASMs; bombs or PGMs; Lepus flares; CBLS; external fuel tanks

DIMENSIONS
	FRS.51	FA.2
Length:	14.5m (47ft 7in)	14.2m (46ft 6in)
Wingspan:	7.7m (25ft 3in)	7.7m (25ft 3in)
Height:	3.7m (12ft 2in)	3.7m (12ft 2in)

FEATURES
Shoulder/swept wing (FA.2 has LERX); single Rolls-Royce Pegasus vectored-thrust turbofan; four nozzles; blown canopy

Sea Harrier FA.2

Sea Harrier FRS.51

Boeing B-52H Stratofortress USA

Long-range bomber

First flown on 15 April 1952 and entered USAF service in 1955. Only the B-52H (102 built 1960-61) remains in service. All aircraft now capable of conventional as well as nuclear role. Many system upgrades in place with more pending.

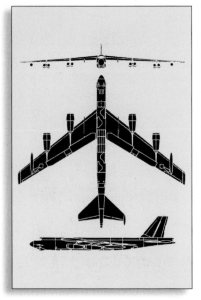

VARIANTS & OPERATORS
B-52H: USAF (94, with plans to reduce to 60)

SPECIFICATIONS
Crew/accommodation: Pilot, co-pilot, three WSOs
Max speed: 516kt (957km/h)
Range: 8,685+nm (16,093+km)

ARMAMENT
Original tail-mounted 20mm M61 cannon now deleted
Bomb bays and two underwing hardpoints
Max weapon load: 24,750kg (60,000 lb)
Representative weapons: 20 AGM-86C CALCM (12 internal, 8 external); nuclear weapons; PGMs; bombs and mines; JDAM, JSOW and JASSM weapons

DIMENSIONS
Length: 49.0m (160ft 11in)
Wingspan: 56.4m (185ft 0in)
Height: 12.4m (40ft 8in)

FEATURES
Shoulder/swept wing; four engine pylons each with two P&W TF33-P-3 turbofans; outboard underwing tanks; tall fin

Boeing (McDonnell Douglas) F-15 Eagle USA

Air superiority fighter

First flown on 27 July 1972 and entered USAF service in 1974. Sold to Israel, Saudi Arabia and Japan (built under licence by Mitsubishi). Last of 894 USAF versions delivered in 1989.

VARIANTS & OPERATORS
F-15A/B: USAF, Israel
F-15C: USAF, Israel, Saudi Arabia
F-15D: USAF, Israel, Saudi Arabia
F-15DJ: Japan
F-15J: Japan

SPECIFICATIONS
Crew/accommodation:
F-15A/C = pilot
F-15B/D/DJ = student and instructor
Max speed: M = 2.5 (800kt, 1,482km/h)
Ferry range: 2,500+nm (4,631+km)

ARMAMENT
Internal gun: one 20mm M61 cannon
Hardpoints: nine
Max weapon load: 10,705kg (23,600 lb) plus four fuselage AAMs
Representative weapons: AIM-7, AIM-9, AIM-120 AAMs; Mk.80 bombs; Paveway LGBs; ECM pods; CFT and external fuel tanks

DIMENSIONS
Length: 19.4m (63ft 9in)
Wingspan: 13.5m (42ft 9in)

Height: 5.6m (18ft 5in)

FEATURES
Twin fins; shoulder swept wings; two P&W F100 turbofans; blown canopy

Boeing (McDonnell Douglas) F-15E Strike Eagle USA

Dual-role attack fighter

Derived from the F-15B, the industry-funded Strike Eagle flew in 1982. First production F-15E flew 11 December 1986 and entered USAF service in 1988. Reduced internal fuel capacity but can used F-15 CFT.

VARIANTS & OPERATORS
F-15E: USAF (235+)
F-15I: Israel (25)
F-15K: South Korea (40)
F-15S: Saudi Arabia (72)

SPECIFICATIONS
Crew/accommodation: All versions = pilot and WSO
Max speed: M = 2.5 (800kt, 1,482km/h)
Radius of Action: 685nm (1,270km)

ARMAMENT
Internal gun: one 20mm M61 cannon
Hardpoints: nine
Max weapon load: 11,113kg (24,500 lb)
Representative weapons: AIM-7, AIM-9, AIM-120 AAMs; nuclear weapons; JDAM bombs; Paveway LGBs; AGM-84 Harpoon; AGM-88 HARM; GBU-15; ECM pods; LANTIRN pods; CFT and external fuel tanks

DIMENSIONS
Length: 19.4m (63ft 9in)
Wingspan: 13.5m (42ft 9in)
Height: 5.6m (18ft 5in)

FEATURES
Twin fins; shoulder swept wings; two P&W F100 (GE F110 in F-15K) turbofans; blown canopy

Boeing (McDonnell Douglas) F/A-18 Hornet USA

Carrier-based attack fighter

Derived from Northrop YF-17 with McDD, first prototype F-18 flew on 18 November 1978. The Hornet entered USN/USMC service from 1980. The last of 1,479 first-generation Hornets delivered in September 2000. Upgrades for Australia, Canada and Spain.

Wingspan: 11.4m (37ft 6in)
Height: 4.7m (15ft 3in)

FEATURES

Twin fins; shoulder swept wings; long LERX; two GE F404-GE-400 turbofans; blown canopy

VARIANTS & OPERATORS

F/A-18A: USN/USMC, Australia, Canada, Spain
F/A-18B: USN/USMC, Australia, Canada, Spain
F/A-18C: USN/USMC, Finland, Kuwait, Switzerland
F/A-18D: USN/USMC, Finland, Kuwait, Malaysia, Switzerland

SPECIFICATIONS

Crew/accommodation:
 F/A-18A/C = pilot
 F/A-18B/D = student and instructor
Max speed: M = 1.8+
Radius of action: 290nm (537km)

ARMAMENT

Internal gun: one 20mm M61 cannon
Hardpoints: seven (plus wingtips)
Max weapon load: 7,031kg (15,500 lb)
Representative weapons: AIM-7, AIM-9, AIM-120 AAMs; bombs; Paveway LGBs; AGMs; ECM pods; designator pods and external fuel tanks

DIMENSIONS

Length: 17.1m (56ft 0in)

Boeing (McDonnell Douglas) F/A-18E/F/G Super Hornet USA

Carrier-based attack fighter

A 'stretched' F/A-18C, the first prototype F-18E flew on 29 November 1995. Super Hornet entered service with the USN in 1999, with combat debut (VFA-115) in November 2002. At present, some 314 Super Hornets are planned (not all funded), plus 90 F/A-18G Growlers, as replacement for EA-6B Prowler SEAD/EW aircraft.

VARIANTS & OPERATORS

F/A-18E: USN/USMC
F/A-18F: USN/USMC
F/A-18G: USN/USMC

SPECIFICATIONS

Crew/accommodation:
  F/A-18E = pilot
  F/A-18F = student and instructor
  F/A-18G = pilot and EWO
Max speed: M = 1.8+
RoA - interdiction: 945nm (1,750km)
RoA - fighter escort: 795nm (1,472km)

ARMAMENT

Internal gun: one 20mm M61A2 cannon
Hardpoints: nine (plus wingtips)
Max weapon load: 8,051kg (17,750 lb)
Representative weapons: AIM-9, AIM-120 AAMs; bombs; Paveway LGBs; AGMs; SLAM-ER; HARM; JSOW; JDAM; ECM pods; designator pods and external fuel tanks

DIMENSIONS

Length: 18.4m (60ft 3in)
Wingspan: 13.6m (44ft 8in)
Height: 4.9m (16ft 0in)

FEATURES

Twin fins; shoulder swept wings; long LERX; two GE F414-GE-400 turbofans; blown canopy

CAC J-7 (F-7) China

Fighter and ground attack aircraft

Chinese variant of MiG-21, in PLAAF service from 1967. Several thousand in various variants produced for China. Current export model is the F-7MG, with a double-delta wingplan, Western avionics and uprated engine. About 400 of all types exported.

VARIANTS & OPERATORS

China **J-7 I/II/III, J-7E/EB, JJ-7** (two-seater built by GAIC); Albania **(F-7A)**; Bangladesh **(F-7MB)**; Egypt **(F-7B)**; Iran **(F-7M)**; Myanmar **(F-7M)**; Pakistan **(F-7P/MP/PG)**; Sri Lanka **(F-7B)**; Sudan **(F-7B)**; Tanzania **(F-7A)**; Zimbabwe **(F-7B/IIN)**.

SPECIFICATIONS

Crew/accommodation:
    J-7/F-7 variants = pilot
    JJ-7 (FT-7) = student and instructor
Max speed **(J-7C)**: M = 2.1
RoA **(F-7M) – interdiction**: 324nm (600km)

ARMAMENT: F-7MG

Internal gun: one 30mm Type 30-1 cannon
Hardpoints: five
Max weapon load: about 1,500kg (3,300 lb)
Representative weapons: PL-7, AIM-9, Magic AAMs; bombs; FFAR pods; external fuel tanks

DIMENSIONS: F-7MG

Length: 12.2m (39ft 11in)
Wingspan: 8.3m (27ft 3in)
Height: 4.1m (13ft 5in)

FEATURES

Low, double-delta wing, swept tailplanes, single LMC (Liyang) WP13F turbojet, nose intake with central radome.

NOT TO BE CONFUSED WITH

MiG-21; CAC/PAC FC-1/JF-17 Xiaolong/Thunder; Dassault Mirage F1

CAC/PAC FC-1/JF-17 Xiaolong/Thunder China/Pakistan

Multi-role attack aircraft

Joint venture between China and Pakistan launched in 1991. First flight on 25 August 2003 with second prototype flying on 9 April 2004.

Chinese avionics with Western radar. China plans for 1,000 aircraft, Pakistan for 150.

VARIANTS & OPERATORS
China: FC-1
Pakistan: JF-17

SPECIFICATIONS
Crew/accommodation: pilot
Max speed: M = 1.6
RoA – fighter: 648nm (1,200km)

ARMAMENT
Gun: one 23mm GSh-23-2 cannon pod on centreline
Hardpoints: seven
Max weapon load: about 3,800kg (8,380 lb)
Representative weapons: PL-12, AIM-9, Magic AAMs; bombs; LGBs; designator pod; external fuel tanks

DIMENSIONS
Length: 14.0m (45ft 11in)
Wingspan: 9.0m (29ft 6in)
Height: 5.1m (16ft 8in)

FEATURES
Low, delta wing; swept tailplanes; single Klimov RD-93 turbofan; side intakes with central radome

Dassault Mirage III/5/50 France

Interceptor and multi-role fighter

Designed as all-weather interceptor (C/O/S), first flown on 17 November 1956. Developed into a two-seat trainer (B/D), long-range fighter bomber (E) and recce (R) aircraft. A total of 1,420 Mirage III/5/50 were built.

VARIANTS & OPERATORS
Mirage IIIB/C/D/E/O/R/S: Argentina, Brazil, France, Pakistan.
Mirage 5A/C/D/E/F/G/M/P/R: Argentina, Chile (aka Elkan), Colombia, Congo (Democratic Republic of, formerly Zaire), Egypt, Gabon, Libya, Pakistan
Mirage 50C/D/E/FC: Chile (aka Pantera) and Venezuela

SPECIFICATIONS
Crew/accommodation:
   All except those B/D models = pilot
   All B/D models = student and instructor
Max speed: M = 2.2 (1,268kt, 2,350km/h)
Radius of action: 700nm (1,300km)

ARMAMENT: MIRAGE 5
Internal gun: two 30mm DEFA cannon
Hardpoints: seven
Max weapon load: 3,800kg (8,370 lb)
Representative weapons: Magic, AIM-9 AAMs; AS-30 AGM on centreline; PGMs; bombs; FFAR pods or external fuel tanks

DIMENSIONS
Length (Mirage IIIE): 15m (49ft 3in)
Length (Mirage 5/50): 15.5m (51ft 0in)
Wingspan (Mirage IIIE/5/50): 8.2m (26ft 11in)
Height (all versions): 4.5m (14ft 9in)

FEATURES
Low, swept delta wing; single SNECMA Atar 9C/9K-50 turbojet

Dassault Mirage F1 France

Air defence/multi-role fighter

Prototype flew on 23 December 1966 and Mirage F-1C entered French service in 1973. Developed into an attack aircraft (A/J), two-seat trainer (B/D), long-range fighter bomber (E) and recce (R) aircraft. A total of 731 were built by 1992.

VARIANTS & OPERATORS

F1-A: Libya (AD)

F1-B: France (B), Jordan (BJ), Libya (BD) and Spain (B/BE)
F1-C: France (C/CR/CT), Greece (CG), Jordan (CJ), Kuwait (CK), Morocco (CH) and Spain (CE)
F1-D: Spain (DDA)
F1-E: Iran (EQ), Jordan (EJ), Libya (ED), Morrocco (EH/EH-2000) and Spain (EDA/EE)
F1-J: Ecuador (JA/JE)

SPECIFICATIONS

Crew/accommodation:
    All except those B/D models = pilot
    All B/D models = student and instructor
Max speed: M = 1.2 (800kt, 1,480km/h)
Radius of action: 378nm (700km)

ARMAMENT

Internal gun: two 30mm DEFA cannon
Hardpoints: seven
Max weapon load: 6,300kg (13,890 lb)
Representative weapons: Magic, AIM-9, Super 530 AAMs; AS 30L AGM; PGMs; ASMs; bombs; FFAR pods; designator, EW and/or recce pods, plus external fuel tanks

DIMENSIONS

Length: 15.2m (49ft 11in)
Wingspan: 8.4m (27ft 7in)
Height: 4.5m (14ft 9in)

FEATURES

Shoulder/swept wing; single SNECMA Atar 9K-50 turbojet; wingtip missiles; sharp pointed nose

Dassault Mirage 2000 France

Air defence/multi-role fighter

Successor to Mirage III/F1, prototype flown on 10 March 1979 and entered French service in 1984. Developed into a two-seat trainer (2000B), multi-role fighter (2000E and 2000-5/-9) and strike/attack aircraft (2000D/N - see next entry). Over 600 are in service or on order.

VARIANTS & OPERATORS

France: 2000B and 2000C (37 converted to 2000-5F)
Abu Dhabi (UAE): 2000DAD/RAD/EAD (33 converted to 2000-9 DAD and 9RAD)
Egypt: 2000EM/BM
Greece: 2000C/2000EG (10 converted to 2000-5 Mk.2), 2000BG and 2000-5 Mk.2
India: 2000H/TH
Peru: 2000P/DP
Qatar: 2000-5EDA/DDA
Taiwan: 2000-5Ei/Di

SPECIFICATIONS

Crew/accommodation:
  All except those B/D models = pilot
  All B/D models = student and instructor
Max speed: M = 2.2
Radius of action: 800nm (1,480km)

ARMAMENT: MIRAGE 2000-5

Internal gun: two 30mm DEFA cannon
Hardpoints: nine
Max weapon load: 7,260kg (16,005 lb)
Representative weapons: Magic, Super 530, Mica AAMs; BAP 100 anti-runway bomb; bombs; Paveway LGBs; FFAR pods; external fuel tanks; designator, EW and/or recce pods

DIMENSIONS

Length: 14.6m (48ft 0in)
Wingspan: 9.1m (29ft 11in)
Height: 5.2m (17ft 1in)

FEATURES

Low delta wing; single SNECMA M53 turbofan; sharp pointed nose

Dassault Mirage 2000D/N France

Strike/attack aircraft

Derived from Mirage 2000B, prototype 2000N nuclear attack version flew on 3 February 1983 and entered service in 1988. Developed into a conventional attack version, the 2000D, first flown on 19 February 1991 and entered service in 1993. In all, 86 2000Ds and 75 2000Ns were delivered.

VARIANTS & OPERATORS

2000D: France
2000N: France

SPECIFICATIONS

Crew/accommodation: Both models = pilot and WSO
Max speed: M = 2.2
RoA (2000-N): 1,800nm (3,333km)

ARMAMENT

No internal gun
Hardpoints: nine
Max weapon load: 7,260kg (16,005 lb)
Representative weapons: Magic 2 AAMs; ASMP; APACHE; AGMs; bombs; Paveway LGBs; FFAR pods; designator, EW and/or recce pods; external fuel tanks

DIMENSIONS

Length: 14.5m (47ft 5in)
Wingspan: 9.1m (29ft 11in)
Height: 5.1m (16ft 10in)

FEATURES

Low delta wing; single SNECMA M53 turbofan; sharp pointed nose (2000D lacks nose pitot tube)

Dassault Rafale France

Multirole fighter

Prototype Rafale A flew on 4 July 1986 and first production Rafale B flown 24 November 1998. Two-seat strike D version preferred to single seater C-model. Carrier-borne M-model entered service 2001. With a requirement of 294, 120 Rafales were on firm order as of December 2004.

VARIANTS & OPERATORS
Rafale B: trainer, France (both services)
Rafale C: French Air Force
Rafale D: French Air Force
Rafale M: French Navy

SPECIFICATIONS
Crew/accommodation:
    Rafale B = student and instructor
    Rafale C/M = pilot
    Rafale D = pilot and WSO
Max speed: M = 1.8 (750kt, 1,390km/h)
Radius of action: 570nm (1055km)

ARMAMENT
Internal gun: one 30mm DEFA cannon
Hardpoints: 12 (plus wingtips)
Max weapon load: 9,500kg (20,944 lb)
Representative weapons: Magic, Mica AAMs; APACHE/SCALP; AGMs; ASMs; PGMs; bombs; Paveway LGBs; designator, EW and/or recce pods; external fuel tanks

DIMENSIONS
Length: 15.3m (50ft 1in)

Wingspan: 10.8m (35ft 5in)
Height: 5.3m (17ft 6in)

FEATURES
Swept nose canards; mid-delta wing; twin SNECMA M88-2 turbofans; chin intakes beneath canards

Dassault Super Etendard France

Carrier-based strike fighter and recce aircraft

Super Etendard prototype flew on 28 July 1974, with deliveries to Aeronavale from May 1982. Upgrade with SLEP and new avionics from 1990, as Super Etendard Modernisé. Sold to Argentina in 1979. Deliveries completed in 1983.

VARIANTS & OPERATORS

Super Etendard/Super Etendard Modernise: French Navy (71)
Super Etendard: Argentine Navy (14)

SPECIFICATIONS

Crew/accommodation: Super Etendard/
  Super Etendard Modernisé = pilot
Max speed: M = 1.0 (637kt, 1,180km/h)
Radius of action: 460nm (850km)

ARMAMENT

Internal guns: two 30mm DEFA cannon
Hardpoints: six
Max weapon load: 2,100kg (4,630 lb)
Representative weapons: Magic AAMs; AM 39 Exocet ASM; 250kg and 400kg bombs; external fuel tanks; EW and/or recce pods

DIMENSIONS

Length: 14.3m (46ft 11in)
Wingspan: 9.6m (31ft 6in)
Height: 3.86m (12ft 8in)

FEATURES

Chubby nose; low swept wing; swept tailplanes; one SNECMA 8K-50 turbojet; fuselage intakes by cockpit

Embraer EMB-314M (A-29) Super Tucano Brazil

Patrol attack fighter

Derived from EMB-312 trainer, the EMB-314M (Brazilian designation = A-29) features a more-powerful PT6A turboprop engine, reprofiled wing and two fuselage extensions. For use in Brazil's SIVAM programme. YA-29 single-seat prototype was rolled-out on 28 May 1999. A trainer version, AT-29, is also being procured. First A-29 delivered 18 December 2003.

VARIANTS & OPERATORS

A-29: Brazilian Air Force (49 on order)
AT-29: Brazilian Air Force (50 on order)
EMB-314M: Dominica (10 on order)

SPECIFICATIONS

Crew/accomodation:
  A-29 = pilot;
  AT-29 = student and instructor
Max speed: 301kt, (557km/h)
Radius of action: 847nm (1,568km)

ARMAMENT

Internal guns: two 12.7mm (0.5in) machine guns
Hardpoints: four
Max weapon load: n/a
Representative weapons: MAA-1 Piranha AAM;
Mk.81 250 lb bombs; Mk.82 500 lb bombs;
BLG-252 cluster weapons and LGBs

DIMENSIONS

Length: 11.4m (37ft 5in)

Wingspan: 11.1m (36ft 6in)
Height: 3.9m (12ft 9in)

FEATURES

Low tapered wing; blown canopy; one P&WC PT6A-68C turboprop

English Electric (British Aerospace) Canberra UK

Bomber, intruder and recce aircraft

First flown on 13 May 1949, the Canberra entered RAF service in 1951. Built in 20 different versions (plus seven in the US) and widely exported. Today, the RAF still uses Canberra PR.9 operationally (including over Afghanistan). Total UK production was 924, 48 in Australia and 403 in the US.

VARIANTS & OPERATORS

UK/RAF: Canberra B.2(TT) (2); T.4 (2); Canberra PR.9 (5)

UK/Qinetic: Canberra B(TT).2 (2)
India: Canberra B(TT).2/PR.57 (3); B(I)TT.58 (10)
Peru: Canberra T.4 (1); T.54 (1); B.52/56 (8/7 delivered); Canberra B(I).12/B(I).68 (9)

SPECIFICATIONS

Crew/accommodation:
    B.2 = pilot and two navigators
    T.4/T.54 = student and instructor (plus one)
    B(I) versions = pilot and navigator
    PR.9 = pilot and navigator
Max speed: 470kt (871km/h)
Radius of action: 700nm (1,296km)

ARMAMENT: B(I).12/68

Internal guns: four 20mm Hispano cannon (optional)
Hardpoints: four in bomb bay, two underwing
Max weapon load: 3,630kg (8,000 lb)
Representative weapons: 500 lb, 1,000 lb and 4,000lb bombs; AS.30 AGM; wingtip fuel tanks and underwing target-towing stores

DIMENSIONS

Length: B(I).12/58/68: 19.9mm (65ft 6in)
    PR.9: 20.3m (66ft 8in)
Wingspan: B(I).12/58/68: 19.5m (64ft 0in)
    PR.9: 20.7m (67ft 10in)
Height: 4.8m (15ft 8in)

FEATURES

Mid-tapered wing; offset canopy on B(I).12/58/68 and PR.9; two mid-wing-mounted Rolls-Royce Avon 206 turbojets

Eurofighter EF2000 Typhoon International

Swing-role fighter

Collaborative venture between Germany (EADS/DASA), Italy (Alenia Aerospazio), Spain (EADS/CASA) and the UK (BAE Systems). The first of seven development aircraft flown on 27 March 1994. Deliveries began from 2003. Austria confirmed order in 2003, Norway and Singapore are considering buying.

VARIANTS & OPERATORS

Austria: 18 aircraft
Germany: 147 single-seaters, 33 two-seaters
Italy: 106 single-seaters, 15 two-seaters
Spain: 72 C.16 single-seaters, 15 CE.16 two-seaters
UK: 195 F.2 single-seaters, 37 T.1 two-seaters

SPECIFICATIONS

Crew/accommodation:
    Single-seater = pilot
    Trainer = student and instructor.
Max speed: M = 2.0
RoA – ground attack: 750nm (1,389km)

ARMAMENT

Internal gun: one 27mm Mauser cannon
Hardpoints: nine
- Max weapon/fuel load: 23,000kg (50,706 lb)
Representative weapons: AIM-120, AIM-9, ASRAAM, IRIS-T AAMs; various bombs, LGBs and PGMs; Storm Shadow AGM (UK); Brimstone ATGW (UK); designator and recce pods plus external fuel tanks

DIMENSIONS

Length: 15.9m (52ft 4in)
Wingspan: 10.9m (35ft 11in)
Height: 5.3m (17ft 4in)

FEATURES

Tall fin; canard; cranked-delta wings; twin Eurojet EJ200 turbojets; underfuselage inlets

Fairchild Republic (Lockheed Martin) A-10A USA

Close-support aircraft

Prototype YA-10A flew on 10 May 1972 and 713 production A-10As were built for the USAF between 1975 and 1983, plus one two-seater.

Many converted to forward observation role as OA-10A. Lockheed Martin to conduct SLEP for service to 2028; may possibly be re-engined.

VARIANTS & OPERATORS
A/OA-10A: USAF (362 remain in service)

SPECIFICATIONS
Crew/accommodation: Pilot
Max speed: 390kt (722km/h)
Radius of action: 540nm (1,000km)

ARMAMENT
Internal gun: one 30mm GAU-8/A cannon
Hardpoints: 11
Max weapon load: 9,450kg (21,000 lb)
Representative weapons: AIM-9 AAMs; Mk.80-series bombs; BLU-27/B Rockeye cluster bombs; Paveway II LGBs; AGM-65 Maverick AGMs; designator and EW/ECM pods; external fuel tanks

DIMENSIONS
Length: 16.3m (53ft 4in)
Wingspan: 17.5m (57ft 6in)
Height: 4.5m (14ft 8in)

FEATURES
Twin fins; low 'plank' wings; twin GE TF34 turbofans on rear-fuselage pods

FMA (LMAA) IA 58 Pucara Argentina

Close-support and recce aircraft

Designed by Argentina's Military Aircraft Factory (FMA) - privatised and re-named Lockheed Martin Aircraft Argentina (LMAA) since 1995 - deliveries of 105 Pucaras to the Argenine Air Force, 1976–86. Developed to IA 58B/C and IA 66 but these only reached prototype stage.

VARIANTS & OPERATORS
IA 58A: Argentina (35 in service) and Uruguay (5)

SPECIFICATIONS
Crew/accommodation:
   IA 58A = Pilot and navigator/WSO,
   IA 58C = pilot
Max speed: 405kt (750km/h)
Radius of action: 350nm (650km)

ARMAMENT
Internal guns: two 20mm Hispano cannon and four 7.62mm machine guns
Hardpoints: three
Max weapon load: 2,000kg (4,410 lb)
Representative weapons: 125kg or 500kg bombs; 2.75in FFAR pods; gun or EW/ECM pods; or external fuel tanks

DIMENSIONS
Length: 14.3m (46ft 9in)
Wingspan: 14.5m (47ft 6in)
Height: 5.4m (17ft 1in)

FEATURES
T-tail; low 'plank' wings; twin Turbomeca Astazou XVIG turboprops on wings

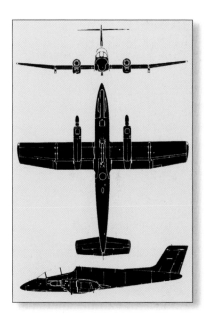

General Dynamics (Lockheed Martin) F-111 USA

Bomber and recce aircraft

Prototype F-111A V-G strike fighter for the USAF flew on 21 December 1964 and 538 F-111s were built for USAF and 24 for RAAF, last deliveries in 1976. USAF EF-111A were withdrawn in 1996. The RAAF bought four F-111As in 1982 and 25 ex-USAG F-111Gs in 1993-98, 10 of which were for spares. RAAF F-111s being upgraded for service to 2020.

VARIANTS & OPERATORS
F-111A(C): RAAF (4)
F-111C: RAAF (13)
F-111G: RAAF (14)
RF-111C: RAAF (4)

SPECIFICATIONS
Crew/accommodation: All versions = pilot and navigator/WSO in a jettisonable escape capsule
Max speed: M = 2.2
Range: 2,750+nm (5,093km)

ARMAMENT
Internal gun: one 20mm M61 cannon (optional)
Hardpoints: eight
Max weapon load: about 14,228kg (31,500 lb)
Representative weapons: AIM-9 AAM; Mk.80-series bombs; Paveway II LGB; AGM-84 Harpoon; EW/ECM or desigator pods; plus external fuel tanks

DIMENSIONS
Length: 22.4m (73ft 6in)
Wingspan: spread 21.3m (70ft 0in)
    fully-swept 10.3m (33ft 11in)
Height: 5.2m (17ft 1in)

FEATURES
Shoulder-mounted variable geometry wings; twin P&W TF30-P-3 turbofans; side-by-side cockpit; wide sleek nose

Grumman (Northrop Grumman) EA-6B Prowler USA

Electronic combat aircraft

Derived from the A-6 Intruder, prototype EA-6B Prowler flown on 25 May 1968 and entered USN service in 1971. Its ALQ-99 tactical jamming system progressively upgraded to ICAP III level. In all, 170 Prowlers were built. Now flown by mixed USN/USAF crews.

VARIANTS & OPERATORS
EA-6B: USN (91 in service)

SPECIFICATIONS
Crew/accommodation: Two pilots and two EWOs
Max speed: 530kt (982km/h)
Radius of action: 878nm (1,627km)

ARMAMENT
No internal gun
Hardpoints: one centreline, four under each wing
Max weapon load: about 4,547kg (10,025 lb)
Representative weapons: AGM-88 HARM plus external fuel tanks

DIMENSIONS
Length: 18.2m (59ft 10in)
Wingspan: 16.1m (53ft 0in)
Height: 4.9m (16ft 3in)

FEATURES
Bulbous fin fairing; swept mid-mounted wings; twin P&W J52 turbojets; lower fuselage intakes; double side-by-side cockpits

Grumman (Northrop Grumman) F-14 Tomcat USA

Carrier-based interceptor and attack fighter

First flown on 21 December 1970, the V-G F-14A entered USN service in 1972. Upgraded and re-engined (F110 replaced TF-30 in F-14B/D models). Iran bought 80 and the USN 632. USB retired F-15A in September 2004, with OSD for F-14B by 2006 and F-14D in 2007.

VARIANTS & OPERATORS
F-14A: Iran (30?), USN (37)
F-14B: USN (65)
F-14D: USN (46)

SPECIFICATIONS
Crew/accommodation: Pilot and WSO
Max speed: (F110 engines) M = 1.9
Range: (external fuel) 1,600nm (2,965km)

ARMAMENT
Internal gun: one 20mm M61 cannon
Hardpoints: six
Max weapon load: 6,577kg (14,500 lb)
Representative weapons: AIM-7, AIM-9, AIM-54 AAMs; Mk.80-series bombs; Rockeye cluster bombs; AGM-88 HARM; AGM-84G SLAM; LGBs; plus designator or recce pods and/or external fuel tanks

DIMENSIONS
Length: 19.1m (62ft 8in)
Wingspan: spread - 19.5m (64ft 1in)
    fully-swept - 11.6m (38ft 2in)
Height: 4.8m (16ft 0in)

FEATURES
Twin fins; variable-geometry wings; twin P&W TF30 or GE F110 turbofans; intakes under wing-root; rear ventral fins

Israel Aircraft Industries Kfir (Lion Cub) Israel

Fighter/attack aircraft

Derived from the Nesher (Mirage 5J) powered by a US J79 turbojet in place of the Atar 9K-50 with an auxiliary air intake forward of the fin root, canard foreplanes and lengthened nose. Prototype Kfir flown in 1973 and was revealed in April 1975. A total of 27 Kfir C1s and 185 C2/TC2s were built, many upgraded to C7/TC7 configuration.

VARIANTS & OPERATORS

Kfir C2: single-seater, Ecuador and Sri Lanka
Kfir TC2: two-seat operational trainer, Ecuador and Sri Lanka
Kfir C7: single seater, Israel, Colombia and Sri Lanka
Kfir TC7: two-seat operational trainer, Israel and Colombia

SPECIFICATIONS

Crew/accommodation:
Kfir C2/C7 = pilot,
Kfir TC2/TC7 = student and instructor
Max speed: 750kt (1,389km/h)
Radius of action: 640nm (1,186km)

ARMAMENT

Internal guns: two 30mm DEFA cannon
Hardpoints: seven
Max weapon load: about 6,085kg (13,415 lb)
Representative weapons: AIM-9 or Python-3/-4 AAMs; Mk.80-series bombs; AGM-45 Shrike; AGM-65 Maverick; GBU-15 PGM; FFAR pods; EW/ECM or designator pods; plus external fuel tanks

DIMENSIONS

Length: 15.7m (51ft 4in)
Wingspan: 8.2m (26ft 11in)
Height: 4.5m (14ft 11in)

FEATURES

Low delta wing; intake-mounted canards; single GE J79-J1E turbojet, with fin-root intake

Lockheed Martin AC-130H/U USA

Special operations gunship

The Hercules gunship concept goes back to the AC-47 of the Vietnam war era. The first C-130H Spectre, fitted with various sensors and a heavy armament, flew in September 1989. The improved AC-130U Spooky, modified by Rockwell North American (now Boeing), flew in December 1990.

VARIANTS & OPERATORS
AC-130H Spectre: USAF (8)
AC-130U Spooky: USAF (13 + 10 more conversions in hand)

SPECIFICATIONS
Crew/accommodation: Three flight crew plus mission crew of 10 (AC-130U) or 11 (AC-130H)
Max speed: 325kt (602km/h)
Range: 2,046nm (3,791km)

ARMAMENT: AC-130U
Internal guns: one 25mm GAU-12/U cannon; one 40mm M2A1 Bofors gun; one 105mm M137A1 howitzer, on port side of fuselage
Hardpoints: four
Representative weapons: use of AGM-114 Hellfire AGM studied; external fuel tanks under wing

DIMENSIONS
Length: 29.8m (97ft 9in)
Wingspan: 40.4m (132ft 7in)
Height: 11.7m (38ft 3in)

FEATURES
High-straight wings; four Allison (Rolls-Royce) T56 turboprops

Lockheed Martin F-16 Fighting Falcon USA

Multi-role fighter

Prototype YF-16A flew on 2 February 1974 and F-16A/B entered USAF from 1979. Progressively developed with Block improvements to current model F-16C/D Block 50/52. The B- and D-models are two-seat trainers. Over 4,410 ordered and 4,144 delivered, the F-16 has sold to 23 nations plus USAF and USN.

VARIANTS & OPERATORS

F-16A/B: USAF, Belgium, Denmark, Egypt, Indonesia, Israel, Italy*, Jordan*, Netherlands, Norway, Pakistan, Portugal, Singapore, Taiwan, Thailand, Venezuela
F-16C/D: USAF, Bahrain, Chile, Egypt, Greece, Israel, Korea (South), Oman, Poland, Singapore, Turkey, UAE
F-16N: USN (no longer in service)
* receiving used F-16s

SPECIFICATIONS

Crew/accommodation:
  F-16A/C/N = pilot
  F-16B/D = student and instructor
Max speed: M = 2.0+
Radius of action: 500+nm (925+km)

ARMAMENT

Internal gun: one 20mm M61 cannon
Hardpoints: nine (plus wingtips)
- Max external load: about 7,226+kg (15,930 lb)
Representative weapons: AIM-9, AIM-120 AAMs; Mk.80-series and cluster bombs; Paveway-series LGBs; AGM-65F Maverick; Penguin ASM; ECM pods; designator pods and external fuel tanks

DIMENSIONS

Length: 15.0m (49ft 4in)
Wingspan: 10.0m (32ft 9in)
Height: 5.1m (16ft 8in)

FEATURES

Swept fin; mid-swept wings; one P&W F100 or GE F110 turbofan; chin intake

NOT TO BE CONFUSED WITH: Mitsubishi F-1; T-50/A-50 Golden Eagle; F-CK-1 Ching-Kuo

Lockheed Martin F/A-22 Raptor USA

Air superiority fighter

Prototype YF-22 flew on 29 September 1990 (with GE YF120 engines) in competiton with Northrop YF-23 for ATF programme. USAF selected YF-23 with P&W YF119 engines on 23 April 1991. Nine EMD F-22As in test, first LRIP batch (10 aircraft) in 2001, against the USAF's reduced requirement of 276. IOT&E from September 2004, with IOC in December 2005.

VARIANTS & OPERATORS
F/A-22A: USAF

SPECIFICATIONS
Crew/accommodation: pilot
Max speed supercruise: M = 1.58
  with reheat: M = 1.7+ at 30,000ft
Radius of action: n/a

ARMAMENT
Internal gun: one 20mm M61A2annon
Hardpoints: four underwing + three internal bays
Max weapon load: external: 2,268kg (5,000 lb)
  internal: n/a
Representative weapons: AIM-9, AIM-120 AAMs; SDB and JDAM-series bombs; LOCAAS; WCMDs; AGM-88 HARM; Paveway III LGB; external fuel tanks

DIMENSIONS
Length: 18.9m (62ft 1in)
Wingspan: 13.6m (44ft 6in)
Height: 5.1m (16ft 8in)

FEATURES
Twin fins; shoulder-swept wings; two P&W F119 turbofans; intake under LERX

Lockheed Martin F-35 Joint Strike Fighter USA

Fighter and attack aircraft

Prototype X-35 flew on 24 October 2000 (with JSF119-PW-611 engine - now F135) in competition with Boeing X-32 for joint USN/USMC/USAF/RN/RAF programme. Flown in three versions: X-35A (CTOL), X-35B (STOVL) and X-35C (CV). X-35 with P&W F135 engines selected on 26 October 2001. Five F-35A, four F-35B and five F-35C for SDD. LRIP was expected in 2006/7 for 459 aircraft in six batches. Overall requirement is 2,593.

VARIANTS & OPERATORS

USAF: 1,763 F-35As required
USN/USMC: 680 F-35B/Cs required
Royal Navy: 60 F-35Bs required
RAF: 90 F-35Bs required
Orders possible from Australia (100), Canada, Denmark, Israel, Italy, the Netherlands, Norway, Singapore and Turkey.

SPECIFICATIONS

Crew/accommodation: pilot
Max speed: M = 1.6
RoA - F-35A: 600+nm (1,111km)
RoA - F-35B: 450+nm (833km)
RoA - F-35C: 700+nm (1,296km)

ARMAMENT

Internal gun: one 25mm GAU-12 cannon (USAF F-35A)
Hardpoints: four/six underwing plus two internal bays
Max weapon load: about 9,072+kg (20,000+ lb)
Representative weapons: ASRAAM, AIM-9, AIM-120C AAMs; AGM-154 JSOW, AGM-158 JASSM, JDAM-series bombs; WCMDs; Paveway-series LGBs; Storm Shadow, external fuel tanks

DIMENSIONS

	F-35A/B	F-35C
Length:	15.6m (51ft 1in)	15.7m (51ft 5in)
Wingspan:	10.7m (35ft 0in)	13.1m (43ft 0in)
Height:	4.6m (15ft 0in)	4.7m (15ft 6in)

FEATURES

Twin fins, shoulder swept-and-tapered wings, 'shark'-bevelled nose, one P&W F135 turbofan, side intakes

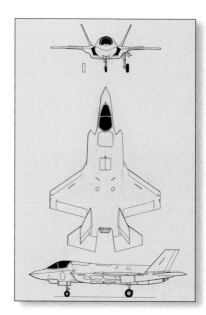

Lockheed Martin F-117A Nighthawk USA

Stealth attack fighter

Prototype Have Blue demonstrator flew in December 1977, with pre-series F-117A flying on 18 June 1981. Enter USAF service on 23 August 1982 and publicly revealed on 10 November 1988. Of a planned 100 aircraft, 59 were built and periodically upgraded.

VARIANTS & OPERATORS
F-117A: USAF

SPECIFICATIONS
Crew/accommodation: Pilot
Max speed: M = 1.0+
Radius of action: n/a

ARMAMENT
No internal gun
Weapons bays but no external hardpoints
Representative weapons: Mk.84 bomb;
BLU-109B, GBU-10, GBU-27 LGBs; AGM-65
Maverick; AGM-88 HARM

DIMENSIONS
Length: 20.1m (65ft 11in)
Wingspan: 13.2m (43ft 4in)
Height: 3.8m (12ft 5in)

FEATURES
Swept butterfly fins; low-swept wings blended to angular fuselage; two GE F404 turbofans

McDonnell Douglas (Boeing)/
BAE Systems AV-8B Harrier GR.7/9 USA

STOVL attack fighter

First YAV-8B demonstrator flown 9 November 1978, with first FSD AV-8B flying on 5 November 1981. Enter USMC service in September 1982. Some USMC upgraded to Night Attack and Harrier II Plus. First RAF Harrier GR.5 flown 30 April 1985 and entered RAF service on 1 July 1987. Three upgrades followed to GR.5A/7/9 configurations. A total of 391 AV-8B/Harrier GR.5/7/9s and 37 TAV-8B/Harrier T.10/12 trainers built by October 1995

VARIANTS & OPERATORS
AV-8B: USMC, Italy, Spain
Harrier GR.5/7/9: RAF
TAV-8B: USMC, Italy, Spain
Harrier T.10: RAF

SPECIFICATIONS
Crew/accommodation:
 AV-8B/Harrier GR.5/7/9 = pilot
 TAV-8B/Harrier T.10/12 = student + instructor
Max speed: 575kt (1,065km/h)
Radius of action: 594nm (1,101km)

ARMAMENT
Internal gun: one 25mm GAU-12/U cannon (USMC), two 25mm Aden cannon (now abandoned by RAF)
Hardpoints: seven (nine on RAF and Harrier II Plus)
Representative weapons: AIM-9; Mk.80-series bombs; AGM-65 Maverick; Paveway LGBs; FFAR pods; Brimstone AAAW; external fuel tanks

DIMENSIONS
Length – AV-8B: 14.1m (46ft 4in)
Length – Harrier GR.5/7/9: 14.4m (47ft 1in)
Wingspan: 9.2m (30ft 4in)
Height: 3.5m (11ft 7in)

FEATURES
Shoulder-swept wings; LERX; one Rolls-Royce Pegasus 11-61 vectored-thrust turbofan

McDonnell Douglas (Douglas) A-4 Skyhawk USA

Attack bomber

XA4D-1 Skyhawk prototype flown on 22 June 1954, with production reaching 2,960 (mostly for the USN/USMC). Sold to nine nations and many upgraded, including Singapore's Skyhawks, re-engined with GE F404 turbofans. Deliveries completed in 1979.

VARIANTS & OPERATORS
Argentina: A-4AR (converted OA/A-4Ms), TA-4AR
Brazil: A-4MB, TA-4MB (ex-Kuwait TA/A-4KUs)
Indonesia: A-4E, TA-4H/J
Israel: A-4H/N, TA-4H/J
Singapore: A-4SU, TA-SU (converted A-4Bs)
USA: TA-4J

SPECIFICATIONS
Crew/accommodation:
A-4AR/E/H/MB/N/SU = pilot
TA-4AR/H/J/SU = student and instructor
Max speed: 561kt, (1,040km/h)
Radius of action: 800nm (1,480km)

ARMAMENT
Internal guns: two 20mm Mk.12 cannon
Hardpoints: five
Max weapon load: 4,528kg (10,000 lb)
Representative weapons: AIM-9 AAMs; AGM-65 Maverick; Paveway LGBs; Mk.80-series bombs; FFAR pods; external fuel tanks and recce pods

DIMENSIONS
Length: 12.3m (40ft 4in)
Wingspan: 8.4m (27ft 6in)
Height: 4.6m (15ft 0in)

FEATURES
Low delta wing; delta tailplanes; one P&W J52-P-408 turbojet; fuselage intakes by cockpit

McDonnell Douglas (Boeing) F-4 Phantom II USA

Multirole fighter

XF4H-1 Phantom prototype flown on 27 May 1958, with production reaching 5,195 of all versions (including Japanese-built examples). Still in service with nine nations and many upgraded. Deliveries completed in 1981.

VARIANTS & OPERATORS

RF-4C: South Korea
F-4D: Iran, South Korea
F-4E: Egypt, Greece, Iran, Israel, South Korea, Turkey
F-4EJkai: Japan
RF-4E: Greece, Iran, Israel, Turkey
RF-4EJkai: Japan
F-4F: Germany
YF-4J, QF-4N/S: USA

SPECIFICATIONS

Crew/accommodation: All models = pilot and WSO
Max speed: M = 2.0+
Radius of action: 618nm (1,145km)

ARMAMENT: F-4E/F

Internal gun: one 20mm M61 cannon
Hardpoints: nine
Max weapon load: 7,250kg (16,000 lb)
Representative weapons: AIM-7, AIM-9, AIM-120 AAMs; AGM-65 Maverick; Paveway LGBs; Mk.80-series bombs; FFAR pods; ECM, recce and designator pods; external fuel tanks

DIMENSIONS

Length: 19.2m (63ft 0in)

Wingspan: 11.8m (38ft 7in)
Height: 5.0m (16ft 5in)

FEATURES

Anhedral tailplane; low swept wing with dihedral outer panels; two P&W J79 turbojets; fuselage intakes by cockpit

Mikoyan-Guryevich (RAC-MiG)
MiG-21 (J-7) 'Fishbed' Russia

Fighter-bomber

Michael J. Gething / Jane's

Ye-6 prototype first flown in late 1957 and the MiG-21 entered Soviet service in 1958. Progressively developed and several thousand sold worldwide. India and Romania (among others) are having major upgrades. Also built in China as J-7 (exported as F-7) where it was further developed is still in production.

VARIANTS & OPERATORS

MiG-21: Afghanistan (21*bis*), Algeria (21*bis*/PFM/UM), Angola (21*bis*/UM), Azerbaijan (21), Bulgaria (21R/MF/*bis*/UM), Cambodia (21*bis*/UM), Congo (21*bis*/UM), Croatia (21*bis*/UM), Cuba (21PFM/MF/*bis*/UM/US), Czech Republic (21MF), Egypt (21PF/PFM/R/MF/UM/US), Ethiopia (21MF/UM), Guinea Republic (21PFM), Hungary (21*bis*/UM), India (21FL/M/MF/*bis*/I/U/UM/US), Laos (21PFM/U), Libya (21*bis*/UM), Madagascar (21FL/U), Mali (21MF/UM), Mozambique (21*bis*), Nigeria (21MF/U), North Korea (21PF/PFM/U), Poland (21R, 21M/MF/*bis*/UM), Romania (21M/MF/UM), Slovak Republic (21MF/UM), Syria (21PF/MF/*bis*/U/UM), Turkmenistan (21), Vietnam (21*bis*/UM), Yemen (21MF/*bis*/U), Yugoslavia (21M/*bis*/UM), Zambia (21MF/US)

J-7/F-7: Albania, Bangladesh, China, Egypt, Iran, Myanmar, Pakistan, Sudan, Sri Lanka, Tanzania, Zimbabwe

SPECIFICATIONS

Crew/accommodation:
  MiG-21 fighter series = pilot
  MiG-21U-series ('Mongol') = student and instructor
Max speed: M = 2.2 (1,159kt, 2,150km/h)
Radius of action: 400nm (740km)

ARMAMENT: MIG-21MF 'FISHBED-J'

Internal gun: one twin-barrel 23mm GSh-23 cannon
Hardpoints: five
Max weapon load: about 1,500kg (3,307 lb) plus centreline tank
Representative weapons: K-13 'Atoll' AAMs; FFAR pods; bombs; external fuel tanks

DIMENSIONS

Length: 15.8m (51ft 8in)
Wingspan: 7.1m (23ft 5in)
Height: 4.1m (13ft 5in)

FEATURES

Swept tailplane; delta wing; one Tumansky R-13 turbojet; nose intake

Mikoyan-Guryevich (RAC-MiG)
MiG-23/27 'Flogger' Russia

Air combat fighter

Jane's/Craig Hoyle

Prototype first flown in June 1967. MiG-23 V-G
interceptor entered Soviet service in 1973.
Progressively developed; 4,000+ sold worldwide.
MiG-27 ground-attack version also developed.

VARIANTS & OPERATORS
MiG-23: Algeria (23BN/MS/UB), Angola
(23/ML/UB), Bulgaria (23BN/MF/ML/MLD/UB),
Cuba (23BN/MF/ML/UB), Ethiopia (23BN/UB), India
(23BN/MF/UB), Kazakhstan (23/MLD/UB), Libya
(23B/MS/UB), Namibia (23), North Korea
(23ML/UB), Russia (23M/UB), Sudan (23B), Syria
(23BN/MF/ML/MS/UB), Turkmenistan (23M/UB),
Yemen (23ML/UB), Zimbabwe (23)
MiG-27: India (27M), Kazakhstan (27M), Russia
(27), Sri Lanka (27M)

SPECIFICATIONS
Crew/accommodation:
    MiG-23/27 fighter series = pilot
    MiG-23UB = student and instructor
Max speed: M = 2.35 (1,350kt, 2,500km/h)
Radius of action: 620nm (1,150km)

ARMAMENT: MIG-23
Internal gun: one twin-barrel 23mm GSh-23L
Hardpoints: six
Max weapon load: 3,00kg (6,615 lb)
Representative weapons: R-23 'Apex', R-60
'Aphid' AAMs; FFAR pods; external fuel tanks

DIMENSIONS
Length: 16.7m (54ft 10in)

Wingspan: spread – 13.9m (45ft 10in)
           swept – 7.8m (25ft 6in)
Height: 4.8m (15ft 9in)

FEATURES
Swept tailplane; shoulder-mounted V-G wing; one
Soyuz/Khachaturov R-35 turbofan; rear ventral fin

Mikoyan-Guryevich (RAC-MiG)
MiG-25 'Foxbat' Russia

Interceptor fighter and recce aircraft

Developed as Ye-155P interceptor, first flown in 1964, the MiG-25BM high-altitude recce version entered Soviet service in 1971. Progressively developed as interceptor (MiG-25P/PD/PDS) with more specialised recce versions (MiG-25R/RB) and two-seat conversion trainer (MiG-25PU/RU). Some 1,186 MiG-25s of all versions built from 1970-1985.

VARIANTS & OPERATORS
Algeria (25PD/PU/RB), Armenia (25), Azerbaijan (25PD/PU/RB/RU), India (25R/RU), Kazakhstan (25PU/RB/RU), Libya (25PD/RB/RU), Russia (25BM/PU/R/RU), Syria (25PD/PU/RB/RU), Turkmenistan (25/PU)

SPECIFICATIONS
Crew/accommodation:
   MiG-25BM/P/PD/R/RB = pilot
   MiG-25PU/UB = student and instructor
Max speed: M = 2.83
Radius of action: 933nm (1,730km)

ARMAMENT: MIG-25P/PD
No internal gun
Hardpoints: four
Max weapon load: 1,800kg (3,968 lb)
Representative weapons: R-23 'Apex', R-40R/R-40T 'Acrid', R-60T 'Aphid', R-73T 'Archer' AAMs; external fuel tanks

DIMENSIONS
Length: 23.8m (78ft 1in)
Wingspan: 14.0m (45ft 11in)
Height: 6.1m (20ft 0in)

FEATURES
Twin fins; shoulder swept wing; two Soyuz/Tumansky R-15B turbojets; angular swept intakes

Mikoyan-Guryevich (RAC-MiG)
MiG-29 'Fulcrum' Russia

Air combat fighter

First flown on 6
October 1977, the
MiG-29 entered Soviet
service in 1983.
Progressively
developed as MiG-
29S-series 'Fulcrum-C'
multi-mission fighter,
MiG-29UB 'Fulcrum-B'
two-seat conversion
trainer and carrier-
borne version,
MiG-29K, plus other
upgrade
developments.
Over 1,100 MiG-29s of
all versions built.

VARIANTS & OPERATORS

Algeria (29S/UB), Bangladesh (29/UB), Belarus
(29S/UB), Bulgaria (29/UB), Cuba (29/UB), Eritrea
(29), Hungary (29/UB), India (29/UB/K), Iran
(29/UB), Kazakhstan (29/UB), Libya (29), Malaysia
(29/UB), Myanmar (29/UB), North Korea (29/UB),
Peru (29S/UB), Poland (29/UB), Russia
(29/S/UB/K), Serbia & Montenegro (29/UB),
Slovak Republic (29/UB), Syria (29/UB),
Turkmenistan (29/UB), Ukraine (29/S/UB), USA
(29/UB), Uzbekistan (29/UB), Yemen (29/UB)

FEATURES

Twin fins; mid-swept wing; two Klimov/Sarkisov
RD-33 turbofans; intakes under LERX

SPECIFICATIONS

Crew/accommodation:
  MiG-29/29S = pilot,
  MiG-29UB = student and instructor
Max speed: M = 2.3 (1,320kt, 2,445km/h)
Radius of action: about 380nm (704km)

ARMAMENT

Internal gun: one 30mm GSh-30-1 cannon
Hardpoints: seven
Max weapon load: about 4,000kg (8,816 lb)
Representative weapons: R-27 'Alamo', R-60T
'Aphid', R-73T 'Archer' AAMs; bombs; FFAR pods;
external fuel tanks

DIMENSIONS

Length: 17.3m (56ft 10in)
Wingspan: 11.4m (37ft 3in)
Height: 4.7m (15ft 6in)

Mikoyan-Guryevich (RAC-MiG)
MiG-31 'Foxhound' Russia

All-weather, all-altitude interceptor fighter

First flown as Ye-155MP interceptor on 16 September 1975, the two-seat MiG-31 entered Soviet service in 1982. Progressively evolved as

interceptor with more missiles and improved radar (MiG-31M).

VARIANTS & OPERATORS
Kazakhstan (34) and Russia (315)

SPECIFICATIONS
Crew/accommodation: Pilot and WSO
Max speed: M = 2.83
Radius of action: 647nm (1,200km)

ARMAMENT
Internal gun: provision for one 23mm GSh-6-23M six-barrel cannon
Hardpoints: ten
Max weapon load: about 2,700kg (5,951 lb)
Representative weapons: R-33 'Amos', R-37 (AA-X-13), R-40R/R-40T 'Acrid', R-60T 'Aphid', R-77 'Adder' AAMs; external fuel tanks

DIMENSIONS
Length: 22.3m (74ft 5in)
Wingspan: 13.5m (44ft 2in)
Height: 6.1m (20ft 2in)

FEATURES
Twin fins; shoulder swept wing; two Aviadvigatel D-30F6 turbojets; angular swept intakes

Mitsubishi F-1 Japan

Close air support fighter

Derived from the Mitsubishi T-2 trainer, the first F-1 flew on 3 June 1975 and entered JASDF service in 1976. The last of 177 aircraft delivered in 1987.

VARIANTS & OPERATORS
Japan

SPECIFICATIONS
Crew/accommodation: Pilot
Max speed: M = 1.6
Radius of action: n/a

ARMAMENT
Internal gun: one 20mm JM61 cannon
Hardpoints: five
Max weapon load: 2,721kg (5,997 lb)
Representative weapons: ASM-1 ASM; bombs, FFAR pods; external fuel tanks

DIMENSIONS
Length: 17.8m (58ft 6in)
Wingspan: 7.9m (25ft 10in)
Height: 4.5m (14ft 8in)

FEATURES
Shoulder swept wing; two Rolls-Royce/Turbomeca Adour 108 turbofans; rear ventral fins

Mitsubishi F-2 Japan

Close air support fighter

Based on F-16C and co-developed with Lockheed Martin, the first F-2A flew on 7 October 1995. A combat-capable two-seater (F-2B) planned. First deliveries to JASDF in September 2000. As of April 2004 45 delivered of 71 on order.

VARIANTS & OPERATORS
Japan

SPECIFICATIONS
Crew/accommodation:
    F-2A = pilot,
    F-2B = student and instructor
Max speed: M = 2.0
Radius of action: n/a

ARMAMENT
Internal gun: one 20mm M61 cannon
Hardpoints: 13
Max weapon load: 6,498kg (14,320 lb)
Representative weapons: AAM-3, AIM-7, AIM-9 AAMs; ASM-1/-2 ASMs; bombs, FFAR pods; external fuel tanks

DIMENSIONS
Length: 15.5m (58ft 6in)
Wingspan: 11.1m (36ft 6in)
Height: 4.9m (16ft 3in)

FEATURES
Mid-swept wing; GE F110 turbofan; chin intake

NAMC Q-5 'Fantan' China

Close air support fighter

The twin-jet attack Q-5, derived from the J-6/MiG-19, first flew on 4 June 1965 and entered service in 1970. Sold to four countries as the A-5 and improved Q-5 II (A-5M) developed but not sold. About 1,000 built.

VARIANTS & OPERATORS
China (Q-5), Bangladesh (A-5), Myanmar (A-5), North Korea (A-5), Pakistan (A-5)

SPECIFICATIONS
Crew/accommodation: Pilot
Max speed: M = 1.12 (643kt, 1,190km/h)
Radius of action: 324nm (600km)

ARMAMENT
Internal gun: one 23mm cannon
Hardpoints: 10
Max weapon load: 2,000kg (4,410 lb)
Representative weapons: PL-2, PL-7, AIM-9, Magic AAMs; bombs; FFAR pods; external fuel tanks

DIMENSIONS
Length: 16.2m (53ft 4in)
Wingspan: 9.7m (31ft 10in)
Height: 4.5m (14ft 9in)

FEATURES
Swept wing; two Shenyang WP6 turbojets; intakes by cockpit; pointed nose

Northrop (N-G) B-2A Spirit USA

Long-range bomber

With a low-observable (stealth) configuration
built as a flying wing, the first B-2A flew on 17
July 1989 and entered USAF service in 1996. Only
21 built but having capability upgrades.

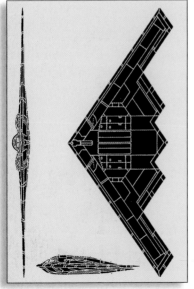

VARIANTS & OPERATORS
USAF

SPECIFICATIONS
Crew/accommodation: Two pilots (plus third seat)
Max speed: n/a
Range (internal fuel): 4,500nm (8,334km)

ARMAMENT
No internal gun
Two weapons bays, each with 8-store rotary
launcher, no external hardpoints
Max weapon load: 18,144kg (40,000 lb)
Representative weapons: AGM-129 ACM; JDAM,
JSOW and JASSM weapons; nuclear and
conventional bombs

DIMENSIONS
Length: 21.0m (69ft 0in)
Wingspan: 52.4m (172ft 0in)
Height: 5.2m (17ft 0in)

FEATURES
No fin; flying wing with blended fuselage
(tadpole-like); serrated trailing edge; four GE F118
turbofans

Northrop (N-G) F-5A/B Freedom Fighter USA

Lightweight fighter-bomber

The N-156C prototype first flew on 30 July 1959 and was widely exported from 1963. Two-seat F-5B flown 24 February 1964. Built under licence in Canada and Spain. Many upgraded. Last of 1,199 F-5A/B delivered in 1976.

VARIANTS & OPERATORS

Botswana **(CF-5A/D)**, Morocco **(F-5A/B, RF-5A)**, Norway **(F-5A/B)**, Philippines **(F-5A/B)**, South Korea **(F-5A/B, EF-5A, RF-5A)**, Spain **(F-5M)**, Thailand **(F-5A/B)**, Turkey **(NF/F-5A/B,RF-5A)**, Venezuela **(VF-5A/D, NF-5B)**, Yemen **(F-5B)**

SPECIFICATIONS

Crew/accommodation:
  F-5A, EF-5A, RF-5A = pilot
  F-5B, F-5M = student and instructor
Max speed: 710kt (1,315km/h)
Range (internal fuel): 485nm (898km)

ARMAMENT

Internal guns: two 20mm cannon
Hardpoints: five (plus wingtips)
Max weapon load: 2,812kg (6,200 lb)
Representative weapons: AIM-9 AAMs; bombs; FFAR pods; external fuel tanks (sometimes on wingtips)

DIMENSIONS

Length: 14.4m (47ft 2in)
Wingspan: 7.7m (25ft 3in)

Height: 4.0m (13ft 2in)

FEATURES

Low tailplane; low swept wing; two GE J85 turbojets

Northrop (N-G) F-5E/F Tiger II USA

Lightweight fighter-bomber

An improved version of the F-5A/B, the first F-5E flew on 11 August 1972 and was widely exported. Two-seat F-5F flown 25 September 1974. Built under licence in Switzerland and Taiwan. Many upgraded. Last of 1,418 F-5E/F delivered in 1989.

VARIANTS & OPERATORS

Austria (F-5E/F – leased), Bahrain (F-5E/F), Brazil (F-5E/F), Chile (F-5E/F), Honduras (F-5E/F), Indonesia (F-5E/F), Iran (F-5E/F), Jordan (F-4E/F), Kenya (F-5E/F), Malaysia (RF/F-5E/F), Mexico (F-5E/F), Morocco (F-5E/F), Saudi Arabia (RF/F-5E/F), Singapore (RF/F-5S/T), South Korea (F-5E/F), Switzerland (F-5E/F), Taiwan (RF/F-5E/F), Thailand (F-5E/F), Tunisia (F-5E/F), USA (F-5E/F), Yemen (F-5E)

SPECIFICATIONS

Crew/accommodation:
   F-5E/S, RF-5E/S Tigereye = pilot
   F-5F/T = student and instructor
Max speed: 710kt (1,315km/h)
Range (internal fuel): 570nm (1,056km)

ARMAMENT

Internal guns: two 20mm cannon (one on F-5F)
Hardpoints: five (plus wingtips)
Max weapon load: 3,175kg (7,000 lb)
Representative weapons: AIM-9 AAMs; bombs; FFAR pods; external fuel tanks

DIMENSIONS

Length: 14.5m (47ft 5in)
Wingspan: 8.1m (26ft 8in)
Height: 4.1m (13ft 4in)

FEATURES

Low tailplane; low swept wing; two GE J85 turbojets; some aircraft have dorsal fin extension

Panavia Tornado IDS/ECR Germany/Italy/UK

Interdictor strike and recce aircraft

First prototype Tornado IDS (aka MRCA) flew on 14 August 1974 and deliveries began in 1980. Built in Germany, Italy and the UK and sold to Saudi Arabia. IDS designated GR.1 by RAF, now upgraded to GR.4. ECR (converted from IDS) developed by Germany and flown 18 August 1988. Last of 795 Tornado IDS/ECRs delivered in 1992. German and Italian Tornados also being upgraded.

VARIANTS & OPERATORS
German Air Force/Navy **(IDS/ECR)**, Italian Air Force **(IDS/ECR)**, RAF **(IDS)**, Saudi Arabia **(IDS)**

SPECIFICATIONS
Crew/accommodation: Pilot and navigator/WSO
Max speed: M = 2.2
Range (internal fuel): 750nm (1,390km)

ARMAMENT
Internal guns: two 27mm BK27 cannon
Hardpoints: seven
Max weapon load: about 7,530kg (16,600 lb)
Representative weapons: AIM-9 AAM; AGM-65 Maverick; AGM-88 HARM; ALARM; Kormoran ASM; Storm Shadow AGM; bombs; rockets; CBLS; ECM, designator and recce pods; external fuel tanks

DIMENSIONS
Length: 16.7m (54ft 10in)
Wingspan: spread - 13.9m (45ft 7in)
spread - 8.6m (28ft 2in)

Height: 5.9m (19ft 6in)

FEATURES
Large fin; V-G wing; two Turbo-Union RB199 turbofans

Panavia Tornado F.3 ADV Germany/Italy/UK

Air defence fighter

Tornado EF.3

First prototype Tornado ADV flew on 27 October 1979. Tornado F.2 (18-only) now out of service, Tornado F.3 (with RB199 104 engines) deliveries began in 1986. Sold to Saudi Arabia (24) and 24 RAF F.3s leased by Italy (now returned). RAF aircraft being upgraded, including six to EF.3. Total of 197 ADVs built.

VARIANTS & OPERATORS
RAF (EF/F.3), Saudi Arabia (F.53)

SPECIFICATIONS
Crew/accommodation: Pilot and navigator/WSO
Max speed: M = 2.2
Range (internal fuel): 1,000+nm (1,853km)

ARMAMENT
Internal gun: one 27mm BK27 cannon
Hardpoints: eight
Max weapon load: 8,500kg (18,740 lb)
Representative weapons: AIM-9, AIM-120, ASRAAM, Skyflash AAMs; ALARM (EF.3); Ariel towed radar decoy; ECM pods; external fuel tanks

DIMENSIONS
Length: 18.7m (61ft 3in)
Wingspan: spread - 13.9m (45ft 7in)
    swept - 8.6m (28ft 2in)
Height: 5.9m (19ft 6in)

FEATURES
Large fin; V-G wing; two Turbo-Union RB199 turbofans

Rockwell (Boeing) B-1B Lancer USA

Long-range bomber

Original B-1A first flew on 23 December 1974 and four prototypes flown. Resurrected in 1981, 100 improved B-1Bs were ordered, the first flying on 18 October 1984. Entered USAF service in May 1985. Deliveries completed in April 1988. Capability upgrades underway.

VARIANTS & OPERATORS
USAF

SPECIFICATIONS
Crew/accommodation: Two pilots, two WSOs
Max speed: M = 1.25
Range (unrefuelled): 6,475nm (12,000km)

ARMAMENT
No internal gun
Weapons bays: three internal plus six external hardpoints
Max weapon load: internal: 34,019kg (75,000 lb)
external: 26,762kg (59,000 lb)
Representative weapons: AGM-86 ALCM; AGM-69 SRAM; nuclear weapons; bombs; JDAM, JSOW, WCMD weapons; mines

DIMENSIONS
Length: 44.8m (147ft 0in)
Wingspan: spread - 41.7m (136ft 8in)
swept - 23.8m (78ft 2in)
Height: 10.4m (34ft 0in)

FEATURES
V-G wing blended to fuselage; four GE F101 turbofans in under fuselage pods; small canards

Rockwell (Boeing) OV-10 Bronco USA

Mulltipurpose COIN aircraft

YOV-10A prototype flown on 16 July 1965 and 271 Broncos entered USMC and USAF service, now withdrawn. Some export sales, some ex-US transfers with 360 built.

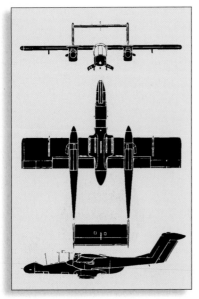

VARIANTS & OPERATORS
OV-10A: Columbia, Morocco, Philippines, Venezuela
OV-10C: Thailand
OV-10E: Venezuela
OV-10F: Indonesia

SPECIFICATIONS
Crew/accommodation: Two pilots
Max speed: 244kt (452km/h)
Radius of action: 198nm (367km)

ARMAMENT
Internal guns: four 7.62mm M60C machine guns
Hardpoints: seven
Max weapon load: 1,633kg (3,600 lb)
Representative weapons: AIM-9 AAM; Mk.80-series bombs; FFAR pods; gun pods; external fuel tank

DIMENSIONS
Length: 12.7m (41ft 7in)
Wingspan: 12.2m (40ft 0in)
Height: 4.6m (15ft 2in)

FEATURES
Twin boom tail; podded fuselage; two Garrett T76 turboprops; fuselage stores sponsons

Saab 37 Viggen Sweden

Fighter, attack and recce aircraft

Michael J. Gething / Jane's

First flown on 8 February 1967, the Viggen produced in five variants: AJ37 attack, SF37 and SH37 recce, SK37 two-seater and JA37 fighter. JA37 to be withdrawn 2005, leaving only SK37 in Swedish service. Last of 329 Viggens delivered in 1990.

VARIANTS & OPERATORS
Sweden (JA37C/D, SK37E)

SPECIFICATIONS
Crew/accommodation:
  JA37 = pilot,
  SK37E = student and WSO
Max speed: M = 2.0+
Radius of action: 540+nm (1,000km)

ARMAMENT: JA37
Internal gun: one 30mm KCA cannon
Hardpoints: seven
Max weapon load: 2,000kg (4,408 lb)
Representative weapons: Skyflash, AIM-9, AIM-120 AAMs; 135mm rockets; ECM pods; external fuel tanks

DIMENSIONS
Length: 15.6m (51ft 1in)
Wingspan: main - 10.6m (34ft 9in)
    fore - 5.4m (17ft 10in)
Height: 5.9m (19ft 4in)

FEATURES
Canard foreplane; delta main wing; one Volvo RM8B turbofan

Saab JAS 39 Gripen Sweden

Interceptor, attack and recce aircraft

First flown on 9 December 1988, the first multi-role Gripen delivered in 1993. Prototype JAS 39B flown 29 April 1996. Sweden has ordered 204. Sold to South Africa (new build) and Czech Republic and Hungary (leased Swedish aircraft).

VARIANTS & OPERATORS
Sweden (JAS 39A/B), Czech Republic, Hungary, Sweden (JAS 39C/D), South Africa (JAS 39X/XT)

SPECIFICATIONS
Crew/accommodation:
    JAS 39A/C/X = pilot,
    JAS 39B/D/XT = student and instructor
Max speed: supersonic
Radius of action: 432nm (800km)

ARMAMENT
Internal gun: one 27mm BK27 cannon
Hardpoints: six (plus wingtips)
Max weapon load: 4,120kg (9,080 lb)
Representative weapons: AIM-9, AIM-120 AAMs; AGM-65 Maverick; RBS 15F; DWS 39; bombs; FFAR pods; ECM and recce pods; external fuel tanks

DIMENSIONS
Length: 14.1m (46ft 3in)
Wingspan: 8.4m (27ft 7in)
Height: 4.5m (14ft 9in)
FEATURES
Canard foreplane; delta main wing; one Volvo RM12 (GE F404) turbofan

Shenyang J-6/F-6 (MiG-19) 'Farmer' China

Interceptor fighter

The J-6 (exported as F-6 and FT-6 trainer) is the Chinese-built version of Russia's MiG-19 first flown in September 1953. The MiG-19 entered Soviet service in 1954 and Russian production of about 2,500 ceased in 1959. The first Chinese J-6 (MiG-19S) flew in December 1961. Several thousand J-6 and variants built by Guizhou and Shenyang up to early-1980s.

VARIANTS & OPERATORS

J-6: China
F-6: Albania, Egypt, Iran, North Korea, Sudan, Tanzania, Zambia.
FT-6: Bangladesh, Egypt, North Korea, Pakistan, Zambia

SPECIFICATIONS

Crew/accommodation:
    J-6/F-6 = pilot,
    FT-6 = student and instructor
Max speed: 738kt (1,452km/h)
Radius of action: 370nm (685km)

ARMAMENT

Internal gun: two/three 30mm NR-30 cannon
Hardpoints: up to eight
Max weapon load: about 500kg (1,123 lb) plus external fuel tanks
Representative weapons: AIM-9 AAM (Pakistan); FFAR pods; bombs

DIMENSIONS

Length: 14.6m (48ft 2in)

Wingspan: 9.0m (29ft 8in)
Height: 3.9m (12ft 8in)

FEATURES

Fin-mounted tailplane; mid swept wing; two Shenyang WP6 (R-9BF) turbojets; nose intake

Shenyang J-8 'Finback' China

Air superiority fighter

First prototype J-8 flown on 5 July 1969 but development delayed. J-8/J-8 I production 1979-1987 (100+). J-8B first flew on 12 June 1984 and 24 reported in service by 1993. J-8B and C production continues and J-8 upgrade developing.

VARIANTS & OPERATORS
China

SPECIFICATIONS
Crew/accommodation: Pilot
Max speed: M = 2.2
Radius of action: 432nm (800km)

ARMAMENT
Internal gun: one 23mm Type 23-3 twin-barrel cannon
Hardpoints: seven
Max weapon load: about 5,400kg (11,902 lb)
Representative weapons: PL-2B, PL-7, R-27 'Alamo' AAMs; bombs; rockets; ECM and recce pods; external fuel tanks

DIMENSIONS
Length: 21.6m (70ft 10in)
Wingspan: 9.3m (30ft 8in)
Height: 5.4m (17ft 9in)

FEATURES
Tailed delta configuration; swept fin; ventral fin; two Liyang WP13A II turbojets; side slab intakes

SEPECAT Jaguar France/UK

Close air support fighter

First prototype Jaguar (E = Ecole or trainer) flown on 8 September 1968 with first production aircraft flying in November 1971. France bought 200 and the UK 202. Sold to Ecuador, India (licence-built by HAL and still in production), Nigeria and Oman. RAF and Omani aircraft upgraded to GR.3A and T.4 configuration. Over 620 produced. OSD for RAF is 2007.

VARIANTS & OPERATORS
Ecuador (**Jaguar EB/ES**), France (**Jaguar A/E**), India (**Jaguar IB/IM/IS**), Nigeria (**Jaguar BN/SN**), Oman (**Jaguar OB/OS**), RAF (**Jaguar B [T.2/4] / S [GR.1/3/3A]**)

SPECIFICATIONS
Crew/accommodation:
    Jaguar A/ES/IM/IS/OS/S/SN = pilot
    Jaguar B/BN/E/EB/IB/OB = student and
instructor
Max speed: M = 1.6 (917kt, 1,699km/h)
Radius of action: 760nm (1,408km)

ARMAMENT
Internal guns: two 30mm Aden cannon
Hardpoints: five (plus overwing pylons)
Max weapon load: 4,536kg (10,000 lb)
Representative weapons: Magic, ASRAAM, AIM-9 AAMs; Sea Eagle ASM; AS.37 Martel ARM; bombs; FFAR pods; ECM and recce pods; external fuel tanks

DIMENSIONS
Length: 16.8m (55ft 2in)

Wingspan: 8.7m (28ft 6in)
Height: 4.9m (16ft 1in)

FEATURES
Shoulder swept wing; two Rolls-Royce/Turbomeca Adour 804/811 turbofans; square lateral intakes; Jaguars A/B/E have pointed nose, others a wedge nose; Jaguar IM has Agave radar nose

Sukhoi Su-17/-20/-22 'Fitter-D/K' Russia

Ground attack and recce fighter

Evolved from the Su-7, the Su-17 featured V-G outer wings and the prototype flew on 2 August 1966. Ground attack, recce and trainer versions were developed. The Su-20/-22 were used exclusively as export designations. Over 2,900 Su-17/-20/-22 'Fitters' were produced.

VARIANTS & OPERATORS

Angola (**Su-22M4/ UM3**), Azerbaijan (**Su-17M**), Bulgaria (**Su-22M4/UM3**), Ethiopia (**Su-22M4**), Georgia (**Su-17**), Libya (**Su-20/-22M/U/UM3**), Peru (**Su-20/-22MU/UM3**), Poland (**Su-22M4/UM3**), Syria (**Su-22M/M4/UM3**), Turkmenistan (**Su-17M/UM3**), Ukraine (**Su-17M3/M4/UM3**), Uzbekistan (**Su-17M3/UM3**), Vietnam (**Su-22M3/M4/UM3**), Yemen (**Su-20/ Su-22M/UM3**)

SPECIFICATIONS

Crew/accommodation:
    All but Su-22U/UM3 = pilot,
    Su-22U/UM3 = student and instructor
Max speed: M = 2.09
Radius of action: about 550nm (1,017km)

ARMAMENT

Internal guns: two 30mm NR-30 cannon
Hardpoints: nine
Max weapon load: 4,250kg (9,370 lb)
Representative weapons: Kh-23 'Kerry', Kh-25 'Karen', Kh-28 'Kyle' AGMs; bombs; rockets; external fuel tanks

DIMENSIONS

Length: 18.8m (61ft 6in)
Wingspan: spread - 10.0m (32ft 10in)
    swept - 8.8m (28ft 9in)
Height: 5.0m (16ft 5in)

FEATURES

V-G wing; one Lyulka AL-21F-3 turbojet; nose intake

Sukhoi Su-24 'Fencer' Russia

Bomber and recce/EW aircraft

An F-111 "lookalike", the Su-24 prototype first flew in January 1970 and by 1980, production running at 70 per year. Also operates as 'buddy'-tanker. About 1,000 Su-24s produced to date.

VARIANTS & OPERATORS

Algeria (Su-24MK), Angola (Su-24), Azerbaijan (Su-24), Belarus (Su-24MK/MR), Iran (Su-24MK), Kazakhstan (Su-24/MR), Libya (Su-24MK), Russia (Su-24/MP/MR), Syria (Su-24MK), Ukraine (Su-24M/MP/MR), Uzbekistan (Su-24/MR)

SPECIFICATIONS

Crew/accommodation: Pilot and WSO
Max speed: M = 2.18
Radius of action: about 565nm (1,050km)

ARMAMENT

Internal gun: one 30mm six-barrel cannon
Hardpoints: nine
Max weapon load: 8,000kg (17,635 lb)
Representative weapons: Kh-23 'Kerry', Kh-25ML 'Karen', Kh-25MP 'Kegler', Kh-29ovod 'Kingbolt, Kh-29 'Kedge', Kh-58 'Kilter' AGMs; bombs; rockets; AAR pod; external fuel tanks

DIMENSIONS

Length: 24.5m (80ft 5in)
Wingspan: spread - 17.6m (57ft 10in)
         swept - 10.4m (34ft 0in)

Height: 5.0m (16ft 3in)

FEATURES

V-G wing; two Saturn/Lyulka AL-21F-3A turbojets; lateral intakes; ventral fins

Sukhoi Su-25 'Frogfoot' Russia

Close air support aircraft

Michael J. Gething / Jane's

Prototype Su-25 first flown on 22 February 1975. Initial production in Tbilisi, Georgia, ended by 1989 but about 50 built/partially-built aircraft remain unsold and Su-25 Scorpion upgrade developed. Russian production at Ulan-Ude finished 1992 but Su-39 upgrade developed. About 1,000 Su-25s produced to date.

VARIANTS & OPERATORS

Angola (Su-25/UB), Armenia (Su-25), Azerbaijan (Su-25), Belarus (Su-25/UBK), Bulgaria (Su-25/UBK), Dem. Rep. of Congo (Su-25), Czech Republic (Su-25/UBK), Eritrea (Su-25K), Georgia (Su-25/UBK/T/TM/Su-39), Kazakhstan (Su-25), Macedonia (Su-25), North Korea (Su-25/UBK), Peru (Su-25), Russia (Su-25/UB/UTG/T/TM/ Su-39), Slovak Republic (Su-25UBK), Turkmenistan (Su-25/UBK), Ukraine (Su-25/UBK/UTG), Uzbekistan (Su-25)

SPECIFICATIONS

Crew/accommodation:
Su-25/T/TM/Su-39 = pilot
Su-25UB/UBK/UTG = student and instructor
Max speed: 526kt (975km/h)
Range: 675nm (1,250km)

ARMAMENT

Internal gun: one 30mm AO-17A two-barrel cannon
Hardpoints: 10
Max weapon load: 4,400kg (9,700 lb)
Representative weapons: R-3S 'Atoll', R-60 'Aphid' AAMs; Kh-23 'Kerry', Kh-25 'Karen', Kh-29 'Kedge' AGMs; LGBs; bombs; rockets; 23mm gun pod; external fuel tanks

DIMENSIONS

Length: 15.5m (50ft 11in)
Wingspan: 14.4m (47ft 1in)
Height: 4.8m (15ft 9in)

FEATURES

Shoulder slightly swept wing; ECM pod wingtips; two Soyuz/Gavrilov R-195 turbojets; lateral intakes and jetpipes

Sukhoi Su-27 'Flanker' Russia

Air superiority fighter and ground attack aircraft

Prototype Su-27 'Flanker-B' first flown on 20 May 1977 and developed as a long-range heavy fighter, as well as an operational trainer – Su-27UB 'Flanker-C'. Further developments described in other entries. Exported and to be built under licence in China as J-11.

VARIANTS & OPERATORS
Angola (Su-27), Belarus (Su-27/UB), China (Su-27/UB), Ethiopia (Su-27), Kazakhstan (Su-27/UB), Russia (Su-27/UB), Ukraine (Su-27/UB), Uzbekistan (Su-27/UB), Vietnam (Su-27/UB)

SPECIFICATIONS
Crew/accommodation:
   Su-27 = pilot
   Su-27UB = student and instructor
Max speed: M = 2.35 (1,350kt, 2,500km/h)
Radius of action: 810nm (1,500km)

ARMAMENT
Internal gun: one 30mm GSh-30-1 cannon
Hardpoints: eight (plus wingtips)
Max weapon load: 4,000kg (8,818 lb)
Representative weapons: R-27 'Alamo', R-33 'Amos', R-60 'Aphid', R-73 'Archer' AAMs; bombs; rockets; 23mm gun pod; external fuel tanks

DIMENSIONS
Length: 21.9m (71ft 11in)
Wingspan: 14.7m (48ft 3in)

Height: 5.9m (19ft 5in)

FEATURES
Twin fins; shoulder swept wing; two Saturn/Lyulka AL-31F turbofans; intakes under fuselage/wing; ventral fins; tailcone between jetpipes

Sukhoi Su-30/-33 'Flanker' Russia

Air superiority fighter and ground attack aircraft

Originally the Su-27PU, the tandem two-seat Su-30 first flew on 31 December 1989 as a long-range interceptor. Su-30M 'Flanker-F' is multirole version, Su-30MKI 'Flanker-H' features canards. Su-33 (Su-27K 'Flanker-D') is carrier-borne version.

VARIANTS & OPERATORS

China (Su-30MKK 'Flanker-G'), India (Su-30MK/MKI/PU), Russia (Su-30/M/-33)

SPECIFICATIONS

Crew/accommodation: Pilot and WSO
Max speed: M = 2.35 (1,350kt, 2,500km/h)
Radius of action: 810nm (1,500km)

ARMAMENT

Internal gun: one 30mm GSh-30-1 cannon
Hardpoints: 10 (plus wingtips)
Max weapon load: 8,000kg (17,635 lb)
Representative weapons: R-27 'Alamo', R-73 'Archer', R-77 'Adder' AAMs; Kh-29 'Kedge', Kh-31 'Krypton', Kh-59 'Kazoo' AGMs; Raduga 3M80E ASM; bombs; rockets; external fuel tanks

DIMENSIONS

Length: 21.9m (71ft 11in)
Wingspan: 14.7m (48ft 3in)
Height: 5.9m (19ft 5in)

FEATURES

Twin fins; shoulder swept wing; two Saturn/Lyulka AL-31F turbofans; intakes under fuselage/wing; ventral fins; tailcone between jetpipes

Sukhoi Su-32/-33U/-34 'Fullback' Russia

Long-range fighter/attack aircraft

Paul Jackson / Jane's

Originally the Su-27IB with side-by-side seating, the Su-34 first flew on 18 December 1993. This configuration developed as Su-32 for land-based maritime attack (not yet in service) and Su-33UB (Su-27KUB) carrier-borne trainer version. Su-34 no longer used.

VARIANTS & OPERATORS
Russia (**Su-32/-33UB**)

SPECIFICATIONS
Crew/accommodation:
    Su-32/-34 = pilot and WSO,
    Su-33UB = student and instructor
Max speed: M = 1.8 (1,025kt, 1,900km/h)
Radius of action: 601nm (1,113km)

ARMAMENT
Internal gun: one 30mm GSh-30-1 cannon
Hardpoints: 10 (plus wingtips)
Max weapon load: 8,000kg (17,635 lb)
Representative weapons: R-73 'Archer', R-77 'Adder' AAMs; ASMs; LGBs; bombs; external fuel tanks

DIMENSIONS
Length: 23.3m (76ft 7in)
Wingspan: 14.7m (48ft 3in)
Height: 6.5m (21ft 4in)

FEATURES
Twin fins; shoulder swept wing; canard foreplanes; two Saturn/Lyulka AL-31F turbofans; intakes under fuselage/wing; ventral fins; tailcone between jetpipes

Sukhoi Su-35/-37 'Flanker-E' Russia

All-weather counter-air fighter

Paul Jackson / Jane's

The Su-35, originally Su-27M, first flew on 28 June 1988. Planned for Russian service but not produced, marketed for export. The Su-37 was a technology demonstrator for vectored-thrust jetpipes, flown in April 1996.

VARIANTS & OPERATORS
Su-35 (and Su-33UB trainer) in service in small numbers with Russia; Indonesia ordered 2 in 2003

SPECIFICATIONS
Crew/accommodation: Pilot
Max speed: M = 2.35 (1,350kt, 2,500km/h)
Range: 2,160+nm (4,000+km)

ARMAMENT
Internal gun: one 30mm GSh-30-1 cannon
Hardpoints: 12 (plus wingtips)
Max weapon load: 8,200kg (18,077 lb)
Representative weapons: R-27 'Alamo', R-40 'Acrid', R-60 'Aphid', R-73 'Archer', R-77 'Adder' AAMs; Kh-25ML 'Karen', Kh-25MP 'Kegler', Kh-29 'Kedge', Kh-31 'Krypton', Kh-59 'Kazoo' AGMs; LGBs; PGMs; bombs; rocket; ECM pods; external fuel tanks

DIMENSIONS
Length: 22.2m (72ft 9in)
Wingspan: 15.2m (49ft 9in)
Height: 6.4m (20ft 10in)

FEATURES
Twin fins; shoulder swept wing; canard foreplanes; two Saturn/Lyulka AL-35F turbofans; intakes under fuselage/wing; ventral fins, tailcone between jetpipes

Tupolev Tu-22M 'Backfire' Russia

MRA bomber and EW aircraft

Michael J. Gething / Jane's

The V-G Tu-22M was first flown on 30 August 1969 and the production Tu-22M-2 entered Russian service in 1975, followed by improved M-3 version in 1983. Tu-22MP is EW/escort jammer aircraft and MR is for maritime recce. Production ceased in 1992 after 497 built.

VARIANTS & OPERATORS
India (**Tu-22M-3**), Russia (**Tu-22M/MR**), Ukraine (**Tu-22M**)

SPECIFICATIONS
Crew/accommodation: Two pilots, navigator, WSO
Max speed: M = 1.88 (1,080kt, 2,000km/h)
Radius of action: 1,300nm (2,410km)

ARMAMENT
Internal gun: one 23mm GSh-23M twin-barrel cannon
Internal weapons bay plus two hardpoints
Max weapon load: 24,000kg (52,910 lb)
Representative weapons: Kh-22 'Kitchen' ASM; Kh-15P 'Kickback' SRAM; Kh-31 'Krypton', Kh-35 'Kayak' AGMs; bombs; mines

DIMENSIONS
Length: 42.5m (139ft 4in)
Wingspan: spread - 34.3m (112ft 6in)
 swept - 23.3m (76ft 5in)
Height: 11.0m (36ft 3in)

FEATURES
Low V-G wing; two Samara/Kuznetsov NK-25 turbofans in fuselage; lateral intakes

Tupolev Tu-95/-142 'Bear' Russia

Long-range bomber and MRA aircraft

The Tu-95 prototype first flew on 12 November 1952 and became operational in Russian service in 1956, with Tu-95MS6 ('Bear-H6') in service from 1984. First Tu-142 ASW version flown July 1968, with the Tu-142M ('Bear-F Mod 2') entering service in 1972. Final aircraft built in 1994.

VARIANTS & OPERATORS
Russia (Tu-95/MR/MS/Tu-142), India (Tu-142M)

SPECIFICATIONS
Crew/accommodation: Two pilots, four WSOs, one gunner
Max speed: 499kt (925km/h)
Radius of action: 3,455nm (6,400km)

ARMAMENT
Internal gun: one/two 23mm cannon
Hardpoints: two plus internal weapon bay
Max weapon load: about 11,000kg (24,244 lb)
Representative weapons: Kh-55 'Kent', Kh-101 ALCMs; Kh-35 'Kayak' ASM; bombs; mines; sonobuoys

DIMENSIONS
Length: 49.1m (161ft 2in)
Wingspan: 50.0m (164ft 2in)
Height: 13.3m (43ft 8in)

FEATURES
Tall fin; shoulder swept wing; four Samara/ Kuznetsov NK-12MP turboprops; nose radome on Tu-95MS; under-fuselage radome on Tu-142M

Tupolev Tu-160 'Blackjack' Russia

Long-range bomber

First flown on 18 or 19 December 1981 and the production Tu-160s entered Soviet service in the Ukraine in May 1987 and in Russia in 1992. After dissolution of Soviet Union, eight Ukrainian aircraft eventually returned to Russia. About 32 of 100 planned aircraft built to 1992, when production ceased.

VARIANTS & OPERATORS
Russia

SPECIFICATIONS
Crew/accommodation: Two pilots, two WSOs
Max speed: M = 2.05 (1,200kt, 2,220km/h)
Radius of action: 1,080nm (2,000km)

ARMAMENT
No internal gun
Two internal weapons bays
Max weapon load: 40,000kg (88,185 lb)
Representative weapons: Kh-55 'Kent', Kh-101 ALCMs; Kh-15P 'Kickback' SRAM

DIMENSIONS
Length: 54.1m (177ft 6in)
Wingspan: spread - 55.7m (182ft 9in)
    swept - 35.6m (116ft 10in)
Height: 13.1m (43ft 0in)

FEATURES
V-G wing blended to fuselage; four Samara NK-321 turbofans under fuselage

Vought (N-G) A-7 Corsair II USA

Attack aircraft

Based on F-8 Crusader, the first A-7A flown on 27 September 1965. In USN service from 1966 and USAF service from 1968, all now withdrawn. A-7A/B/Cs powered by P&W TF30, A-7D/E/H/J by Allison (Rolls-Royce) TF41(Spey). Last of 1,541 delivered in 1982, with last re-manufactured A-7P finished in 1985.

VARIANTS & OPERATORS
TA-7C: Greece, Thailand
A-7E: Greece, Thailand
A-7H: Greece
TA-7H: Greece

SPECIFICATIONS
Crew/accommodation:
 A-7E/H = pilot,
 TA-7C/H = student and instructor
Max speed: 600kt (1,112km/h)
Radius of action: about 700nm (1,296km)

ARMAMENT
Internal gun: one 20mm M61 cannon
Hardpoints: eight
Max weapon load: 6,805kg (15,000 lb)
Representative weapons: AIM-9 AAMs; LGBs; PMGs; Mk.80-series bombs; FFAR pods; external fuel tanks

DIMENSIONS
Length: 14.1m (46ft 1in)
Wingspan: 11.8m (38ft 9in)
Height: 4.9m (16ft 0in)

FEATURES
Shoulder swept wing; one Allison TF41 (Spey) turbofan; chin intake in nose

Xian H-6 (Tu-16) 'Badger' China/Russia

Medium bomber/MRA aircraft

The H-6 is the Tu-16, first flown (as Tu-88) on 27 April 1952, built under licence in China. Used by both PLAAF and APN. Chinese production ceased in late-1980s.

VARIANTS & OPERATORS
China (H-6, H-6 III)

SPECIFICATIONS
Crew/accommodation: Two pilots, one navigator/bombardier, three gunners
Max speed: 566kt (1,050km/h)
Range: 3,885nm (7,200km)

ARMAMENT
Internal guns: seven 23mm AM-23 cannon
Internal bomb bay plus two hardpoints
Max weapon load: 9,000kg (19,800 lb)
Representative weapons: Kh-26 'Kingfisher' ASM; nuclear and conventional bombs

DIMENSIONS
Length: 34.8m (114ft 2in)
Wingspan: 33.0m (108ft 3in)
Height: 10.4m (34ft 0in)

FEATURES
Mid swept wing with trailing edge fairings; two Mikulin RD-3M-500 turbojets; wing root intakes, glazed nose

MILITARY
TRAINING
AIRCRAFT

Aermacchi MB-326 Italy

Advanced trainer/light attack aircraft

Prototype MB-326 first flown on 10 December 1957. Licence-built as AT-26 Xavante by EMBRAER of Brazil and as Impala I/II by Atlas (Denel) in South Africa. Total of 736 built.

VARIANTS & OPERATORS

MB-326: Argentina, Brazil, Dem. Rep. Congo, Ghana, Paraguay, Togo, Tunisia, Zambia
MB-326K series: Dem. Rep. Congo, Ghana, Tunisia
MB-326L series: Tunisia

SPECIFICATIONS

Crew/accommodation:
MB-326/L = student and instructor,
MB-326K = pilot
Max speed: 496kt (871km/h)
Radius of action: 145nm (268km)

ARMAMENT: MB-326K SERIES

Internal guns: two 30mm DEFA cannon
Hardpoints: six (plus wingtip tanks)
Max weapon load: 1,814kg (4,000 lb)
Representative weapons: Magic AAMs; AS 11/12 AGMs; bombs; FFAR pods; gun and recce pods; external fuel tanks

DIMENSIONS

Length: 10.7m (35ft 0in)
Wingspan: 10.8m (35ft 7in)
Height: 3.7m (12ft 2in)

FEATURES

Low/straight wing; one Rolls-Royce Viper 632 turbojet; wingtip tanks

Aermacchi MB-339 Italy

Advanced FLI trainer/light attack aircraft

Prototype MB-339 first flown on 12 August 1976. MB-339CD/FD series feature digital avionics. Orders book (including deliveries) is 219.

VARIANTS & OPERATORS
MB-339A series: Eritrea, Ghana, Italy, Malaysia, Nigeria, Peru, UAE (Dubai)
MB-339C series: Eritrea, Italy
MB-339FD: Venezuela
MB-339PAN: Italy

SPECIFICATIONS
Crew/accommodation: Student and instructor
Max speed: 500kt (926km/h)
Radius of action: 255nm (472km)

ARMAMENT
No internal gun
Hardpoints: six (plus wingtip tanks)
Max weapon load: 1,814kg (4,000 lb)
Representative weapons: Magic, AIM-9 AAMs; AGM-65 Maverick; Marte ASM; bombs; FFAR pods; gun and recce pods; external fuel tanks

DIMENSIONS
Length: 11.2m (36ft 10in)
Wingspan: 11.2m (36ft 10in)
Height: 3.9m (12ft 11in)

FEATURES
Low/straight wing; raised canopy; one Rolls-Royce Viper 680 turbojet; wingtip tanks

Aermacchi M-346 Italy

Advanced jet trainer

A comprehensively re-designed and westernised version of the Russo-Italian Yak-130D development (see p. 417) to meet requirements of the Eurotrainer group. The prototype Yak-130D first flew on 25 April 1996. Aermacchi announced M-346 version in July 2000. First of three Italian prototypes flew on 15 July 2004 with initial production predicted from 2007.

VARIANTS & OPERATORS
M-346: none (as of December 2004)

SPECIFICATIONS
Crew/accommodation: Student and instructor
Max speed: 585kt (1,083km/h)
Range: 1,020nm (1,889km) - internal fuel

ARMAMENT
Internal gun: none
Hardpoints: nine (including wingtips)
Max weapon load: 3,000kg (6,614 lb)
Representative weapons: AAMs; AGMs; FFAR pods; gun pods; external fuel tanks

DIMENSIONS
Length: 11.5m (37ft 9in)
Wingspan: 9.7m (31ft 10in)
Height: 4.9m (16ft 4in)

FEATURES
Low swept wing; tandem cockpit; two Honeywell F124-GA-200 turbofans; underwing root intakes/exhausts

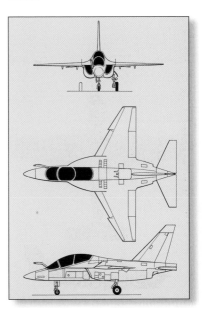

Aermacchi (SIAI-Marchetti) SF.260 Italy

Aerobatic and weapons trainer

Michael J. Gething

Designed as a civil trainer and first flown on 15 July 1964, the first military version - SF.260M - flown on 10 October 1970. The SF.260TP, powered by an Allison (now R-R) 250-B17D turboprop engine, flown in 1980. Over 650 of all types built. Italy to replace surviving 21 SF.260AM with 30 new-production SF.260EA aircraft.

VARIANTS & OPERATORS
SF.260AM: Italy
SF.260C: Burundi, Tunisia
SF.260D: Belgium, Turkey
SF.260E: Mauritania, Mexico, Uruguay, Venezuela
SF.260F: Zimbabwe
SF.260M: Belgium, Indonesia, Zambia, Zimbabwe
SF.260TP: Ethiopia, Philippines, UAE (Dubai), Zambia, Zimbabwe
SF.260W: Burundi, Chad, Indonesia, Libya, Tunisia, Uganda, Zimbabwe

SPECIFICATIONS
Crew/accommodation: Student and instructor
Max speed: 235kt (436km/h)
Range: 890nm (1,650km)

ARMAMENT
No internal gun
Hardpoints: two or four
Max weapon load: 300kg (661 lb)
Representative weapons: FFAR pods, gun pods, target towing kit, external fuel tanks

DIMENSIONS
Length: 7.1m (23ft 3in)
Wingspan: 8.3m (27ft 4in)
Height: 2.4m (7ft 11in)

FEATURES
Swept fin; low straight wing with dihedral; wingtip tanks; side-by-side cockpit; one Textron Lycoming O-540-E4A5 piston engine

Aero Vodochody L-29 Delphin Czech Republic

Basic/advanced jet trainer

Prototype XL-29 first flown on 5 April 1959 with first production aircraft flying in April 1963. Large orders from Soviet Union and Warsaw Pact plus other. Total of 3,665 built with production ending in 1974.

VARIANTS & OPERATORS

L-29: Azerbaijan, Czech Republic, Ghana, Mali, Romania, Slovak Republic, Syria

SPECIFICATIONS

Crew/accommodation: Student and instructor
Max speed: 42kt (820km/h)
Range: 480nm (894km)

ARMAMENT

No internal gun
Hardpoints: two (plus wingtip tanks)
Max weapon load: 260kg (573 lb)
Representative weapons: bombs; FFAR pods; external fuel tanks

DIMENSIONS

Length: 10.8m (35ft 5in)
Wingspan: 10.3m (33ft 9in)
Height: 3.1m (10ft 3in)

FEATURES

T-tail; mid straight wing; one M 701c turbojet; wingtip tanks

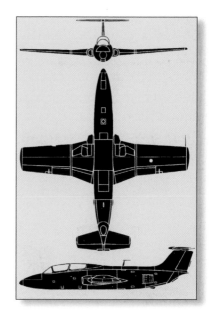

Aero Vodochody L-39/-139/-59/-159 Czech Republic

Advanced jet trainer and light attack aircraft

L-39 first flown on 4 November 1968 and
selected to replace L-29 in Soviet Union. L-39Z
series are armed. L-139 has Honeywell TFE731
engine. L-39MS/L-59 has improved Czech engine.
A total 2,938 of all versions built. Work on L-159
ALCA (Advanced Light Combat Aircraft) began in
1992. Two-seater L-159B flown 2 August 1997,
first production L-159A flown 20 October 1999.

VARIANTS & OPERATORS

L-39: Armenia, Azerbaijan, Bangladesh,
Turkmenistan
L-39C: Afghanistan, Algeria, Cuba, Czech
Republic, Ethiopia, Georgia, Krygizia, Lithuania,
North Korea, Russia, Slovak Republic, Ukraine,
Vietnam, Yemen
L-39MS: Czech Republic, Slovak Republia
L-39V: Slovak Republic
L-39ZA: Algeria, Bangladesh, Bulgaria, Cambodia,
Czech Republic, Lithuania, Nigeria,Romania,
Slovak Republic, Syria, Thailand, Uganda
L-39ZO: Hungary, Iraq, Libya, Syria
L-59: Egypt, Tunisia
L-159A/B ALCA: Czech Republic

SPECIFICATIONS

Crew/accommodation: L-39/-59/-159B = student
and instructor; L-159A = pilot
Max speed: L-39/-139/-59 - 340kt (630km/h);
L-159 - 505kt (936km/h)
RoA: L-39/-139/-59 - 401nm (743km); L-159 -
380nm (705km)

ARMAMENT: L-159A

Internal gun: none
Hardpoints: seven (plus wingtip tanks)
Max weapon load: 2,340kg (5,159 lb)
Representative weapons: AAMs; AGMs, PGMs,
bombs or FFAR pods; external fuel tanks; gun,
ECM or designator pods

DIMENSIONS

	L-39/-139/-59	L-159
Length:	12.1m (39ft 9in)	12.7m (41ft 9in)
Wingspan:	9.5m (31ft 3in)	9.5m (31ft 3in)
Height:	4.8m (15ft 8in)	4.8m (15ft 8in)

FEATURES

Low/straight wing; wingtip tanks; one turbofan
engine (AI 25 TL in L-39; DV-2 in L-39MS/-59;
Honeywell F124-GA-100 in L-159); intakes behind
canopy; long pointed nose

AIDC AT-3 Tzu-Chiang Taiwan

Operational trainer/close air support aircraft

Prototype flown on 16 September 1980 with production from 1984. AT-3A is single-seater (prototype only), AT-3B is trainer. Last of 60 delivered in 1990.

VARIANTS & OPERATORS
AT-3B RoCAF: (Taiwan)

SPECIFICATIONS
Crew/accommodation:
AT-3A = pilot, AT-3B = student and instructor
Max speed: 488kt (904km/h)
Range: 1,230nm (2,279km)

ARMAMENT
No internal gun but provision for underfuselage gun pod
Hardpoints: five (plus wingtips)
Max weapon load: 2,721kg (6,000 lb)
Representative weapons: HF 2 ASM; bombs; FFAR pods; flares; external fuel tanks

DIMENSIONS
Length: 12.9m (42ft 4in)
Wingspan: 10.46m (34ft 4in)
Height: 4.4m (14ft 4in)

FEATURES
Low/straight wing; long forward fuselage; twin Honeywell TFE731 turbofans; wing root intakes

Avione IAR-99 Soim Romania

Basic/advanced jet trainer/light attack aircraft

Prototype flown on 21 December 1985 with production of 20 from 1988. Elbit is working with Avione on an avionics/cockpit upgrade for a further 18.

VARIANTS & OPERATORS
IAR-99: Romania

SPECIFICATIONS
Crew/accommodation:
IAR-99 = student and instructor
Max speed: 467kt (865km/h)
Range: 593nm (1,100km)

ARMAMENT
Internal gun: removeable ventral 23mm GSh-23 cannon pod
Hardpoints: four
Max weapon load: 2,000kg (4,408 lb)
Representative weapons: bombs; FFAR pods; gun pods; external fuel tanks

DIMENSIONS
Length: 11.0m (36ft 1in)
Wingspan: 9.8m (32ft 4in)
Height: 3.9m (12ft 9in)

FEATURES
Low/straight wing; raised cockpit; one Rolls-Royce Viper 632 turbojet; wing root intakes

BAC (BAE Systems) 167 Strikemaster UK

Basic/advanced jet trainer/light attack aircraft

Derived from BAC 145 Jet Provost T.5 (now withdrawn), the first Strikemaster was flown on 26 October 1967. A total of 155 were built.

VARIANTS & OPERATORS
Ecuador (Mk.89), Sudan (Mk.90)

SPECIFICATIONS
Crew/accommodation: Student and instructor
Max speed: 467kt (865km/h)
Range: 593nm (1,100km)

ARMAMENT
Internal guns: two 7.62mm FN machine guns
Hardpoints: eight (plus wingtip tanks)
Max weapon load: 1,360kg (3,000 lb)
Representative weapons: bombs; FFAR pods; recce pods; external fuel tanks

DIMENSIONS
Length: 11.0m (36ft 1in)
Wingspan: 9.8m (32ft 4in)
Height: 3.9m (12ft 9in)

FEATURES
Low/straight wing; side-by-side cockpit; one Rolls-Royce Viper 535 turbojet; lateral intakes

BAE Systems (HSA) Hawk 50/60/100 UK

Advanced jet trainer

The prototype HS.1182 Hawk was first flown on 21 August 1974 and entered RAF service as the Hawk T.1 (Series 50) in 1976. Followed by 60 and 100 series, plus US Navy T-45 Goshawk (see next entry). A total of 770 have been ordered across all versions.

VARIANTS & OPERATORS
Series 50: Finland, Indonesia, Kenya, UK
Series 60: Kuwait, Saudi Arabia, South Korea, UAE (Abu Dhabi/Dubai), Zimbabwe
Series 100: Australia, Bahrain, Canada, India, Indonesia, Malaysia, Oman, South Africa, UAE (Abu Dhabi), UK

SPECIFICATIONS
Crew/accommodation: Student and instructor
Max speed: 575kt (1,065km/h)
Radius of action: 345nm (638km)

ARMAMENT
No internal gun
Hardpoints: five (plus wingtips)
Max weapon load: 3,000kg (6,614 lb)
Representative weapons: centreline 30mm gun pod; AIM-9 AAM; AGM-65 Maverick AGM; bombs; FFAR pods; CBLS; external fuel tanks

DIMENSIONS
Length: 10.8m (35ft 4in)
Wingspan: 9.4m (30ft 9in)
Height: 4.0m (13ft 1in)

FEATURES
Low swept wing; tandem cockpit; single Rolls-Royce/Turbomeca Adour turbofan

BAE Systems (HSA)/Boeing (McDD) T-45 Goshawk UK/USA

Intermediate/advanced jet trainer

The prototype of the carrier-capable T-45 Goshawk was first flown on 16 April 1988, with T-45A deliveries to USN from 1992 and T-45C (with glass cockpit) from 1997. A total of 187 are planned.

VARIANTS & OPERATORS
US Navy

SPECIFICATIONS
Crew/accommodation:
Student and instructor
Max speed: 575kt (1,065km/h)
Radius of action: 345nm (638km)

ARMAMENT
No internal gun
Hardpoints: three
Max weapon load: n/a
Representative weapons: bombs; FFAR pods; external fuel tanks

DIMENSIONS
Length: 12.0m (35ft 4in)
Wingspan: 9.4m (30ft 10in)
Height: 4.3m (14ft 0in)

FEATURES
Low swept wing; tandem cockpit; arrester hook; nose leg catapult strut; single Rolls-Royce/Turbomeca Adour turbofan

Beagle (BAE Systems) Bulldog 120 UK

Primary trainer

Paul Jackson/Jane's

First flight of Beagle-built Bulldog on 19 May 1969 and first RAF Bulldog T.1 version flown on 30 January 1973. Last RAF Bulldogs withdrawn 2001. A total of 184 built.

VARIANTS & OPERATORS
Kenya (**Model 127**), Lebanon (**Model 126**), Malta (**ex-RAF T.1**)

SPECIFICATIONS
Crew/accommodation: Student and instructor
Max speed: 210kt (389km/h)
Range: 540nm (1,000km)

ARMAMENT
No internal guns
Hardpoints: two
Max weapon load: 290kg (640 lb)
Representative weapons: FFAR pod; gun pod; SAR equipment.

DIMENSIONS
Length: 7.1m (23ft 3in)
Wingspan: 10.0m (33ft 0in)
Height: 2.3m (7ft 6in)

FEATURES
Low/straight wing with slight dihedral; side-by-side cockpit; fixed tricycle undercarriage; one Avco Lycoming IO-360-A1B6 piston engine

Beech (Raytheon) T-34 Mentor USA

Primary trainer/light strike aircraft

First flight of the Beech Model 45 (Continental O-470-13A piston engine) was on 2 December 1948 and first YT-34A USAF version in May 1950. USAF took 450 T-34A and USN 423 T-34Bs. First flight of YT-34C Turbo-Mentor on 21 September 1973. By April 1990, 1,465 T-34s delivered from US plus 50 Fuji T-3s, licence-built in Japan.

VARIANTS & OPERATORS

T-34A/B: Argentina, Bolivia Colombia, Indonesia
VT-34A: Venezuela
T-34C: Algeria, Argentina, Ecuador, Gabon, Indonesia, Morocco, Peru, Taiwan, Uruguay, USA
NT-34C: USA
Fuji T-3: Japan

SPECIFICATIONS

Crew/accommodation: Student and instructor
Max speed: 280kt (518km/h)
Range: 708nm (1,311km)

ARMAMENT: T-34C-1

No internal guns
Hardpoints: four
Max weapon load: 544kg (1,200 lb)
Representative weapons: AGM-22 AGM; practice bombs; FFAR pod; gun pod.

DIMENSIONS

Length: 8.8m (28ft 8in)
Wingspan: 10.2m (33ft 4in)
Height: 2.9m (9ft 7in)

FEATURES

Low/straight wing with dihedral; tandem cockpit; one P&WC PT6A-25 turboprop

Canadair CL-41/CT-114 Tutor Canada

Basic jet trainer/light strike aircraft

First flight of the CL-41 prototype was on 13 January 1960 and first CT-114 version in October 1963. Canada took 190 CT-114 Tutors and Malaysia 20 CL-41Gs. Production ended in 1966 at 212 aircraft.

VARIANTS & OPERATORS
CT-114: Canada (with Snowbirds aerobatic display team)

SPECIFICATIONS
Crew/accommodation: Student and instructor
Max speed: 407kt (755km/h)
Range: n/a

ARMAMENT: CL-41G
No internal guns
Hardpoints: four
Max weapon load: 1,590kg (3,500 lb)
Representative weapons: bombs; FFAR pod; gun pod; external fuel tanks

DIMENSIONS
Length: 9.8m (32ft 0in)
Wingspan: 11.1m (36ft 6in)
Height: 2.8m (9ft 4in)

FEATURES
T-tail; low/straight wing; lateral intake, side-by-side cockpit; one GE J85-J4 turbojet

CASA (EADS) C-101 Aviojet Spain

Basic/advanced trainer/attack aircraft

First flight of the C-101 prototype was on 27 June 1977 and 88 delivered C-101 (E.25 Mirlo) to Spain. Assembled under licence in Chile by ENAER. Production ended in 1997 at 151 aircraft.

VARIANTS & OPERATORS
C-101BB: Honduras, Chile (T-36)
C-101CC: Jordan, Chile (A-36)
C-101EB: Spain

SPECIFICATIONS
Crew/accommodation: Student and instructor
Max speed: 450kt (834km/h)
Range: 260nm (482km)

ARMAMENT: A-36
Internal gun: provision for ventral gun pack (one 20mm cannon or two 7.62mm machine guns)
Hardpoints: six
Max weapon load: 2,250kg (4,960 lb)
Representative weapons: AIM-9 AAM; AGM-65 Maverick, bombs; FFAR pods; external fuel tanks

DIMENSIONS
Length: 12.5m (41ft 0in)
Wingspan: 10.6m (34ft 9in)
Height: 4.2m (13ft 11in)

FEATURES
Low/straight wing; lateral intake; tandem cockpit; one Honeywell TFE731 turbofan

Cessna T-37 'Tweety Bird' USA

Basic/advanced trainer/attack aircraft

Michael J. Gething

First flown on 12 October 1954, the T-37 remains the basic jet trainer of the USAF and other. Prototype YAT-37D attack version flown 22 October 1963 and produced as A-37 Dragonfly. Production of 1,272 T-37/A-37 aircraft ended in 1977.

VARIANTS & OPERATORS
A-37B: Chile, Colombia, Ecuador, Guatemala, Honduras, Peru, El Salvador, South Korea, Thailand, Uruguay
T-37B/C: Bangladesh, Colombia, Germany, Greece, Morocco, Pakistan, South Korea, Turkey, USA

SPECIFICATIONS
Crew/accommodation:
A-37 = two pilots, T-37 = student and instructor
Max speed: 455kt (843km/h)
Range: 399nm (740km)

ARMAMENT: A-37
Internal gun: one 7.62mm GAU-2B/A Minigun
Hardpoints: eight (plus wingtip tanks)
Max weapon load: 2,574kg (5,680 lb)
Representative weapons: Mk.81/82 bombs; FFAR pods; gun pods; external fuel tanks

DIMENSIONS
Length: 8.6m (28ft 3in)
Wingspan: 10.9m (35ft 10in)
Height: 2.7m (8ft 10in)

FEATURES
Low/straight wing; wingtip tanks; wing root intakes,; side-by-side cockpit; one GE J85-GE-17A turbojet

Dassault/Dornier Alpha Jet France/Germany

Advanced trainer/close air support aircraft

The first prototype (of four) was flown on
26 October 1973, and entered service with
France (as a trainer) and Germany (CAS now
withdrawn). Production of 504 Alpha Jets ended
in 1991.

VARIANTS & OPERATORS
Belgium, Cameroun, Egypt, France, Morocco,
Nigeria, Portugal, Qatar, Thailand, Togo, UK

SPECIFICATIONS
Crew/accommodation:
Student and instructor
Max speed: 560kt (1,038km/h)
Range: 315nm (583km)

ARMAMENT
Internal gun: one 30mm DEFA or 27mm Mauser
cannon in underfuselage pod
Hardpoints: five
Max weapon load: 2,500kg (5,510 lb)
Representative weapons: Magic, AIM-9 AAMs;
AGM-65 Maverick; Mk.81/82 bombs; FFAR pods;
recce and gun pods; external fuel tanks

DIMENSIONS
Length: 11.8m (38ft 6in)
Wingspan: 9.1m (29ft 10in)
Height: 4.2m (13ft 9in)

FEATURES
Shoulder swept wing; lateral intakes; tandem
cockpit; two SNECMA/Turbomeca Larzac 04–
C6/20 turbofans

EMBRAER EMB-312 Tucano Brazil

Turboprop trainer

Powered by a PT6A turboprop, the EMB-312 Tucano first flew on 16 August 1980 and entered Brazilian service in 1983. Shorts produced a modified version with the Honeywell TPE331 turboprop as the S312 Tucano T.1 for RAF. A stretched version, EMB-314 became the EMB-314M/AT-29 for Brazil. A total of 650 produced, plus demonstrators.

VARIANTS & OPERATORS
EMB-312: Angola, Argentina, Brazil, Colombia, Egypt, France, Honduras, Iran, Paraguay, Peru, Venezuela
S312: Kenya, Kuwait, RAF

SPECIFICATIONS
Crew/accommodation: Student and instructor
Max speed: 280kt (519km/h)
Range: 995nm (1,843km)

ARMAMENT
No internal gun
Hardpoints: four
Max weapon load: 1,000kg (2,204 lb)
Representative weapons: Mk.81 250 lb bombs; FFAR pods; gun pods; practice bombs

DIMENSIONS
Length: 9.9m (32ft 4in)
Wingspan: 11.1m (36ft 6in)
Height: 3.4m (11ft 2in)

FEATURES
Low tapered wing; blown tandem canopy; one P&WC PT6A-25C turboprop

ENAER T-35 Pillan Chile

Basic trainer

First flown on 6 March 1981, deliveries to Chile began in 1985. Exported to Spain and around Latin America. Single-seat and turboprop versions developed but not sold. Production of 146 to 1991, plus eight ordered in 1998.

VARIANTS & OPERATORS
Chile, Dominican Republic, Ecuador, Guatemala, Panama, Paraguay, El Salvador, Spain

SPECIFICATIONS
Crew/accomodation: Student and instructor
Max speed: 241kt, (446km/h)
Range: 680nm (1,260km)

ARMAMENT
No internal gun
Hardpoints: nil
Max weapon load: nil
Representative weapons: nil

DIMENSIONS
Length: 8.8m (29ft 0in)
Wingspan: 11.1m (36ft 6in)
Height: 2.6m (8ft 8in)

FEATURES
Low tapered wing; blown tandem canopy; one Textron Lycoming IO-540-K1K5 piston engine

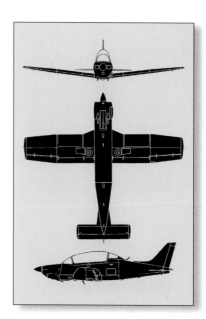

FMA (Lockheed Martin) IA 63/AT-63 Pampa Argentina

Basic/advanced jet trainer

The prototype IA 63 Pampa first flew on 6 October 1984 with deliveries to Argentina from 1987. In 2001, AT-63 light attack variant launched at Paris air show. Production of 18 IA 63s, with 20 orders for AT-63.

VARIANTS & OPERATORS
Argentina

SPECIFICATIONS
Crew/accomodation: Student and instructor
Max speed: 445kt, (825km/h)
Range: 1,090nm (2,018km)

ARMAMENT
No internal gun
Hardpoints: seven
Max weapon load: 2,290kg (5,047 lb)
Representative weapons: AAMs; AGMs; bombs, FFAR pods; gun pods; external fuel tanks

DIMENSIONS
Length: 10.9m (35ft 9in)
Wingspan: 9.7m (31ft 9in)
Height: 4.3m (14ft 1in)

FEATURES
Shoulder straight wing; tandem canopy; one Honeywell TFE731-2-2N turbofan; lateral intakes

Fouga (Aerospatiale) CM-170 Magister France

Basic/advanced jet trainer

The prototype CM-170-01 Magister first flew on 23 July 1952 with deliveries to France from 1956. Built under licence in Finland, Germany and Israel. Production reached 921 of all versions.

tanks; tandem canopy; one Turbomeca Mabore II/III/IV turbojet

VARIANTS & OPERATORS
Belgium, Cameroun, Israel, Lebanon, Morocco

SPECIFICATIONS
Crew/accomodation:
Student and instructor
Max speed: 350kt, (650km/h)
Range: 675nm (1,250km)

ARMAMENT
Internal guns: two 7.62mm machine guns
Hardpoints: four (plus wingtip tanks)
Max weapon load: 100kg (220 lb)
Representative weapons: AS-11 AGMs; 110 lb bombs; FFAR pods; gun pods

DIMENSIONS
Length: 10.0m (33ft 0in)
Wingspan: 11.4m (37ft 5in)
Height: 2.8m (9ft 2in)

FEATURES
No fin, butterfly tail; mid straight wing; wingtip

Hindustan Aeronautics Ltd HJT-16 Kiran India

Basic/advanced jet trainer

The prototype Kiran first flew on 4 September 1964 with deliveries of the Mk.I version to India from 1968. Mk.IA featured one hardpoint under

each wing, the Mk.II had two. Production reached 250 of all versions.

VARIANTS & OPERATORS
India

SPECIFICATIONS
Crew/accomodation: Student and instructor
Max speed: 463kt (858km/h)
Range: 332nm (615km)

ARMAMENT: MK.II
Internal guns: two 7.62mm machine guns
Hardpoints: four
Max weapon load: 1,000kg (2,204 lb)
Representative weapons: 250kg bombs; FFAR pods; CBLS; external fuel tanks

DIMENSIONS
Length: 10.2m (33ft 7in)
Wingspan: 10.7m (35ft 1in)
Height: 3.6m (11ft 11in)

FEATURES
Low mid straight wing; side-by-side canopy; one Rolls-Royce Viper 11 (Mk.I/IA) or Orpheus 701 turbojet (Mk.II)

Hindustan Aeronautics Ltd HJT-36 Sitara India

Basic jet trainer

Work on this Kiran replacement began 1997. Requirement for IAF (187) and Indian Navy (24) approved in Jan 2001. Initial contract (16 for IAF) announced February 2003. First flown on 7 March 2003. Deliveries to start before end 2004.

NOT TO BE CONFUSED WITH
Aermacchi S.211/311; FMA (LMAA) IA-63 Pampa; Dassault/Dornier Alpha Jet

VARIANTS & OPERATORS
Indian Air Force
Indian Navy

SPECIFICATIONS
Crew/accomodation: Student and instructor
Max speed: M = 0.75
Endurance: 2 hours

ARMAMENT
No internal gun
Hardpoints: four plus centreline
Max weapon load: 1,000kg (2,204 lb)
Representative weapons: gun pods; rocket pods; bombs; external tanks

DIMENSIONS
Length: 10.9m (35ft 11in)
Wingspan: 10.0m (32ft 9in)
Height: 4.4m (14ft 5in)

FEATURES
Low swept wing; tandem canopy; swept tail; one SNECMA/Larzac 04-H20; bifurcated intakes behind canopy

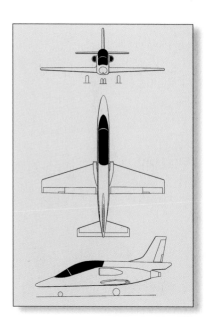

Kawasaki T-4 Japan

Intermediate jet trainer

First flight of XT-4 on 29 July 1985, with deliveries from 1988. Equips JASDF Blue Impulse aerobatic team. Similar to Alpha Jet in appearance. Production of 212 complete.

VARIANTS & OPERATORS
T-4 Japan

SPECIFICATIONS
Crew/accommodation: Student and instructor
Max speed: 560kt (1,038km/h)
Range: 900nm (1,668km)

ARMAMENT
No internal gun
Hardpoints: three
Max weapon load: n/a
Representative weapons: ECM pods, towed targets; external fuel tanks

DIMENSIONS
Length: 13.0m (42ft 8in)
Wingspan: 9.9m (32ft 7in)
Height: 4.6m (15ft 1in)

FEATURES
Tall fin; shoulder swept wing; tandem cockpit; two Ishikawajima-Harima F3-IHI-30 turbofans; lateral intakes

KAI (Daewoo) KT-1 Woong-Bee South Korea

Basic/advanced trainer/attack aircraft

Michael J. Gething/Jane's

The KTX-1 prototype first flew on 12 December 1991 and the KT-1 was ordered into production in 1999 (85 on order) plus seven for Indonesia. An FAC version, KOX-1 is being developed (20 required).

VARIANTS & OPERATORS
KT-1 South Korea, Indonesia

SPECIFICATIONS
Crew/accommodation: Student and instructor
Max speed: 350kt (648km/h)
Range: 900nm (1,668km)

ARMAMENT
No internal gun
Hardpoints: four
Max weapon load: n/a
Representative weapons: FFAR pods; gun pods; external fuel tanks

DIMENSIONS
Length: 10.3m (33ft 8in)
Wingspan: 10.6m (34ft 9in)
Height: 3.7m (12ft 0in)

FEATURES
Low/straight wing; tandem cockpit; one P&WC PT6A-62A turboprop

KAI T-50 (A-50) Golden Eagle South Korea

Advanced jet trainer/light attack aircraft

Initiated in 1992 by Samsung (now KAI) with assistance from Lockheed Martin (as offset for RoKAF F-16 programme). Maiden flight on 20 August 2002 and three others since flown (including one LIFT version). First 25 T-50s ordered by RoKAF in December 2003 (25 more required plus 44 A-50 attack variants). Offered for export as F-5/T-38 replacement.

VARIANTS & OPERATORS
T-50: South Korea

SPECIFICATIONS
Crew/accommodation: Student and instructor
Max speed: M = 1.5
Range: 1,400nm (2,592km)

ARMAMENT: LIFT/A-50
Internal gun: 20mm Gatling-type cannon (in port LERX)
Hardpoints: seven (including wingtips)
Max weapon load: 4,309kg (9,500 lb)
Representative weapons: AIM-9 AAMs; AGM-65 Maverick; cluster munitions; ACMI pod; external fuel tanks

DIMENSIONS
Length: 13.1m (43ft 1in)
Wingspan: 9.5m (31ft 0in)
Height: 4.9m (16ft 2in)

FEATURES
Similar to F-16 - swept wing (with LERX) and fin; tandem cockpit; intakes under LERX; one GE F404-GE-102 turbofan

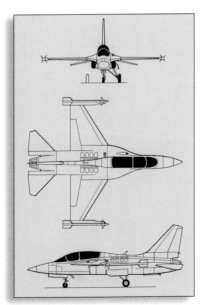

Lockheed AT/T-33 (CT-133 Silver Star) USA

Basic/advanced jet trainer

Derived from the P-80 Shooting Star, the prototype TF-80C was first flown on 22 March 1948 and later re-designated T-33. Lockheed produced 5,691 aircraft. Licence-built by Canadair as the CT-133 Silver Star (656) and Kawasaki of Japan (210) the last of which flew in 1959.

VARIANTS & OPERATORS

T-33A: Bolivia, South Korea, Thailand
AT-33A: Mexico
AT-33AN Silver Star: Bolivia
CT-33SF: Bolivia

SPECIFICATIONS

Crew/accommodation: Student and instructor
Max speed: 486kt (900km/h)
Range: 1,169nm (2,165km)

ARMAMENT: T-33

Internal guns: two 0.50in M3 machine guns
Hardpoints: wingtip tanks only
Max weapon load: nil
Representative weapons: nil

DIMENSIONS

Length: 11.5m (37ft 8in)
Wingspan: 11.8m (38ft 10in)
Height: 3.5m (11ft 8in)

FEATURES

low/straight wing; tandem cockpit; one Allison J-23 or Rolls-Royce Nene turbojet; low lateral intakes

Mitsubishi T-2 Japan

Advanced jet trainer

Japan's first supersonic trainer flew on 20 July 1971 and entered JASDF service in 1975. The last of 96 aircraft delivered in 1988. Similar to Jaguar E in appearance.

VARIANTS & OPERATORS
Japan

SPECIFICATIONS
Crew/accommodation: Pilot
Max speed: M = 1.6
Radius of action: n/a

ARMAMENT
Internal gun: one 20mm JM61 cannon
Hardpoints: five
Max weapon load: 2,721kg (5,997 lb)
Representative weapons: bombs; FFAR pods; external fuel tanks

DIMENSIONS
Length: 17.8m (58ft 6in)
Wingspan: 7.9m (25ft 10in)
Height: 4.4m (14ft 2in)

FEATURES
Shoulder swept wing; two Rolls-Royce/Turbomeca Adour 108 turbofans; rear ventral fins

Nanchang CJ-6 (Yak-18 'Max') China

Basic trainer

Air Forces Monthly

First Yak-18 prototype flown in 1945, it was progressively developed to the Yak-18T, with some 8,000 of all versions produced. China licence-produced the Yak-18 from 1954, then further developed it as the Nanchang CJ-6, building 1,796 by 1986.

Zhuzhou (SMPMC) HS6A radial engine; large tandem canopy

VARIANTS & OPERATORS
Yak-18A: Laos, Mali
Yak-18T: Turkmenistan
CJ-6: North Korea

SPECIFICATIONS
Crew/accommodation: Student and instructor
Max speed: 155kt (286km/h)
RoA: n/a

ARMAMENT
No internal gun
Hardpoints: none
Max weapon load: nil
Representative weapons: n/a

DIMENSIONS
Length: 8.5m (27ft 9in)
Wingspan: 10.2m (33ft 5in)
Height: 3.2m (10ft 8in)

FEATURES
Straight wing; straight fin and tailplane; one

Nanchang K-8 Karakorum 8 China

Basic jet trainer/light attack aircraft

Originally a collaborative project with Pakistan, the first K-8 flew on 21 November 1990. Six preproduction K-8s delivered to Pakistan from 1994. Re-engined with Russian AI-25 engine as K-8J for Chinese use, about 30 delivered.

VARIANTS & OPERATORS
China, Egypt, Morocco, Myanmar, Namibia, Pakistan, Sri LankaZambia

SPECIFICATIONS
Crew/accommodation: Student and instructor
Max speed: 512kt (950km/h)
Range (internal fuel): 842nm (1,560km)

ARMAMENT
Internal gun: one 23mm cannon in centreline gun pod
Hardpoints: four
Max weapon load: 943kg (2,080 lb)
Representative weapons: PL-7 AAM; bombs; FFAR pods; external fuel tank

DIMENSIONS
Length: 11.6m (38ft 1in)
Wingspan: 9.6m (34ft 7in)
Height: 4.2m (13ft 10in)

FEATURES
Low tapered wing; tandem cockpit; one Honeywell TFE731 or Progress AI-25 turbofan; lateral intakes

Northrop (N-G) T-38 Talon USA

Supersonic jet trainer

A private venture, the T-38 Talon prototype first flew on 10 April 1959 and entered USAF service in 1961. Developed into the F-5 series fighters. T-38C upgrade by McDonnell Douglas (Boeing) ordered in 1996 – over 200 delivered. Last of 1,187 Talons delivered in 1972.

VARIANTS & OPERATORS
Germany (**T-38A**), South Korea (**T-38**), Turkey (**T-38A**), USA (**T-38A/B/C, AT-38B**)

SPECIFICATIONS
Crew/accommodation: Student and instructor
Max speed: M = 1.23+
Range (internal fuel): 955nm (1,700km)

ARMAMENT
No internal gun
Hardpoints: one (AT-38B only)
Max weapon load: n/a
Representative weapons: n/a

DIMENSIONS
Length: 14.1m (46ft 4in)
Wingspan: 7.7m (25ft 3in)
Height: 3.9m (12ft 10in)

FEATURES
Low tailplane; low swept wing; two GE J85 turbojets

PAC Mushak
(Saab MFI-17 Supporter) Pakistan (Sweden)

Light trainer/observation aircraft

Günter Endres

First flown as MFI-17 on 9 April 1973. Built under licence in Pakistan as Mushak, then upgraded as Shabaz and Super Mushak Agile. Over 295 built as at 2000.

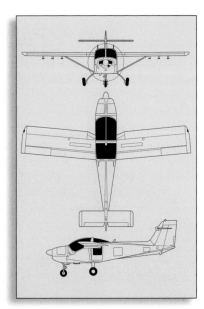

VARIANTS & OPERATORS
Mushak: Iran, Oman, Pakistan, Syria
Super Mushak: Oman, Pakistan
MFI-17: Denmark, Norway, Uganda, Zambia

SPECIFICATIONS
Crew/accommodation: Student and instructor (plus one other)
Max speed: 196kt (363km/h)
Range (internal fuel): n/a

ARMAMENT
No internal gun
Hardpoints: nil
Max weapon load: nil
Representative weapons: nil

DIMENSIONS
Length: 7.0m (22ft 11in)
Wingspan: 8.8m (29ft 0in)
Height: 2.6m (8ft 6in)

FEATURES
High tailplane; shoulder slightly forward swept wing; fixed tricyle undercarriage; one Textron Lycoming IO-360 piston engine

Pacific Aerospace CT4 Airtrainer New Zealand

Basic trainer

A re-design of the Victa Aircruiser (first flown on 12 February 1972), 114 CT4A/B trainers built by 1977. CT4C turboprop prototype (not produced). CT4E with bigger engine in production from 1998 with 24 orders.

VARIANTS & OPERATORS
New Zealand (CT4E), Thailand (CT4A/B/E)

SPECIFICATIONS
Crew/accommodation: Student and instructor
Max speed: 230kt (426km/h)
Range (internal fuel): 520nm (963km)

ARMAMENT
No internal gun
Hardpoints: nil
Max weapon load: nil
Representative weapons: nil

DIMENSIONS
Length: 7.3m (23ft 9in)
Wingspan: 7.9m (26ft 0in)
Height: 2.6m (8ft 6in)

FEATURES
Low tapered wing; side-by-side cockpit; fixed tricyle undercarriage; one Textron Lycoming AEIO-540 piston engine

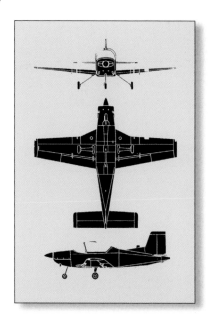

Pilatus PC-7 Turbo Trainer Switzerland

Basic trainer

Air Forces Monthly

The PC-7 first flew on 18 August 1978 with deliveries from December 1978. The Mk.II M version flown 28 September 1992, the 60 SAAF version being named Astra. A total of 448 PC-7s and 66 PC-7 Mk.II built.

VARIANTS & OPERATORS

PC-7: Angola, Austria, Bolivia, Botswana, Chad, Chile, France, Guatemala, Iran, Malaysia, Mexico, Myanmar, Netherlands, Switzerland, UAE (Abu Dhabi), Uruguay

PC-7 Mk.II: Brunei, Malaysia, South Africa

SPECIFICATIONS

Crew/accommodation: Student and instructor
Max speed: 270kt (500km/h)
Range (internal fuel): 1,420nm (2,630km)

ARMAMENT

No internal gun
Hardpoints: four (locally installed on Iranian aircraft)
Max weapon load: n/a
Representative weapons: n/a

DIMENSIONS

Length: 9.8m (32ft 1in)
Wingspan: 10.4m (34ft 1in)
Height: 3.2m (10ft 6in)

FEATURES

Low tapered wing; tandem cockpit; one P&WC PT6A-62 turboprop

Pilatus PC-9 Advanced Turbo-Trainer Switzerland

Advanced turboprop trainer

Derived from the PC-7, the PC-9 was first flown on 7 May 1984 with deliveries from 1986. The PC-9 Mk.II version developed by Raytheon (Beech) as T-6A Texan II (see p. 411). PC-9M has enlarged dorsal fairing (and cockpit layout) of PC-7 Mk II. Over 260 PC-9s built, plus US production.

NOT TO BE CONFUSED WITH
PC-7; Raytheon T-6; EMBRAER EMB-312/314

VARIANTS & OPERATORS
PC-9: Angola, Cyprus, Iraq, Myanmar, Saudi Arabia, Switzerland
PC-9/A: Australia, Thailand
PC-9M: Croatia, Ireland, Oman, Slovenia

SPECIFICATIONS
Crew/accommodation: Student and instructor
Max speed: 320kt (593km/h)
Range (internal fuel): 830nm (1,537km)

ARMAMENT
No internal gun
Hardpoints: provision for six
Max weapon load: n/a
Representative weapons: n/a

DIMENSIONS
Length: 10.3m (32ft 3in)
Wingspan: 10.1m (33ft 2in)
Height: 3.3m (10ft 9in)

FEATURES
Enlarged dorsal fin; low tapered wing; tandem cockpit; one P&WC PT6A-62 turboprop

Pilatus PC-21 Switzerland

Advanced turboprop trainer

Development began in 1999 and prototype PC-21 was first flown on 1 July 2002. Based on PC-7/-9 experience but with 21st century design, materials and technology. Intended for advanced pilot training and pilot/WSO weapons training at turboprop (rather than jet) costs. Ready for production by end 2004. Initial markets seen in Australia, South Africa and UK.

VARIANTS & OPERATORS
PC-21: none as of December 2004.

SPECIFICATIONS
Crew/accommodation: Student and instructor
Max speed: 370kt (685km/h)
Range (internal fuel): n/a

ARMAMENT
No internal gun
Hardpoints: one centreline and four wing stores stations
Max weapon load: n/a
Representative weapons: n/a

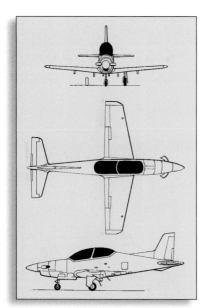

DIMENSIONS
Length: 11.2m (36ft 8in)
Wingspan: 8.8m (28ft 9in)
Height: 3.9m (12ft 10in)

FEATURES
Low tapered wing; swept fin and tailplane; tandem cockpit; one P&WC PT6A-68B turboprop

PZL-Warszawa PZL-130TC-1 Orlik Poland

Basic trainer

Michael J. Gething

Derived from the piston-engined PZL-130, the prototype turboprop conversion used a PT6A and was first flown on 18 July 1986. PZL-130TB with M601 turboprop flew 17 September 1991 and nine built. Eight TBs upgraded to PZL-130TC-1 plus 15 new-builds. PZL-130TC-2 has PT6A-25 turboprop and advanced avionics.

VARIANTS & OPERATORS
Poland

SPECIFICATIONS
Crew/accommodation: Student and instructor
Max speed: 200kt (371km/h)
Range (internal fuel): 761nm (1,410km)

ARMAMENT
No internal gun
Hardpoints: six
Max weapon load: 800kg (1,764 lb)
Representative weapons: bombs; FFAR pods; gun pods.

DIMENSIONS
Length: 8.3m (27ft 2in)
Wingspan: 8.6m (28ft 2in)
Height: 3.0m (9ft 8in)

FEATURES
Low tapered wing; tandem cockpit; one Walter M 601 T turboprop

RAC-MiG Advanced Trainer (MiG-AT) Russia

Advanced jet trainer

One of two designs selected for final evaluation as successor to L-29/L-39 in Russian service. The prototype was first flown on 21 March 1996. Several variants proposed with Russian or French engines and avionics. No firm production order yet but three development aircraft flown and initial order of 12-16 in build against a Russian requirement of 200-250 aircraft.

VARIANTS & OPERATORS
Russia

SPECIFICATIONS
Crew/accommodation: Student and instructor
Max speed: 540kt (1,000km/h)
Range: 647nm (1,200km)

ARMAMENT
No internal gun
Hardpoints: seven
Max weapon load: 2,000kg (4,410 lb)
Representative weapons: AAMs; AGMs; bombs; FFAR pods; gun pods; external fuel tanks

DIMENSIONS
Length: 12.0m (39ft 5in)
Wingspan: 10.2m (33ft 4in)
Height: 4.4m (14ft 6in)

FEATURES
Low tapered wing with wingroot engine pods; two Turbomeca-SNECMA Larzac 04-R20 turbofans; tandem canopy

Raytheon (Beech) T-6 Texan II USA

Advanced turboprop trainer

Derived from the PC-9 (see p. 407) under an agreement between Pilatus and Raytheon (Beech) to bid for joint USAF/USN JPATS requirement. Selected in June 1995. Production prototype T-6A flown 15 July 1998, first deliveries from March 2000. Requirement for USAF (454) and USN (328), with export sales to Canada (24 - designated CT-156 Harvard II) and to Greece (45). Armed T-6B version being promoted.

VARIANTS & OPERATORS
T-6A: Greece, USN, USAF
CT-156: Canada

SPECIFICATIONS
Crew/accommodation: Student and instructor
Max speed: 316kt (585km/h)
Range (internal fuel): 850nm (1,574km)

ARMAMENT: T-6B
No internal gun
Hardpoints: three under each wing
Max weapon load: 1,040kg (2,293 lb)
Representative weapons: n/a

DIMENSIONS
Length: 10.3m (32ft 3in)
Wingspan: 10.1m (33ft 2in)
Height: 3.3m (10ft 9in)

FEATURES
Enlarged dorsal fin; low tapered wing; tandem cockpit; one P&WC PT6A-68 turboprop

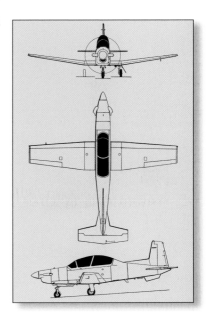

Rockwell (Boeing) T-2 Buckeye USA

Jet trainer

Elias Daloumis

The prototype T2J-1 Buckeye was first flown on 31 January 1958. Early T-2A/B models withdrawn from USN service, with the remaining T-2Cs awaiting replacement by the T-45. The last of 550 Buckeyes was completed in 1976.

VARIANTS & OPERATORS
Greece (T-2C/E), USN (T-2C), Venezuela (T-2D)

SPECIFICATIONS
Crew/accommodation: Student and instructor
Max speed: 460kt (582km/h)
Range: 930nm (1,722km)

ARMAMENT: T-2E
No internal gun
Hardpoints: six (plus wingtip tanks)
Max weapon load: 1,588kg (3,500 lb)
Representative weapons: AGMs; bombs; FFAR pods; gun pods; external fuel tanks

DIMENSIONS
Length: 11.7m (38ft 3in)
Wingspan: 11.6m (38ft 1in)
Height: 4.5m (14ft 9in)

FEATURES
Mid tapered wing with tip tanks; tandem canopy; two GE J85 turbojets; fuselage chin intakes

Saab 105 (Sk 60) Sweden

Basic/advanced jet trainer/light attack and recce aircraft

Michael J. Gething/Jane's

The prototype Saab 105 was first flown on 29 June 1963, and 190 were built for Sweden, 106 of which have been re-engined with FJ44 turbofans. Austria took 40 105ÖE (or 105XT) versions with GE J85 turbojets.

VARIANTS & OPERATORS
Austria (105ÖE), Sweden (Sk 60 RM 15A/E)

SPECIFICATIONS
Crew/accommodation: Student and instructor
Max speed: 432kt (1,800km/h)
Range (internal fuel): 1,350nm (2,500km)

ARMAMENT
No internal gun
Hardpoints: six
Max weapon load: 700kg (1,543 lb)
Representative weapons: bombs; FFAR pods; gun pods.

DIMENSIONS
Length: 10.8m (35ft 4in)
Wingspan: 9.5m (31ft 2in)
Height: 2.7m (8ft 9in)

FEATURES
Shoulder swept wing; side-by-side cockpit; two Williams-Rolls FJ44 turbofans

Slingsby T67 Firefly UK

Basic trainer

Michael J. Gething/Jane's

The current T67-series are composite-built versions of the original wooden T67A (itself a licence-built Fournier RF6B first flown in 1980). The first T67M military variant on 5 December 1982 and is available with various engine configurations. Used for military training in the

UK, but aircraft are civilian-owned and operated. To 1999, 265 had been built and Jordan ordered 16 T67M-260s in 2001.

VARIANTS & OPERATORS

T67: Canada
T67M-160: UK
T67M-200: Belize, UK
T67M-260: Bahrain, UK, Jordan

SPECIFICATIONS

Crew/accommodation: Student and instructor
Max speed: 195kt (361km/h)
Range: 407nm (753km)

ARMAMENT

No internal gun
Hardpoints: nil
Max weapon load: nil
Representative weapons: nil

DIMENSIONS

Length: 7.6m (24ft 10in)
Wingspan: 10.6m (34ft 9in)
Height: 2.4m (7ft 9in)

FEATURES

Low wing; side-by-side cockpit; one Textron Lycoming AEIO-540-D4A4 piston engine; fixed tricycle undercarriage

SOCATA (Aerospatiale) TB 30 Epsilon France

Basic trainer

The TB 30 Epsilon prototype first flew on 22 December 1979 and, as a result of initial trials, the design was refined. Entered French service in 1984. A total of 174 were built.

VARIANTS & OPERATORS
TB30: France, Portugal, Togo.

SPECIFICATIONS
Crew/accommodation: Student and instructor
Max speed: 281kt (530km/h)
Range: n/a

ARMAMENT
No internal gun
Hardpoints: four
Max weapon load: 300kg (661 lb)
Representative weapons: FFAR pods, gun pods, practice bomb carriers.

DIMENSIONS
Length: 7.6m (24ft 10in)
Wingspan: 7.9m (26ft 0in)
Height: 2.7m (8ft 9in)

FEATURES
Low wing; tandem cockpit; one Textron Lycoming AEIO-540-L1B5D piston engine

SOKO G-4 Super Galeb Bosnia-Herzegovina

Armed jet trainer

The prototype Super Galeb was first flown on 17 July 1978, entering service with Yugoslavia in 1981. Armed during the 1991 war with Croatia. Exact number built remains unkown.

VARIANTS & OPERATORS

Bosnia-Herzegovina (Republika Srpska), Myanmar, FRY (Serbia/Montenegro)

SPECIFICATIONS

Crew/accommodation: Student and instructor
Max speed: M = 0.9
Range: 701nm (1,300km)

ARMAMENT

Internal gun: one GSh-23L twin barrel cannon in ventral pack
Hardpoints: four
Max weapon load: 1,500kg (3,306 lb)
Representative weapons: R-60 'Aphid', R-73T 'Archer' AAMs; AGM-65B Maverick; bombs; FFAR pods; external fuel tanks

DIMENSIONS

Length: 12.2m (40ft 2in)
Wingspan: 9.9m (32ft 5in)
Height: 4.3m (14ft 1in)

FEATURES

Tailplane anhedral; low swept wing; tandem canopy; one Rolls-Royce Viper 632 turbojet; lateral intakes

Yakovlev Yak-130 Russia/Italy

Advanced jet trainer

Piotr Butowski

Developed in partnership between Russia's Yakovlev (now owned by Irkut) and Aermacchi of Italy as a potential replacement for Russia's L-29/L-39 trainers, the Yak-130D development aircraft first flew on 25 April 1996. Design refined and each partner took their own variant forward as Yak-130 and M-346 (see pp. 417 and 375 respectively). First series-configured Yak-130 flew on 30 April 2004.

VARIANTS & OPERATORS
Yak-130: Russia (expected)

SPECIFICATIONS
Crew/accommodation: Student and instructor
Max speed: 572kt (1,060km/h)
Range: 1,079nm (2,00km)

ARMAMENT
No internal gun
Hardpoints: seven (plus optional wingtips)
Max weapon load: 3,000kg (6,614 lb)
Representative weapons: AAMs; AGMs; FFAR pods; gun pods; external fuel tanks

DIMENSIONS
Length: 11.5m (37ft 9in)
Wingspan: 9.7m (31ft 10in)
Height: 4.8m (15ft 8in)

FEATURES
Low swept wing; tandem cockpit; two ZMKB Progress AI-222-25 (DV-2S / RD-35) turbofans; underwing root intakes/exhausts; bevelled nose chine

COMBAT
SUPPORT
AIRCRAFT

Airbus A310 MRTT France/Germany/Spain/UK

AAR tanker/transport

Developed by Europe's Airbus Industrie as an AAR tanker variant of the A310 airliner (aka MRT), the first (of four) MRTT conversions for Germany flew on 20 December 2003, with Canada ordering a similar conversion for two of its CC-150 Polaris MRTs in late 2001.

VARIANTS & OPERATORS
A310MRT/MRTT: Canada, Germany

SPECIFICATIONS
Payload/Accommodation: 3 or 4 flight crew plus 214 passengers or 36 tonnes cargo
Disposable fuel: 28,000kg (61,729 lb)
Max speed: M = 0.8
Range: 4,800nm (8,889km)

DIMENSIONS
Length: 47.4m (155ft 5in)
Wingspan: 43.9m (144ft 0in)
Height: 15.8m (51ft 10in)

FEATURES
Low swept wing; two GE CF6 turbofans; underwing AAR pods and/or tail-mounted AAR boom

Airtech CN-235M Indonesia/Spain

Transport/MPA

A collaborative venture between IPTN of Indonesia and CASA (EADS) of Spain, the prototype CN-235 first flew on 11 November 1983, entering service in both countries in 1991. Also developed as an MPA. Some 249 military and 45 civil versions built.

VARIANTS & OPERATORS

CN-235-10: Spain
CN-235: Botswana, Brunei, Colombia, Ecuador, Gabon, Jordan, Saudi Arabia, Turkey, UAE (Abu Dhabi), USA
CN-235M-100: Chile, Ecuador, France, Indonesia, Morocco, Oman, Papua New Guinea, South Africa, South Korea, Spain
CN-235M-200: Colombia, Thailand
CN-235M-220: Malaysia, Pakistan, South Korea
CN-235-300: Austria
CN-235MP: Ireland, USA
CN-235MPA: Indonesia

SPECIFICATIONS

Payload/Accommodation: 2 flight crew and 1 loadmaster plus 46 paratroopers or 6,000kg (13,227 lb) cargo
Sensors (MPA): Search radar, FLIR turret, ESM/DAS.
Armament (M-series): Six underwing hardpoints for ASMs or ASW torpedoes.
Max speed: 240kt (445km/h)
Range: 2,400nm (4,445km)

DIMENSIONS

Length: 21.4m (70ft 2in)
Wingspan: 25.9m (84ft 8in)
Height: 8.2m (26ft 10in)

FEATURES

High tail; shoulder tapered wing; two GE CT7-9C turboprops; fuselage undercarriage fairings

Alenia G222 (C-27) Italy

Tactical transport

First G222 flown on 18 July 1970, Italy took
delivery of the first military transport version in
1976. Sold in several versions to several countries,
including R-R Tyne-engined version for Libya and
C-27 Spartan for USAF (now withdrawn).
Production ceased in 1993 after 111 built.

VARIANTS & OPERATORS
G222: Argentina, Nigeria, Thailand, Tunisia,
Venezuela
G222T: Libya
G222AAA: Italy
G222RM: Italy
G222TCM: Italy
G222VS: Italy

SPECIFICATIONS
Payload/Accommodation: 3 flight crew and 1
loadmaster plus 53 troops, 40 paratroopers or
9,000kg (19,840 lb) cargo
Max speed: 291kt (540km/h)
Range: 740nm (1,371km)

DIMENSIONS
Length: 22.7m (74ft 5in)
Wingspan: 28.7m (94ft 2in)
Height: 9.8m (32ft 2in)

FEATURES
High tail; shoulder tapered wing; two GE T64-GE-
P4D turboprops; fuselage undercarriage fairings

Alenia/Lockheed Martin C-27J Spartan Italy/USA

Tactical transport

A collaborative venture between Alenia and Lockheed Martin, the C-27J merges engines, avionics and systems from the C-130J with the G222. Prototype C-27J (a converted G222) first flown on 24 September 1999. Italy ordered 12 in 1999 and sales of 500 expected over 20 years.

VARIANTS & OPERATORS
C-27J: Italy, Greece (on order)

SPECIFICATIONS
Payload/Accommodation: 2 flight crew and 1 loadmaster plus 53 troops, 40 paratroopers or 10,000kg (22,046 lb) cargo
Max speed: 325kt (602km/h)
Range: 1,350nm (2,500km)

DIMENSIONS
Length: 22.7m (74ft 5in)
Wingspan: 28.7m (94ft 2in)
Height: 9.8m (32ft 2in)

FEATURES
High tail; shoulder tapered wing; two Rolls-Royce AE 2100D2 turboprops; fuselage undercarriage fairings

Antonov An-12 (Y-8) 'Cub' Ukraine

Tactical transport

Paul Jackson/Jane's

Derived from the An-10 airliner, the An-12 was first flown with NK-4 turboprops in 1958, and later re-engined with Ivchenko AI-20A/M turboprops. In service from 1959, some 900 were built to 1973, including an EW version. Widely exported and licence-built in China as Y-8.

VARIANTS & OPERATORS
An-12: Algeria, Angola, Azerbaijan, Belarus, Ethiopia, Kazakhstan, Russia, Turkmenistan, Ukraine, Uzbekistan, Yemen
Y-8: China, Myanmar, Sri Lanka, Sudan

SPECIFICATIONS
Payload/Accommodation: 5 flight crew and 1 rear gunner plus 90 troops, 60 paratroopers or 20,000kg (44,090 lb) cargo
Max speed: 419kt (777km/h)
Range: 1,942nm (3,600km)

DIMENSIONS
Length: 33.1m (108ft 7in)
Wingspan: 38.0m (124ft 8in)
Height: 12.2m (40ft 0in)

ARMAMENT
Two 23mm NK-23 cannon in tail turret

FEATURES
High tail; shoulder tapered wing; anhedral on outer wing panels; four Ivchenko AI-20 turboprops; fuselage undercarriage fairings

Antonov An-24 'Coke', An-26 'Curl', An-32 'Cline' Ukraine

Tactical transport/freighter/survey aircraft

Michael J. Gething/Jane's

The prototype An-24 was first flown on 20 December 1959 and entered service from 1963. Production of about 1,200 ended in 1979, although continued in China (as Y-7) into the mid-1990s. The An-26 freighter (Y-7H-500 in China) and first shown in 1969. The An-32 is derived from the An-26 and first flew on 9 July 1976 and 346 produced to 1997.

VARIANTS & OPERATORS

An-24: Armenia, Azerbaijan, Belarus, Cambodia,

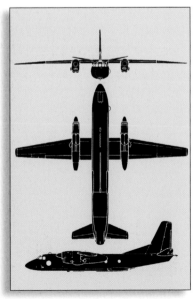

China, Congo, Cuba, Czech Republic, Guinea-Bisseau, Guinea Republic, Kazakhstan, Laos, Mali, Mongolia, North Korea, Romania, Russia, Slovak Republic, Syria, Turkmenistan, Uzbekistan, Yemen

An-26: Angola, Belarus, Bulgaria, Cape Verde, Chad, China, Cuba, Czech Republic, Ethiopia, Hungary, Kazakhstan, Laos, Libya, Lithuania, Madagascar, Mali, Mongolia, Mozambique, Nicaragua, Niger, Poland, Romania, Russia, Serbia & Montenegro, Slovak Republic, Syria, Ukraine, Uzbekistan, Vietnam, Yemen, Zambia

An-32: Angola, Armenia, Bangladesh, Croatia, Cuba, Equatorial Guinea, Ethiopia, India, Mexico, Peru, Russia, Sri Lanka, Ukraine, USA

SPECIFICATIONS

Payload/Accommodation: 5 or 6 flight crew plus (An-24) 36-44 passengers or (An-26) 4,500kg (9,920 lb) cargo; (An-32) 3 or 4 flight crew plus 50 passengers, 42 paratroops or 7,500kg (16,525 lb) cargo

	An-24	An-32
Max speed:	243kt (450km/h)	286kt (530km/h)
Range:	296nm (550km)	971nm (1,800km)

DIMENSIONS

	An-24	An-32
Length:	23.5m (77ft 2in)	23.7m (77ft 8in)
Wingspan:	29.2m (95ft 9in)	29.2m (95ft 9in)
Height:	8.3m (27ft 3in)	8.7m (28ft 8in)

FEATURES

Dihedral tail; shoulder tapered wing; (An-24/-26) two Progress/Ivchenko AI-24A or (An-32) two AI-20D5 turboprops

Antonov An-70 Ukraine

Wide-body transport/freighter

Paul/Jackson/Jane's

The prototype An-70 was first flown on 16 December 1994 and lost on 10 February 1995. Second prototype flown 24 April 1997 with third prototype (An-70T commercial) variant due to fly in 2002. Production of 10 authorised 1999, requirement for Russia is 164 with 65 for Ukraine, plus 100 civil freighters.

VARIANTS & OPERATORS
An-70: Russia, Ukraine

SPECIFICATIONS
Payload/Accommodation: 3 flight crew and 1 loadmaster plus provision for 300 troop seats, 214 stretchers or 47,000kg (103,615 lb) cargo
Max speed: 432kt (800km/h)
Range: 4,319nm (8,000km)

DIMENSIONS
Length: 40.7m (133ft 7in)
Wingspan: 44.1m (144ft 7in)
Height: 16.4m (53ft 9in)

FEATURES
Shoulder tapered wing; four Progress/Ivchenko D27 propfans with eight-bladed propellers; fuselage undercarriage fairings

BAE Systems (HSA) Nimrod MR.2/MRA.4 UK

MPA and ASW aircraft

Derived from the de Havilland Comet 4C airliner to become the HS.801 Nimrod, the prototype first flew on 23 May 1967 and entered RAF service from 1969. In all 49 Nimrods were built - 46 MR.1 and three R.1 ELINT aircraft - of which 35 MR.1s were converted to MR.2 standard. Of these one has been converted to R.1 standard (to replace a crashed aircraft) and 12 MR.2s are now being re-manufactured to MRA.4 configuration. First flight on 26 August 2004.

VARIANTS & OPERATORS
Nimrod R.1: UK
Nimrod MR.2P: UK
Nimrod MRA.4: UK

SPECIFICATIONS
Payload/Accommodation: 3 flight crew and 9 mission specialists
Hardpoints: one under each wing for Harpoon ASMs or AIM-9 AAMs (two per wing for MRA.4); fuselage sonobuoy launchers; lower fuselage bomb bay for mines, depth charges or Stingray torpedoes for a max payload of 6,120kg (13,500 lb)
Max speed: 500kt (926km/h)
Ferry range: 5,000nm (9,265km)

DIMENSIONS
Length: 39.4m (129ft 1in)
Wingspan: 35.0m (114ft 10in)
Height: 9.1m (29ft 8in)

FEATURES
Fin-top ESM pod; mid swept wings; with wingtip ESM pods; four Rolls-Royce Spey Mk.207 (MR.2) or BMW R-R BR710 (MRA.4) turbofans in wing root; tail MAD boom

Nimrod MR.2

BAE Systems (Vickers) VC10 C.1K & K.2/3/4 UK

Transport/tanker aircraft

Derived from the civil VC10, first flown on 29 June 1962, and entered RAF service from 1965. The RAF took 14 VC10 C.1 transports, 13 of which later converted to C.1K tanker/ transports. Later ex-civil airliners converted to VC10 K.2 (5), K.3 (4) and K.4 (5) tankers.

VARIANTS & OPERATORS
VC10 C.1K: UK
VC10 K.2/3/4: UK

SPECIFICATIONS
Payload/Accommodation: 4/5 flight crew plus (C.1K) plus 137-146 passengers

	VC10 C.1K/K.2	VC10 K.3/4
Max speed:	494kt (914km/h)	494kt (914km/h)
Range:	4,692nm (8,690km)	4,692nm (8,690km)

DIMENSIONS

	VC10 C.1K/K.2	VC10 K.3/4
Length:	48.4m (158ft 8in)	52.3m (171ft 8in)
Wingspan:	44.6m (146ft 2in)	44.6m (146ft 2in)
Height:	12.0m (39ft 6in)	12.0m (39ft 6in)

FEATURES
Swept T-tail; low swept wings; with underwing AAR pods; four rear-fuselage Rolls-Royce Conway Mk.301 turbofans

Beriev (BETAIR) Be-200 Altair Russia

Multi-role amphibian

Derived from the A-40/Be-42 (see entry in Third Edition), which first flew in A-40 guise on 8 December 1986, the slightly smaller Be-200 made its 'official' first flight on 17 October 1998. Although initially developed as a fire-fighting water bomber, the Be-200 has been considered for SAR and ASW duties but the most likely military use could be from the Russian Border Guards as a patrol aircraft. Five firm orders from Russia's Ministry of Emergency Situations, as of October 2003, although some export interest expressed.

VARIANTS & OPERATORS

Be-200ChS: Russia

SPECIFICATIONS

Payload/Accommodation: 2 flight crew, plus mission specialists, with maximum payload of 7,500kg (16,534 lb) of cargo or 72 passengers plus 2 cabin crew
Max level speed: 388kt (720km/h)
Range: 2,078nm (3,850km)

DIMENSIONS

Length: 31.4m (103ft 1in)
Wingspan: 38.8m (107ft 6.5in)
Height: 8.9m (29ft 2.5in)

FEATURES

T-tail; shoulder swept wing with winglets, underwing floats; two upper-rear-fuselage-mounted ZMKB Progress D-436TP turbofans; (optional nose AAR probe)

Beriev (Ilyushin) A-50 'Mainstay' Russia

AEW&C aircraft

Developed from the Il-76 (which see) as an AEW&C aircraft, the prototype A-50 was first flown on 19 December 1978. Has Liana or Vega-M Shmell-II AEW radar in rotating radome above fuselage. Indian aircraft to have IAI Phalcon radar. About 28 produced.

VARIANTS & OPERATORS
A-50: China, India, Russia

SPECIFICATIONS
Payload/Accommodation: 5 flight crew and 10 systems operators
Max speed: 425kt (785km/h)
Range: 2,753nm (5,100km)

DIMENSIONS
Length: 46.6m (152ft 10in)
Wingspan: 50.5m (165ft 8in)
Height: 14.8m (48ft 5in)

FEATURES
T-tail; shoulder swept wing; four Aviadvigatel D-30KP-2 turbofans; radar 'flying saucer' above rear fuselage; fuselage undercarriage fairings

Boeing (McDonnell Douglas) C-17 Globemaster III USA

Strategic transport aircraft

Developed as C-X from early 1980s, the first flight

of the C-17A took place on 15 September 1991, with first deliveries to USAF from 1993. USAF has over 100 of 120 on order delivered. Four Boeing-owned aircraft leased to RAF will be bought, plus a fifth aircraft. A further 60 ordered for USAF in 2002.

VARIANTS & OPERATORS
C-17A: UK, USA

SPECIFICATIONS
Payload/Accommodation: 2 flight crew and 1 loadmaster, plus 154 passengers, 102 paratroops or a max of 76,655kg (169,000 lb) of cargo
Max speed: M = 0.77
Range: 2,400nm (8,704km)

DIMENSIONS
Length: 53.0m (174ft 0in)
Wingspan: 51.7m (169ft 9in)
Height: 16.8m (55ft 1in)

FEATURES
T-tail; shoulder swept wing with winglet tips; four wing-mounted P&W F117-PW-100 (PW2040) turbofans; fuselage undercarriage sponsons

Boeing E-3 Sentry AWACS USA

AEW&C aircraft

Based on the airframe of the Boeing 707-320B airliner fitted with AN/APY-1 'flying saucer' radome over the rear fuselage, the first prototype, designated EC-137D flew on 5 February 1972. The first E-3A Sentry flew in 1975 and entered USAF service in 1977. British, French and Saudi E-3s powered by CFM56 turbofans. Production ceased in 1992 with 68 built. Many being upgraded.

VARIANTS & OPERATORS
E-3A: NATO, Saudi Arabia
E-3B/C: USAF
E-3D: UK
E-3F: France

SPECIFICATIONS
Payload/Accommodation: 4 flight crew plus 13 mission specialists
Max speed: 460kt (853km/h)
Endurance: over 11h

DIMENSIONS
Length: 46.6m (152ft 11in)
Wingspan: 44.4m (145ft 9in)
Height: 12.7m (41ft 9in)

FEATURES
Low swept wing; radome over rear fuselage; four

P&W TF33-PW-100 or CFM International F108 (CFM 56) turbofans, two under each wing

Boeing E-6A Mercury TACAMO II USA

Communications relay aircraft

Based on the airframe of the E-3 Sentry and fitted with an AVLF communications relay system, the first prototype E-6 flew on 1 June 1987. It replaced EC-130Q Hercules TACAMO in USN service from 1989. A total of 16 produced. Now undergoing upgrade.

VARIANTS & OPERATORS
E-6A: USN

SPECIFICATIONS
Payload/Accommodation: 4 flight crew plus 8 mission specialists
Max speed: 530kt (981km/h)
Endurance: over 15h

DIMENSIONS
Length: 46.6m (152ft 11in)
Wingspan: 45.2m (148ft 2in)
Height: 12.9m (42ft 5in)

FEATURES
Low swept wing; radome over rear fuselage; four CFM International F108-CF-100 (CFM56-2A-2) turbofans, two under each wing

Boeing E-767 AWACS / KC-767 tanker USA

AWACS and tanker aircraft

Based on the airframe of the Boeing 767-200ER airliner and fitted with the AN/APY-2 radar the first prototype E-767 (for Japan) flew on 10 October 1994. With four E-767s in service, Japan plans to buy four more, plus four of the KC-767 AAR tanker variant. Italy has selected the KC-767, while USAF plans to acquire the type are in limbo.

VARIANTS & OPERATORS
E-767: Japan
KC-767: Italy, Japan, USA (none yet in service)

SPECIFICATIONS
Payload/Accommodation (AWACS): 2 flight crew plus up to 19 mission specialists
Max speed: over 434kt (805km/h)
Range: 5,000nm (9,260km)

DIMENSIONS
Length: 48.5m (159ft 2in)
Wingspan: 47.6m (156ft 1in)
Height: 15.8m (52ft 0in)

FEATURES
Low swept wing; 'flying-saucer' radome over rear fuselage; two GE CF6-80C2B6FA turbofans

Boeing KC-135 Stratotanker USA

AAR tanker aircraft

Michael J. Gething/Jane's

Based on Boeing's Model 367-80 - which spawned the Model 707 airliner (USAF = C-137, USN = C-18) with a wider-diameter fuselage - which first flew on 15 July 1954, the KC-135 Stratotanker is fitted with the Flying Boom refuelling system. Boeing and IAI have sold several tanker conversions of the Model 707 airliner. The

KC-135 has been in USAF service since 1957, taking 732 Stratotankers (of which the KC-135R is the major variant today) and France bought 12 C-135F tankers.

VARIANTS & OPERATORS

C-135F/FR: France
KC-135E: USAF
KC-135R: France, Singapore, Turkey, USAF
KC-137: Brazil, Venezuela
KC-707: Israel
KE-3A: Saudi Arabia
707 tanker: Australia, Chile, Colombia, Iran, Italy, Peru, South Africa, Spain

SPECIFICATIONS

Payload/Accommodation: 4 flight crew plus 1 boom operator
Max speed: 530kt (982km/h)
Range: 2,997nm (5,552km)

DIMENSIONS

Length: 41.5m (136ft 3in)
Wingspan: 39.9m (130ft 10in)
Height: 12.3m (40ft 7in)

FEATURES

Low swept wing; flying boom under rear fuselage (some aircraft have underwing refuelling pods); four CFM International F108 (CFM56) or P&W TF33 (JT3D) turbofans

Boeing C-135 series USA

Special mission aircraft

As well as the KC-135, the USAF bought 88 non-tanker C-135s. These were adapted for a variety of special missions including airborne command post, ELINT, radio relay, range monitoring, SIGINT, trials, weather reconnaissance and VIP transport. The major variants (albeit built in small numbers) are detailed below.

antennae on nose and fuselage; four P&W J57 turbojets, P&W TF33 (JT3D) or CFM International F108 (CFM56) turbofans – two under each wing

VARIANTS
C-135B/C/E, EC-135E/K/N, RC-135S Cobra Ball, RC-135U Combat Sent, RC-135V Rivet Joint, TC-135W, WC-135C/W – all in US service

SPECIFICATIONS
Payload/Accommodation: 4 flight crew plus various mission specialists

	EC-135K	RC-135V
Max speed:	530kt (982km/h)	535kt (991km/h)
Range:	2,997nm (5,552km)	4,913nm
(9,100km)		

DIMENSIONS

	EC-135K	RC-135V
Length:	41.5m (136ft 3in)	49.9m (163ft 9in)
Wingspan:	39.9m (130ft 10in)	44.4m (145ft 8in)
Height:	12.3m (40ft 7in)	12.9m (42ft 4in)

FEATURES
Low swept wing; various non-standard radomes/

CASA (EADS) C-212 Aviocar Spain

Light multirole transport

First flown on 26 March 1971, the C-212 has
evolved through four major variants. It has been
adapted for roles including transport, paratrooper,
freighter, ambulance, photographic aircraft,
ELINT/ECM and ASW/MPA. Production of Series 100
(153 built) and Series 200 (211 built) ended. Over
460 Series 300/400 for military/civil use sold. Built
under licence in Indonesia.

VARIANTS & OPERATORS

C-212-100: Chile, Indonesia, Jordan, Portugal,
Spain, Thailand
C-212-200: Angola, Argentina, Chile, Colombia,
Indonesia, Mexico, Panama, Paraguay, South
Africa, Spain, Sweden, Thailand, Uruguay, USA,
Venezuela, Zimbabwe
C-212-300: Angola, Argentina, Bolivia, Botswana,
Chile, Colombia, France, Lesotho, Panama,
Portugal, South Africa, Thailand
C-212-300MP: Angola
C-212-400: Dominican Republic, Lesotho,
Suriname, Venezuela
C-212-400MP: Venezuela

SPECIFICATIONS

Payload/Accommodation: 2 flight crew plus 25
passengers or 2,700kg (5,952 lb) of freight
Max speed: 200kt (370km/h)
Range: 233nm (431km)
Weapons (when carried): two fuselage
hardpoints for machine gun or rocket pods, for
250kg (551 lb) each

DIMENSIONS: SERIES 300/400

Length: 16.1m (53ft 0in)
Wingspan: 20.3m (66ft 6in)
Height: 6.6m (21ft 8in)

FEATURES

Shoulder straight wing; winglets on Series
300/400 aircraft; two Honeywell TPE331-10R-
513C turboprops

CASA (EADS) C-295M Spain

Multirole transport

Derived from the CN-235M, the C-295M was first flown on 28 November 1997. Like the C-212 and CN-235M, can be adapted for roles including tactical transport, paratrooper, freighter and MPA. Spain ordered nine in April 1999 and a market of 300 is foreseen.

VARIANTS & OPERATORS

C-295M: Brazil, Spain, UAE (Abu Dhabi)

SPECIFICATIONS

Payload/Accommodation: 2 flight crew plus up to 78 passengers, 48 paratroopers or 7,500kg (16,535 lb) of freight
Max speed: 260kt (481km/h)
Range: 728nm (1,348km)

DIMENSIONS

Length: 24.4m (80ft 2in)
Wingspan: 25.8m (84ft 8in)
Height: 8.6m (28ft 2in)

FEATURES

Shoulder tapered wing; fuselage undercarriage fairings; two P&WC PW127G turboprops

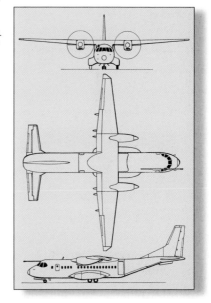

Dassault (Breguet) Atlantic 1 & 2 France

First flown, as Breguet BR 1150, on 21 October 1961, the Franco-German Atlantic 1 entered French Navy service in 1965. German, Italian and Pakistani aircraft since upgraded. Production of Atlantic 1 (87 built) ended in 1974. France converted 28 to Atlantique 2 configuration, the first of which entered service in 1990.

VARIANTS & OPERATORS
Atlantic 1: Germany, Italy, Pakistan
Atlantique 2: France

SPECIFICATIONS
Payload/Accommodation: 2 flight crew plus 10 mission crew.
Max speed: 300kt (556km/h)
Range: 4,200nm (7,778km)
Weapons: bomb bay for bombs, depth charges or homing torpedoes; plus underwing hardpoints for rockets and ASMs

DIMENSIONS: ATLANTIC 1
Length: 31.8m (104ft 2in)
Wingspan: 36.3m (119ft 1in)
Height: 11.3m (37ft 2in)

FEATURES
Straight mid-wing; ECM dome atop fin; tail MAD boom; two SNECMA-built Rolls-Royce Tyne RTy.20 Mk.21 turboprops

de Havilland Canada (Bombardier)
DHC-4A Caribou Canada

STOL transport

The prototype DHC-4 first flew on 20 July 1958 and as the Caribou, flew in Canadian and US Army (later USAF) service and was exported for military and civil use. Pen Turbo Aviation has trialled a prototype Turbo-Caribou conversion with P&WC PT6A engines. Total of 307 Cariboux produced.

VARIANTS & OPERATORS
DHC-4: Australia, Costa Rica

SPECIFICATIONS
Payload/Accommodation: 2 flight crew plus 32 troops, 26 paratroops or 3,965kg (8,740 lb) of freight
Max speed: 188kt (347km/h)
Range: 210nm (390km)

DIMENSIONS
Length: 22.1m (72ft 7in)
Wingspan: 29.1m (95ft 7in)
Height: 9.7m (31ft 9in)

FEATURES
High straight wing; high beaver-tail; two P&W R-2000-7M2 piston engines

de Havilland Canada (Bombardier)
DHC-5 Buffalo Canada

All-weather STOL transport

Developed from the DHC-4, the DHC-5 prototype first flew with GE CT-64 turboprops on 9 April 1964 and served in Canadian and US Army (later USAF) service as well as being widely exported (with GE CT-82 turboprops). Production (126 built) ended in 1986.

VARIANTS & OPERATORS
DHC-5D: Brazil, Cameroun, Canada (CC-115), Congo (Dem.Rep), Ecuador, Egypt Indonesia, Kenya, Mexico, Sudan, Tanzania, Togo

SPECIFICATIONS
Payload/Accommodation: 2 flight crew and crew chief, plus 41 troops, 35 paratroops or 8,164kg (18,000 lb) of freight
Max speed: 252kt (467km/h)
Range: 225nm (415km)

DIMENSIONS
Length: 24.1m (79ft 0in)
Wingspan: 29.3m (96ft 0in)
Height: 8.7m (28ft 8in)

FEATURES
High wing; T-tail; two GE CT-82-4 turboprops

Douglas DC-3 Dakota / C-47 Skytrain USA

Multirole transport

The ubiquitous DC-3 Dakota first flew on 18 December 1935 and the last Douglas-built version (total 10,629) was completed in 1946. Many others built in Russia and China as the Li-2. Some aircraft have been converted to turboprop power in the USA (Basler Turbo-67) and South Africa (C-47TP).

VARIANTS & OPERATORS

C-47: Congo (Dem.Rep), Greece, Haiti, Honduras, Indonesia, Madagascar, Mexico, Thailand, Venezuela
C-47TP: South Africa
Dakota C.III: UK (BBMF)
Turbo AC-47: Colombia
Turbo-67: Bolivia, Colombia, El Salvador, Guatemala, Malawi, Mali, Mauritania, Thailand

SPECIFICATIONS

Payload/Accommodation: 2 flight crew and 21 passengers
Max speed: 199kt (368km/h)
Range: 1,306nm (2,420km)

DIMENSIONS

Length: 19.6m (64ft 5in)
Wingspan: 28.9m (95ft 0in)
Height: 5.2m (16ft 11in)

FEATURES

Low tapered wing; tailwheel undercarriage; two Wright Cyclone GR-1820-G102A, P&W Twin Wasp R-1830-S1C3G piston engines or P&WC PT6A-65AR/-67R turboprops

EMBRAER EMB-145 (R-99) Brazil

Surveillance aircraft

EMB-145SA

The EMB-145 is derived from the ERJ-145 regional airliner, which first flew on 17 November 1995. The EMB-145SA (R-99A) is an AEW and surveillance aircraft equipped with the Erieye dorsal radar (five ordered) and the EMB-145RS (R-99B) is a remote sensing variant (three ordered) for Brazil's SIVAM programme. Greece and Mexico have ordered variants.

VARIANTS & OPERATORS
EMB-145MP: Mexico
EMB-145RS: Brazil
EMB-145SA: Brazil, Greece, Mexico

SPECIFICATIONS
Payload/Accommodation: 2 flight crew and 4-6 mission systems operators
Max speed: 450kt (833km/h)
Range: 1,600nm (2,963km)

DIMENSIONS
Length: 29.9m (98ft 0in)
Wingspan: 20.0m (65ft 9in)
Height: 6.8m (22ft 2in)

FEATURES
Low swept wing; T-tail, dorsal radar antenna (R-99A); belly-mounted radome and fuselage antenna just forward of wing root (R-99B); two rear-fuselage-mounted Rolls-Royce/Allison AE 3007A1 turbofans

EMB-145RS

Fokker F27 / Fokker 50/60 The Netherlands

MPA and transport aircraft

Michael J. Gething/Jane's

The prototype F27 first flew on 24 November 1955, while its follow-on Fokker 50 flew on 28 December 1985. A successful civil airliner (Friendship), the F27 was adapted as a military transport (Troopship) and the MPA role (Maritime Enforcer). It was built under licence in the USA as the Fairchild-Hiller FH-227. The Fokker 50 and 60 were modern equivalents, falling victim to the bankruptcy of the manufacturer in 1996-97. Production of the F27 (786 built) ended in 1986; the Fokker 50/60 (209) in 1997.

VARIANTS & OPERATORS

F27: Algeria, Angola, Argentina, Bolivia, Finland, Ghana, Guatemala, Iceland, Indonesia, Iran, Myanmar, Pakistan, Peru, Philippines, Senegal, Spain, Thailand, Uruguay, USA (C-31A)
Fokker 50: Netherlands, Singapore, Taiwan, Tanzania, Thailand
Fokker 60: Netherlands
FH-227: Myanmar

SPECIFICATIONS

Payload/Accommodation: 2 flight crew and 52 passengers, 6,261kg (13,804 lb) freight or (for MPA variant) 4-6 mission systems operators
Hardpoints (MPA): 2 x 907kg (2,000 lb) fuselage; 6 x underwing - inner 295kg (650 lb), centre 680kg (1,500 lb) and outer 113kg (250 lb)
Weapons (MPA): Homing torpedoes; depth charges; AGMs; ASMs; external fuel tanks

	F27 SERIES	FOKKER 50
Max speed:	259kt (480km/h)	282kt (522km/h)
Range (MPA):	2,698nm (5,000km)	1,700nm (3,148km)

DIMENSIONS

	F27 SERIES	FOKKER 50
Length:	23.6m (77ft 3in)	25.3 (82ft 10in)
Wingspan:	29.0m (95ft 2in)	29.0m (95ft 2in)
Height:	8.7m (28ft 6in)	8.3m (27ft 3in)

FEATURES

High tapered wing; dorsal fin fillet; two wing-mounted Rolls-Royce Dart Mk.552 (F-27/FH-227) or two P&WC PW125B (Fokker 50/60) turboprops; some MPAs have belly radome

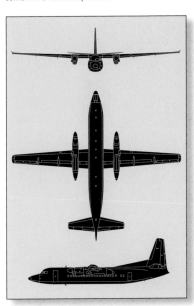

Grumman (N-G) OV-1 Mohawk USA

Observation aircraft

Horacio J. Clariá

First flown on 14 April 1959, as an observation and intelligence-gathering platform for the US Army. Progressively upgraded but now withdrawn from service. Some transferred to Argentina and South Korea. Production of the Mohawk (380 built) ended in 1970.

VARIANTS & OPERATORS
OV-1D: Argentina, South Korea

SPECIFICATIONS
Payload/Accommodation: 2 flight crew and specialised mission equipment and cameras
Max speed: 265kt (491km/h)
Range: 878nm (1,627km)
Hardpoints: two under each wing for sensor pods and external fuel tanks

DIMENSIONS
Length: 12.5m (41ft 0in)
Wingspan: 14.6 (48ft 0in)
Height: 3.9m (12ft 8in)

FEATURES
Mid slightly-swept wing; bulged side-by-side canopy in nose; triple fin; two wing-mounted Lycoming T53-L-701 turboprops

Grumman (N-G) S-2 Tracker USA

MPA & ASW aircraft

A carrier-borne ASW aircraft for the USN, the Tracker was first flown on 4 December 1952, as the XS2F-1. Widely exported and progressively upgraded, including re-engining with turboprops by Marsh Aviation. Production of the Tracker (1,269 built) ended in 1967.

VARIANTS & OPERATORS
S-2E: South Korea
S-2F: Thailand
S-2T: Argentina, Taiwan

SPECIFICATIONS
Payload/Accommodation: 2 flight crew and 2 mission specialists
Hardpoints: three under each wing for bombs, torpedoes, rockets and external fuel tanks, plus bomb bay for homing torpedoes and depth charges for a max payload of 2,182kg (4,810 lb)

	S-2E	S-2T
Max speed:	230kt (426km/h)	260kt (481km/hr)
Range:	1,128nm (2,095km)	1,390nm (2,581km)

DIMENSIONS
Length: 13.3m (43ft 6in)
Wingspan: 22.1m (72ft 7in)
Height: 5.1m (16ft 7in)

FEATURES
Tapered shoulder wing; bulged side-by-side canopy; two wing-mounted (S-2E) Wright R-1820-82 radial engines or (S-2T) AlliedSignal (Garrett) TPE331-15AW turboprops

IAI (Boeing) Phalcon 707 Israel

AEW aircraft

Specifically developed for Chile, this is an IAI conversion of a Boeing 707-320C airliner fitted with the Phalcon solid-state phased array radar located in antennas located in the nose and large forward fuselage panniers. First flown on 12 May 1993 and delivered to Chile in 1995. One built.

VARIANTS & OPERATORS
Phalcon 707: Chile

SPECIFICATIONS
Payload/Accommodation: 3 flight crew and 13 mission specialists
Max speed: 545kt (1,010km/h)
Range: 5,000nm (9,265km)

DIMENSIONS
Length: 46.6m (152ft 11in)
Wingspan: 44.4m (145ft 9in)
Height: 12.9m (42ft 5in)

FEATURES
Swept low wing; with four wing-mounted P&W JT3D-7 turbofans; large nose radome; forward fuselage side panniers with radomes fore and aft

Ilyushin Il-18/-20/-22 'Coot' Russia

Airborne command post and recce aircraft

These non-transport military developments of the Il-18D 'Coot' airliner (see p. 95), first flown on 4 July 1957, have been converted for specialised roles. Serial production of the Il-18 ceased in 1969, after 565 had been built.

VARIANTS & OPERATORS
Il-18 'Coot': China Kazakhstan, North Korea, Russia
Il-20M 'Coot-A': Russia
Il-22M-11 'Coot-B/-C': Belarus, Russia, Ukraine

SPECIFICATIONS
Payload/Accommodation: 5 flight crew plus mission specialists (or 65 passengers); specialised SIGINT, ELINT, SLAR and camera sensor payloads
Max speed: 364kt (675km/h)
Range: 3,508nm (6,500km)

DIMENSIONS
Length: 35.9m (117ft 9in)
Wingspan: 37.4m (122ft 8in)
Height: 10.2m (33ft 4in)

FEATURES
Tapered low wing; with four wing-mounted Ivchenko AI-20 turboprops; under-fuselage 'canoe' radome

Ilyushin Il-38 'May' Russia

MPA and ASW aircraft

Derived from the Il-18D 'Coot' airliner (see p. 95), this MPA version first flew on 27 September 1961, and serves with the naval air arms of India and Russia. Now in process of receiving a sensor upgrade. A total of 57 built.

VARIANTS & OPERATORS
Il-38: India, Russia

SPECIFICATIONS
Payload/Accommodation: 3 flight crew plus 9 mission specialists; specialised ASW and surveillance sensor payloads
Max speed: 390kt (722km/h)
Range: 3,887nm (7,200km)

DIMENSIONS
Length: 39.6m (129ft 10in)
Wingspan: 37.4m (122ft 8in)
Height: 10.2m (33ft 4in)

FEATURES
Tapered low wing; with four wing-mounted Ivchenko AI-20M turboprops; round radome under forward fuselage; tail MAD boom

Ilyushin Il-76MD 'Candid-B' & Il-78M 'Midas' Russia

Transport and tanker aircraft

This military transport (also built as a civil freighter – see p. 54), first flew on 25 March 1971. It has been developed into into the A-50 'Mainstay' AEW&C version by Beriev (see p. 429) and also the 'Midas' three-point AAR tanker. Over 850 of all versions built.

VARIANTS & OPERATORS

Il-76: Algeria, Angola, Belarus, China, India, Iran, Libya, North Korea, Russia, Syria, Ukraine, Yemen
Il-78: Algeria, India, Russia, Ukraine

SPECIFICATIONS

Payload/Accommodation: 5 flight crew plus 2 loadmasters; plus 47,000kg (103,615 lb) freight; 'Midas' has two underwing and one rear-fuselage AAR pods
Max speed: 459kt (850km/h)
Range: 2,051nm (3,800km)
Armament: Twin 23mm GSh-23 guns in tail turret

DIMENSIONS

Length: 46.6m (152ft 10in)
Wingspan: 50.5m (165ft 8in)
Height: 14.8m (48ft 5in)

FEATURES

T-tail; shoulder swept wing; four Aviadvigatel

D-30KP-2 turbofans under wings; glazed lower nose with radome under forward fuselage

Kawasaki C-1A Japan

Transport aircraft

The first prototype XC-1 military transport first flew on 12 November 1970. The EC-1 ECM training version with a large bulbous nose radome and two smaller forward fuselage side radomes was converted from one transport. A total of 31 built.

VARIANTS & OPERATORS

C-1A: Japan
EC-1: Japan

SPECIFICATIONS

Payload/Accommodation: 5 flight crew plus 11,900kg (26,235 lb) freight
Max speed: 435kt (806km/h)
Range: 1,810nm (3,353km)

DIMENSIONS

Length: 29.0m (95ft 2in)
Wingspan: 30.6m (100ft 5in)
Height: 26.5m (86ft 11in)

FEATURES

T-tail; shoulder swept wing; two Mitsubishi (P&W) JT8D-M-9 turbofans under wings

Lockheed S-3B Viking USA

Carrier-borne ASW aircraft

Prototype first flown 21 January 1972 and entered USN service in 1974. A total of 187 S-3As built, including five US-3A COD versions and one KS-3A dedicated AAR tanker. First flight of developed S-3B on 13 September 1984 and 122 A-models brought up to this standard (in service), plus 16 to ES-3B EW standard (now withdrawn).

GE TF34-GE-2 turbofans; retractable MAD tail boom; bulged side-by-side canopy

VARIANTS & OPERATORS
S-3B: USA

SPECIFICATIONS
Payload/Accommodation: 2 flight crew and 2/3 mission specialists
Max speed: 450kt (834km/h)
Range: 2,000nm (3,706km)
Hardpoints: one under each wing for mines, Harpoon/SLAM ASMs, external tanks or 'buddy' AAR pod; fuselage sonobuoy launchers; fuselage bomb bay for mines, depth charges or torpedoes

DIMENSIONS
Length: 16.3m (53ft 4in)
Wingspan: 20.9m (68ft 8in)
Height: 6.9m (22ft 9in)

FEATURES
Shoulder swept wing; four underwing-mounted

Lockheed U-2S USA

High-altitude recce aircraft

The prototype 'Dragon Lady' was first flown on 4 August 1955 and an unspecified number built for USAF and CIA use. The U-2R flew in 1967 and 12 were procured. Another 37 versions built from 1979, comprising 16 U-2Rs, one U-2RT trainer, 16 TR-1As, two TR-1B trainers and two ER-2s for NASA. From 1994, remaining aircraft re-engined as U-2S/TU-2S and are now undergoing a cockpit avionics upgrade.

VARIANTS & OPERATORS
U-2S: USA
TU-2S: USA

SPECIFICATIONS
Payload/Accommodation: U-2S = pilot;
   TU-2S = pilot and instructor
Max speed: 673+kt (692+km/h)
Range: 2,605+nm (4,830+km)
Hardpoints: one under each wing for mission pods of various sensor equipment, plus fuselage-mounted sensors

DIMENSIONS
Length: 19.2m (63ft 0in)
Wingspan: 31.4m (103ft 0in)
Height: 4.9m (16ft 0in)

FEATURES
Shoulder tapered wing; some aircraft have wing pods; one GE F118-GE-101 turbofan; various radomes/antennas, depending on configuration

Lockheed Martin C-5 Galaxy USA

Bulk military freighter

Michael J. Gething/Jane's

First flown on 30 June 1968, the C-5A Galaxy entered USAF service in 1969 with the improved C-5B from 1984. A third iteration is now under development involving an avionics upgrade and new engines to be designated C-5M. A total of 81 C-5As and 50 C-5Bs built.

VARIANTS & OPERATORS
C-5A/B/C: USA

SPECIFICATIONS
Payload/Accommodation: 5 flight crew plus 118,387kg (261,000 lb) freight
Max speed: 496kt (919km/h)
Range: 5,618nm (10,411km)

DIMENSIONS
Length: 75.5m (247ft 10in)
Wingspan: 67.9m (222ft 8in)
Height: 19.8m (65ft 1in)

FEATURES
T-tail; shoulder swept wing; four GE TF39-GE-1C turbofans under wings; lower fuselage undercarriage fairings

Lockheed Martin C-130A/B/E/H Hercules USA

Transport & special mission aircraft

Rightfully known as 'ubiquitous', the prototype YC-130 first flew on 23 August 1954 and entered USAF service in 1956. The C-130 was developed through many versions and specialised variants and sold worldwide. All USAF, USN and USMC versions of the Hercules (other than the J-model - see separate entry) will receive an Avionics Modernisation Program. In all, 2,156 first generation Hercules (not the J-model) were built, comprising two YC-130s, 231 C-130As, 230 C-130Bs, 491 C-130Es, 1,089 C-130Hs and 113 L-100 civil freighters.

VARIANTS & OPERATORS

Algeria (C-130H/H-30, L-100-30), Argentina (C-130B/H, KC-130H, L-100-30), Australia (C-130H, EC-130H), Austria (C-130K), Bangladesh (C-130B), Belgium (C-130H), Bolivia (C-130B/H), Botswana (C-130F), Brazil (C-130E/H, KC-130H), Cameroun (C-130H/ H-30), Canada (C-130E/ H/H-30), Chad (C-130A/H/H-30), Chile (C-130B/H), Colombia (C-130B/H), Congo [Dem. Rep] (C-130H), Ecuador (C-130B/H, L-100-30), Egypt (C-130H/H-30, VC-130H), Ethiopia (C-130B), France (C-130H/H-30), Gabon (L-100-30),

Greece (C-130B/H), Honduras (C-130A), Indonesia (C-130B/H/H-30, KC-130B, L-100-30), Iran (C-130E/H), Israel (C-130E/H, EC-130, KC-130H), Italy (C-130H), Japan (C-130H), Jordan (C-130H), Kuwait (L-100-30), Libya (C-130H, L-100-20/-30), Malaysia (C-130H/H-30/H-MP, KC-130H), Mexico (C-130A/E, L-100-30), Morocco (C-130H, KC-130H), Netherlands (C-130H-30), New Zealand (C-130H), Niger (C-130H), Nigeria (C-130H/H-30), Norway (C-130H), Oman (C-130H), Pakistan (C-130B/E, L-100), Peru (C-130A, L-100-20), Philippines (C-130B/H/K, L-100-20), Portugal (C-130H/H-30), Romania (C-130B/H), Saudi Arabia (C-130E/H/H-30, KC-130H, VC-130H, L-100-30), Singapore (C-130H, KC-130B/H), South Africa (C-130B/F), South Korea (C-130H/H-30), Spain (C-130H/ H-30, KC-130H), Sri Lanka (C-130K), Sudan (C-130H), Sweden (C-130E/H), Taiwan (C-130H/HE, EC-130H), Thailand (C-130H/H-30), Tunisia (C-130B/H), Turkey (C-130B/E), UAE/Abu Dhabi (C-130H), UAE/ Dubai (C-130H-30, L-100-30), Uruguay (C-130B), UK (C-130K/ K-30), USA (AC-130H/U [see earlier separate entry], C-130E/H/T,

DC-130A, EC-130E/H, HC-130H/N/P, KC-130F/R/T/T-30, LC-130H/R, MC-130E/H/P, NC-130A/H, TC-130G, WC-130H), Venezuela (C-130H), Yemen (C-130H)

SPECIFICATIONS

Payload/Accommodation: 5 flight crew plus (standard) 94 troops, 64 paratroopers or 19,356kg (42,673 lb) freight or (-30 models) 128 troops, 92 paratroops or 17,645kg (38,900 lb) freight
Max speed: 325kt (602km/h)
Range: 4,250nm (7,876km)

DIMENSIONS

Length (standard): 29.8m (97ft 9in)
Length (-30 models): 34.4m (112ft 9in)
Wingspan: 40.4m (132ft 7in)
Height: 11.7m (38ft 3in)

FEATURES

Shoulder straight wing; with four wing-mounted Allison (R-R) T56-A-15 turboprops; underwing fuel tanks; lower fuselage undercarriage fairings

Lockheed Martin C/CC-130J/J-30 Hercules II USA

Transport & special mission aircraft

The 'next-generation' first C-130J Hercules II flew on 5 April 1996 (a USAF evaluation aircraft). The UK placed the first formal order for 15 C-130J-30s (Hercules C.4) and 10 C-130Js (Hercules C.5). In the USA, the Air National Guard and Air Force Reserve Command took the first USAF aircraft. As of December 2004, 180 Hercules IIs were on order, with 119 delivered.

VARIANTS & OPERATORS

C-130J: Italy, UK, USAF
C-130J-30: Australia, Denmark, Italy, UK
CC-130J: USAF
EC-130J: USAF
HC-130J: USCG
KC-130J: USMC
WC-130J: USAF

SPECIFICATIONS

Payload/Accommodation: 2 flight crew plus loadmaster with (C-130J) 94 troops, 64 paratroopers or 18,955kg (41,790 lb) freight or (C-130J-30) 128 troops, 92 paratroops or 17,264kg (38,061 lb) freight
Max speed: 348kt (645km/h)
Range: 2,835nm (5,250km)

DIMENSIONS

Length (C-130J): 29.8m (97ft 9in)
Length (C-130J-30/CC-130J): 34.4m (112ft 9in)
Wingspan: 40.4m (132ft 7in)
Height: 11.7m (38ft 3in)

FEATURES

Shoulder straight wing; with four wing-mounted Rolls-Royce (Allison) AE2100D3 turboprops; lower fuselage undercarriage fairings

Lockheed Martin P-3 Orion USA

MPA/ASW and special mission aircraft

Converted from the Electra airliner, the first YP-3A flew on 25 November 1959 and entered USN service in 1962. The P-3A and B-models were followed by the P-3C plus three Update configurations. Sold widely, many Orions are being further upgraded. A total of were 650 built.

VARIANTS & OPERATORS
Argentina (P-3B), Australia (AP-3C, EP-3C, P-3W, TAP-3B), Brazil (P-3A/B), Canada (CP-140 Aurora, CP-140A Arcturcus), Chile (P-3A, UP-3A), Germany (P-3C), Greece (P-3B), Iran (P-3F), New Zealand (P-3K), Norway (P-3C/N), Pakistan (P-3C), Portugal (P-3P), South Korea (P-3C), Spain (P-3A/B), Thailand (P-3T, UP-3T), USA (UP-3A, VP-3A, P-3B, UP-3B, P-3C, EP-3C, NP-3C/D)

SPECIFICATIONS
Payload/Accommodation: 3 flight crew and 7 mission specialists
Max speed: 411kt (761km/h)
Range: 2,070nm (3,835km)
Hardpoints: three under each wing for mines, Harpoon/SLAM ASMs or AIM-9 AAMs; rear fuselage sonobuoy launchers; fuselage bomb bay for mines, depth charges or torpedoes for a max payload of 3,290kg (7,252 lb)

DIMENSIONS
Length: 35.6m (116ft 10in)
Wingspan: 30.4m (99ft 8in)

Height: 10.3m (33ft 8in)

FEATURES
Low tapered wing; four wing-mounted Allison (Rolls-Royce) T56-A-14 turboprops; tail MAD boom; various radomes and antennas for special mission aircraft

McDonnell Douglas KC-10A Extender USA

Tanker/transport aircraft

Michael J. Gething/Jane's

Based on the DC-10-30F airliner, the first KC-10A flew on 12 July 1980 and entered USAF service in 1981. A number now equipped to carry Flight Refuelling Mk32B AAR pods. Last of 60 Extenders delivered in 1990. In 1995, the Netherlands took delivery of two KDC-10 tankers converted from civil airliners but essentially similar to the Extender.

VARIANTS & OPERATORS
KC-10A: USA
KDC-10: Netherlands

SPECIFICATIONS
Payload/Accommodation: 3 flight crew and boom operator plus 76,843kg (169,409 lb) cargo
Max speed: 530kt (982km/h)
Range: 3,797nm (7,032km)
Hardpoints: one under each wing for AAR pods

DIMENSIONS
Length: 55.3m (182ft 7in)
Wingspan: 50.4m (165ft 4in)
Height: 17.7m (58ft 1in)

FEATURES
Low swept wing; two wing-mounted and one fin-mounted GE CF6-50C2 turbofans; Advanced Aerial Refuelling Boom under tail; some underwing AAR pods

Northrop Grumman E-2C Hawkeye USA

Airborne early warning and control aircraft

The prototype E-2A first flew on 21 October 1960, followed by E-2B upgrade and prototype E-2C on 20 January 1971. AEW radar progressively improved from AN/APS-120 through -125, -138, -139 to AN/APS-145. Latest version known as Hawkeye 2000. Modest exports. A total of 211 built or on order.

VARIANTS & OPERATORS
E-2C: Egypt, France, Japan, Singapore, USN
E-2T: Taiwan
TE-2C: USN

SPECIFICATIONS
Payload/Accommodation: 2 flight crew plus 3 mission specialists
Max speed: 338kt (626km/h)
Ferry range: 1,541nm (2,854km)

DIMENSIONS
Length: 17.6m (57ft 9in)
Wingspan: 24.6m (80ft 7in)
Height: 5.6m (18ft 4in)

FEATURES
Four fins; tapered wing; two wing-mounted Allison (Rolls-Royce) T56-A-427 turboprops; 'flying saucer' rotodome above fuselage

Northrop Grumman (Boeing) E-8 Joint STARS USA

Ground surveillance/battle management aircraft

Converted from Boeing 707-300 series airliners and fitted with AN/APY-3 SLAR in 'canoe' fairing under forward fuselage, the first flight of E-8A full-scale development aircraft in Joint STARS configuration was 22 December 1988. In addition to two E-8A development aircraft and one E-8C permanent testbed, a total of 17 E-8C production aircraft are funded.

VARIANTS & OPERATORS
E-8A/C: USAF

SPECIFICATIONS
Payload/Accommodation: 4 flight crew plus 18 mission specialists (plus some reserve crew for long missions)
Max speed: M = 0.84
Endurance: 11h on internal fuel

DIMENSIONS
Length: 46.6m (152ft 11in)
Wingspan: 44.4m (145ft 9in)
Height: 12.9m (42ft 6in)

FEATURES
Swept wing; four underwing-mounted P&W TF33-P-102C turbofans; 'canoe' radome below forward fuselage

Raytheon (Beech) C-12 & RC-12 Guardrail USA

Transport and ELINT aircraft

Two distinct military variants have evolved from the Beech (Super) King Air 200, which first flew on 27 October 1972: the C-12 Huron utility transports for the USAF (UC-12 for the USN/USMC) and the RC-12 Guardrail special mission aircraft for the US Army. Over 1,789 aircraft (of all variants) built.

VARIANTS & OPERATORS

King Air 200: Algeria, Argentina, Australia, Bolivia, Botswana, Chile, Colombia, Ecuador, Ireland, Israel, Macedonia, Malaysia, Mexico, Morocco, Netherlands, New Zealand, Pakistan, Peru, South Africa, Sri Lanka, Sweden, Thailand, Togo, Turkey, Uruguay, Venezuela.
C-12A/R/AP Huron: Greece
C-12C/D/F Huron: USAF
C-12R: US Army
UC-12B/F/M: USN, USMC
RC-12D/K: Israel, US Army
RC-12F/H/M/N/P/Q: US Army

SPECIFICATIONS

Payload/Accommodation: 2 flight crew plus (UC/C-12) seven passengers or (RC-12) various mission specialists
Max speed: 292kt (541km/h)
Range: 1,850nm (3,426km)

DIMENSIONS

Length: 13.4m (43ft 10in)
Wingspan: 16.6m (54ft 6in)
Height: 4.5m (14ft 10in)

FEATURES

T-tail; tapered wing; two wing-mounted P&WC PT6A-42 turboprops; RC-12 has wingtip tanks and various wing- and fuselage-mounted radomes and antenna sets (depending on variant)

Raytheon (Bombardier) Sentinel R.1 USA

Ground surveillance aircraft

Raytheon Systems Limited was chosen as the preferred bidder for the UK MoD's ASTOR programme in June 1999, providing five Bombardier Global Express airframes as platforms for a ground surveillance radar system with SAR/MTI modes, and associated communications.

An aerodynamically representative airframe was flown 3 August 2001, with the first production airframe (ZJ690) making its maiden flight on 26 May 2004. Sentinel enters RAF service with 5 Sqn on 1 April 2005, with IOC expected by the end of 2005 and delivery of the fifth aircraft due in 2007.

VARIANTS & OPERATORS
Sentinel R.1: RAF

SPECIFICATIONS
Payload/Accommodation: 2 flight crew plus 3 mission specialists
Max speed: 505kt (935km/h)
Range: 5,320nm (9,852km)

DIMENSIONS
Length: 30.3m (99ft 5in)
Wingspan: 28.7m (94ft 0in)
Height: 8.2m (26ft 1in)

FEATURES
Low, swept wing with winglets; two tail-mounted Rolls-Royce Deutschland BR710 turbofans; swept T-tail with swept anhedral; dorsal radome on forward fuselage; ventral canoe-antenna

NOT TO BE CONFUSED WITH
Cessna 750 Citation X; Gulfstream Aerospace Gulfstream IV or Gulfstream V

Saab 340 AEW&C (S 100B Argus) Sweden

Transport and AEW&C aircraft

Derived from the Saab 340 airliner, which first flew on 25 January 1983, the AEW&C (S 100B) version was first flown (minus Ericsson PS-890 Erieye SLAR antenna) on 17 January 1994. Six ordered for the Swedish Air Force, plus one 340B for Royal/VIP duties. Production ceased in 1999 with 459 aircraft (civil and military) built, including the three test aircraft.

VARIANTS & OPERATORS
S 340B: Sweden
S 340 AEW&C: Greece, Sweden

SPECIFICATIONS
Payload/Accommodation: 2+1 flight crew, plus (VIP) about 20 passengers or (S 100B) up to 10 mission specialists
Max speed: 272kt (504km/h)
Range: 940nm (1,566km)

DIMENSIONS
Length: 19.7m (64ft 8in)
Wingspan: 21.4m (70ft 4in)
Height: 6.9m (22ft 6in)

FEATURES
Tapered wing; two wing-mounted GE CT7-5A2 turboprops; above-fuselage lateral antenna for radar; rear fuselage ventral fins

ShinMaywa US-1A Japan

SAR amphibian

First flown on 16 October 1974, 17 have been delivered to the JMSDF (first delivery 1975) with a further four planned. Now undergoing an upgrade of mission system and new Rolls-Royce AE2100J turboprops. First flown as US-1AKai on 18 December 2003.

VARIANTS & OPERATORS
US-1A/US-1AKai: Japan

SPECIFICATIONS
Payload/Accommodation: 9 crew, plus 20 seated survivors
Max speed: 276kt (511km/h)
Range: 2,060nm (3,817km)

DIMENSIONS
Length: 33.5m (109ft 9in)
Wingspan: 33.1m (108ft 9in)
Height: 9.9m (32ft 8in)

FEATURES
T-tail; tapered wing; four wing-mounted GE T64-IHI-10J turboprops (Rolls-Royce AE2110Js on US-1AKai); bulged nose radome; underwing floats

Transall C.160 France/Germany

Transport aircraft

Developed by the Transall (Transporter Allianz) group, the first prototype C.160 flew on 25 February 1963. The first production batch of 169 aircraft completed by 1972. First of a second series (C.160NG) for France flown on 9 April 1981 and 29 completed by 1985.

VARIANTS & OPERATORS

C.160D: Germany, Turkey
C.160F/R: France
C.160G Gabriel: France
C.160H Asarte: France
C.160NG: France

SPECIFICATIONS

Payload/Accommodation: 3 flight crew, plus 93 seated troops, 61-88 paratroops or up to 8,000kg 17,637 lb) cargo; assorted mission specialists for C.160G/H versions
Max speed: 277kt (513km/h)
Range: 2,750nm (5,095km)

DIMENSIONS

Length: 32.4m (106ft 3in)
Wingspan: 40.0m (131ft 3in)
Height: 11.6m (38ft 3in)

FEATURES

High tapered wing; two wing-mounted Rolls-Royce Tyne RTy.20 Mk.22 turboprops; various antenna/radomes on C.160G Gabriel

MILITARY
HELICOPTERS

Aerospatiale (Eurocopter) SA 313/315
Alouette II/ Lama France

General purpose helicopter

First flown as the Sud-Aviation SE 3130 on 12 March 1955, the Alouette II became the SA 313 under Aerospatiale. The SA 315B Lama has the reinforced airframe of the SA 313 with rotor system and Artouste engine of the SA 316 (see p. 250). Licence-built in Brazil by Helibras as the Gaviao, in India by HAL as the Cheetah and in Romania by IAR-Brazov. With the Astazou engine, the Alouette II is re-designated SA 318C. A total of 1,534 Aloutte IIs (of all versions) were built.

VARIANTS & OPERATORS
SA 313: Germany, Guinea-Bisseau, Lebanon, Tunisia, UK (Alouette AH.2)
SA 315B: Angola (Lama), Argentina (Lama), Bolivia (Gaviao and Lama), Chile (Lama), Ecuador (Lama), Morocco (Lama), India (Cheetah), Namibia (Cheetah), Nepal (Cheetah), Pakistan (Lama), Peru (Lama), Togo (Lama)
SA 318C: Belgium, Cameroun, Congo, Dominican Republic, Senegal, Turkey

SPECIFICATIONS
Crew/accommodation: 1 pilot plus 4 passengers or 1,135kg (2,500 lb) external sling load
Max speed: 110kt (205km/h)
Range: 278nm (515km)

DIMENSIONS
Main rotor diameter: 11.0m (36ft 2in)
Length: 12.9m (42ft 5in)
Height: 3.1m (10ft 2in)

FEATURES
Bubble canopy; open rear fuselage; single Turbomeca Artouste IIC.6/IIIB (SA 313/315) or Astazou IIA (SA 318) turboshaft; skid undercarriage

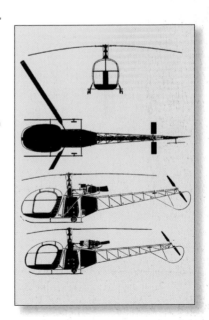

Aerospatiale (Eurocopter) SA 316/319
Alouette III France

General purpose helicopter

First flown as the Sud-Aviation SE 3160 on 28 February 1959, the Alouette III became the SA 316 under Aerospatiale. It was a development of the Alouette II with a larger cabin, greater power, improved equipment and higher performance. The SA 319B Alouette III is powered by the Astazou engine. The SA 316/319B has been licence-built in India (as the Chetak), Romania (IAR-316) and Switzerland. A total of 1,455 Alouette IIIs of all types were built.

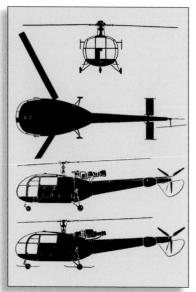

VARIANTS & OPERATORS

SA 316: Angola (IAR-316), Argentina, Austria, Burundi, Chad, China, Congo (Dem.Rep.), Ecuador, Ethiopia, France, Gabon, Ghana, Guinea-Bissau, Guinea Republic (IAR-316), India (Chetak & Lancer), Indonesia, Ireland, Jordan, Lebanon, Malaysia, Malta, Mauritius, Nambibia, Nepal, Netherlands, Pakistan (SE 3160, IAR-316 and SA 316), Portugal, Romania (IAR-316), Senegal, South Africa, Sri Lanka, Suriname, Swaziland, Switzerland, Tunisia, Venezuela, Zimbabwe.

SA 319: Albania, Austria, Belgium, Cameroun, France, Greece, India, Pakistan, South Korea.

SPECIFICATIONS

Crew/accommodation: 1 pilot plus 6 passengers plus 750kg (1,650 lb) external sling load
Max speed: 113kt (210km/h)
Range: 290nm (540km)

ARMAMENT (WHEN FITTED)

Internal gun (if fitted): cabin-mounted 7.62mm machine gun or 20mm MG 151/20 cannon
Hardpoints: up to four on cabin-mounted pylons
Representative weapons: four AS 11 or two AS 12 missiles

DIMENSIONS

Main rotor diameter: 11.0m (36ft 2in)
Length: 12.8m (42ft 1in)
Height: 3.0m (9ft 10in)

FEATURES

Rounded, glazed nose; single Turbomeca Artouste IIIB (SA 316) or Astazou XIV (SA 319) turboshaft; wheeled undercarriage

Aerospatiale (Eurocopter) SA 321 Super Frelon France

Heavy-duty helicopter

Derived from the smaller Frelon, the Super Frelon (originally designated SE 3210) first flew on 7 December 1962. Developed in troop carrier and naval ASW versions, it was licence-produced in China as the Changhe Z-8. Over 100 Super Frelons of all versions were built.

VARIANTS & OPERATORS
SA 321: France, Libya
Z-8: China

SPECIFICATIONS
Crew/accommodation: 3 flight crew plus 27-30 passengers or 5,000kg (11,023 lb) internal or external cargo
Max speed: 148kt (275km/h)
Range: 549nm (1,020km)

ARMAMENT: SA 321G/H
Hardpoints: up to four
Representative weapons: four homing torpedoes or two AM-39 Exocet ASMs

DIMENSIONS
Main rotor diameter: 18.9m (62ft 0in)
Length: 23.0m (75ft 7in)
Height: 6.8m (22ft 2in)

FEATURES
Boat-hull bottom to fuselage; nose radome, rear-fuselage sponsons; three Turbomeca Turmo IIIC turboshafts; wheeled undercarriage

Aerospatiale (Eurocopter) SA 330 Puma France

Medium transport helicopter

Developed for a French Army requirement, the prototype Puma flew on 15 April 1965. Chosen for the RAF, Westland and Aerospatiale formed a joint programme to produce the Puma for the RAF (as well as the SA 341 Gazelle and WG 13 Lynx for the French and British services). Licence-built in Romania (which is now putting 24 through the Puma SOCAT upgrade); assembled in Indonesia; and re-manufactured in South Africa (as the Oryx). Production ceased in 1987 with 697 Pumas of all versions built.

VARIANTS & OPERATORS

Argentina (SA 330L), Cameroun (SA 330C), Chile (SA 330F,L), Congo (Dem.Rep. - SA 330C), Ethiopia (SA 330H), France (SA 330B,Ba), Gabon (SA 330C), Guinea Rep. (IAR-330), Indonesia (NAS 330J,L), Kenya (SA 330H, IAR-330), Kuwait (SA 330F/H), Lebanon (SA 330L), Malawi (SA 330J), Mexico (SA 330S), Morocco (SA 330C,F,G), Nepal (SA 330), Oman (SA 330J), Pakistan (SA 330J), Philippines (SA 330L), Portugal (SA 330S), Romania (IAR-330), Spain (SA 330H,J), Sudan (IAR-330), Turkey (SA330L) UAE - Abu Dhabi (SA 330C,F, IAR-330), UK (SA 330E Puma HC.1)

SPECIFICATIONS

Crew/accommodation: 2 (+1) flight crew plus 16-20 passengers or 3,200kg (7,055 lb) external slung cargo
Max speed: 158kt (294km/h)
Range: 309nm (572km)

ARMAMENT: PUMA SOCAT

Internal gun: Giat 20mm cannon in undernose turret
Hardpoints: up to four on cabin pylons
Representative weapons: AAMs; ATGWs; 57mm or 70mm rocket pods

DIMENSIONS

Main rotor diameter: 15.0m (49ft 2in)
Length: 18.5m (59ft 6in)
Height: 5.1m (16ft 10in)

FEATURES

Air intakes over cabin; rear-fuselage sponsons; two Turbomeca Turmo IVC turboshafts; wheeled undercarriage; tailplane to port of boom; tail rotor to right

Aerospatiale (Eurocopter) SA 341/342 Gazelle France

Light utility helicopter

The Gazelle prototype was first flown on 7 April 1967 and the SA 341 became part of the Westland/Aerospatiale joint programme (with the SA 330 Puma and WG 13 Lynx for the French and British services). Features an enclosed tail rotor known as a 'fenestron'. The SA 342 has an improved powerplant and highter take-off weight. Licence-built by Soko in Yugoslavia. Over 800 Gazelles of all versions built.

VARIANTS & OPERATORS
Angola (SA 242L), Bosnia-Herzegovina (SA 341H, SA 342L), Burundi (SA 342L), Cameroun (SA 342L), China (SA342L), Cyprus (SA 343L), Ecuador (SA 342K,L), Egypt (SA 342K,L), France (SA 341F, SA 342L,M), Gabon (SA 342L), Guinea Rep. (SA 342L), Ireland (SA 342L), Kuwait (SA 342L), Lebanon (SA 342L), Libya (SA 342L), Morocco (SA 342K,L), Qatar (SA 342L), Syria (SA 342L), UAE (Abu Dhabi - SA 342L), UK (SA 342B, Gazelle AH.1), Yugoslavia (SA 341H, SA 342L)

SPECIFICATIONS
Crew/accommodation: 1 or 2 flight crew plus 3 passengers
Max speed: 167kt (310km/h)
Range: 194nm (360km)

ARMAMENT: SA 342L/M
Hardpoints: up to four on cabin pylons
Representative weapons: Mistral AAMs; AS 11, AS 12 or HOT ATGWs; 2.75in or 67mm rocket pods

DIMENSIONS
Main rotor diameter: 10.5m (34ft 5in)
Length: 12.0m (39ft 4in)
Height: 3.1m (10ft 3in)

FEATURES
Glazed cabin; one Turbomeca Astazou IIIA (SA 341) or Astazou XIVM (SA 342L) turboshaft with upturned exhaust; skid undercarriage; fenestron in tailboom

Agusta (A-W) A 109 Italy

Light utility helicopter

The prototype A 109A, powered by an Allison 250 turboshaft engine, was first flown on 4 August 1971 with deliveries starting in 1976. Progressively developed (including re-engining with PW 206 or Arriel) and sold widely on both civil and military markets. Over 600 A 109s of all versions built or on order.

VARIANTS & OPERATORS
Argentina (A 109A), Belgium (A 109HA, HO), Ghana (A 109), Honduras (A 109E Power), Italy (A 109A, A-II, C, CM, E Power), Libya (A 109A), Malaysia (A 109E Power), Nigeria (A 109E Power), Peru (A 109K2), South Africa (A 109LUH), Sweden (A 109M), Turkey (A 109A), UAE (Dubai - A 109K2), UK (A 109A), USA (MH-68 Power), Venzuela (A 109A)

SPECIFICATIONS
Crew/accommodation: 1 or 2 flight crew plus 6 or 7 passengers
Max speed: 168kt (311km/h)
Range: 352nm (652km)

ARMAMENT: A 109CM/HA
Internal guns: cabin-mounted 7.62mm or 12.7mm machine gun
Hardpoints: two lateral pylons
Max weapon load: 600kg (1,322 lb)
Representative weapons: TOW ATGWs; 2.75in or 81mm rocket pods; 12.7mm machine gun pod

DIMENSIONS
Main rotor diameter: 11.0m (36ft 1in)
Length: 11.4m (37ft 6in)
Height: 3.5m (11ft 6in)

FEATURES
Slender fuselage; tailboom has upper and ventral fin; port tail rotor; two Allison 250-C turboshafts; retractable wheel undercarriage

Agusta (A-W) A 129 Mangusta Italy

Light attack helicopter

The Mangusta prototype first flew on 11
September 1983 with deliveries starting in 1990.
Standard tandem cockpit and powered by two
Gem 1004 turboshafts. Multirole and shipborne
plus international versions (with T800 turboshafts)
developed but not sold. Only 60 A 129s built to
date.

VARIANTS & OPERATORS

A 129: Italy

SPECIFICATIONS

Crew/accommodation: 2 flight crew
Max speed: 159kt (294km/h)
Range: 303nm (561km)

ARMAMENT

Internal guns: 20mm cannon in nose turret on
International version
Hardpoints: four pylons
Max weapon load: 1,000kg (2,204 lb)
Representative weapons: Stinger or Mistral
AAMs; TOW ATGWs; 2.75in, 70mm or 81mm
rocket pods; 12.7mm machine gun or 20mm
cannon pods

DIMENSIONS

Main rotor diameter: 11.9m (39ft 0in)
Length: 14.3m (46ft 10in)
Height: 2.3m (9ft 0in)

FEATURES

Tandem cockpit; port tail rotor; two Rolls-Royce
Gem 1004 (A 129) or LHTEC T800-LHT-800 (A 129
International) turboshafts; fixed wheel
undercarriage

AgustaWestland Industries (EHI)
EH 101 Merlin Italy/UK

Multirole helicopter

Royal Navy service in 2002. A total of 112 EH 101s of all versions built or on order.

Evolved as a joint project between Agusta of Italy and the UK's Westland to produce a Sea King Replacement helicopter from 1981, the first EH 101 (known as the first pre-production aircraft - PP1) flown on 9 October 1987. Nine PP aircraft flown in three main configurations: naval, utility and civil. The Merlin HM.1 ASW version entered

VARIANTS & OPERATORS

Series 100: Denmark (SAR), Italy (ASW/ASVW = Mk 110; AEW = Mk 112), UK (Merlin HM.1 = Mk 111)
Series 300: Commercial passenger version – no orders as yet
Series 400: Italy (Utility = Mk 410), Portugal, UK (Merlin HC.3 = Mk 411)
Series 500: Japan (Tokyo Police = Mk 510)
AW320: Canada (Cormorant)

SPECIFICATIONS

Crew/accommodation: 2 pilots plus specialised mission crew or 30 passengers (Series 300) or 30–45 troops
Max speed: 167kt (309km/h)
Radius of action (SAR): 350nm (648km)

ARMAMENT

Internal gun: provision for a nose-mounted 0.5in (12.7mm) machine gun chin turret
Hardpoints: four (plus optional two)
Max weapon load: four torpedoes = 960kg (2,116 lb)
Representative weapons: Marte Mk 2 ASMs; Sting Ray, Mk 46 or MU90 torpedoes; depth charges; FFAR pods

DIMENSIONS

Main rotor diameter: 18.6m (61ft 0in)
Length: 22.8m (74ft 10in)
Height: 6.6m (21ft 9in)

FEATURES

Starboard tailplane; port tail rotor, three Rolls-Royce/Turbomeca RTM 322-01/8 (UK versions) or GE T700-GE-T6A/A1 (Canadian/Italian versions) turboshafts; retractable undercarriage

Bell AH-1 HueyCobra/SuperCobra USA

Attack helicopter

Max weapon load: 1,556kg (3,430 lb)
Representative weapons: Sidewinder AAMs; TOW or Hellfire ATGWs; Maverick AGMs; 2.75in rocket pods; 12.7mm machine gun or 20mm cannon pods

DIMENSIONS
Main rotor diameter: 14.6m (48ft 0in)
Length: 17.7m (58ft 0in)
Height: 4.4m (14ft 7in)

FEATURES
Lateral intakes behind tandem cockpit; port tail rotor; two GE T700-GE-401 turboshafts; skid undercarriage

The Model 209 AH-1G HueyCobra first flew on 7 September 1965 and was a dedicated helicopter gunship seeing service in the Vietnam war. Evolved and upgraded as an ATGW-armed anti-tank helicopter, and built under licence Japan (AH-1S) and Taiwan (AH-1W). The USMC is now upgrading 180 AH-1W SuperCobras to the AH-1Z configuration. Over 2,060 of all variants built.

VARIANTS & OPERATORS
AH-1E: Bahrain
AH-1F: Israel, Jordan, Pakistan, South Korea, Thailand
AH-1J: Iran, South Korea
AH-1P: Turkey
AH-1S: Israel, Japan, Turkey
AH-1W: Taiwan, Turkey, USA
AH-1Z: USA (not yet in service)
TAH-1P: Bahrain, Turkey

SPECIFICATIONS
Crew/accommodation: 2 flight crew
Max speed: 222kt (411km/h)
Radius of action: 125nm (232km)

ARMAMENT: AH-1Z
Internal gun: M197 20mm cannon in nose turret
Hardpoints: six pylons

Bell UH-1 Iroquois/Bell 204/205 USA

Utility helicopter

The first XH-40 prototype flew on 22 October 1956 and, after development as the Model 204, the UH-1A Iroquois entered US Army service in 1959. Subsequent versions of the 204 were designated UH-1B/C/E/F/L/M, HH-1K and TH-1F/L, all affectionately known as 'Huey'. The Model 205 (UH-1D/H/V, EH-1H and HH-1H) featured a longer fuselage and flew on 16 August 1961. Licence built in Germany, Italy, Japan and Taiwan, almost

10,000 of all UH-1/204/205 variants were built.

VARIANTS & OPERATORS
AB 204ASW/B: Turkey, Yemen
205A/AB 205/A/B: Brazil, Greece, Indonesia, Iran, Italy, Libya, Mexico, Morocco, Myanmar, Oman, Pakistan, Panama, Singapore, Thailand, Tunisia, Turkey, UAE (Dubai), Venezuela, Zambia
UH-1B: Paraguay, Venezuela
UH-1D: Germany, Venezuela
UH-1H: Argentina, Australia, Bolivia, Bosnia-Herzegovina, Brazil, Chile, Colombia, Cyprus, Dominican Rep., El Salvador, Georgia, Greece, Guatemala, Honduras, Japan, Jordan, Lebanon, Macedonia, New Zealand, Pakistan, Panama, Papua New Guinea, Paraguay, Peru, Philippines, Singapore, South Korea, Spain, Taiwan, Thailand, Tunisia, Turkey, Uruguay, USA, Venezuela
UH-1J: Japan
UH-1M: El Salvador
UH-1V: Bosnia-Herzegovina, USA

SPECIFICATIONS
Crew/accommodation: 2 flight crew plus 8 passengers (204) and 11-14 passengers (205)
Max speed (UH-1C): 128kt (238km/h)
Range (UH-1C): 332nm (615km)

ARMAMENT (OPTIONAL)
Internal gun: 7.62mm, 12.7mm machine guns or 20mm cannon in cabin
Hardpoints: four pylons
Max weapon load: N/A
Representative weapons: 2.75in, 68mm, 71mm, 81mm rocket pods; 12.7mm machine gun or 20mm cannon pods

DIMENSIONS: UH-1D
Main rotor diameter: 14.6m (48ft 0in)
Length: 16.4m (53ft 11in)
Height: 4.1m (13ft 5in)

FEATURES
Squat fuselage; tail rotor - port on 204, starboard on 205; one Lycoming T53-L turboshaft; skid undercarriage

Bell UH-1N/Y Iroquois/Bell 212/AB 212 USA

Utility helicopter

Derived from the UH-1H/Model 205, fitted with two PT-6T turboshafts in Turbo Twin Pac configuration, the first Model 212 (UH-1N) flew on 16 April 1969 and entered service a year later. The USMC is having 100 UH-1Ns upgraded to UH-1Y configuration with two GE T700 engines. Licence-built by Agusta in Italy (AB 212), versions include AB 212ASW and AB 212EW variants. Almost 500 of all variants built.

VARIANTS & OPERATORS
212/AB 212: Argentina, Austria, Bahrain, Bangladesh, Brunei, Colombia, Ecuador, Greece, Guatemala, Iran, Italy, Lebanon, Libya, Mexico, Morocco, Oman, Panama, Peru, Saudi Arabia, South Korea, Spain, Sri Lanka, Sudan, Thailand, UAE (Dubai), Uganda, Uruguay, UK, Venezuela, Yemen, Zambia
212ASW/AB 212ASW: Greece, Iran, Italy, Peru, Spain, Thailand, Turkey, Venezuela
AB 212EW: Greece, Turkey
HH-1N: USA
UH-1N: Colombia, USA
UH-1Y: USA

SPECIFICATIONS
Crew/accommodation: 2 flight crew plus up to 14 passengers
Max speed: 100kt (185km/h)
Range: 227nm (420km)

DIMENSIONS
Main rotor diameter: 14.7m (48ft 2in)

Length: 17.6m (57ft 3in)
Height: 4.5m (14ft 10in)

FEATURES
Above cabin intakes; starboard tail rotor; two P&WC PT6T-3B turboshafts in Turbo Twin Pac; skid undercarriage

Bell 214 USA

Utility helicopter

The basic Model 214A, which first flew on 15 March 1974, was developed for Iran, with the 214ST (Stretched Twin) flying in February 1977. Bell later developed the 214ST as a commercial Super Transport, retaining the designator letters. Over 400 214s of all variant were built.

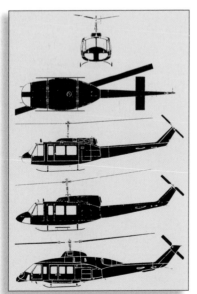

VARIANTS & OPERATORS
214A/C: Iran
214ST: Albania, Brunei, Iran, Peru, Thailand, UAE (Dubai), Venezuela

SPECIFICATIONS
Crew/accommodation: 2 flight crew plus up to 18 passengers
Max speed: 140kt (259km/h)
Range: 439nm (813km)

DIMENSIONS
Main rotor diameter: 15.8m (52ft 0in)
Length: 18.9m (62ft 2in)
Height: 4.8m (15ft 10in)

FEATURES
Streamlined; stretched fuselage, starboard tail rotor; two GE CT7-2A turboshafts; skid or wheeled undercarriage

Bell 412/AB 412 USA

Utility helicopter

The Model 412 is essentially a 212 with a four-bladed rotor (which can be retrofitted to 212s), first flying in August 1979. Production transferred to Canada in 1989. Licence-built by IPTN in Indonesia and by Agusta (as the AB 412) in Italy. Over 580 Model 412s of all variant were built.

VARIANTS & OPERATORS

412: Bahrain, Botswana, Canada, Chile, Colombia, Cyprus, Czech Rep., El Salvador, Eritrea, Gabon, Georgia, Ghana, Guatemala, Guyana, Honduras, Italy (plus CP and HP), Jamaica, Lesotho, Norway, Peru, Philippines, Poland, Saudi Arabia, Slovenia, South Korea, Sri Lanka, Sweden, Tanzania, Thailand, UAE (Dubai), Uganda, Venezuela
412EP: Turkey, UAE (Dubai), UK (Griffin HT.1)
412SP: Italy, Netherlands, Uganda, Zimbabwe

SPECIFICATIONS

Crew/accommodation: 1 or 2 flight crew plus up to 14 passengers
Max speed: 122kt (226km/h)
Range: 402nm (745km)

ARMAMENT: AB 412 GRIFFON

Internal gun: 12.7mm machine gun turret under nose
Hardpoints: two pylons
Max weapon load: N/A
Representative weapons: Sea Skua ASMs; TOW ATGWs; 2.75in or 81mm rocket pods; 25mm cannon pods

DIMENSIONS

Main rotor diameter: 14.0m (46ft 0in)
Length: 17.1m (56ft 2in)
Height: 4.6m (15ft 0in)

FEATURES

Above cabin intakes; starboard tail rotor; two P&WC PT6T-3B turboshafts in Turbo Twin Pac; skid or wheeled undercarriage

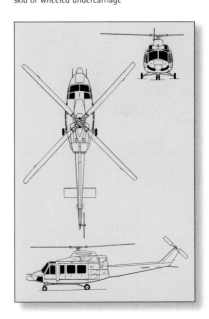

Bell OH-58D Kiowa/Bell 406CS USA

Light attack/scout helicopter

The OH-58D was derived from the OH-58A/B/C (Model 206 Jetranger – which see) under the US AHIP programme. The prototype first flew on 6 October 1983, with deliveries to US Army from 1985. Many upgraded to Kiowa Warrior configuration. A similar version developed for export a Model 406CS Combat Scout. Some 439 OH-58D/406CSs were built or on order.

VARIANTS & OPERATORS
406CS: Saudi Arabia
OH-58D: Taiwan, USA
TH-57A: USA
TH-67A: Taiwan, USA

SPECIFICATIONS
Crew/accommodation: 2 pilots
Max speed: 122kt (226km/h)
Range: 130nm (241km)

ARMAMENT
Hardpoints: two pylons
Max weapon load: N/A
Representative weapons: Stinger AAMs; Hellfire ATGWs; 2.75in rocket pods; 0.5in (12.7mm) machine gun pod

DIMENSIONS
Main rotor diameter: 10.7m (35ft 0in)
Length: 12.6m (41ft 2in)
Height: 3.9m (12ft 10in)

FEATURES
MMS above rotor head; 'tadpole' fuselage; port tail rotor; one Rolls-Royce (Allison) 250-C30R turboshaft; skid undercarriage

Bell/Boeing V-22 Osprey USA

Utility tilt-rotor aircraft

Based on the experience from the Bell XV-15 programme, the JVX project proceeded as a joint Bell/Boeing partnership. The first of five V-22 prototypes made its maiden flight on 19 March 1989 (all since retired). The first LRIP MV-22B for the USMC flown in April 1999. Three crashes in 2000 caused a hiatus in the programme but the technical problems have now been resolved. Funding for 76 MV-22Bs and seven CV-22Bs has been allocated to FY 2005.

VARIANTS & OPERATORS
CV-22B: USAF – 50 required for special missions
CV-22B: USN – 48 required for C-SAR
MV-22B: USMC – 360 required for transport

SPECIFICATIONS
Crew/accommodation: 2 pilots plus crew chief and up to 24 combat-equipped troops
Max speed: 305kt (565km/h)
Range (VTO): 515nm (953km)

ARMAMENT
Internal gun: possibly a 7.62mm or 0.5in (12.7mm) machine gun in nose turret

DIMENSIONS
Rotor diameter: 11.6m (38ft 1in)
Length (wings folded): 19.2m (63ft 0in)
Height (nacelles vertical): 6.7m (22ft 1in)

FEATURES
Twin fins; two Rolls-Royce (Allison) T406-AD-400 turboshafts in rotating nacelles at wingtips; retractable wheeled undercarriage

Boeing (Hughes/McDD) AH-64 Apache USA

Attack/recce helicopter

Originally the Hughes Model 77, the YAH-63 prototype first flew on 30 September 1975. The first AH-64A entered US Army service in January 1984. Development of the D-model with a Longbow MMW radar above the rotorhead, began in 1990 and entered US Army service in 1998. Licence-built by Fuji in Japan and in UK by AgustaWestland as WAH-64D, having been re-engined with Rolls-Royce/ Turbomeca RTM 322

engines. Over 1,069 Apaches of all versions built or on order.

VARIANTS & OPERATORS

AH-64A: Egypt, Greece, Israel, Japan, Saudi Arabia, UAE (Abu Dhabi), USA
AH-64D: Israel, Kuwait, Netherlands, Singapore, USA
WAH-64D: UK (Apache AH.1)

SPECIFICATIONS

Crew/accommodation: 2 pilots
Max speed: 197kt (365km/h)
Range (AH-64D): 220nm (407km)

ARMAMENT

Internal gun: M230 30mm Chain Gun in undernose mounting
Hardpoints: four (+ two planned) pylons
Max weapon load: N/A
Representative weapons: Mistral, Sidewinder, Starstreak or Stinger AAMs; Hellfire ATGWs; 2.75in FFAR pods

DIMENSIONS

Main rotor diameter: 14.6m (48ft 0in)
Length: 17.8m (58ft 3in)
Height (AH-64D): 4.9m (16ft 3in)

FEATURES

Tandem cockpit; two GE T700-GE-701C turboshafts; port tail rotor; fixed wheeled undercarriage

Boeing CH-46 Sea Knight/Vertol 107 USA

Transport helicopter

Originally the Vertol Model 107, the twin-rotor prototype first flew on 22 April 1958. Entered USMC service in 1961 and progressively upgraded. Built under licence by Kawasaki in Japan. A total of 700 helicopters of all versions built.

VARIANTS & OPERATORS
107: Canada (CH-113A), Japan, Saudi Arabia, Sweden (incl. 107-II)
CH-46D/E: USMC, USN
HH-46D: USMC
UH-46D: USN

SPECIFICATIONS
Crew/accommodation: 3 flight crew plus 25 troops
Max speed: 144kt (267km/h)
Range: 206nm (383km)

ARMAMENT - nil

DIMENSIONS
Rotor diameter (CH-46D): 15.5m (51ft 0in)
Length: 25.7m (84ft 4in)
Height: 5.1m (16ft 8in)

FEATURES
Twin rotor configuration; two GE T58-GE-11 turboshafts; rear-fuselage sponsons; fixed tricycle wheeled undercarriage

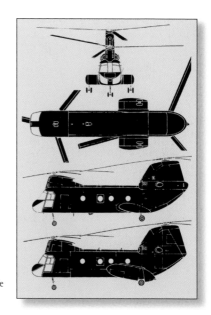

Boeing CH-47 Chinook USA

Transport helicopter

The maiden flight of the Vertol 107's 'big brother', the YCH-47A Chinook, was on 21 September 1961 and was progressively developed through B- and C-models. Built under licence by Kawasaki of Japan and Meridionali of Italy. The US Army re-manufactured 479 CH-47A/B/Cs to D-model configuration from 1982 and now, pending design of a new helicopter, these D-models being upgraded to CH-47F ICH standard, first delivered on 21 July 2004. US Special Operations Command operates the MH-47E variant to be upgraded to MH-47G standard. Over 1,164 Chinooks of all versions built or on order.

VARIANTS & OPERATORS
234MLR Chinook: Taiwan
414 Chinook HC.2/2A/3: UK
CH-47C: Egypt, Iran, Italy, Libya, Morocco
CH-47C+: Italy
CH-47D: Australia, Egypt, Greece, Netherlands, Singapore, South Korea, Spain, Thailand, USA
MH-47E: USA
CH-47F: USA
CH-47SD: Greece, Taiwan
CH-47J/JA: Japan

SPECIFICATIONS
Crew/accommodation: 2 pilots plus crew chief plus 33-55 troops
Max speed: 154kt (285km/h)
Radius of action (MH-47E): 505nm (935km)

ARMAMENT
Internal guns: two or three pintle-mounted 7.62mm M134 Miniguns or 0.5in (12.7mm) machine guns in cabin

DIMENSIONS
Rotor diameter: 18.3m (60ft 0in)
Length: 30.1m (98ft 11in)
Height: 5.7m (18ft 11in)

FEATURES
Twin rotor configuration; two Honeywell (Lycoming) T55-L-712 turboshafts; fuselage sponsons; fixed wheeled undercarriage

Bolkow (MBB/Eurocopter) BO 105 Germany

Light utility helicopter

First flown as the Bolkow BO 105 on 16 February 1967, the manufacturer was absorbed into MBB then Eurocopter. Developed for the anti-tank role as the PAH-1 for Germany. Built under licence by Dirgantara in Indonesia and KAI in South Korea. Over 1,300 BO 105s of all versions were built.

VARIANTS & OPERATORS

BO 105: Macedonia
BO 105ATH: Spain
BO 105C/CB/CBS: Bahrain, Brunei, Chile, Colombia, Czech Rep., Jordan, Indonesia, Lesotho, Mexico, Netherlands, Nigeria, Peru, Philippines, South Korea, Spain, Sudan, Sweden, Trinidad and Tobago, UAE (Abu Dhabi/Dubai)
BO 105D: Nigeria
BO 105GSH/LOH: Spain
BO 105LS/LSA: Chile, Peru
BO 105M (VBH): Germany
BO 105P (PAH-1): Germany
BO 105S: Chile, Indonesia, Lesotho
Super Five: Bahrain

SPECIFICATIONS

Crew/accommodation: 2 pilots
Max speed (PAH-1): 119kt (220km/h)
Range: 300nm (555km)

ARMAMENT: PAH-1

Hardpoints: two external pylons
Max weapon load: N/A
Representative weapons: six HOT ATGWs

DIMENSIONS

Main rotor diameter: 9.8m (32ft 3in)
Length: 11.9m (38ft 11in)
Height: 3.0m (9ft 11in)

FEATURES

Slim tailboom; port tail rotor; two Allison 250-C20B turboshafts; skid undercarriage

Denel (Atlas) AH-2A Rooivalk South Africa

Attack helicopter

Designed as a Combat Support Helicopter for the SAAF (hence its previous designation CSH-2), the prototype Rooivalk (Red Kestrel) first flew on 11 February 1990. It uses many reverse-engineered and locally-built components from the dynamics system of the SA 330 Puma. A second prototype was followed by a pre-production aircraft, with the SAAF ordering a dozen. The Rooivalk is being actively promoted for export.

VARIANTS & OPERATORS
AH-2A: SAAF

SPECIFICATIONS
Crew/accommodation: 2 pilots
Max speed (PAH-1): 167kt (309km/h)
Range: 720nm (1,335km)

ARMAMENT
Internal gun: F2 20mm cannon in undernose turret
Hardpoints: six pylons (three on each stub wing)
Max weapon load: 2,032kg (4,480 lb)
Representative weapons: Mistral AAMs; Mokapa ATGWs; 68mm FFAR pods

DIMENSIONS
Main rotor diameter: 15.6m (51ft 1in)
Length: 18.7m (61ft 5in)
Height: 5.2m (17ft 0in)

FEATURES
Tandem cockpit; starboard tail rotor; port tailplane; two Turbomeca Makila 1K2 turboshafts; fixed wheeled undercarriage

Eurocopter AS 532 Cougar (Super Puma)
EC 725 Cougar RESCO France

Michael J. Gething

Medium transport helicopter

The SA 330 Puma was further developed as the AS 332 Super Puma (with the Makila engine), which first flew on 13 September 1978. Military versions re-designated AS 532 Cougar in 1990. Development Cougar Mk II flown in February 1987. The AS 532UL Horizon has a battlefield surveillance radar. Licence-built in Indonesia by Dirgantara (IPTN) and TAI in Turkey; assembled in Spain by EADS/CASA and some SA 330s re-manufactured as (AS 332) Oryx in South Africa. Over 565 Super Pumas/Cougars of all versions built or on order.

VARIANTS & OPERATORS
Argentina (AS 332B), Brazil (AS 332M, AS 532/UC/UE), Cameroun (AS 332L), Chile (AS 332B/M), China (AS 332L), Congo Dem. Rep. (AS 332L), Ecuador (AS 332B), France (AS 332C/L, AS 532A2UL, EC 725), Germany (AS532U2), Greece (AS 332C, AS 532), Iceland (AS 332L), Indonesia (NAS 332B/L1), Japan (AS 332L), Jordan (AS 332M), Kuwait (AS 532SC), Malawi (AS 332), Mexico (AS 332L), Netherlands (AS 532U2), Nepal (AS 332L), Nigeria (AS 332B), Oman (AS 332C/L), Saudi Arabia (AS 532AL/A2), Singapore (AS 332M, AS 532UL), Slovenia (AS 352AL), South Africa (Oryx), South Korea (AS 332L), Spain (AS 332B/M, AS 532UC/UL), Sweden (AS 532), Switzerland (AS 332M), Thailand (AS 332L), Turkey (AS 532AL/UL), UAE (Abu Dhabi – AS 332L, AS 532SC/UC), Venezuela (AS 332B, AS 532), Zimbabwe (AS 532)

SPECIFICATIONS
Crew/accommodation: 2 (+1) flight crew

plus 21 passengers or 4,500kg (9,920 lb) external slung cargo
Max speed: 170kt (315km/h)
Range: 656nm (1,215km)

ARMAMENT (OPTIONAL)
Hardpoints: two pylons
Representative weapons: Exocet ASMs; FFAR pods; 20mm cannon or 12.7mm machine gun pods; homing torpedoes

DIMENSIONS
Main rotor diameter (Cougar Mk II): 16.2m (53ft 1in)
Length: 19.5m (63ft 11in)
Height: 5.0m (16ft 5in)

FEATURES
Air intakes over cabin; rear-fuselage sponsons; two Turbomeca Makila 1A2 turboshafts; retractable wheeled undercarriage; starboard tailplane; port tail rotor

Eurocopter AS 550/555 Ecureuil/Fennec France

Light utility helicopter

First flight of AS 350 Ecureuil (Squirrel) powered by a Lycoming LTS101 engine on 27 June 1974, and second prototype Ecureuil flew with the production-standard Turbomeca Arriel 1A engine in February 1975. A twin-engined version, designated AS 355, flew on 28 September 1979. Military versions produced after 1990 re-designated AS 550/555 Fennec respectively. Built under licence in Brazil, while China's CHAIC Z-11 would appear to be a copy. Over 2,250 AS 350/550/555s built or on order.

VARIANTS & OPERATORS

Albania **(AS 350B)**, Algeria (AS 350B), Argentina **(AS 350BA, AS 555MN)**, Australia **(AS 350BA)**, Benin **(AS 350B)**, Botswana **(AS 350B/BA)**, Brazil **(AS 550A2, HB 350B/BA/L1, HB 355FS/F2)**, Burkina Faso **(AS 350B)**, Burundi **(AS 350B)**, Cambodia **(AS 350B)**, Central African Rep. **(AS 350B)**, China **(Z-11)**, Colombia **(AS 555SN)**, Comores **(AS 350B)**, Denmark **(AS 550C2)**, Djibouti **(AS 355F)**, Ecuador **(AS 350B)**, France **(AS 350B/BA, AS 355F, AS 550U2, AS 555AN/UN/U2)**, Gabon **(AS 350B, AS 355F)**, Guinea Rep. **(AS 350B)**, Ireland **(AS 355N)**, Jamaica **(AS 355N)**, Malawi **(AS 350B)**, Mali **(AS 350B)**, Mauritius **(AS 555)**, Mexico **(AS 355F, AS 550)**, Nepal **(AS 350B)**, Paraguay **(HB 350B)**, Rwanda **(AS 355F)**, Singapore **(AS 550A2/C2)**, Thailand **(AS 350B/BA)**, Tunisia **(AS 350B)**, UAE **(Abu Dhabi - AS 350B)**, UK **(AS 355BA Squirrel HT.1/2, AS 355F1 Twin Squirrel)**, Venezuela **(AS 355F)**

SPECIFICATIONS

Crew/accommodation: 1 pilot and second front seat plus 4 passengers or 907kg (2,000 lb) cargo sling
Max speed: 155kt (287km/h)
Range: 362nm (670km)

ARMAMENT: AS 550C3

Hardpoints: two
Max weapon load: N/A
Representative weapons: TOW ATGMs; one torpedo; FFAR pods; 7.62mm or 12.7mm machine gun or 20mm cannon pods

DIMENSIONS

Main rotor diameter: 10.7m (35ft 1in)
Length: 12.9m (42ft 5in)
Height: 3.4m (10ft 11in)

FEATURES

Starboard tail rotor; one Turbomeca Arriel 1D1 or 2B (AS 350/550) or two Turbomeca Arrius 1A turboshafts (AS 355/555); skid undercarriage

Eurocopter AS 565 Panther (Dauphin 2) France

General purpose helicopter

Max weapon load: N/A
Representative weapons: AS-15TT ASMs, torpedoes; 7.62mm or 12.7mm machine gun or 20mm cannon pods

DIMENSIONS
Main rotor diameter: 11.9m (39ft 2in)
Length: 13.7m (45ft 0in)
Height: 4.1m (13ft 4in)

First flight of AS 365N Dauphin 2 on 31 March 1979, and developed for several naval, army and air force roles. Bought by US Coast Guard as AS 366G1 (HH-65). Re-designated as AS 565 Panther in 1990. Built under licence in China by HAMC as the Z-9. Over 500 Dauphin 2/Panthers of all variants built or on order.

FEATURES
Fenestron tail rotor; two Turbomeca Arriel 1C2 or 2C turboshafts; retractable wheeled undercarriage

VARIANTS & OPERATORS
Angola (AS 565AA/UA), Argentina (AS 365N), Brazil (AS 565UP), Cambodia (AS 365), Cameroun (AS 365N), Congo (AS 365C), Côte d'Ivoire (AS 365C), China (Z-9/9A), France (AS 365F/N, AS 565MA), Iceland (AS 365N), Ireland (AS 365F), Israel (AS 565SA) Mexico (AS 365), Morocco (AS 365N), Romania (AS 365N), Saudi Arabia (AS 365N, AS 565SA), UAE (Abu Dhabi - AS 565SB), UAE (Dubai - AS 365N), UK (AS 365N), Uruguay (AS 365N), USA (HH-65A Dolphin)

SPECIFICATIONS
Crew/accommodation: 1 pilot and second front seat plus up to 12 passengers or 1,600kg (3,525 lb) cargo sling
Max speed: 155kt (287km/h)
Range: 464nm (859km)

ARMAMENT: AS 365N
Hardpoints: four on two pylons

Eurocopter AS 665 Tigre/Tiger France/Germany

Multirole combat helicopter

The prototype of the Franco-German AS 665 Tigre/Tiger multi-role combat helicopter first flew on 27 April 1991. Original requirement for 427 (France 75 HAP, 140 HAC and Germany 212 PAH-2, now UHT) reduced and now stands at 115 HAP (70 ordered to date), 100 HAC (10 ordered) and 212 UHT (80 ordered). Australia selected Tiger in 2001 and Spain in 2003. First production Tiger

(UHT destined for the German Army) flown 2 August 2002.

VARIANTS & OPERATORS
Tiger UHT: Germany
Tigre HAC: France
Tigre HAD: Spain
Tigre HAP: France
Tigre HCP: Australia

SPECIFICATIONS
Crew/accommodation: 2 pilots
Max speed: 175kt (322km/h)
Range: 432nm (800km)

ARMAMENT
Internal gun (HAP/HCP): Giat 30mm cannon in undernose turret
Hardpoints: four on two pylons
Max weapon load: N/A
Representative weapons: Mistral or Stinger AAMs; Hellfire (RAAF), HOT or Trigat ATGWs; FFAR pods; 12.7mm machine gun or 20mm cannon pods; external fuel tanks

DIMENSIONS
Main rotor diameter: 13.0m (42ft 8in)
Length: 15.8m (51ft 10in)
Height: 4.3m (14ft 2in)

FEATURES
Tandem cockpit; twin-finned tailplanes; starboard tail rotor; two MTU/Rolls-Royce/Turbomeca MTR 390 turboshafts; fixed wheeled undercarriage

Hindustan Aeronautics Ltd Dhruv ALH India

Multirole utility helicopter

Designed in India, with German assistance, the first prototype ALH flew on 20 August 1992. The Indian Air Force requires 60 utility Dhruvs, as it has been named, the Indian Army 120 while the Indian Navy and the Coast Guard will have 120 and seven naval variants respectively. The first seven production aircraft were delivered in April 2002. A tandem-cockpit light combat variant is proposed, awaiting go-ahead.

Length: 15.9m (52ft 1in)
Height: 4.9m (16ft 1in)

FEATURES
Side-by-side cockpit; twin-finned tailplanes; starboard tail rotor; two Turbomeca TM 333-2B turboshafts; skid undercarriage (utility); retractable wheeled undercarriage (naval)

VARIANTS & OPERATORS
Druhv – utility: India
Druhv – naval: India

SPECIFICATIONS
Crew/accommodation: 2 pilots plus 12-14 passengers or 1,500 kg (3,307 lb) external cargo sling
Max speed: 178kt (330km/h)
Range: 432nm (800km)

ARMAMENT
Internal gun: provision for 20mm cannon under nose
Hardpoints: four on two pylons
Max weapon load: N/A
Representative weapons: AAMs; ASMs; ATGWs; torpedoes; depth charges; 68mm or 71mm FFAR pods; 12.7mm machine gun or 20mm cannon pods

DIMENSIONS
Main rotor diameter: 13.2m (43ft 4in)

Kaman SH-2G Super Seasprite USA

Naval helicopter

First flown on 2 July 1959, 184 of the early SH-2A/B models were built 1961-1963. All were converted to twin-T58 UH-2C configuration, some later modified as LAMPS Mk1 (SH-2D). Returned to production in 1981 as the SH-2F for the USN and all C-models were upgraded to F-models. Only six SH-2G versions with two T700 engines were built new for the USN but 18 SH-2Fs were converted to SH-2G standard. Withdrawn from US service by June 2001. Export sales of G-models are converted SH-2Fs, except New Zealand which ordered four new-builds.

VARIANTS & OPERATORS

SH-2G: Australia, Egypt, New Zealand, Poland

SPECIFICATIONS

Crew/accommodation: 2 pilots plus tactical co-ordinator
Max speed: 138kt (256km/h)
Range: 478nm (885km)

ARMAMENT

Internal gun: provision for 7.62mm machine gun in cabin
Hardpoints: two pylons
Max weapon load: N/A
Representative weapons: Maverick AGMs, Penguin or Sea Skua ASMs; Hellfire ATGWs; torpedoes; external fuel tanks

DIMENSIONS

Main rotor diameter: 13.5m (44ft 4in)
Length: 16.1m (52ft 9in)
Height: 4.6m (15ft 0in)

FEATURES

Side-by-side cockpit; port tail rotor; two GE T700-GE-401 turboshafts; retractable wheeled undercarriage

Kamov Ka-25 'Hormone' Russia

Naval helicopter

The prototype Ka-25 'Hormone' first flew in 1961 and featured a pair of co-axial main rotors, with no tailboom. The main version ('Hormone-A') is a shipborne ASW helicopter, while the 'Hormone-B' is configured to provide over-the-horizon targeting information for ship-launched cruise missiles. The 'Hormone-C' is a specialised SAR version. About 140 were built between 1966 and 1973.

VARIANTS & OPERATORS

Ka-25 'Hormone': India, Ukraine
Ka-25BSh 'Hormone-A': Syria
Ka-25BShZ 'Hormone': Russia
Ka-25PL 'Hormone-A': Russia, Vietnam
Ka-25PS 'Hormone-C': Russia
Ka-25T 'Hormone-B': Russia

SPECIFICATIONS

Crew/accommodation: 2 pilots plus up to 12 passengers or fewer mission specialists
Max speed: 119kt (220km/h)
Range: 216nm (400km)

ARMAMENT

Hardpoints: two weapons bays
Max weapon load: N/A
Representative weapons: torpedoes; depth charges; external fuel tanks

DIMENSIONS

Rotor diameter (each): 15.7m (51ft 8in)
Length: 9.7m (31ft 9in)
Height: 5.4m (17ft 8in)

FEATURES

Side-by-side cockpit; undernose radome; triple fin configuration; two Glushenkov GTD-3F turboshafts; fixed wheeled undercarriage

Kamov Ka-27/-28/-32 'Helix-A/-D/-C' Russia

Naval helicopter

A prototype 'Helix-A', designated Ka-25-2, first flew on 8 August 1973 and featured a dipping-sonar facility. Later re-designated Ka-27, the main production 'Helix-A' usually operated in pairs, flying from larger ships and carriers. The Ka-27PS 'Helix-D' was a dedicated SAR version and the Ka-28 was the export designation for the 'Helix-A'

with the civil variant being designated Ka-32 'Helix-C'. About 267 Ka-27/-28s were built.

VARIANTS & OPERATORS
Ka-27 'Helix': Algeria, Ukraine
Ka-27PL 'Helix-A': Russia
Ka-27PS 'Helix-D': Russia
Ka-28 'Helix': China, India, Vietnam
Ka-32T 'Helix-C': Algeria, Laos, South Korea, USA, Vietnam

SPECIFICATIONS
Crew/accommodation: 2 pilots plus one mission specialist
Max speed: 146kt (270km/h)
Range: 432nm (800km)

ARMAMENT
Hardpoints: one weapons bay
Max weapon load: (Ka-28) 1,000kg (2,205 lb)
Representative weapons: torpedoes; depth charges; bombs; external fuel tanks

DIMENSIONS
Rotor diameter (each): 15.9m (52ft 2in)
Length: 11.3m (38ft 0in)
Height: 5.5m (17ft 10in)

FEATURES
Side-by-side cockpit; undernose radome; triple fin configuration; two Klimov TV3-117V turboshafts; fixed wheeled undercarriage

Kamov Ka-29/-31 'Helix-B' Russia

Naval assault helicopter

A prototype 'Helix-B', designated Ka-252TB, first flew on 28 July 1976 and was later re-designated Ka-29TB. Entered service from 1985. The Ka-31 (formerly known as the Ka-29RLD) was a specialised AEW/EW variant sold to India. About 61 Ka-29/-31 were built.

FEATURES

Wider side-by-side cockpit; nose pitot tube; triple fin configuration; two Klimov TV3-117V turboshafts; fixed wheeled undercarriage

VARIANTS & OPERATORS

Ka-29TB 'Helix-B': Russia, Ukraine
Ka-31: India

SPECIFICATIONS

Crew/accommodation: 2 pilots plus (Ka-29) 16 assault troops or (Ka-31) mission specialists
Max speed: 151kt (280km/h)
Range: 248nm (460km)

ARMAMENT

Internal gun: 7.62mm machine gun on starboard door
Hardpoints: four on outrigger pylons plus weapons bay
Max weapon load: 1,800kg (3,968 lb)
Representative weapons: AT-6 'Spiral' ATGWs; torpedoes; bombs; rocket pods; 23mm or 30mm gun pods; external fuel tanks

DIMENSIONS

Rotor diameter (each): 15.9m (52ft 2in)
Length: 11.3m (38ft 0in)
Height: 5.4m (17ft 8in)

Kamov Ka-50/-52 'Hokum-A/-B' Russia

Close support helicopter

The single-seat prototype 'Hokum', designated V-80, first flew on 17 June 1982 and was later re-designated Ka-50. The subject of much evaluation (against the Mi-28 'Havoc') and export promotion, it appears Russian Army Aviation has chosen the Ka-50 for limited production. The Ka-52 features a side-by-side cockpit.

VARIANTS & OPERATORS
Ka-50 'Hokum-A': Russia
Ka-52 'Hokum-B': Russia

SPECIFICATIONS
Crew/accommodation: Ka-50: 1 pilot on Zvelda K-37-800 ejection seat; Ka-52: 2 pilots on same ejection seats
Max speed: 210kt (390km/h)
Range: 595nm (1,100km)

ARMAMENT
Internal gun: 30mm cannon on starboard fuselage
Hardpoints: four pylons on stub wings
Max weapon load: 3,000kg (6,610 lb)
Representative weapons: AA-11 'Archer' AAMs; AS-12 'Kegler' ARMs; AT-6 ATGWs; 80mm or 122mm rocket pods; FAB-500 bombs; external fuel tanks

DIMENSIONS
Rotor diameter (each): 14.5m (47ft 7in)
Length: 16.0m (52ft 6in)
Height: 4.9m (16ft 2in)

FEATURES
E-O fairings under nose; small twin fin tailplane; single main fin; two Klimov TV3-117VMA turboshafts; retractable wheeled undercarriage

Kawasaki OH-1 Japan

Scout/observation helicopter

The prototype XOH-1 was first flown on 6 August 1996. Features 'fenestron'-type tail fan and E-O sensor mounted forward of rotor mast below main rotor. Of a requirement of 150-200 for the JGSDF, 24 (including four flying prototypes) have been ordered to FY04.

FEATURES
Tandem cockpit; 'fenestron-type' tail rotor in main fin; two Mitsubishi TS1-10QT turboshafts; fixed wheeled undercarriage

VARIANTS & OPERATORS
OH-1: Japan

SPECIFICATIONS
Crew/accommodation: 2 pilots
Max speed: 150kt (277km/h)
Range: 297nm (550km)

ARMAMENT
Hardpoints: two pylons under each stub-wing
Max weapon load: 132 kg (291 lb)
Representative weapons: Type 91 IR-guided AAMs

DIMENSIONS
Main rotor diameter: 11.6m (38ft 1in)
Length: 12.0m (39ft 4in)
Height: 3.4m (11ft 2in)

MD Helicopters (Hughes/McDD)
MD 500/530 Defender USA

Scout/attack helicopter

First flown as the Hughes OH-6A Cayuse (Model 500) on 27 February 1963 and was developed into the civil MD 500 by 1968, with the MD 500D flying in 1984. Specialised anti-tank, gunship and naval variants developed, based on civil models, while AH-6/MH-6 versions used by US Special Forces and known as 'Little Birds'. Built under licence by Kawasaki in Japan and BredaNardi in Italy. Development of the NOTAR applied to the design led to the MD 520N, the MD 600N and MH-90 Enforcer (Explorer). Over 1,430 helicopters from OH-6A to MD 530F were built.

VARIANTS & OPERATORS
Argentina (MD 500C/D/E, MD 530F), Belgium (MD 520N), Chile (MD 530F), Colombia (MD 500/D/E/M, MD 530F), Costa Rica (MD 500E), Croatia (MD 500/D), Denmark (MD 500M), El Salvador (MD 500D/E), Finland (MD 500D/E), Honduras (MD 500D), Italy (NH 500D/E/M/MC/MD), Japan (OH-6D/DA/J), Jordan (MD 500D), Kenya (MD 500D/MD-TOW/ME), Malta (NH 500HM), Mexico (MD 500E, MD 530F/MG), North Korea (MD 500D/E), Peru (MD 500D), Philippines (MD 520MG), South Korea (MD 500MD/MD-ASW/MD-TOW), Spain (MD 500), Taiwan (MD 500MD), Turkey (MD 600N), USA (AH-6G/J, MH-6G/J)

SPECIFICATIONS
Crew/accommodation: 1 or 2 pilots plus up to 4 passengers or 907kg (2,000lb) external slung cargo
Max speed: 130kt (241km/h)
Range: 213nm (428km)

ARMAMENT
Hardpoints: two pylons under stub-wings
Max weapon load: N/A
Representative weapons: Stinger AAMs; TOW ATGWs; 2.75in FFAR pods; 7.62mm machine gun pods

DIMENSIONS
Main rotor diameter: 8.0m (26ft 4in)
Length: 7.6m (24ft 0in)
Height: 2.6m (8ft 8in)

FEATURES
'Tadpole' cabin; slim tail boom with T-tail; port tail rotor (NOTAR on MD 520/600N and MH-90); one Rolls-Royce (Allison) 250-C20B turboshaft; skid undercarriage

Mil Mi-6 'Hook' Russia

Heavy transport helicopter

At the time of its first flight on 5 June 1957, the Mi-6 was the world's largest helicopter. Developed to the Mi-10 "Flying Crane" and Mi-22 'Hook-C' command support helicopters. More than 800 built for civil and military use, ending in 1981.

VARIANTS & OPERATORS

Mi-6 'Hook-A': Belarus, China, Kazakhstan, Laos, Russia, Ukraine, Uzbekistan, Vietnam
Mi-6VKP 'Hook-B': Russia, Ukraine
Mi-6AYa (Mi-22) 'Hook-C': Belarus, Russia, Ukraine, Uzbekistan

SPECIFICATIONS

Crew/accommodation: 5 flight crew plus 70 combat troops or 8,000kg (17,637 lb) external slung cargo
Max speed: 162kt (300km/h)
Range: 540nm (1,000km)

ARMAMENT

Internal gun: some have 12.7mm nose-mounted machine gun

DIMENSIONS

Main rotor diameter: 35.0m (114ft 10in)
Length: 41.7m (136ft 11in)
Height: 9.9m (32ft 4in)

FEATURES

Long fuselage/tail boom; starboard tail rotor; stub wings; two Soloviev D-25 V (TV-2BM) turboshafts; fixed wheeled undercarriage

Mil Mi-8/-17/-171/-172 'Hip' Russia

Heavy assault helicopter

The first prototype Mi-8 'Hip-A' was flown on 24 June 1961. Production undertaken by Mil (Moscow), Ulan-Ude and Kazan. Many variants were developed and the second-generation 'Hip', designated Mi-17 'Hip-H', using an Mi-8 airframe and Mi-14 powerplant and dynamic components, first flew on 17 August 1975, but designated Mi-8MT for Russian service. There are many versions and sub-variants under varying Mi-8/-17 designations, plus the Mi-9 'Hip-G' dedicated airborne command post variant. Further improved versions (Mi-171/172) continue to be developed. This helicopter family has been widely exported with over 11,000 (about 3,700 Mi-8T and 7,300 Mi-17) built by Ulan-Ude and 7,300 Mi-8/-17/171/-172 from Kazan.

VARIANTS & OPERATORS

Mi-8 'Hip': Albania, Algeria, Angola, Azerbaijan, Belarus, Bhutan, Bosnia-Herzegovina, Republika Srpska (Bosnia-Herzegovina), Burkina Faso, Cambodia, China, Croatia, Cuba, Czech Republic, Dijbouti, Egypt, Estonia, Ethiopia, Finland, Georgia, Guinea-Bisseau, Hungary, India, Kazakhstan, Kyrgizia, Laos, Latvia, Libya, Lithuania, Macedonia, Maldives, Mali, Moldova, Mongolia, Mozambique, Namibia, North Korea, Peru, Poland, Romania, Russia, Serbia and Montenegro, Slovak Republic, Sudan, Syria, Tajikistan, Turkmenistan, Ukraine, USA, Uzbekistan, Vietnam, Yemen
Mi-9 'Hip-G': Armenia, Belarus, Hungary, Czech Republic, Hungary, Kazakhstan, Russia, Ukraine
Mi-17 'Hip-H': Algeria, Angola, Armenia, Bangladesh, Bosnia-Herzegovina, Bulgaria, Burkina Faso, Cambodia, China, Colombia, Costa Rica, Croatia, Cuba, Czech Republic, Djibouti, Eritrea, Ethiopia, Georgia, Hungary, India, Kazakhstan, Kenya, Kyrgizia, Laos, Macedonia, Mexico, Myanmar, Nepal, Nicaragua, Pakistan, Peru, Poland, Romania, Russia, Rwanda, Serbia and Montenegro, Slovak Republic, Sri Lanka, Syria, Turkey, Uganda, Ukraine, USA, Uzbekistan, Vietnam
Mi-171 'Hip': Algeria, Angola, Ecuador, Iran, Malaysia, Myanmar, Nigeria, Slovak Republic

SPECIFICATIONS

Crew/accommodation: 2 pilots and (Mi-8T 'Hip-C') up to 24 troops and (Mi-17-1V) up to 30 troops, or 3,000kg (6,614 lb) external cargo sling
Max speed: 135kt (250km/h)
Range: 545nm (1,010km)

ARMAMENT: Mi-8TB 'HIP-E'

Internal gun: one 12.7mm machine gun in nose
Hardpoints: six on outrigger pylons
Max weapon load: N/A
Representative weapons: AT-2 Swatter ATGWs; 57mm rocket pods

DIMENSIONS

Main rotor diameter: 21.3m (69ft 10in)
Length (overall, rotors turning): 25.3m (83ft 1in)
Height (overall, rotors turning): 5.5m (18ft 2in)

FEATURES

Round windows on military cabin; square windows on civil variants; starboard tail rotor on Mi-8; port tail rotor on Mi-17; two Klimov TV2-117AG (Mi-8) and TV3-117MT (Mi-17) turboshafts; fixed wheeled undercarriage

NOT TO BE CONFUSED WITH

Mil-14 'Haze'; Aerospatiale SA 330; Eurocopter AS.332/532 Super Puma/Cougar

Mil Mi-24/-25/-35 'Hind' Russia

Attack/assault helicopter

First prototype flown on 19 September 1969 and entered service from 1972. Progressively developed with various sensor and armament fits.

Export designations are Mi-25 and Mi-35. Russia now initiating upgrade programme of Mi-24P 'Hind-F' to Mi-24PN standard. More than 2,500 Mi-24 'Hinds' of all variants produced, many now being upgraded. Remains in low volume production with Rosvertol for domestic and export use.

VARIANTS & OPERATORS

Mi-24 'Hind': Algeria, Angola, Armenia, Azerbaijan, Belarus, Bulgaria, Burundi, Congo (Dem. Rep.), Côte d'Ivoire, Croatia, Cuba, Czech Republic, Eritrea, Ethiopia, Georgia, Guinea Republic, Hungary, India, Kazakhstan, Krygizia, Libya, Macedonia, Mexico, Namibia, Nigeria, North Korea, Poland, Russia, Rwanda, Sierra Leone, Slovak Republic, Sri Lanka, Sudan, Syria, Tajikistan, Tanzania, Turkmenistan, Ukraine, USA, Uzbekistan, Vietnam, Yemen
Mi-24K 'Hind-G2': Armenia, Belarus, Macedonia, Russia, Ukraine
Mi-24RKR 'Hind-G1': Armenia, Belarus, Russia, Ukraine
Mi-25: France, India, Libya, Mozambique, Nicaragua, Peru, Syria, Yemen
Mi-35: Bosnia-Herzegovina, Cyprus, India, Libya, Nigeria, Zimbabwe

SPECIFICATIONS

Crew/accommodation: pilot and WSO
Max speed: Mi-24P – 172kt (320km/h);
        Mi-35M – 167kt (310km/h)
Combat radius:
Mi-24P on internal fuel – 86nm (160km);
Mi-24P with 4 external tanks – 155nm (288km)

ARMAMENT

Internal gun: one 12.7mm four-barrel
Gatling-type machine gun in undernose turret
(Mi-24/25); twin-barrel 23mm gun (Mi-35)
Hardpoints: four pylons on stub wings, and twin
rails under endplate
Max weapon load: Mi-24P - 2,400kg (5,291 lb);
Mi-35M - 2,860kg (6,305 lb)
Representative weapons: AA-8 'Aphid', AA-11
'Archer' or 9M39 Igla-V AAMs; AT-2 'Swatter'
(Mi-24/25); AT-6 'Spiral'(Mi-35) ATGWs; 57mm
rocket pods; 80mm, 130mm or 240mm rockets;
twin-barrel 23mm gun pod; various bombs;
external fuel tanks

DIMENSIONS

	Mi-24P	Mi-35M
Main rotor diameter:		
	17.3m (56ft 9in)	17.2m (56ft 5in)
Length (overall, rotors turning):		
	21.4m (70ft 0in)	21.3m (69ft 10in)
Height (overall, rotors turning):		
		5.0m (16ft 5in)

FEATURES

Tandem cockpit; undernose sensor fairings on
some versions; port tail rotor; two Klimov
TV3-117MT turboshafts; fixed wheeled
undercarriage

Mil Mi-14 'Haze' Russia

Attack/assault helicopter

Essentially an Mi-8 with a boat-hull lower fuselage (in the manner of a Sea King) and Mi-17 engines, first flown in September 1969, the 'Haze' was developed for ASW and SAR work. At least 250 were produced.

VARIANTS & OPERATORS
Mi-14: Ukraine, USA
Mi-14PL 'Haze-A': Bulgaria, Cuba, Ethiopia, Libya, North Korea, Poland, Russia, Syria
Mi-14PS 'Haze-C': Poland, Russia

SPECIFICATIONS
Crew/accommodation: 2 pilots and 2 mission specialists plus up to 10 survivors
Max speed: 124kt (230km/h)
Range: 612nm (1,135km)

ARMAMENT: Mi-14PL 'HAZE-A'
Hardpoints: N/A
Max weapon load: N/A
Representative weapons: torpedoes; depth charges; nuclear depth bomb

DIMENSIONS
Main rotor diameter: 21.9m (69ft 10in)
Length: 25.3m (83ft 1in)
Height: 6.9m (22ft 9in)

FEATURES
Round windows on cabin; boat-type hull; rear fuselage sponsons; port tail rotor; two Klimov TV3-117MT turboshafts; retractable wheeled undercarriage

Mil Mi-28 'Havoc' Russia

Attack helicopter

First prototype flew on 10 November 1982 and was considered an "Apache-lookalike". Basic Mi-28A selected for pre-series production but not initiated. Mi-28N Night Hunter developed and as of January 2004 was being considered as a 'next generation attack helicopter'.

VARIANTS & OPERATORS
Mi-28 'Havoc': Russia

SPECIFICATIONS
Crew/accommodation: 2 pilots
Max speed: 162kt (300km/h)
Range: 234nm (435km)

ARMAMENT
Internal gun: one 30mm cannon in under-nose turret
Hardpoints: two pylons under each stub-wing
Max weapon load: 11,500kg (24,961lb)
Representative weapons: Vikhr, Igla-V or AT-6 'Spiral' ATGWs; 80mm or 122mm rocket pods; 23mm cannon pods; mine dispensers

DIMENSIONS
Main rotor diameter: 17.2m (56ft 5in)
Length: 17.0m (55ft 10in)
Height: 4.7m (15ft 5in)

FEATURES
Angular fuselage; starboard tail rotor; port tailplane; two laterally-mounted Klimov TV3-117VMA turboshafts; fixed wheeled undercarriage

NH Industries NH 90 France/Germany/Italy/Netherlands/Portugal

Medium transport/naval helicopter

The first of five prototype NH90s (NATO Helicopter for the 1990s) flew in France on 18 December 1995. Originally a four-nation collaborative venture, Portugal joined in 2001. Two versions are being developed: the tactical transport helicopter (TTH) and the NATO frigate helicopter (NFH). The first production NH90 flew on 4 May 2004. As of July 2004, there are 345 firm orders and options on a further 86, with Australia selecting the NH90 in September 2004

VARIANTS & OPERATORS

NH 90 NFH: France, Germany, Italy, Netherlands, Norway, Sweden
NH 90 TTH: Finland, France, Germany, Greece, Italy, Oman, Portugal, Sweden

SPECIFICATIONS

Crew/accommodation: 2 flight crew plus mission specialists (NFH) or 14-20 troops (TTH)
Max speed: 157kt (291km/h)
Range: 650nm (1,203km)

ARMAMENT

Internal gun(s): 7.62mm machine gun(s) in door mountings
Hardpoints: two pylons
Max weapon load: 4,600kg (10,143 lb)
Representative weapons: ASV - Marte Mk 2/S ASMs; ASW - torpedoes; depth charges

DIMENSIONS

Main rotor diameter: 16.3m (53ft 5in)
Length: 19.6m (64ft 2in)
Height: 4.1m (13ft 5in)

FEATURES

Side-by-side cockpit; port tail rotor; starboard tailplane; two RTM 322 or GE T700-T6E turboshafts; fuselage sponsons for retractable wheeled undercarriage

NOT TO BE CONFUSED WITH

Agusta A139; Eurocopter AS332/532 Super Puma/ Cougar; Sikorsky S-92

PZL Swidnik (Mil) Mi-2 'Hoplite' Russia/Poland

Light helicopter

Grzegorz Holdanowicz

First flown in Russia on 22 September 1962 but production and marketing assigned to Poland in 1964. Built in ambulance, agricultural, naval, SAR, troop transport, combat support and anti-tank versions. Over 5,450 Mi-2s of all versions built.

VARIANTS & OPERATORS

Mi-2: Algeria, Armenia, Azerbaijan, Cuba, Czech Republic, Djibouti, Estonia, Georgia, Ghana, Hungary, Latvia, Libya, Lithuania, Mexico, Myanmar, North Korea, Poland, Russia, Slovak Republic, Syria, Ukraine, USA

SPECIFICATIONS

Crew/accommodation: 1 pilot plus up to 8 passengers
Max speed: 113kt (210km/h)
Range (internal fuel): 237nm (440km)

ARMAMENT: MI-2URP

Hardpoints: four on outrigger pylons
Max weapon load: N/A
Representative weapons: AT-3 Sagger ATGWs or Strela 2 AAMs

DIMENSIONS

Main rotor diameter: 14.5m (47ft 7in)
Length: 17.4m (57ft 2in)
Height: 3.8m (12ft 4in)

FEATURES

Short cabin; starboard tail rotor; two Isotov GTD-350 turboshafts; fixed wheeled undercarriage

PZL Swidnik W-3 Sokol Poland

Multi-purpose helicopter

Grzegorz Holdanowicz

Clearly showing its Mi-2 grandparentage, the prototype W-3 first flew on 16 November 1979, several versions were produced and other, one-off specialised variants evaluated. Over 124 W-3s built or on order.

VARIANTS & OPERATORS

W-3 Sokol: Myanmar, Poland
W-3A Sokol: Czech Republic
W-3RM Anakonda: Poland
W-3W Sokol: Poland

SPECIFICATIONS

Crew/accommodation: 2 flight crew plus 12 passengers
Max speed: 140kt (260km/h)
Range: 402nm (745km)

ARMAMENT: W-3W

Internal gun: twin-barrel 23mm cannon (starboard side)
Hardpoints: four on cabin pylons
Max weapon load: N/A
Representative weapons: 57mm or 80mm rocket pods

DIMENSIONS

Main rotor diameter: 15.7m (51ft 6in)
Length: 18.80m (61ft 8in)
Height: 5.1m (16ft 10in)

FEATURES

Sharp nose; starboard tail rotor; two WSK-PZL Rzeszow PZL-10W turboshafts; fixed wheeled undercarriage

Sikorsky S-61/SH-3 Sea King USA

Amphibious ASW/SAR helicopter

The prototype S-61 (initial military designation HSS-2) was first flown on 11 March 1959 and featured a 'boat-hull' fuselage. It entered USN service in September 1961 (later being designated SH-3). Developed into several versions and licence-built in Italy by Agusta, in Japan by Mitsubishi and the UK by Westland (see p. 516). Over 1,030 versions of the S-61/SH-3 were produced.

VARIANTS & OPERATORS

Argentina (S-61D-4/r, ASH-3H, SH-3D/H), Brazil (ASH-3D/SH-3D), Canada (SH-3/CH-124), Denmark (S-61A), Egypt (AS-61), Iran (AS-61A-4, ASH-3D), Italy (AS-61A-4, ASH-3D/H), Japan (S-61A/AH, HSS-2B), Libya (AS-61A-4), Malaysia (AS-61N Nuri, S-61A-4 Nuri), Namibia (S-61L), Peru (AS-61D, ASH-3D), Saudi Arabia (AS-61A-4), Spain (H-3, SH-3), USA (NVH-3A, SH-3H, UH-3H, VH-3A/D), Venezuela (AS-61D)

SPECIFICATIONS

Crew/accommodation: 2 pilots and 2 WSOs
Max speed: 144kt (267km/h)
Range: 542nm (1,005km)

ARMAMENT: SH-3D/H

Internal guns: provision for door-mounted 7.62mm Miniguns
Hardpoints: four
Max weapon load: 381 kg (840 lb)
Representative weapons: AS 12, Marte Mk 2 or Exocet ASMs; torpedoes; depth charges

DIMENSIONS

Main rotor diameter: 18.9m (62ft 0in)
Length: 22.1m (72ft 8in)
Height: 5.1m (16ft 10in)

FEATURES

'Boat-hulled' fuselage; port tail rotor; two GE T58-GE-10 turboshafts; outrigger sponsons for retractable wheeled undercarriage

Sikorsky S-61R/HH-3 (Pelican) USA

Amphibious SAR helicopter

Derived from the S-61, the S-61R, with a tail-ramp at the rear fuselage and re-designed tail boom, first flew on 17 June 1963. It entered USAF service as the CH-3C transport and, later, as the HH-3 SAR version, and attained the nickname 'Jolly Green Giant' for its rescue missions. Built under licence by Agusta in Italy as the AS-61R (HH-3F). Over 100 AS/S-61R/HH-3E/F were produced.

VARIANTS & OPERATORS
Argentina (S-61R), Italy (HH-3F Pelican), Tunisia (HH-3E)

SPECIFICATIONS
Crew/accommodation: 3 flight crew plus 25-30 troops
Max speed: 141kt (261km/h)
Range: 770nm (1,427km)

ARMAMENT
Internal guns: provision for door-mounted 7.62mm machine guns

DIMENSIONS
Main rotor diameter: 18.9m (62ft 0in)
Length: 22.3m (73ft 0in)
Height: 5.5m (18ft 1in)

FEATURES
'Boat-hulled' fuselage with tail ramp; port tail rotor; starboard tailplane; two GE T58-GE-100 turboshafts; rear fuselage sponsons for retractable wheeled undercarriage

Sikorsky S-65/CH-53 Sea Stallion USA

Assault transport helicopter

Michael J. Gething

A step up from the S-61R/CH-3 and using some S-64 Skycrane components, the first CH-53A flew on 14 October 1964 and entered USMC service as the Sea Stallion in 1966. Adopted by the USAF as a successor to its SAR HH-3E, the HH-53 was nicknamed "Super Jolly". The MH-53J Pave Low III is a Special Operations version. Licence-built in Germany by VFW-Fokker (now part of Eurocopter). Some 522 S-65/CH-53s of all versions were built.

VARIANTS & OPERATORS
Germany (CH-53G), Iran (RH-53D), Israel (CH-53D Yasur 2000), USA (CH-53D, MH-53J/M)

SPECIFICATIONS
Crew/accommodation: 3 flight crew plus up to 37 troops
Max speed: 170kt (315km/h)
Range: 468nm (869km)

ARMAMENT: MH-53J
Internal guns: three 7.62mm or 0.5in (12.7mm) machine guns in fuselage and on ramp

DIMENSIONS
Main rotor diameter: 22.0m (72ft 3in)
Length: 26.9m (88ft 3in)
Height: 7.6m (24ft 115n)

FEATURES
Long cabin with tail ramp; port tail rotor; starboard tailplane; two pod-mounted GE T64-GE-6 turboshafts; centre-fuselage sponsons for retractable wheeled undercarriage

Sikorsky S-80/SH-53E Super Stallion USA

Assault and MCM helicopter

Essentially a three-engined version of the S-65/CH-53, the prototype S-80/CH-53E first flew on 1 March 1974. The CH-53E Super Stallion replaced CH-53Ds in USMC service, while in the USN, the MH-53E Sea Dragon replaced the RH-53D in the MCM role. US versions being upgraded. Some 237 S-80/CH/MH-53s were produced although a major upgrade and/or new production is in prospect.

VARIANTS & OPERATORS
Japan (MH-53EJ), USA (CH-53E, MH-53E)

SPECIFICATIONS
Crew/accommodation: 3 flight crew plus up to 55 troops or various towed MCM devices
Max speed: 170kt (315km/h)
Range (ferry): 1,120nm (2,074km)

ARMAMENT
Internal guns: provision for three 7.62mm or 0.5in (12.7mm) machine guns in fuselage and on ramp
Hardpoints: two on sponsons
Representative stores: external fuel tanks

DIMENSIONS
Main rotor diameter: 24.1m (79ft 0in)
Length: 30.2m (99ft 0in)
Height: 9.0m (29ft 5in)

FEATURES
Long cabin with tail ramp; canted fin with port tail rotor; starboard tailplane; three GE T64-GE-416/-416A turboshafts; centre-fuselage sponsons for retractable wheeled undercarriage

Sikorsky S-70A/UH-60 Black Hawk USA

Battlefield helicopter

ARMAMENT (OPTIONAL)

Internal guns: provision for two 7.62mm Miniguns or 0.5in (12.7mm) GECAL 50 machine guns in fuselage doors
Hardpoints: four mounted on the outrigger ESSS
Max weapon load (ESSS): 2,268kg (5,000 lb)
Representative weapons (ESSS): Stinger AAMs; Hellfire ATGWs; 2.75in FFAR pods; mine dispensers; ECM pods; external fuel tanks

DIMENSIONS

Main rotor diameter: 16.7m (53ft 8in)
Length: 19.8m (64ft 10in)
Height: 5.1m (16ft 10in)

FEATURES

Side-by-side cockpit; square windows in fuselage; starboard tail rotor; full tailplane at base of fin; two GE T700-GE-700/-701 turboshafts; fixed wheeled undercarriage

First flown on 17 October 1974, the YUH-60A was declared the winner of the US Army's UTTAS competition on December 1976. The Black Hawk entered US Army service in 1979 and has evolved into many specialised variants, including EW, medevac, C-SAR and Special Forces. Sikorsky is now producing the latest UH-60M configuration. Export variants are designated S-70A, while the naval version is S-70B (SH-60) – see next entry. Over 2,000 S-70A/UH-60 versions have been built or are on order.

VARIANTS & OPERATORS

Argentina (**S-70A**), Australia (**S-70A**), Austria (**S-70A**), Bahrain (**UH-60A/L**), Brazil (**S-70A**), Brunei (**S-70A**), Chile (**S-70A**), China (**S-70C**), Colombia (**UH-60A/L**), Egypt (**S-70A, UH-60L**), Israel (**S-70A, UH-60A**), Japan (**UH-60J**), Jordan (**S-70A**), Malaysia (**S-70A**), Mexico (**S-70A**), Morocco (**S-70A**), Philippines (**S-70A**), Saudi Arabia (**S-70A**), South Korea (**UH-60P**), Taiwan (**S-70C/C-6/C(M)**), Thailand (**S-70A**), Turkey (**S-70A**), USA (**AH-60L, CH-60S, EH-60A, HH-60G/L, MH-60G/K/L, UH-60A/L/M/Q, VH-60N**)

SPECIFICATIONS

Crew/accommodation: 3 flight crew plus 11 troops or 4,082kg (9,000 lb) external cargo sling
Max speed (UH-60L/Q): 194kt (359km/h)
Range (with external tanks): 1,200nm (2,222km)

Sikorsky S-70B/SH-60 Seahawk USA

Naval helicopter

Winner of the USN's LAMPS Mk III contest in 1977, the first YSH-60B (S-70B) Seahawk prototype flew on 12 December 1979. In USN service since 1983, the Seahawk has been developed into various specialised models for frigate and carrier-borne ASW, C-SAR, vertrep, and customs roles. Over 400 S-70B/SH-60 versions have been built or are on order.

VARIANTS & OPERATORS
Australia (S-70B), Greece (S-70B), Japan (SH-60J), Spain (S-70B), Thailand (S-70B), Turkey (MH-60S), USA (CH-60S, HH-60H/J, MH-60R/S, NSH-60B, SH-60B/F/R)

SPECIFICATIONS
Crew/accommodation: 2 flight crew plus mission specialists or 4,082kg (9,000 lb) external cargo sling
Max speed: 160kt (296km/h)
Range (interal fuel): 319nm (592km)

ARMAMENT
Internal guns: (HH-60H) two 7.62mm M60D machine guns in fuselage doors
Hardpoints: two on the rear fuselage
Max weapon load: N/A
Representative weapons: Mk 46/50/54 torpedoes; MCM equipment; ECM pods; external fuel tanks

DIMENSIONS
Main rotor diameter: 16.7m (53ft 8in)
Length (SH-60B): 12.3m (40ft 11in)
Height: 5.2m (17ft 0in)

FEATURES
Side-by-side cockpit; square windows in fuselage; starboard tail rotor; full tailplane at base of fin; two GE T700-GE-700/-701 turboshafts; fixed wheeled undercarriage (tailwheel further forward than UH-60)

Westland (A-W) WG.13 Lynx/Super Lynx UK

Naval and battlefield helicopter

Representative weapons:
battlefield: HOT, Hellfire or TOW ATGWs; FFAR pods; 7.62mm machine gun or 20mm cannon pods;
naval-ASW: Mk 44/46, A244S or Sting Ray torpedoes; depth charges;
naval-ASV: Sea Skua, Penguin or Marte ASMs; 7.62mm machine guns or 20mm cannon pods

The third type covered by the 1968 Westland/Aerospatiale joint programme for the French and British services, the first of 13 WG.13 Lynx prototypes flew on 21 March 1971. Developed in army (battlefield) and naval versions, the first Royal Navy Lynx HAS.2 entered service in 1977. Subsequently upgraded and evolved (including BERP main rotors), the latest Super Lynx can be powered by the LHTEC CTS-800-4N engines. Over 430 Lynx/Super Lynx have been built or are on order.

DIMENSIONS

	Army/Navy	Super Lynx
Main rotor diameter:	12.8m (42ft 0in)	12.8m (42ft 0in)
Length:	15.1m (49ft 9in)	15.2m (50ft 0in)
Height:	3.5m (11ft 6in)	3.7m (12ft 0in)

FEATURES

Side-by-side cockpit; square windows in fuselage; port tail rotor; starboard tailplane; two Rolls-Royce Gem 42-1 turboshafts; skid (army) or fixed wheeled undercarriage (naval and AH.9)

VARIANTS & OPERATORS

Brazil (**Super Lynx Mk 21A**), Denmark (**Mk 90, Super Lynx Mk 90B**), France (**Mk 4(FN)**), Norway (**Mk 86**), Germany (**Mk 88, Super Lynx Mk 88A**), Malaysia (**Super Lynx 300**), Netherlands (**SH-14D**), Nigeria (**Mk 89**), Oman (**Super Lynx 300**), Portugal (**Mk 95**), South Africa (**Mk 64**), South Korea (**Mk 99/99A**), Thailand (**Super Lynx 300**), UK (**AH.7/9, HAS.3/ICE/S/SGM/S(ICE), HMA.8, Mk 5X**)

SPECIFICATIONS

Crew/accommodation: 1 pilot and 1 WSO (naval) or 2 pilots plus 10 troops (battlefield)

	Army/Navy	Super Lynx
Max speed:	145kt (269km/h)	138kt (256km/h)
Radius of action:	292nm (540km)	320nm (593km)

ARMAMENT

Internal gun: provision for door-mounted 7.62mm GPMG or 0.5in (12.7mm) M3 machine gun
Hardpoints: two pylons (battlefield), or four (naval)
Max weapon load: 3,949kg (8,707 lb) battlefield or 4,618kg (10,181 lb) naval

Westland (A-W) WS-61 Sea King UK

Naval and battlefield helicopter

Many variants upgraded including addition of BERP main rotors. Some 328 Sea King/ Commando variants have been built by Westland in the UK.

VARIANTS & OPERATORS

Australia (Sea King Mk 50);
Belgium (Mk 48);
Egypt (Commando Mk 1/2, Sea King Mk 47);
Germany (Mk 41);
India (Mk 42);
Norway (Mk 43A/B);
Pakistan (Mk 45);
Qatar (Commando Mk 2/3);
UK (Sea King AEW.2A, HAR.3/3A, HAS.5U/6, HC.4, HU.5, Mk 4X, ASaC.7)

Westland acquired licence to built/develop the S-61 (see p. 299) in 1959 and the first production Westland Sea King HAS.1 flew on 7 May 1969. Several variants developed, including AEW, ASaC, ASW, ASV and troop transport (Commando).

SPECIFICATIONS

Crew/accommodation: 2 pilots plus 2 WSOs (ASW/ASVW) or 2 pilots plus 28 troops (Sea King HC.4/Commando) or 3,628 kg (8,000 lb) external slung cargo
Max speed: 122kt (226km/h)
Range (Commando): 300nm (556km)

ARMAMENT

Internal gun: one 7.62mm GPMG, starboard door mounted
Hardpoints: four
Max weapon load: N/A
Representative weapons: Sea Eagle or Exocet ASMs; Mk 46, A224S, Sting Ray torpedoes; depth charges

DIMENSIONS

Main rotor diameter: 18.9m (62ft 0in)
Length: 22.1m (72ft 8in)
Height: 5.1m (16ft 10in)

FEATURES

'Boat-hulled' fuselage; port tail rotor; two Rolls-Royce Gnome H.1400-1T turboshafts; outrigger sponsons for retractable wheeled undercarriage

Glossary of Acronyms and Terms

A-W	AgustaWestland (now wholly owned by Finmeccanica of Italy)
AAAW	Advanced Anti-Armour Weapon (became Brimstone)
AAM	Air-to-Air Missile
AAR	Air-to-Air Refuelling
ACM	Advanced Cruise Missile (US designation = AGM-129)
ACMI	Air Combat Manoeuvring Instrumentation (pod)
ADV	Air Defence Variant (of Tornado), RAF designations = Tornado F.2/2A, F.3 or EF.3
AEW	Airborne Early Warning
AEW&C	Airborne Early Warning and Control
AGM	Air-to-Ground Missile (also used in US designations)
AH	Army Helicopter (UK designator)
AHIP	Army Helicopter Improvement Programme (for US Army OH-58 Kiowa)
AIDC	Aerospace Industrial Development Corporation (Taiwan)
AIM	Air Interception Missile (used in US designations)
aka	also known as
ALARM	Air-Launched Anti-Radar Missile
ALCM	Air-Launched Cruise Missile
ALH	Advanced Light Helicopter (HAL Druhvs)
AMRAAM	Advanced Medium-Range Air-to-Air Missile (US designation = AIM-120)
An	Antonov (Ukrainian design bureau)
APACHE	Armement Propulsée A CHarges Ejectables - French weapons dispenser weapon from which StormShadow/SCALP EG weapons are derived.
APN	Aviation of the People's Navy (China's naval air arm)
ARM	Anti-Radar Missile
ASaC	Airborne Surveillance and Control (UK designator applied to what was the Sea King AEW.7, now ASaC.7)
ASM	Anti-Ship Missile
ASMP	Air-Sol-Moyenne Portée - French nuclear stand-off missile
ASRAAM	Advanced Short-Range Air-to-Air Missile
ASTOR	Airborne STand-Off Radar
ASV	Anti-Surface Vessel
ASVW	Anti-Surface Vessel Warfare
ASW	Anti-Submarine Warfare
ATGW	Anti-Tank Guided Weapon
AVLF	Airborne Very Low Frequency - communications system used to communicate with submerged USN submarines
AWACS	Airborne Warning And Control System - the USAF programme which led to the E-3 Sentry and often incorrectly used as the aircraft name itself.
B	Bomber (US designation prefix)
BAC	British Aircraft Corporation

BAe	British Aerospace
BBMF	Battle of Britain Memorial Flight
Be	Beriev (Russian design bureau)
BERP	British Experimental Rotorcraft Programme
C	Cargo (transport) - UK designator and US prefix
CAC	Chengdu Aircraft Industrial Corporation (China)
CALCM	Conventional (-armed) Air-Launched Cruise Missile (US designation = AGM-86C/D)
CAS	Close Air Support (also known as ground attack)
CBLS	Carrier, Bomb, Light Stores (a practice bomb carrier)
CFT	Conformal Fuel Tank (used on F-15)
CHAIC	CHanghe Aircraft Industries Corporation (China)
CIA	Central Intelligence Agency (US)
COD	Carrier On-board Delivery
COIN	COunter INsurgency
C-SAR	Combat Search-And-Rescue
DAS	Defensive Aids Suite
DHI	Daewoo Heavy Industries (South Korea)
E-O	Electro-Optical equipment (FLIRs or laser rangefinder)
EADS	European Aeronautic and Defence Systems Company
ECM	Electronic CounterMeasures
ECR	Electronic Combat and Reconnaissance (variant of Tornado)
EMD	Engineering, Manufacture and Development (i.e. pre-production/pre-series)
EMBRAER	EMpresa BRasiliera de AERonautica (Brazil)
ENAER	Empresa Nacional de AERonautica (Chile)
ESM	Electronic Support Measures
ESSS	External Stores Support System (for S-70A/UH-60)
EW	Electronic Warfare
EWO	Electronic Warfare Officer
F	Fighter (UK & US designator)
FAC	Forward Air Control (or Controller)
FFAR	Folding-Fin Aerial Rocket (pod)
FLI	Fighter Lead-In (trainer)
FLIR	Forward-Looking InfraRed (thermal sensor)
FMA	Spanish acronym for Military Aircraft Factory, now Lockheed Martin Aircraft Argentina SA
FRY	Federal Republic of Yugoslavia
FSD	Full Scale Development
GE	General Electric (US)
GPMG	General Purpose Machine Gun (UK weapon)

Glossary of Acronyms and Terms

GR   Ground-attack and Recconaissance (UK designator)

HAC   Hélicoptère Anti-Char (anti-tank helicopter), version of Tigre/Tiger

HAD   Hélicoptère d'Attaque et de Destruction (attack helicopter) more powerful version of Tigre/Tiger

HAL   Hindustan Aeronautics Limited (India)

HAMC   Harbin Aircraft Manufacturing Corporation (China)

HAP   Hélicoptère d'Appui et de Protection (escort/fire support helicopter), version of Tigre/Tiger

HARM   High-speed Anti-Radar Missile (US designation = AGM-88)

HAS   Helicopter Anti-Submarine (UK designator)

HC   Helicopter Cargo (UK designator)

HCP   Hélicoptère de Combat Polyvalent (multirole combat helicopter) applied to Tigre/Tiger

HMA   Helicopter, Maritime Attack (UK designator)

HOT   French ATGW acronym from Haut subsonique Optiquement téléguidé tiré d'un Tube = subsonic optically-tracked tube-launched [anti-tank missile]

HSA   Hawker Siddeley Aviation (UK)

IAI   Israel Aircraft Industries

ICH   Improved Cargo Helicopter (US Army name for CH-47F)

IDS   InterDictor Strike (variant of Tornado)

IOT&E   Initial Operational Test and Evaluation (USAF term)

ISD   In-Service Date

JASDF   Japanese Air Self-Defense Force (air force)

JASSM   Joint Air-to-Surface Stand-off Missile (US designation = AGM-158)

JDAM   Joint Direct Attack Munition, being a GPS-guidance package added to existing bomb bodies, US designations being GBU-29 (with Mk.81 bomb), GBU-30 (Mk.82), GBU-31 (Mk.83) and GBU-32 (Mk 84 or BLU-109/B) and GBU-35 (BLU-110/B)

JGSDF   Japanese Ground Self-Defense Force (army)

JMSDF   Japanese Maritime Self-Defense Force (navy)

JPATS   Joint Primary Aircraft Training System (USAF/USN)

JSF   Joint Strike Fighter (USAF/USN/USMC/RN/RAF)

JSOW   Joint Stand-Off Weapon, US designations being AGM-154A (with 145 BLU-97/B bomblets), AGM-154B (with six BLU-108/B bomblets) and AGM-154C (with BROACH penetrating warhead)

JVX   Joint Vertical eXperimental - the tiltrotor project which became the V-22 Osprey

K   Kerosene (tanker - UK designator)

Ka   Kamov (Russian design bureau)

KAI   Korean Aerospace Industries (South Korea)

LAMPS   Light Airborne Multi-Purpose System (Mk I = SH-2F/G Seasprite; Mk III = SH-60B Seahawk)

LANTIRN   Low Altitude Navigation Targeting InfraRed at Night (a twin-pod configuration)

LERX   Leading-Edge Root eXtension

LGB   Laser-Guided Bomb

LHTEC   Light Helicopter Turbine Engine Company (US), joint venture between Rolls-Royce (formerly Allison) and Honeywell (formerly Garrett)

LIFT   Lead-In Fighter Trainer

LOCAAS   LOw-Cost Autonomous Attack System

LRIP   Low-Rate Initial Production

MAD   Magnetic Anomoly Dectector

MBB   Messerschmitt Bolkow Blohm (Germany)

McDD   McDonnell Douglas (US)

MCM   Mine CounterMeasures

Medevac   Medical evacuation

MiG   Mikoyan-Guryevich (Russian design bureau)

Mi   Mil (Russian design bureau)

MLU   Mid-Life Update

MMS   Mast-Mounted Sight

MMW   MilliMetric (or MilliMetre) Wave (as AN/APG-78 Longbow radar for the AH-64D Apache Longbow helicopter)

MPA   Maritime Patrol Aircraft

MR   Maritime Reconnaissance (UK designator)

MRA   Maritime Reconnaissance and Attack (UK designator)

MRCA   Multi-Role Combat Aircraft (re-named Tornado)

MRT   Multi-Role Transport

MRTT   Multi-Role Tanker/Transport

MTI   Moving Target Indication

MTU   Motoren und Turbinen Union (Germany)

N/A (or n/a)   Not Available or Not Applicable

N-G   Northrop Grumman (US)

NAMC   Nanchang Aircraft Manufacturing Company (China)

NASA   National Aeronautics And Space Administration (US)

NFH   Naval Frigate Helicopter (NH 90 variant)

NOTAR   NO TAil Rotor - patented tail stabilisation system developed for MD 500-type helicopter

Glossary of Acronyms and Terms

OSD	Out-of-Service Date
P&W	Pratt & Whitney (US)
P&WC	Pratt & Whitney Canada
PAC	Pakistan Aeronautical Complex
PAH	PanzerAbwehr-Hubschrauber (Army [anti-] tank helicopter)
Panavia	Tri-national consortium formed to produce Tornado, comprising MBB of Germany (now EADS/DASA), Aeritalia of Italy (now Alenia Aerospazio) and BAC (now BAE Systems)
PLAAF	People's Liberation Army - Air Force (China)
PGM	Precision-Guided Munition
PZL	Polskie Zaklady Lotnicze (Polish Aviation Factory)
Q	US designation prefix for drone-configured aircraft
R	Radio (ELINT/SIGINT) - UK designator applied to versions of the Nimrod and Sentinel
RAAF	Royal Australian Air Force
RAC-MiG	Russian Aircraft Corporation-MiG (RSK-MiG in Russian - the manufacturing organisation teamed with the Mikoyan-Gurevich design bureau)
RAF	Royal Air Force
Recce	Reconnaissance
RoA	Radius of Action
RoCAF	Republic of China (Taiwan) Air Force
RoKAF	Republic of Korea (South Korea) Air Force
S	Sikorsky (model designator, e.g. S-70)
SAAF	South African Air Force
SAR	Search-And-Rescue; Synthetic Aperture Radar
SCALP	Systéme de Croisiére conventional Autonome a Longue Portée de precision - French derivative of APACHE weapon
SDB	Small Diameter Bomb
SDD	System Design and Development (taken over from EMD)
SEPECAT	Societe Europeane de Production de l'Avion Ecole et Combat Appui Tactique = European company to produce the training and tactical combat aircraft (50:50 Anglo-French company responsible for Jaguar, with BAC (now BAE Systems) and Breguet (now Dassault)
SIFICAP	Sistema de Fiscalizacao e Controlo das Activades da Pesca – Portuguese acronym meaning System of Supervision and Fishing Activity Control. Relates to EH 101 Mk 515
SIVAM	SIstema de Vigilancia da AMazonia - Brazil's surveillance programme for its Amazon region

SLAM	Stand-off Land Attack Missile (US designation = AGM-84G)
SLAM ER	Stand-off Land Attack Missile - Expanded Response (US designation = AGM-84H)
SLAR	Sideways-Looking Airborne Radar
SLEP	Service (or Structural) Life Extension Programme
SNECMA	Société Nationale d'Etude et de Construction de Moteurs d'Aviation (France)
SOCAT	Romanian acronym for the IAR-Brasov/Elbit upgrade of 24 IAR-330L Pumas with modern avionics and armament
SRAM	Short-Range Attack Missile
STOL	Short Take-Off and Landing
STOVL	Short Take-Off Vertical Landing
Su	Sukhoi (Russian design bureau)
T	Trainer (UK & US designator)
TACAMO	TAke CHarge And Move Out - USN AVLF relay system
TOW	Tube-launched, Optically-tracked, Wire-guided (ATGW), designation = BGM-71
TTH	Troop Transport Helicopter (NH 90 variant)
Tu	Tupolev (Russian design bureau)
UAE	United Arab Emirates
UHT	UnterstützungHubschrauber Tiger - final anti-tank/fire support configuration of German Army Tiger, replacing original PAH-2
USAF	United States Air Force
USMC	United States Marine Corps
USN	United States Navy
UTTAS	Utility Tactical Transport Aircraft System
V-G	Variable-Geometry (i.e. swing-wing)
Vertrep	Vertical Replenishment (at sea)
VC	Vickers Commercial (as in VC 10)
VLF	Very Low Frequency radio transmission band
VTO	Vertical Take-Off
WCMD	Wind-Corrected Munition Dispenser, being an add-on to the US series of CBU-78/B, CBU-87/B CEM and CBU-98/B Gator cluster munitions.
WSO	Weapons System Operator
X	US designation prefix for experimental aircraft
Y	US designation prefix for developmental aircraft

International Civil Aircraft Markings

AP	Pakistan			
A2	Botswana	I	Italy	
A3	Tonga Friendly Islands			
A40	Oman	JA	Japan	
A5	Bhutan	JU	Mongolia	
A6	United Arab Emirates	JY	Jordan	
A7	Qatar	J2	Djibouti	
A8	Liberia	J3	Grenada	
A9C	Bahrain	J5	Guinea Bissau	
		J6	St. Lucia	
B	China	J7	Dominica	
B–H	Hong Kong	J8	St. Vincent & Grenadines	
B–M	Macau/Macao			
B	China – Taiwan	LN	Norway	
		LV	Argentina	
C	Canada	LX	Luxembourg	
CC	Chile	LY	Lithuania	
CN	Morocco	LZ	Bulgaria	
CP	Bolivia			
CS	Portugal	N	USA	
CU	Cuba			
CX	Uruguay	OB	Peru	
C2	Nauru	OD	Lebanon	
C3	Andorra	OE	Austria	
C5	Gambia	OH	Finland	
C6	Bahamas	OK	Czech Republic	
C9	Mozambique	OM	Slovakia	
		OO	Belgium	
D	Germany	OY	Denmark, including Greenland and Faroe Islands	
DQ	Fiji			
D2	Angola			
D4	Cape Verde Islands	P	Korea, North	
D6	Comoros	PH	Netherlands	
		PJ	Netherlands Antilles	
EC	Spain	PK	Indonesia	
EI	Eire	PP/PR/PT	Brazil	
EK	Armenia	PZ	Suriname	
EP	Iran	P2	Papua New Guinea	
ER	Moldova	P4	Aruba	
ES	Estonia			
ET	Ethiopia	RA	Russian Federation	
EW	Belarus	RDPL	Laos	
EX	Kyrgyzstan	RP	Philippines	
EY	Tajikistan			
EZ	Turkmenistan	SE	Sweden	
E3	Eritrea	SP	Poland	
		ST	Sudan	
F	France	SU	Egypt	
		SU–Y	Palestine	
G	Great Britain	SX	Greece	
		S2	Bangladesh	
HA	Hungary	S5	Slovenia	
HB	Switzerland and Liechtenstein	S7	Seychelles	
HC	Ecuador	S9	Sao Tomé & Principe	
HH	Haiti			
HI	Dominican Republic	TC	Turkey	
HK	Colombia	TF	Iceland	
HL	Korea, South	TG	Guatemala	
HP	Panama	TI	Costa Rica	
HR	Honduras	TJ	Cameroon	
HS	Thailand	TL	Central African Republic	
HV	Vatican	TN	Congo Brazzaville	
HZ	Saudi Arabia	TR	Gabon	
H4	Solomon Islands	TS	Tunisia	

International Civil Aircraft Markings

TT	Chad		4K	Azerbaijan
TU	Ivory Coast		4L	Georgia
TY	Benin		4R	Sri Lanka
TZ	Mali		4X	Israel
T2	Tuvalu			
T3	Kiribati		5A	Libya
T7	San Marino		5B	Cyprus
T8A	Palau		5H	Tanzania
T9	Bosnia-Herzegovina		5N	Nigeria
			5R	Madagascar
UK	Uzbekistan		5T	Mauritania
UN	Kazakhstan		5U	Niger
UR	Ukraine		5V	Togo
			5W	Western Samoa
VH	Australia		5X	Uganda
VN	Vietnam		5Y	Kenya
VP-A	Anguilla			
VP-B	Bermuda		6O	Somalia
VP-C	Cayman Islands		6V	Senegal
VP-F	Falkland Islands		6Y	Jamaica
VP-G	Gibraltar			
VP-L	British Virgin Islands		7O	Yemen
VP-M	Montserrat		7P	Lesotho
VQ-T	Turks & Caicos Islands		7Q	Malawi
VT	India		7T	Algeria
V2	Antigua & Barbuda		8P	Barbados
V3	Belize		8Q	Maldives
V4	St. Kitts & Nevis		8R	Guyana
V5	Namibia		9A	Croatia
V6	Micronesia		9G	Ghana
V7	Marshall Islands		9H	Malta
V8	Brunei		9J	Zambia
			9K	Kuwait
ZA/XB/XC	Mexico		9L	Sierra Leone
XT	Burkina Faso		9M	Malaysia
XU	Cambodia		9N	Nepal
XY	Myanmar		9Q/9T	Congo, Democratic Republic
			9U	Burundi
YA	Afghanistan		9V	Singapore
YI	Iraq		9XR	Rwanda
YJ	Vanuatu		9Y	Trinidad & Tobago
YK	Syria			
YL	Latvia			
YN	Nicaragua			
YR	Romania			
YS	El Salvador			
YU	Serbia and Montenegro			
YV	Venezuela			
Z	Zimbabwe			
ZA	Albania			
ZK	Cook Islands			
ZK	New Zealand			
ZP	Paraguay			
ZS/ZU	South Africa			
Z3	Macedonia			
3A	Monaco			
3B	Mauritius			
3C	Equatorial Guinea			
3D	Swaziland			
3X	Guinea			

National Military Aircraft Markings

Afghanistan: Air Force

Albania: Air Force

Algeria: Air Force

Angola: Air Force

Argentina: Air Force
and Army

Argentina: Navy

Argentina: Coast Guard

Armenia: Air Force

Australia: Air Force
and Navy

Australia: Army

Australia: Low Visibility

Austria: Air Force

Azerbaijan: Air Force

Bahamas: Defence Force

Bahrain: Air Force
and Navy

Bangladesh: Defence Force

Belarus: Air Force

Belgium: Air Force
and Army

Belgium: Navy Flight

Belgium: Luchtkadetten

Belgium: Police

Belize: Defence Force

Benin: Armed Forces

Bolivia: Air Force

No Marking

Bolivia: Army

Bosnia–Herzegovina:
Air Force

Bosnia–Herzegovina:
Serbian Republic

Botswana: Defence Force

Brazil: Air Force

Brazil: Navy 1

Brazil: Navy 2

Brazil: Army

Brunei: Air Force

Bulgaria: Air Force
and Navy

Burkina Faso: Air Force

Burkina Faso: Air Force
(alternate)

Burundi: Army Air Arm

Cambodia: Air Force

Cameroun: Air Force

Cameroun: Government

National Military Aircraft Markings

Canada: Air Command

Canada: Low Visibility

Cape Verde: Air Force

Central African Republic: Air Arm

Chad: Air Arm

Chile: Air Force

Chile: Air Force Low Visibility

Chile: Navy

Chile: Army

Chile: Presidential/ VIP Transport

Chile: Prefectura Aéreopolicial de los Carabineros

Chile: Prefectura Aéreopolicial de los Carabineros (dark background)

China: Air Force and Navy

Colombia: Air Force, Navy Army and Police

Colombia: Low Visibility

Colombia: Navy

Comoros: Air Arm

Congo: Air Force

Congo Deocratic Republic: Air Force

Costa Rica: Public Security

Côte d'Ivoire: Air Force

Croatia: Air Force

Cuba: Air Force

Cyprus: Air Force

Czech Republic: Air Force

Czech Republic: Low Visibility

Czech Republic: Police

Denmark: Air Force Navy and Army

Djibouti: Air Force

Dominican Republic: Air Force

Ecuador: Air Force

Ecuador: Navy

Egypt: Air Force and Navy

Egypt: Air Force (Special)

Egypt: VIP Transports
No Marking

Equatorial Guinea: National Guard

Eritrea: Air Force

Estonia: Air Force

Ethiopia: Air Force

Finland: Air Force and Army

National Military Aircraft Markings

France: Air Force, Army Gendarmerie and CEV

France: Navy

France: Gendarmerie (Supplemental)

Gabon: Air Force, Army and Presidential Guard

Gabon: Gendarmerie

Georgia: Navy

Germany: Air Force, Navy and Army

Germany: Navy (Supplemental)

Ghana: Air Force

Greece: Air Force, Navy and Army

Greece: Navy Low Visibility

Greece: Coast Guard

Guatemala: Air Force

Guinea Bissau: Air Force

Guinea Republic: Air Force

Guyana: Defence Force

Haiti: Air Corps

Honduras: Air Force

Hungary: Air Force

Iceland: Coast Guard

India: Air Force and Army

India: Navy

India: Coast Guard

Indonesia: Air Force

Indonesia: Air Force Low Visibility

Indonesia: Navy

Indonesia: Army

Indonesia: Police

Iran: Air Force

Iraq: Air Force

Ireland: Air Corps

Israel: Air Force

Italy: Air Force, Carabinieri and Guardia di Finanza

Italy: Navy

Italy: Capitanerie di Porto

Jamaica: Defence Force

Japan: Air Force Navy and Army

Jordan Air Force

Kazakhstan: Air Force

Kazakhstan: Government
No Marking

524

National Military Aircraft Markings

Kenya: Air Force

Korea, North: Air Force

Korea, South: Air Force

Korea, South: Navy

Korea, South: Army

Kuwait: Air Force

Kyrgizia: Air Force

Laos: Air Force

Latvia: Air Force

Lebanon: Air Force

Lesotho: Defence Force

Liberia: Army

Libya: Air Force
Navy and Army

Lithuania: Air Force

Lithuania: National
Defence Service

Luxembourg: NATO
AEW Force

Macedonia: Air Force

Macedonia: Alternative

Macedonia:
Low Visibility

Madagascar: Air Force

Malawi: Air Force

Malaysia: Air Force

Malaysia:
Low Visibility

Malaysia:
Government/VIP

Malaysia: Air Force
(Alternate)

Malaysia: Navy

Malaysia: Fire and
Rescue Department

Mali: Air Force

Malta: Armed Forces

Mauritania: Air Force

Mauritius: Coast Guard

Mexico: Air Force

Mexico: Air Force
Low Visibility

Mexico: Navy

Mexico: Navy 2

Moldova: Air Force

Mongolia: Air Force

Morocco: Air Force
and Gendarmerie

Mozambique: Air Force

Myanmar: Air Force

National Military Aircraft Markings

No Marking

Namibia: Air Force

NATO: AEW Force

Fin Marking

Nepal: Air Force

Netherlands: Air Force and Navy

Netherlands: Low Visibility

Fin Marking

New Zealand: Air Force

Fin Marking

New Zealand: Low Visibility

Nicaragua: Air Force

Fin Marking

Niger: National Squadron

Fin Marking

Nigeria: Air Force

Nigeria: Government (Supplemental)

Fin Marking

Nigeria: Navy

Norway: Air Force

Norway: Low Visibility

Fin Marking

Oman: Air Force

Oman: Low Visibility

Fin Marking

Pakistan: Air Force and Army

Fin Marking

Pakistan: Navy

Fin Marking

Panama: Air service

Fin Marking

Papua New Guinea: Defence Force

Fin Marking

Paraguay: Air Force

Fin Marking

Paraguay: Navy

Fin Marking

Peru: Air Force

Fin Marking

Peru: Navy

Peru: Army

Philippines: Air Force

No Marking

Philippines: Government

Philippines: Navy

Fin Marking

Poland: Air Forces, Navy Army and Interior Ministry

Fin Marking

Poland: Marine Search and Rescue

Fin Marking

Portugal: Air Force Navy and Army

Portugal: Navy (Supplemental)

Fin Marking

Qatar: Air Force

Romania: Air Force and Navy

Russia: Air Force Navy and Army

Fin Marking
No Marking

Russia: (Supplemental/alternate)

Fin Marking

Russia: Navy (Supplemental)

Fin Marking

Rwanda: Air Force

Fin Marking

El Salvador: Air Force

Fin Marking

Saudi Arabia: Air Force

National Military Aircraft Markings

Saudi Arabia: Air Force
Low Visibility

Saudi Arabia: Navy

Saudi Arabia: Land Forces

Senegal: Air Force

Serbia & Montenegro:
Air Force

Seychelles: Air Force

Sierra Leone: Air Force

Singapore: Air Force

Singapore:
Low Visibility

Slovak Republic: Air Force

Slovenia: Defence Force

Somalia: Aeronautical Corps

South Africa: Air Force

South Africa:
Low Visibility

Spain: Air Force
and Army

Spain: Navy

Spain: Navy
(Supplemental, optional)

Sri Lanka: Air Force

Sudan: Air Force

Suriname: Air Force

Swaziland: Defence Force

Sweden: Air Force,
Navy and Army

Sweden: Low Visibility

Switzerland: Air Force

Syria: Air Force
and Navy

Taiwan: Air Force
Navy and Army

Taiwan: Low Visibility

Tajikistan: Air Force

Tanzania: Air Force

Thailand: Air Force
and Army

Thailand: Navy

Togo: Air Force

Tonga: Defence Service

Trinidad & Tobago:
Defence Force

Tunisia: Air Force

Turkey: Air Force,
Navy and Army

Turkmenistan: Air Force

Uganda: Air Force

Ukraine: Air Force

Ukraine: Army

National Military Aircraft Markings

Ukraine: Navy

Ukraine: Navy

United Arab Emirates: Air Force

United Arab Emirates: Dubai Police Force

United Arab Emirates: Low Visibility

United Kingdom: Air Force and QinetiQ

United Kingdom: Air Force, Low Visibility

United Kingdom: Navy

United Kingdom: Army

United States: Air Force, Navy/Marine Corps

United States: Coast Guard

United States: Low Visibility 1

United States: Low Visibility 2

United States: Low Visibility 3

United States: Low Visibility 4

United States: Army

Uruguay: Air Force

Uruguay: Navy 1
No Marking

Uruguay: Navy 2

Uzbekistan: Air Force

Venezuela: Air Force, Navy and Army

Venezuela: Air Force and Navy (Supplemental)

Venezuela: Navy (Supplemental)

Vietnam: Air Force

Yemen: Air Force

Zambia: Air Force

Zimbabwe: Air Force